Quotes for Pr

The world of networking continues to advance, and
by advancements like Kubernetes and Linux contain
practices a necessity to fully maximize Cisco IOS-X
find this book to be an exceptionally insightful guid
vating, orchestrating, and developing operational best practices for containerizing and
instantiating applications and network services. I recommend it highly, as it is written by
the engineers who have the best real-world experience of designing and troubleshooting
these architectures.

—*Tom Berghoff, Senior Vice President, Customer Experience, Cisco Systems*

Time-to-value realization for our customers is key to achieving their business outcomes
with our solutions. The book that Yogesh and Nagendra have written will allow our
customers to maximize their investment by leveraging Cisco solutions in a unique and
innovative way. The passion that Yogesh and Nagendra bring to this topic through this
book will jump off the page at you. Please enjoy this well-written book, as it will help to
ensure that you realize maximum value from the investments you have made in this Cisco
solution.

—*Marc Holloman, Vice President, Customer Experience, Cisco Systems*

With the introduction of software-defined networking (SDN), we knew that the way we
build and operate networks was never going to be the same. For the network to keep up
with the speed of business, major changes had to happen at every layer of the enterprise
stack. With this book, the reader will get an insider look at the innerworkings of the technologies enabling this change. Two experts in the field present solutions and technologies
for successful virtualization and orchestration of network resources and applications on
Cisco platforms. A must-read for every network technology participant in the digital
transformation journey.

—*Hazim Dahir, Distinguished Engineer, Customer Experience, Cisco Systems*

At last, a comprehensive overview of containerization in networking context. Written by
two of the foremost experts, this book is a must for every cloud architect and network
architect contemplating the usage of containerized apps on Cisco routers for on-board
computing-related use cases such as efficient network operations.

—*Rajiv Asati, CTO/Distinguished Engineer, Customer Experience, Cisco Systems*

To digitize and disrupt legacy business models, agile organizations require a flexible and
scalable infrastructure. Containers provide portability, protection, and design resiliency to
modern network infrastructures. Learn to leverage the power of containers on the Cisco
Systems platforms from two of its leading minds. As authors, patent developers, and principle engineers at Cisco, Nagendra and Yogesh are uniquely qualified to explain how you,
too, can build, test, deploy, and manage application hosting on your Cisco-enabled infrastructure. I rely on their expertise daily and, through this book, you will, too!

—*Chris Berriman, Senior Director, Customer Experience, Cisco Systems* and author
    of Networking Technologies, Fundamentals of Network Management and Cisco
    Network Management Solutions

As society becomes more dependent on the benefits of the digital economy, enterprise leaders need to be informed of the technological capabilities available to meet their customers' demand. In this book, two of the most prolific principal engineers and technologists at Cisco, Nagendra Kumar Nainar and Yogesh Ramdoss, provide a clear introduction into one of the major innovations fundamental to the digital economy: cloud computing and virtualization. The work is superb in content, covering the basics of container orchestration and networking from a technically agnostic perspective while progressing to show the unique capabilities and benefits of using Cisco technology. For the leader responsible for digital transformation, this book will provide actionable insights through real-world scenarios and a future look to the possibilities ahead.

—*Hector Acevedo, Senior Director, Customer Experience, Cisco Systems*

Containers in Cisco IOS-XE, IOS-XR, and NX-OS: Orchestration and Operation

Yogesh Ramdoss (CCIE No. 16183)
Nagendra Kumar Nainar
(CCIE No. 20987, CCDE No. 20190014)

Cisco Press

Hoboken, New Jersey

Containers in Cisco IOS-XE, IOS-XR, and NX-OS: Orchestration and Operation

Yogesh Ramdoss (CCIE No. 16183)

Nagendra Kumar Nainar (CCIE No. 20987, CCDE No. 20190014)

Copyright© 2021 Cisco Systems, Inc.

Published by:
Cisco Press

3 2022

Library of Congress Control Number: 2020906738

ISBN-13: 978-0-13-589575-7

ISBN-10: 0-13-589575-8

Warning and Disclaimer

Trademark Acknowledgments

Special Sales

For information about buying this title in bulk quantities, or for special sales opportunities (which may include electronic versions; custom cover designs; and content particular to your business, training goals, marketing focus, or branding interests), please contact our corporate sales department at corpsales@pearsoned.com or (800) 382-3419.

For government sales inquiries, please contact governmentsales@pearsoned.com.

For questions about sales outside the U.S., please contact international@pearsoned.com.

Feedback Information

At Cisco Press, our goal is to create in-depth technical books of the highest quality and value. Each book is crafted with care and precision, undergoing rigorous development that involves the unique expertise of members from the professional technical community.

Readers' feedback is a natural continuation of this process. If you have any comments regarding how we could improve the quality of this book, or otherwise alter it to better suit your needs, you can contact us through email at feedback@ciscopress.com. Please make sure to include the book title and ISBN in your message.

We greatly appreciate your assistance.

Editor-in-Chief: Mark Taub

Alliances Manager, Cisco Press: Arezou Gol

Director, ITP Product Management: Brett Bartow

Executive Editor: Nancy Davis

Managing Editor: Sandra Schroeder

Development Editor: Rick Kughen

Project Editor: Mandie Frank

Copy Editor: Gill Editorial Services

Technical Editors: Richard Furr; Rahul Nimbalkar

Editorial Assistant: Cindy Teeters

Designer: Chuti Prasertsith

Composition: codeMantra

Indexer: Erika Millen

Proofreader: Charlotte Kughen

CISCO.

Americas Headquarters
Cisco Systems, Inc.
San Jose, CA

Asia Pacific Headquarters
Cisco Systems (USA) Pte. Ltd.
Singapore

Europe Headquarters
Cisco Systems International BV Amsterdam,
The Netherlands

Cisco has more than 200 offices worldwide. Addresses, phone numbers, and fax numbers are listed on the Cisco Website at **www.cisco.com/go/offices**.

Cisco and the Cisco logo are trademarks or registered trademarks of Cisco and/or its affiliates in the U.S. and other countries. To view a list of Cisco trademarks, go to this URL: www.cisco.com/go/trademarks. Third party trademarks mentioned are the property of their respective owners. The use of the word partner does not imply a partnership relationship between Cisco and any other company. (1110R)

Credits

Figure 1-5   Screenshot of Linux processor output © Canonical Ltd

"cloud computing is defined as a model for enabling convenient, on-demand network access to a shared pool of configurable computing resources that can rapidly provisioned and released with minimal management effort or service provider interaction."   NISt

About the Authors

Yogesh Ramdoss (CCIE No. 16183) is a principal engineer with the Cisco Customer Experience (CX) organization focusing on data center technologies such as Nexus switching platforms (standalone as well as VXLAN fabric), application-centric infrastructure (ACI), and hyperconverged infrastructure HyperFlex. Associated with Cisco since 2003, Yogesh is a distinguished speaker at Cisco Live, where he shares his knowledge and educates customers and partners on data center platforms and technologies, telemetry, analytics, network programmability, and various troubleshooting and packet capturing tools. He is a machine and behavior learning coinventor.

Nagendra Kumar Nainar (CCIE No. 20987, CCDE No. 20190014) is a principal engineer with the Cisco Customer Experience (CX) organization (formerly TAC), focusing on enterprise networking. He is the coinventor of more than 100 patent applications on various cutting-edge technologies and the coarchitect for various recent technologies. He has coauthored multiple Internet RFCs and IEEE papers. Serving as Technical Program Committee (TPC) member for various IEEE and other international conferences, he is an active speaker in various industry forums.

About the Technical Reviewers

Richard Furr, CCIE No. 9173 (R&S & SP), is a technical leader of the Cisco Customer Experience (CX) organization, providing support for customers and TAC teams around the world. Richard has authored and acted as a technical editor for several Cisco Press publications. During the past 19 years, Richard has provided support to service provider, enterprise, and data center environments resolving complex problems with routing protocols, MPLS, IP Multicast, IPv6, and QoS.

Rahul Nimbalkar is a technical leader with Cisco, where he has worked since 2001. He has been working on LXC (guestshell, OAC) and Docker containers as well as virtualization technologies on the Cisco NX-OS data center switches. Most recently he designed and implemented Docker container support on the standalone NX-OS 9000 series and has been working on the NX-OSv, the virtual machine version of the NX-OS switch.

Dedications

Yogesh: I dedicate this book to my parents, Ramdoss Rajagopal and Bhavani Ramdoss, who have given me the best things in the world and taught me to do the right things to the people around us. I further dedicate this book to my wife, Vaishnavi, and our children, Janani and Karthik, for their patience and support throughout the authoring process. Finally, I want to dedicate this book to my ex-manager Mike Stallings, for several years of his support and encouragement to start this project.

Nagendra: This book is dedicated to my mother and father for their encouragement and support throughout my life. I am what I am today because of the guidance and support from you. This book is further dedicated to my wife, Lavanya, and my daughter, Ananyaa, who are the driving factors of my life. Lavanya, your patience and understanding are a great support for me to do things beyond my capacity. Ananyaa, I love you to the core. This book is also dedicated to my ex-manager, Mike Stallings. Mike, you are one of the greatest managers, and I am glad that I had an opportunity to work with you.

Acknowledgments

Yogesh: My heartfelt thanks to my manager Hector Acevedo for his trust and support. I am thankful to my coauthor, Nagendra Kumar Nainar, for his guidance, and to my technical reviewers, Richard Furr and Rahul Nimbalkar, for providing valuable comments and feedback. I would like to extend my thanks to Christopher Hart for helping me build, test, and validate deployment scenarios and use cases for this book. Last but not least, I would like to thank Carlos Pignataro, who has been mentoring me and providing career guidance for so many years.

Nagendra: First, I would like to thank my mentor, Carlos Pignataro, for his mentoring and career guidance. Your guidance and advice always played a key role in my career. I would like to thank my manager, Chris Berriman, for his support and flexibility. Your trust in me and the flexibility you offer is encouraging, and it motivates me to explore different opportunities.

I would like to thank my coauthor and good friend, Yogesh Ramdoss, who completed this book on time. I would like to thank Richard Furr and Rahul Nimbalkar for the high-quality technical review performed on our writeup. You improved the quality of the content.

I also would like to thank Akshar Sharma, who helped me significantly with various XR content, and Akram Sheriff, who helped with IoT-related content.

I would like to thank Ajitha Buvanachandran for the tremendous help in reviewing my work. I would like to thank Poornima Nandakumar and Satish Manchana for helping me with various virtualization use cases.

Contents at a Glance

Reader Services

Register your copy at www.ciscopress.com/title/9780135895757 for convenient access to downloads, updates, and corrections as they become available. To start the registration process, go to www.ciscopress.com/register and log in or create an account*. Enter the product ISBN 9780135895757 and click Submit. When the process is complete, you will find any available bonus content under Registered Products.

*Be sure to check the box that you would like to hear from us to receive exclusive discounts on future editions of this product.

Contents

Icons Used in This Book

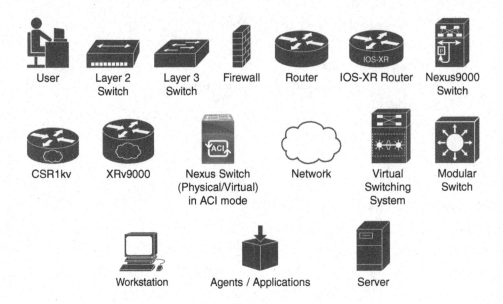

Command Syntax Conventions

The conventions used to present command syntax in this book are the same conventions used in the IOS Command Reference. The Command Reference describes these conventions as follows:

- **Boldface** indicates commands and keywords that are entered literally as shown. In actual configuration examples and output (not general command syntax), boldface indicates commands that are manually input by the user (such as a **show** command).

- *Italic* indicates arguments for which you supply actual values.

- Vertical bars (|) separate alternative, mutually exclusive elements.

- Square brackets ([ ]) indicate an optional element.

- Braces ({ }) indicate a required choice.

- Braces within brackets ([{ }]) indicate a required choice within an optional element.

Foreword

What do rhinos, Internet RFCs, memory buffers, and volunteering have in common? In that intersection, you will find Nagendra and Yogesh!

A few years ago, Nagendra, Yogesh, and I met when we were providing direct customer support on networking infrastructure. It was the common passion for technology as well as for customer service that brought us together.

At that time, virtual local area networks (VLANs), then followed by encapsulations or "tunnels," were network virtualization technologies. Fast-forwarding, we can see how the technology landscape and ecosystem has dramatically evolved and reinvented itself. Virtualization has multiplied and expanded into many areas of networking, storage, and computing, including containerized network functions.

This book guides and shepherds the reader through the evolution of virtualization technologies with depth and breath. It invites images both historical and futuristically visionary. Explaining design principles and considerations of end-to-end network virtualization and controller architectures, it challenges the reader through the mystical twists of context virtualization, recursing through a software stack as if it were a Möbius strip and creating dimensional layers on a topology.

Not content with abstraction alone, this book teaches the concrete art and engineering of configuring container orchestration and management—where the network is the node, and the node is the network. It describes how to create bendable cloud-native network functions, which are utilized for lifecycle management and service automation. Then, to make Cloud real, this book instructs network wizards and software geeks how to realize these container-based orchestration architectures in Cisco network operating system software and platforms. Because the end goal is to conjure applications that were not possible before, this book covers several application developer tools, resources, and real-life container deployment use cases.

Switching contexts—no pun intended—what do technology and helping others have in common? Everything! And as technology reinvented itself, so did the focus area and the meaning of their careers.

Yogesh not only masters all interface counters in Nexus fabric platforms, but bends packet captures and embedded diagnostic tools and configures Layer 2 (L2) Data Center Interconnect (DCI). He also applies his skills and experience to design and deploy networks, ad honorem, for the Food Bank of Central and Eastern North Carolina. He leads selflessly.

Nagendra's technical and architectural accomplishments include coinventing several patented applications—in fact, he is currently the top inventor in the Cisco Customer Experience team—and coauthoring Internet RFC standards. I'm honored to have part-nered in white-boarding some of those with him. However, what makes me prouder is that together we painted houses for refugee resettlement. When I asked Nagendra for help in a hackathon in Bangalore, India, for the Cisco Sustainable Impact program, he jumped at the chance. For techno-conservation including saving rhinos and other endangered species, and for encouraging social responsibility, he engaged immediately with no second thought.

The seeds of the technology that the two authors are showing in this book might have always been there, but it needed thought leaders to reinvent it to accommodate its fast-paced growth. Similarly, Nagendra and Yogesh, throughout the years, have reinvented themselves as technologists and as leaders, continually growing. Professional portability is reached with technology-agnostic technical skills, as they evidence from VLANs to containers. And they further extrapolated that to food banks and techno-conservation.

I am grateful to Yogesh and Nagendra for contributing to the industry and sharing in writing this book on container orchestration!

Carlos Pignataro
Distinguished Engineer and CTO, Emerging Technologies and Incubation, Cisco Systems
Adjunct Faculty, North Carolina State University
Fellow, National Academy of Inventors
Volunteer

Introduction

The introduction of cloud computing and virtualization is one of the radical innovations that the industry has witnessed recently. These technologies have allowed the industry to decouple the services from the proprietary hardware and allowed the users to instantiate workflows on any supported compute platforms. Although toolsets such as Linux Containers (LXC) and Kernel Virtual Machine (KVM) were developed to instantiate any workloads as virtual machines, recent developments, such as Docker and Kubernetes, allow the user to develop and instantiate these workloads as containers. Containerizing the applications and network services (NFV) is the goal the industry is moving toward for the agility and efficiency properties.

Cisco IOS-XE, IOS-XR, and NX-OS Architecture have been augmented with compute virtualization capabilities to accommodate native and third-party container hosting that allows the users to containerize and instantiate applications or network services. The Software Development Kit (SDK) Cisco offers can be used to develop applications from scratch to instantiate on Cisco IOS-XE, IOS-XR, and NX-OS platforms natively by leveraging the built-in application hosting capabilities.

This book explains the architecture and capabilities of Cisco products, Container infrastructure configuration, activation, orchestration, and operational activities. It acts as a complete guide to deploying and operating applications and network services that are hosted on Cisco platforms. This book is the first and the only comprehensive guide featuring Cisco IOS-XE, IOS-XR, and NX-OS architecture that supports deployment of various virtual and containerized network services and the container orchestration tools to instantiate and operate them.

Goals and Methods

The primary goal of this book is to introduce you to the new application hosting capabilities and the built-in toolkits that can be used to build, orchestrate, and operate applications or services by leveraging compute resources in Cisco platforms.

This book introduces readers to the fundamentals of virtualization and associated concepts and how virtualization and SDN are related to the Cisco IOS-XE, IOS-XR, and NX-OS platforms. This book explores different orchestration tools (for example, LXC, KVM, Docker, and Kubernetes) for workload instantiation (as virtual machines or containers) and different modes of enabling the interworkload communication. It takes a deep dive into application hosting capabilities for each of the mentioned Cisco platforms. Furthermore, it covers available Cisco and open-source tools and resources that application developers can leverage to build and test applications before hosting them on the respective platforms. Beyond explaining the platform capabilities and the methods to host applications, this book offers multiple real-world use cases in which these applications are used in day-to-day network operations.

How This Book Is Organized

Although you could read this book cover to cover, it is designed to be flexible and allow you to easily move between chapters and sections of chapters to cover just the material you need, when you need it.

Part I, "Virtualization and Containers," is an overview of the evolution of virtualization technologies and different orchestration tools and networking concepts that are broadly applicable for hosting a virtual service in any compute platform.

- Chapter 1, "Introduction to Virtualization": This chapter starts by describing the evolution of computing technologies and then introduces the motivation, business drivers, and concept of computing virtualization. It also describes the architecture, principles, and various types of virtualization.

- Chapter 2, "Virtualization and Cisco": This chapter describes the history of virtualization in the Cisco core routing and switching products and discusses how infrastructure virtualization is being achieved in these platforms. This chapter continues to introduce the software-defined networking (SDN) concepts, associated protocols, Cisco and open-source controllers, function virtualization, and trending technologies.

- Chapter 3, "Container Orchestration and Management": This chapter describes the cloud-native reference model and how the model is used to develop cloud-native services and help the industry migrate from virtual to cloud-native network functions. It explains different orchestration tools and the applicability of these tools for workload instantiation on Cisco platforms.

- Chapter 4, "Container Networking Concepts": This chapter describes the fundamentals of container networking and how the underlying kernels use the network namespaces to create resource isolation. This chapter digs deep into different container networking models for each orchestration method and explains all the supported modes in Cisco platforms along with the relevant configuration to enable the container networking modes.

Part II, "Container Deployment and Operation in Cisco Products," discusses fundamentals of IOS-XE, IOS-XR, and NX-OS architecture; various container capabilities natively available in related platforms; and how to leverage them to host applications to perform day-to-day operations.

- Chapter 5, "Container Orchestration in Cisco IOS-XE Platforms": This chapter starts with a quick introduction to the architecture of IOS-XE and its key components and functions. Next, it explains how the architecture enables application hosting with support for various types of applications. It offers sample steps to enable, install, activate, and orchestrate the containers (such as LXC) and how to leverage them to host simple applications.

- Chapter 6, "Container Orchestration in Cisco IOS-XR Platforms": This chapter introduces the IOS-XR architecture and the latest enhancements to support application hosting capabilities for native or third-party services. The chapter further explains different methods of hosting the application using orchestration tools, such as LXC and Docker, along with the relevant network configurations. This chapter concludes by explaining the basic management aspects of the hosted applications.

■ Chapter 7: "Container Orchestration in Cisco NX-OS Platforms": This chapter introduces users to the fundamentals of the NX-OS architecture and the benefits this architecture brings to hosting applications natively. It discusses various container capabilities, such as Guest Shell, Bash, Docker, and more, and covers the steps to activate and configure them and host applications. The chapter concludes with an explanation of how a Docker container running in a Nexus platform can be orchestrated with Kubernetes.

■ Chapter 8: "Application Developers' Tools and Resources": In this chapter, you will learn various Cisco as well as open-source tools and resources available to application developers to develop, test, and host applications in Cisco IOS-XE, IOS-XR, and NX-OS platforms. It provides details on the software development environment and toolkits that are built into these platforms.

■ Chapter 9: "Container Deployment Use Cases": This chapter introduces various real-world use cases for Day-0, Day-1, and Day-2 operations and explains the applicability of the use cases with deployment examples on Cisco IOS-XR, IOS-XE, and NX-OS platforms.

■ Chapter 10: "Current NFV Offering and Future Trends in Containers": This chapter starts by introducing various open-source and certified third-party applications that are readily available for hosting on Cisco platforms for some common use cases. It continues by explaining different NFV services currently offered by Cisco and highlights some virtualization trends.

## Chapter 1

Introduction to Virtualization

In this chapter, you will learn the following:

■ The history behind the evolution of computer and virtualization technology

■ Architecture, components, and types of virtualization

■ Introduction to the different types of virtualization, such as virtual machines and containers

■ Virtualization scale and design considerations

■ Data plane techniques to protect the network edge and core, including the different router interface types

■ Techniques to protect the network and to mitigate a network attached within the data plane by using control plane techniques

■ Layer 2 Ethernet techniques to protect switched-Ethernet LANs

History of Computer Evolution

In this modern world, super computers, smartphones, and other smart devices used in daily life are the sequels of the historical evolution that has materialized in the past 100 years. The evolution of computers spans from punch-card based computer models to the discrete transistor-based models, and an active community of inventors continuously works hard on the next-gen model.

With the exponential increase in the volume of data, even simple tasks such as data sorting have become challenging—and sometimes even not humanly possible. For example, during the late 1880s, the US government struggled to sort the US Census results because the volume of data that needed to be sorted took years to be tabulated. Tabulating the results was taking longer than the time between census surveys, causing the data to be outdated by the time it was finished. This basic, yet critical, government requirement led to the invention of the early punch-card computers, which were invented by Herman Hollerith and were known as Hollerith Cards. These machines were analog computers that used a piece of paper to store and read the data in binary format. The data was represented in binary format using a punched hole to mean **0** and the absence of a hole to mean **1**. In the 1930s, when electrically powered analog computers were slowly evolving, British mathematician Alan Turing introduced the principle of modern computers that resulted in the advent of digital computers.

The celebrated Turing Machine was built using the modern principles, and this machine played a key role in WWII. The early digital computers built around this time were electromechanical, and they used a blend of electric rotary switches and electromagnetic relays to perform arithmetic and other complex sequence of calculations on the punch card data. The electromagnetic relays were then replaced by vacuum tubes or electron tubes that controlled the flow of electric current between electrodes in an evacuated container or valve. The vacuum tube computer model laid the foundation for some of the general-purpose computers in the 1940s, such as the Electronic Numerical Integrator and Computer (ENIAC).

Although these tube machines offered substantial improvements to the computing performance, these improvements came with a cost. ENIAC was the first entirely electronic computer, and it was built with an astounding estimate of about 18,000 vacuum tubes, more than 7000 diodes, 70,000 resistors, and 5 million soldered joints, all of which covered more than 1800 square feet of floor space. Running this device consumed 160 kilowatts of electrical power. The energy consumed by the computer, the amount of heat produced from the electric consumption, and the colossal size of these computers were some of the hindrances that led the industry experts to look for an alternative.

Transistors, invented by Bell Labs, unleashed an unprecedented development in the electronic world. Transistors are semiconductors that act as a relay that controls the electronic transmission of signals. While transistors transmitted electric signals in a controlled manner, they were tiny compared to earlier vacuum tubes. Replacing vacuum tubes with transistors reduced the size of the computers from room-sized to palm-sized.

When processors were built with transistors, Intel's Gordon Moore predicted that the number of transistors in a chip would double every two years while the price would continually decrease. His prediction has proven true for the past 50 years. The Intel 4004 processor, which was introduced in 1971, was built with fewer than 2500 transistors. Recent processors, such as the Intel Quad Core i7, are built with more than one billion transistors. This is a typical example of a single innovation driving a cascade of related revolutionary changes.

History of Virtualization

Thanks to transistors, most people now own three smart connected devices. By 2021, some experts say each person in North America will have about 13 smart connected devices. However, this wasn't the situation when computers were evolving from vacuum tubes to transistors. The electromechanical computers built with vacuum tubes were costly, which meant users had to share computing resources via service bureaus and Tymshare.

The concept of virtualization dates back to the early 1960s when IBM's Cambridge Scientific Center developed the Control Program (CP) hypervisor that allowed users to create multiple independent virtual machines; the underlying hardware was known as Cambridge Monitor System (CMS). Various versions of CMS/CP were developed, which resulted with the introduction of S/360 and S/370 systems. Virtualization was one of the more popular areas for research during the 1970s, and entire conferences were dedicated in the interest of these researchers. Figure 1-1 illustrates the evolution of virtualization.

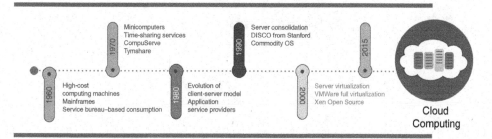

Figure 1-1 *Evolution of Virtualization*

In the 1980s, virtualization started fading away as computer hardware became dramatically cheaper with the advancement of the transistor-based processors. It was the evolution of the server/client–based data consumption model. The revolutionary start of the dotcom bubble in the early 1990s increased the demand for computing capacity and led to the consolidation of computing resources such as application servers.

Experts from Stanford University published a paper on DISCO (see https://dl.acm.org/doi/pdf/10.1145/265924.265930) that proposed the concept of introducing a new software layer between the hardware and the operating system to act as a hypervisor to allow multiple copies of commodity operating systems to share the underlying hardware resource. DISCO was demonstrated on an experimental cache-coherent, non-uniform memory access (ccNUMA) machine. In 1998, VMware came up with a full-stack virtualization model that eliminated the need for a commodity operating system as a guest OS. Instead, the hypervisor allowed users to run any operating system as the guest OS.

In the early 2000s, Xen was introduced by the University of Cambridge as an open-source hypervisor for hardware virtualization. In 2006, Amazon announced a limited public beta test of Elastic Compute Cloud (EC2) deployment on Xen hypervisors.

Motivation and Business Drivers for Virtualization

As businesses have increased their reliance on the IT infrastructure, virtualization has become a driving force. At one end of the spectrum, users from a diverse set of departments can have full access to specific applications; at the other end of the spectrum, users in the same group can have varying levels of privileges to access the same application. For example, the email server needs to be accessed by all users in all groups; however, sensitive financial information needs to accessible only by a select group of financial users.

Figure 1-2 illustrates the business drivers that led to virtualization. They are further articulated in the coming sections.

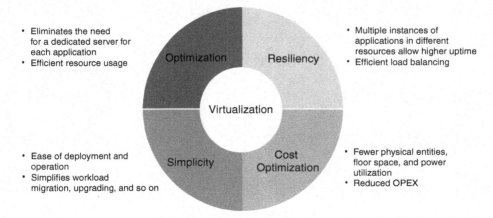

Figure 1-2   *Business Drivers for Virtualization*

Resource Optimization

Capacity management is an integral part of the Information Technology Infrastructure Library (ITIL) framework that is used to plan and manage the resources required to deliver IT services based on business demands.

Capacity planning uses a top-down approach that estimates the capacity needs based on the business requirement and drills down further to component or configuration items. In other words, capacity planning involves identifying the group of users required to access a service based on business requirements and designing the service configuration to satisfy that need.

Typically, most users in a large enterprise are required to access the email service, whereas other services, such as the recruitment portal, are accessed only by the Human Resources (HR) team. This means a powerful, high-performance email server is needed while the recruitment portal needs only a moderate performance server. Although capacity planning is undeniably useful, there are additional operational challenges that IT administrators face:

- **Efficient server consolidation:** As a best practice, the configuration of any server is chosen such that the average resource utilization does not exceed more than 60 to 70 percent, which allows services to scale during unpredicted traffic bursts.

■ **Efficient resource utilization:** Capacity planning that is done based on utilization trends and projected growth might not optimally utilize the resource. For example, an enterprise intranet portal is accessed intensively during events such as quarterly financial result announcements or performance bonus announcements but is only sporadically accessed the rest of the time. In a large enterprise data center, it is common to see thousands of servers hosting different applications. The magnitude of resource inefficiency increases with the number of sporadically utilized applications. Powering off some or all these application servers during off business hours is not an option because it increases the operational overhead.

These challenges make achieving resource efficiency difficult for IT administrators and are among the motivations for using virtualization.

Resilience

Expansion of business-critical applications affects the health of the applications and business revenue. This in turn creates a challenge for IT administrators to avoid business disruptions and failures and handle them swiftly when they do occur.

Consequently, such business-critical applications are always expected to be available to end users, which means resiliency-based capacity planning and positioning is critical, and the single-point-of-failure risk must be mitigated. Failure of a physical server, a rack, a building, or even a site must not affect the ability of users to reach business-critical applications.

The most obvious solution for the challenge is to run multiple instances of the business-critical applications in different servers positioned in different sites or data centers. As you might imagine, this eventually amplifies the cost involved and creates resource efficiency challenges. Running a moderately utilized application on more than one physical server prevents IT administrators from realizing resource efficiency.

Simplicity and Cost Optimization

Ease of workload provisioning and operation is a critical necessity for successful IT infrastructure management. In a physical infrastructure environment, scaling a workload up or down is not an easy task. It is not only a matter of identifying the right hardware configuration. Integrating the applications into the business ecosystem also involves time-consuming tasks such as hardware procurement and shipment to the site and installation and configuration of the servers.

Although the initial provisioning is challenging, the operational activities, such as migrating the workload or application to a different server for policy or performance adherence, presents a similar challenge. One obvious option is to increase the workforce of the IT operation team, but doing so is a trade-off between cost and simplicity.

Following are some of the most common questions raised while designing an IT infrastructure:

■ How can the hardware procurement cost be reduced?

■ How can the hardware maintenance cost be reduced?

- How is it possible to efficiently utilize resources without compromising business needs?

- How is it possible to provide efficient and scalable business resiliency?

Although virtualization has existed since the late 1960s, the need to resolve these issues has paved the way to full-blown virtualization.

Virtualization—Architecture Definition and Types

Virtualization is the ability to decouple the software from the underlying hardware infrastructure to create a virtual environment and run specific applications as virtual entities. With this modularity and versatility, virtualization has transitioned into a mainstream technology for many data centers and enterprise networks and has allowed them to integrate and manage business-critical workloads at the desired scale while still reducing the initial and operational expenditures.

Architecture and Components

In the computing world, the microprocessors that evolved from the 8086, 80286, and 80386 processors are collectively referred to as x86, which is the dominant architecture in use today. The x86 architecture offers four levels of privileges, with Ring 0 being the most privileged level and Ring 4 being the least privileged level (see Figure 1-3). The global description table (GDT) that defines the characteristics of each memory area includes an **IO Privilege Level (IOPL)** flag of size 2 bits that defines the access privileges.

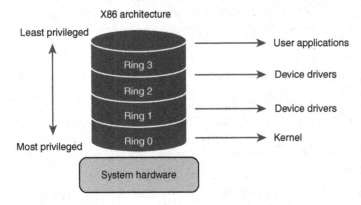

Figure 1-3 *x86 Architecture*

From the virtualization architecture point of view, four types of virtualization exist. They are described below and shown in Figure 1-4.

- **Full virtualization:** Full virtualization employs a combination of binary translation and direct-execution techniques to provide the appearance of full virtualization. The binary translation technique involves modified x86 software (also known as hypervisor software) that translates the sequence of instructions from the guest OS to instructions that can be interpreted by the target computer. In this approach, the guest OS is completely abstracted from the underlying hardware, with the virtualization software acting as a median that translates the instruction from the guest OS and caches the results between the hardware and the guest OS. The guest OS does not need modification to support virtualization. Usually, the guest OS is not even aware that it is running in a virtual environment.

■ **Paravirtualization:** Paravirtualization, also known as OS Assisted Virtualization, is a technique in which the guest OS is customized to replace the instructions with hypercalls. Unlike full virtualization, the paravirtualization technique does not need a dedicated hypervisor because the guest OS is augmented with hypercall instructions and thus provides direct control over the underlying hardware resources. While this technique can exhibit comparatively better performance, it is poor in terms of backward compatibility and does not scale because it requires guest OS–level modifications.

■ **Hardware-assisted virtualization:** Hardware-assisted virtualization is a platform or hardware virtualization approach that leverages the extended virtualization capabilities of the underlying processors. Hardware vendors such as Intel and AMD came up with CPUs that natively support virtualization and eliminate the need for binary translation or paravirtualization. This technique includes introducing a new privilege mode as the ROOT mode that can be considered as a layer between Ring 0 and the underlying hardware layer. The hypervisor or the Virtual Machine Monitor (VMM) runs in this new layer and allows the guest OS to run on Ring 0.

■ **Nested virtualization:** Nested virtualization instantiates a virtual entity within another virtual device. This method allows the guest OS to act as a virtualization host and installs the hypervisor software on a guest OS, which in turn is running on another hypervisor. Typically, nested virtualization is not used to run production workloads. However, this is an excellent platform that is useful for testing or learning purposes. Cisco Virtual Internet Routing Lab (VIRL) is a good example of an application that leverages nested virtualization. Cisco VIRL is a Linux-based distribution (Lubuntu) that runs on a bare metal or ESXi host as a virtual machine and allows users to simulate multiple virtual Cisco devices on the VIRL environment.

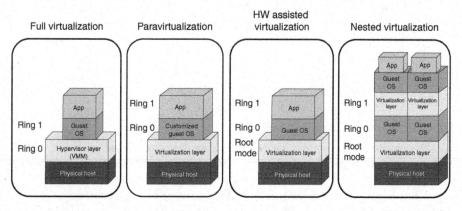

Figure 1-4 *Types of Virtualization Architecture*

Depending on the type of processor and the hypervisor used, one or more of the preceding types of virtualization can be realized. Figure 1-5 shows output from a Linux server that depicts the capability of the processor to support virtualization.

```
                    :~$ lscpu
Architecture:          x86_64
CPU op-mode(s):        32-bit, 64-bit
Byte Order:            Little Endian
CPU(s):                24
On-line CPU(s) list:   0-23
Thread(s) per core:    2
Core(s) per socket:    6
Socket(s):             2
NUMA node(s):          2
Vendor ID:             GenuineIntel
CPU family:            6
Model:                 44
Model name:            Intel(R) Xeon(R) CPU        X5660  @ 2.80GHz
Stepping:              2
CPU MHz:               2793.112
BogoMIPS:              5585.94
Virtualization:        VT-x
L1d cache:             32K
L1i cache:             32K
L2 cache:              256K
L3 cache:              12288K
NUMA node0 CPU(s):     0,2,4,6,8,10,12,14,16,18,20,22
NUMA node1 CPU(s):     1,3,5,7,9,11,13,15,17,19,21,23
Flags:                 fpu vme de pse tsc msr pae mce cx8 apic sep mtrr pge mca
cmov pat pse36 clflush dts acpi mmx fxsr sse sse2 ss ht tm pbe syscall nx pdpe1g
b rdtscp lm constant_tsc arch_perfmon pebs bts rep_good nopl xtopology nonstop_t
sc aperfmperf eagerfpu pni pclmulqdq dtes64 monitor ds_cpl vmx smx est tm2 ssse3
 cx16 xtpr pdcm pcid dca sse4_1 sse4_2 popcnt aes lahf_lm ssbd ibrs ibpb stibp k
aiser tpr_shadow vnmi flexpriority ept vpid dtherm ida arat
                    :~$
```

Figure 1-5   *Linux Processor Output*

Types of Virtualization

Based on the granularity of the stack and components, virtualization is arguably classified in as many as seven different types. For the sake of simplicity, the following three most distinct and well-known categories are covered in the coming sections:

- Server virtualization

- Network virtualization

- Storage virtualization

Server Virtualization

Server virtualization is the first and the most dominant use of virtualization that allows users to run end-user application services, such as a web server or a file server, in the emulated hardware environment as shown in Figure 1-6. The introduction of virtualization-powered processors, such as Intel-VT and AMD-V, encouraged the implementation of server virtualization in x86 architecture.

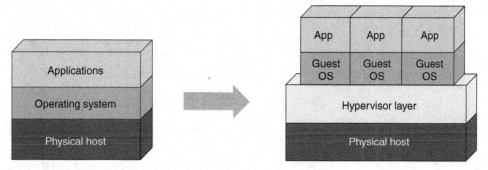

Figure 1-6 *Server Virtualization*

As mentioned in the previous section, the hypervisor layer plays a key role in virtualization. This is a software layer that abstracts the underlying hardware resources and presents them as virtual resources—such as vCPU—to the server operating system running on top of it. Virtual CPU (vCPU) is a logical time-shared entity that provides a dedicated processing time slot on the physical CPU. The availability and number of physical CPUs and the cores per CPU decide the number of vCPUs that can be simulated on the processor. Online vCPU calculators are useful for estimating the number of virtual servers that can be hosted on a physical server with specific processor configurations.

Based on their abilities, hypervisors are classified into two types, as shown in Figure 1-7.

- Native hypervisor

- Hosted hypervisor

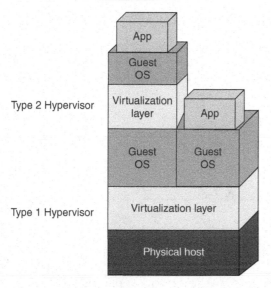

Figure 1-7 *Types of Hypervisor*

Cisco Unified Computing System (UCS) is one of the platforms that supports the following types of hypervisors:

- **Native hypervisor:** Also known as a type 1 hypervisor, a native hypervisor is VMM software that is installed directly on top of bare-metal hardware and acts as the host operating system. VMware ESXi and Microsoft Hyper-V are two of the available native hypervisors. Typically, these hypervisors come with a server manager that acts as a front-end tool for creating or deleting virtual servers. Although these hypervisors are free to download and install, the server manager requires paid licensing. Linux KVM, on the other hand, is an open-source native hypervisor that is developed and managed by open community contributors, and it is freely available. Because native hypervisors can run directly on top of the bare-metal server, they offer high scalability and other advanced features that make it one of the best hypervisors for enterprise-grade deployments.

- **Hosted hypervisor:** Also known as a type 2 hypervisor, a hosted hypervisor is software that is installed on an existing host operating system and runs like any other application on top of the host operating system. Unlike a native hypervisor, the hosted hypervisor does not require a licensed server manager to administrate the servers, which means it is less expensive compared to the native hypervisor. A type 2 hypervisor enables nested virtualization provisioning; in fact, a type 2 hypervisor is required to implement nested virtualization. VMware Fusion and VirtualBox are two such hosted hypervisors.

Network Virtualization

A traditional enterprise network includes much more than basic routing and switching. It is not unusual to see an enterprise network built with a composite set of network appliances. Each of those network appliances is built by defining relevant operational characteristics to satisfy specific business needs. For example, Cisco ASA 5506 is an enterprise-class firewall appliance that is built to provide security, encryption, and access-control functionalities. Similarly, Cisco WAAS is a WAN optimization appliance that is built to optimize WAN throughput (see Figure 1-8).

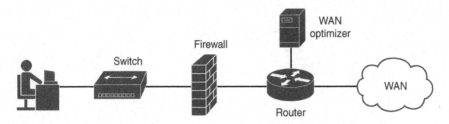

Figure 1-8   *Typical Branch Site*

The current deployment model to insert service appliances such as firewalls is to position the appliances inline to the data path of the traffic. This depends on the order in which the network service should be applied to the data traffic. One typical example is shown in Figure 1-8. User traffic must be optimized only if the firewall rules allow the traffic flow. This requirement means the firewall policy must be applied before the WAN optimization service is applied. Applying WAN optimization before firewall policies may result in a flow that is optimized by the WAN optimizer and dropped by the firewall appliance. This static nature of service insertion does not scale and requires meticulous design to position the services based on the business intent. Any change in the order of services requires moving the physical position of the appliances in the data path.

The benefits of virtualization are applicable for both the server and the network arena. The industry moved toward virtualizing the network function for several reasons, such as the need to control traffic between multitenant virtual servers that reside on the same physical servers.

As shown in Figure 1-9, if the traffic between the Enterprise-Green and the Enterprise-Red virtual servers must apply stringent policies, the traffic needs to traverse a physical network appliance, such as a firewall with all the relevant policies configured. Applying the virtualization concept to network appliances will introduce additional benefits that manifest as strong business drivers for network virtualization.

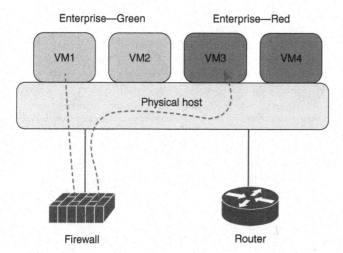

Figure 1-9 *Network Virtualization*

Network function virtualization (NFV) decouples the network function from the underlying proprietary hardware and runs the network function as a virtual network appliance on a supported hypervisor. NFV is not just limited to virtualizing the network function. NFV can virtualize a physical network node into multiple virtual nodes or combine multiple physical network nodes and create one virtual node. In the past decade, Cisco has pioneered some of these architectures that are available in many Cisco products. More details about network virtualization in Cisco are explained in Chapter 2, "Virtualization and Cisco."

Storage Virtualization

Back in the 1880s, analog computers used punch cards to store binary data. Since the 1950s, data storage techniques have evolved from magnetic tapes to floppy disks and then CD-ROMs. Currently, data storage is completely offloaded to the cloud and allows the user to access the data anytime from anywhere. If you are an iPhone or an Android user, your photos are likely uploaded to the cloud, alleviating the need to store them on your device. (Whether the data is safe in the cloud is a different story.)

The evolution from punch cards to the cloud shown in Figure 1-10 is both exciting and radical.

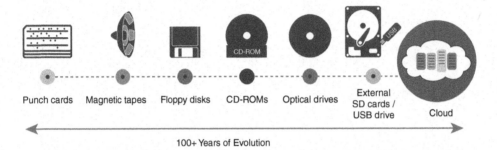

Figure 1-10   *Storage Evolution*

Today, it is hard to imagine the use of such punch cards or even a floppy disk to store data now that data can be transported on a thumb-sized USB drive. The fact that floppy disks are no more in use reminds me of one of the famous IT jokes where a current generation kid was surprised seeing a floppy disk and asked, "You 3D printed the Save icon?"

The use of external storage is not a new concept, and it is a widespread practice in large data center deployments. Data storage disks have been decoupled from the physical servers that allowed users to access their data from different applications with redundancy. These external data stores are arrays of disks that act as block devices that handle the raw data. File systems, such as FAT-32 and NTFS, are layered on top of these block devices to store the actual data, and the file systems define the format of the data stored on the block devices. Two common storage deployment models are storage area networks (SANs) and network-attached storage (NAS):

- **Storage area network (SAN):** In this deployment model, servers are configured to access an array of block devices over the network. SAN access can be provided by fiber channel or Ethernet-based iSCSI access channels. Because the access is provided only to the block devices, the applications using the block devices are responsible for layering the relevant file systems on top of the block devices.

- **Network-attached storage (NAS):** In this deployment model, servers are configured to access the file system itself instead of the block devices so that the file systems are ready to mount and use. NAS services, such as AFS, FTP, and NFS, can be imagined as another server that resides within the network but provides only the file system for data storage.

With the evolution of server virtualization, workloads are being migrated from physical machines to virtual machines, and the ability to virtualize storage is critical for the success of server virtualization. Storage virtualization allows the operators to partition the disk arrays into virtual block devices with their own file systems. Such virtual storage is then coupled with one or more virtual machines.

Connecting the Dots with Cloud Computing

Cloud computing is often misinterpreted as virtualization. Technically, they are not the same. However, virtualization lays the foundation to realize the benefits of cloud computing. According to the National Institute of Standards and Technology (NIST), "cloud computing is defined as a model for enabling convenient, on-demand network access to a shared pool of configurable computing resources that can be rapidly provisioned and released with minimal management effort or service provider interaction."

The term "cloud" is a metaphor that refers to a collective set of shared physical computers and storage devices that are connected through the Internet and offers a plethora of ever-evolving services. Cloud computing is a general term that loosely refers to computing resources in the cloud. Cloud computing is powered by a blend of Service Oriented Architecture (SOA) and virtualization. The prime reason for the success of cloud computing is that it instantiates on-demand, cost-effective, and flexible virtual computing resources that are offered by virtualization and that are combined with a loosely integrated suite of SOA. As cloud computing has moved from concept to product, many existing and new providers devised a plethora of cloud-based service offerings.

Amazon and Google Cloud are real-world examples of cloud providers that offer varying degrees of cloud services. Back in the physical computing days, it took days—or in worst case, even months—to integrate a computer server into production because it involved designing the server with the desired specifications, such as CPU, memory, storage, and so on, and install the relevant software and applications. In the era of cloud computing, the same task involves a few clicks and takes just a few seconds to minutes. Following are some of the key characteristics of cloud computing:

- **On-demand and self-service:** Cloud computing allows users to spin up the resources as needed or required and shut them down when not required with minimal or no dependency on the cloud provider.

- **Flexible resource availability:** Cloud computing allows users to scale the workload up or down dynamically based on need in a matter of few seconds.

- **Multitenancy:** Multitenancy allows users to run the workload on a virtual environment that is shared by other tenants without security concerns.

- **Maintenance:** Maintenance allows users to offload resource maintenance to providers, which means issues in the underlying resources are outside the scope of the users and do not increase the management overhead for users.

- **Reliability:** Failure of the underlying server is nearly seamless to users because failed workloads are dynamically reprovisioned on other available physical hosts.

Computing Virtualization Elements and Techniques

Computing or server virtualization provides resource abstraction at varying granularity, which results in different by-products that satisfy different types of computing use cases.

Virtual Machines

A virtual machine is the first by-product of server virtualization technology that emulates a computer as a virtual entity on a physical server. Virtual machines are self-contained systems with their own share of virtual resources and their own guest operating system (guest OS). By leveraging the hypervisor, multiple virtual machines running distinct guest operating systems are instantiated on the same physical host operating system, as shown in Figure 1-11.

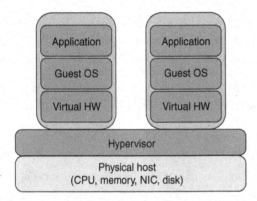

Figure 1-11   *Virtual Machines*

The guest operating system is packaged in a file format that includes the configuration and properties for the virtual machine that is instantiated using the image file. Different types of file formats are available for packaging and distributing virtual machine guest OSs. The file format defines the lists of requested resource specifications, such as vCPU, vMemory, vNIC ports, serial ports, and parallel ports, along with the initial configuration required for the bootup and operation of the virtual machine.

Open Virtualization Format (OVF) is an open standard format for software packaging. OVF uses the following structure:

- One instance of the OVF descriptor file with the .ovf extension (mandatory file)

- OVF manifest with the .mf extension (optional)

- OVF certificate with the .cert extension (optional)

- Disk image files (optional)

- Resource files such as ISO images (optional)

The OVF descriptor file is composed of the metadata for the OVF package that is encoded in an extensible human-readable XML schema. Optionally, a disk format is defined in the package that describes the virtual HDD for the virtual machine. Although there are different types of disk formats, not all formats are supported by all the hypervisors. Virtual Machine Disk (VMDK) is one of the most used formats that is supported by many of the hypervisors. Qcow2 is another format that is represented in fixed-size block devices. Qcow2 format is supported by the QEMU processor emulator that KVM, an open-source hypervisor, uses.

One of the most painful and stressful situations for any user is to lose the machine containing their data. It can take days to recover from the grief. Imagine a situation in which a user has provisioned a virtual machine and taken hours or days to identify and install the right set of binaries and software and then abruptly loses the virtual machine. Rebuilding the lost virtual machine takes the same amount of time and energy. Most hypervisors, however, allow you to take a snapshot of a virtual machine with all the installed application binaries that can be reinstantiated in the same or a different physical host. These snapshots are stored as disk images that contain the configuration files and the data. Usually, these snapshots are saved as VMDK or Qcow2 disk images.

Most hypervisors also support duplication of the virtual machine by instantiating different instances of the virtual machine from a snapshot image. Some hypervisors also allow you to duplicate the machine using a template; this is known as virtual machine cloning. Virtual machine cloning allows the hypervisor to take a snapshot of a running virtual machine and clone the snapshot into multiple instances. This allows users to realize various benefits, such as workload migration, demand-based workload scaling, and more.

Each virtual machine is assigned with one or more virtual network interface cards (vNICs) for network connectivity as defined in the descriptor file. vNIC is a software version of the NIC with its own MAC and IP address. The traffic load on the respective vNIC varies depending on the application enabled or the service offered by the virtual machine. The performance of the virtual machine is directly affected by the type of vNIC used in the virtual machine and its ability to handle the traffic load. Continuous enhancement has been performed to improve the performance of vNIC with the help of a hardware-accelerated NIC and with the new generation smart NICs. Hardware-accelerated NICs are interface cards with the capability to offload some responsibilities, such as decryption or frame checksum verification. Smart NIC is powered with an ARM-based processor that can perform more advanced offloading from both the control plane and the data plane process.

Containers

In the past decade, the application development model has changed from a monolithic to a microservice architecture for scalability and agility. As an application that is built based on the monolithic architecture, all the software functional components, such as user authentication, ordering, and payments, are integrated as one single linear application. Changes to the existing code or the introduction of a new feature instigate many challenges that affect the development lifecycle.

The microservices architecture, on the other hand, decomposes each functional component into a lightweight service and uses well-defined APIs for inter-service communication. A collection of such lightweight microservices is integrated as a software application. The microservice architecture grants great modularity that allows software developers to address the challenges faced with monolithic development. This microservice architecture is further enhanced to run services as virtual entities on different physical hosts and use network-based APIs for interservice communication. Although this enhancement is astonishing, running a virtual machine for each service is costly in terms of resources and does not justify the benefits. This is where containers come into the picture.

The containers shown in Figure 1-12 are lightweight virtual entities that are packages of binaries and libraries required to run the relevant application or service.

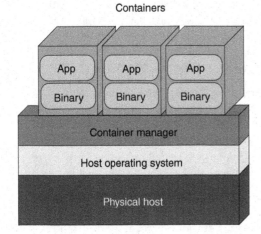

Figure 1-12   *Container Architecture*

Virtual machines and containers are similar in terms of resource governance, but containers do not need their own guest OS, so it is not technically accurate to say that containers are lightweight virtual machines. Because containers share the same host operating system, the container manager uses kernel namespaces and control groups—also known as cgroups—to provide isolation between the containers and to allow the containers to run in the user mode.

Control groups (cgroups) are a kernel feature written in 2006 that groups the collection of processes that can share the system resource and limits the resource utilization between such groups. Cgroups are responsible for allocating resources such as CPU time, memory, network resources, and the like.

Namespace is another kernel feature that offers isolation between processes by running them in different namespaces. The group of processes in one namespace cannot see or use the resources in other namespaces.

LXC is a virtualization method that allows you to provision containers on a Linux distribution by using the lxd daemon as the container manager and libvirt as the container driver. Figure 1-13 shows a snapshot of the Linux commands for installing and provisioning LXC containers.

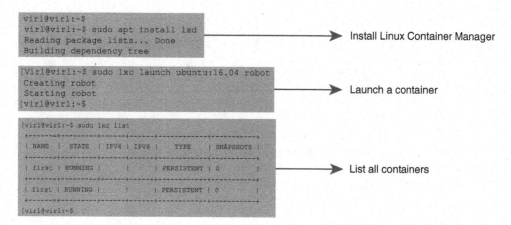

Figure 1-13 *LXC Command Output*

Serverless Computing

In most of the XaaS offerings, such as PaaS, SaaS, IaaS, and so on, one of the virtual entities, such as a virtual machine or a container, offers the service. More simply, a computing resource is enabled to provide any such XaaS. Generally, the offered services are densely used and thus, a dedicated computing resource is required to continuously execute the function. However, other use cases sporadically use the computer resource. ETL (Extract, Transform, and Load) is one such use case in which the data transform function is executed only when required. Running a computer resource for such a sporadically used service is expensive. In the recent past, FaaS (function as a service) began evolving as a service option suitable for such sporadically used services. FaaS leverages serverless computing. However, serverless computing does not mean there is no need for a server or a computer resource to run such services. Instead, the computer resource is invoked and used only when the need arises.

FaaS, as the name says, is a simple functional code that is invoked only when a request is received. The functional code is developed by the end user based on the end user's requirements, using programming languages such as C, C++, and Python. The function is provisioned in the cloud without dedicated server resources, and the code is associated with an invoke function. The invoke function, managed by the cloud provider, invokes and executes the function only when it receives a request. This eliminates the need for an always-on server or other virtual entity. This allows users to focus on the business logic and app development instead of spending energy to manage servers. Two such FaaS options are AWS Lambda and Azure Function. Apache OpenWhisk is an open source, distributed, serverless platform.

Although some say serverless computing is the next generation application development model that is superseding microservice architecture, it is too early to conclude if this is true.

Virtualization Scale and Design Consideration

Some of the critical characteristics that should be considered while designing and deploying the virtualization environment are listed in the following sections.

High Availability

It is annoying to see "Service Unavailable" error messages popping up on an ATM machine while you are trying to draw some cash. A 404 error is equally annoying when you are trying to make your mortgage or credit card payment. Both problems are caused by the lack of service availability when users need it.

High availability is a design characteristic to ensure the availability of the offered service for end users, and it is measured by the uptime of the service. This candidly reflects the quality of the offered service. In a banking environment, the application that is used to host the user portal or the dashboard is a critical service that cannot afford downtime. In any IT company, the build server on which the application development is ported and committed is a critical one that the business cannot afford to lose, even for seconds. However, other internal low-priority services—such as a vacation request portal—can run with acceptable downtime because they do not have a critical effect on the business. While designing the infrastructure, due diligence must be given for high-priority services by considering service redundancy.

High availability must be designed by considering failures from different layers and aspects. Running the same application as two processes (active and standby) in the same virtual machine provides process-level redundancy. However, if the virtual machine fails, both processes will be lost. Cloning and running the application as two different virtual machine instances provides virtual machine–level redundancy, but they both must not run on the same physical host. It is a common practice to deploy disaster recovery sites in different parts of the geographic area by running the same instances of business-critical services so that any failures due to natural disaster in one geographical area does not stop the business. In short, high availability design that avoids any single point of failure is a compelling business requirement for IT infrastructure design.

Although high availability is not specific to end applications (remember the ATM example?), virtualization capability delivers high availability by instantiating more than one virtual machine or containers in different physical hosts. Advanced features, such as virtual machine cloning or using a virtual machine template, come in handy in such situations because they allow you to provision multiple instances of the same virtual machine or appliances in a matter of seconds.

Workload Distribution

Although service resiliency is achieved by running multiple instances of the same application in different environments, utilization efficiency depends on the high availability deployment model. There are two types of high availability deployment models:

- **Active-standby:** In active-standby mode, one of the services or the virtual machine acts as the primary service and takes all the load while the other instance of the virtual machine acts as a backup that takes over the role of primary service only when the primary is down. It is a common practice in data centers or disaster recovery sites to provision both active and standby services with the same IP address and the GW connected to the primary service advertises a more specific prefix. Traffic flows are redirected to stand by only if the primary service is down. This model is not as efficient as the standby virtual machine, and the service consumes computer and other resources even when the primary service is taking all the traffic load.

- **Active-active:** In active-active mode, the workload is distributed to both the virtual machines, which improves the efficiency drastically and yet provides high availability because one virtual machine is available even if the other fails. The characteristics of virtualization to instantly provision the virtual machine or container help users create multiple instances and configure them for efficient load distribution.

Resource Utilization

For the past two decades, resource utilization has been one of the benefits associated with the deployment of virtualization. Efficiently utilizing available IT resources is a critical business component that is directly reflected in revenue. By the end of the year, most of the employees are on vacation, which reduces server workload. Therefore, it is a common practice to shut down data centers during that time of year to save power, money, and the environment. However, resource efficiency can be realized on a per-day basis, too. It is common to see a heavy workload on the employee portal during business hours but minimal or no load during off-business hours.

The characteristics of virtualization that allow users to provision instant virtual machines or containers help to dynamically scale the service up or down based on the workload. During business hours, multiple instances of the virtual machine running business-critical applications can be deployed for load distribution, while the numbers can be drastically scaled down during off-business hours. This elastic nature of virtualization helps users utilize the resources efficiently, and the business can proudly claim that it is eco-friendly.

Multitenancy in Virtualization

A "tenant" is a term used to refer to an individual who pays and temporarily possesses some resources from the proprietor. A simple example is someone who rents land or a house from the landlord and pays on a monthly basis. Multitenancy is a related term for multiple tenants who temporarily possess their own share of the resources from the same proprietor. A housing apartment complex in which multiple tenants have their own living spaces while sharing some common spaces is a typical example. Figure 1-14 shows an example of multitenancy in the cloud.

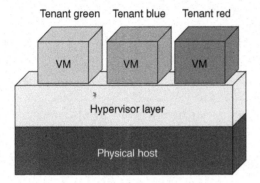

Figure 1-14   *Multitenancy in the Cloud*

In a cloud computing environment, multitenancy is not new; it is a common practice for efficiently utilizing resources. Most of the XaaS services that cloud providers offer are multitenancy aware. Provisioning and running virtual machines that belong to different customers on the same physical host or data center is a classic example for multitenancy. The degree of multitenancy varies depending on the type of service offered. With infrastructure as a service (IaaS) or even bare metal as a service (BMaaS), multitenancy is all about running multiple virtual machines that belong to different tenants. With software as a service (SaaS), the granularity is at the software level where the provider creates a different user account for each tenant in the same application.

Multitenancy eventually comes with a stringent security tightening requirement. Communication between virtual machines that belong to different tenants (intertenant communication) must undergo tight scrutiny of security policies. The ability of virtualization natively helps to provide multitenant services by segregating the resources without compromising security.

It is a common misconception that multitenancy is intended only for public clouds where the cloud provider and the tenants belong to different administrative domains. Multitenancy-based service deployments in private clouds are equally common and efficient. In a private cloud where the cloud and the services belong to the same administrative domain, different departments are considered tenants that share the resources but require controlled communication between those tenants.

Summary

Although virtualization is not a new concept, it is irrefutably one of the radical innovations in the past couple of decades. Inevitably, virtualization has aided numerous businesses and has paved the way for other service offerings that span different business verticals. Virtualization is now an integral part of any infrastructure design.

This chapter discussed the evolution of virtualization and emphasized the types of virtualization with the applicable components and use cases. The next four chapters will explain the virtualization applicability of Cisco products.

References in This Chapter

Arena, Simone, Falkner, Matthias, Zacks, David, and Szigeti Tim. *Cisco Digital Network Architecture: Intent-Based Networking for the Enterprise*, First Edition. Hoboken, New Jersey: Cisco Press, 2018.

Santana, G. A. *Data Center Virtualization Fundamentals: Understanding Techniques and Designs for Highly Efficient Data Centers with Cisco Nexus, UCS, MDS, and Beyond*, First Edition. Hoboken, New Jersey: Cisco Press, 2013.

Moreno, Victor and Reddy, Kumar. *Network Virtualization*. Hoboken, New Jersey: Cisco Press, 2006.

Chapter 2

Virtualization and Cisco

In this chapter, you will learn the following:

- History of virtualization in the core routing and switching products of Cisco

- How the infrastructure virtualization is achieved and applied to enterprise and service-provider segments

- Software-defined networking (SDN) and its various key enablers

- SDN Controllers and associated protocols and various open-source SDN Controllers

- The roles played by APIs and various programmability elements in the era of virtualization

- Proprietary Cisco SDN Controllers for enterprise and data centers and modern-day network design with network functions virtualization (NFV)

- Trending technologies built on virtualization and SDN

History of Virtualization in Cisco

Chapter 1, "Introduction to Virtualization," discussed the history behind virtualization, cloud computing, and different milestones crossed by those technologies to reach its current state. It also briefly discussed container capabilities and how containers allow you to build and offer virtual services. In this chapter, you learn how virtualization is applicable to the Cisco network platforms and infrastructure.

Network Infrastructure Virtualization

Historically, VLANs (Virtual LANs) were a key concept in the early days of virtualization days. VLANs take a physical entity (LAN) and virtualize an Ethernet switching infrastructure to create multiple logical segments.

As you learned in Chapter 1, necessity is responsible for many inventions. The necessity of VLANs is to scale the deployments. As you know, broadcasts are a well-known way for devices to communicate among themselves—Address Resolution Protocol (ARP), Dynamic Host Configuration Protocol (DHCP), address assignments, and so on. As more devices are added to the switch and the network grows, broadcast traffic grows exponentially.

In Figure 2-1, four PCs are connected to an unmanaged switch, and VLAN is not implemented. If PC A sends a broadcast frame, besides PC B, it will be forwarded to PCs C and D even though they are not in the same subnet.

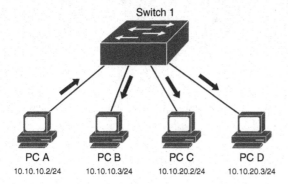

Figure 2-1   *Unmanaged Ethernet Switch*

VLANs within a standalone switch are easily understandable, but how do you extend the VLANs to multiple switches to scale the deployment? The answer is a VLAN Trunking protocol like Dot1Q (or 802.1Q) or the Cisco Inter-Switch Link (ISL). These protocols add a special header (referred as a **dot1Q** or **ISL** header) to the original frame to virtualize the switching infrastructure into multiple logical segments, as illustrated in Figure 2-2. Figure 2-3 illustrates how a regular Ethernet frame adds a dot1Q header to identify the traffic in a specific VLAN.

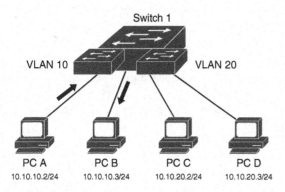

Figure 2-2   *Ethernet Switch with VLANs*

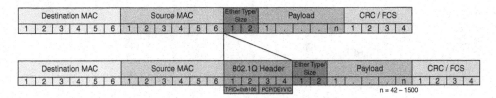

Figure 2-3 *VLAN Dot1Q Header*

While virtualizing a given LAN infrastructure into multiple logical segments helps to scale the network, it also keeps up the integrity of broadcast domains (by not forwarding traffic from one to another) and simplifies managing the network. Most importantly, VLANs and the Dot1Q header are completely transparent to users (see Figure 2-4).

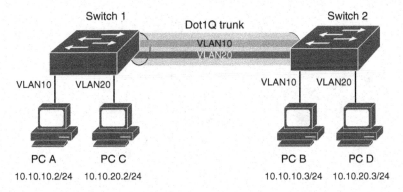

Figure 2-4 *Dot1Q Trunking*

You can extend the same idea and apply it to various protocols and standards, such as Virtual Route Forwarding (VRF). VRF virtualizes a single routing device to support multiple virtual routing instances and keeps them logically separated from each other.

In Figure 2-5, Gig0/1 and Gig0/3 are assigned to VRF RED, whereas Gig0/2 and Gig0/4 are assigned to VRF BLUE. For each VRF created, the router will have a dedicated routing and forwarding resources, which contains the routing information base, routing table, ARP table, adjacency table, and so on.

In Figure 2-6, using the dedicated forwarding resources, the router forwards the traffic between network A and C and between network B and D, but it isolates them from each other. This VRF concept, which is usually referred to as **VRF-Lite**, basically virtualizes one physical routing device into multiple virtual routing devices.

If you extend this concept, Multiprotocol Label Switching VPN (MPLS VPN) segments a large routed network into multiple logical networks allocated for individual user groups.

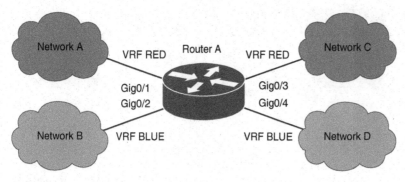

Figure 2-5   *Virtualizing a Router with VRF-Lite*

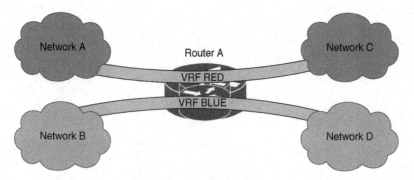

Figure 2-6   *Dedicated Forwarding Services*

In Figure 2-7, Customers A, B, and C are identified with dedicated VRFs A, B, and C, respectively, at the Provider Edge PE-A router, which adds MPLS labels to the packet headers to differentiate the traffic in a VRF from other VRFs. The routers in the provider network exchange information on labels allocated to send and receive traffic between them. As an end result, the traffic received by PE-A in VRF A is forwarded across the provider network to PE-B, which in turn correctly identifies the traffic originated by CE-A in VRF A and forwards them to CE-D in VRF A. This MPLS VPN network is transparent to customers, and it virtualizes one common physical routing infrastructure to provide exclusive private service to customers connecting their sites across the service provider network. The concepts of VLANs, VRFs, and MPLS VPNs virtualize one physical entity such as an MPLS network in our case to multiple logical entities.

Network Device Virtualization

Starting with VLAN and VRFs, several technologies have evolved in the data center and enterprise networking domain. For example, multiple stacked switches act as one larger logical switch (see Figure 2-8). With the single unified control plane and management interface, all the switches in the stack run the same version of the software and communicate with each other through stack cables connecting their backplanes.

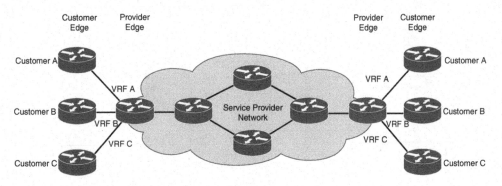

Figure 2-7   *User Segmentation with MPLS VPN*

Figure 2-8   *Stacking with Ethernet Switches*

In Figure 2-8, physical switches' backplanes are connected with stacking cables to build a stack of four switches. This stack will have a unified management interface and appear as one logical device to all the neighboring devices running Layer 2 or Layer 3 protocols, such as Spanning Tree Protocol, Link Aggregation Control Protocol (LACP), and Open Shortest Path First (OSPF).

In terms of network device virtualization, the Virtual Switching System (VSS) technology is a significant milestone where two physical Catalyst 6500 switches are brought together as one logical switch with a unified control plane (see Figure 2-9). They communicate through a channel/link between the two physical switches called a Virtual Switch Link (VSL) using a proprietary handshaking protocol—Virtual Switch Link Protocol (VSLP). VSS is a game changer in network virtualization because building out a virtual domain from two physical switches has been made easy and seamless. This increases the available bandwidth by having all ports (which were in Spanning Tree Protocol blocking states before) in use. This in turn makes the core network highly available with sub-second convergence; above all, it supports in-service software upgrade (ISSU) and related in-service maintenance activities.

Through the VSLP protocol, the switches negotiate and define their roles. One of them becomes Active and the other becomes Standby. Both switches have a unified control plane, which is on the active switch. The data plane in both switches is active and forwards the traffic.

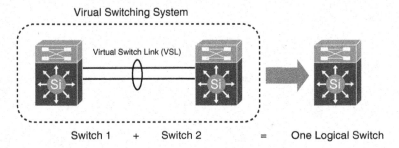

Figure 2-9   *Virtual Switching System*

When two physical switches become one logical switch—by bundling the links of a distribution switch connected to VSS with a port channel—it removes the spanning-tree blocking port on the distribution switch, doubling the bandwidth available.

In Figure 2-10, Switches SW1 and SW2 are brought together to build VSS Domain 100. The ports Gig1/6/1, 1/9/1 in physical switch 1, and ports Gig2/6/1 and 2/9/1 in SW2 are configured as one logical LACP port-channel 2, connecting to a neighboring switch's SW3 ports Gig1/0/1-4. In SW3, VSS appears as one switch for any Layer 2 or Layer 3 control plane protocols, such as Spanning Tree Protocol, Cisco Discovery Protocol, OSPF, and so on.

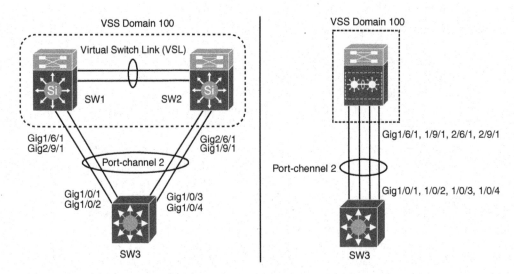

Figure 2-10   *VSS and Neighboring Device—Physical and Logical View*

Virtual PortChannel (vPC) supported in Nexus data center switching platforms is another method of forming a single Layer 2 logical entity, but it uses two separate control planes that are operating in unison. Just as with VSS, a vPC domain appears as a single virtual switch for the Layer 2 devices connected to them, but it appears as two different routers for Layer 3 devices because control planes are individually present in each vPC switch (see Figure 2-11).

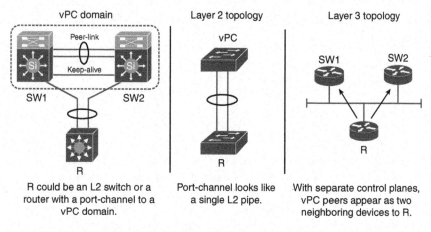

Figure 2-11 *Nexus Virtual PortChannel (vPC)*

As you see in Figure 2-11, a vPC domain consists of two vPC peer switches connected via a peer link. These two vPC peer switches communicate over a peer link using a proprietary protocol called Cisco Fabric Services (CFS). Also, parallel to the vPC peer link, there is a peer keepalive link that is used to take corrective measures when issues are experienced by the vPC peers communicating over a peer link.

Virtual Device Context (VDC) is a mechanism that converts one physical device into one or more logical devices, as illustrated in Figure 2-12. Each logical device (also referred as VDC instance) has its own independent set of VLANs, VRFs, OSPF, BGP processes, and a dedicated domain to manage it. When VDCs are created in a switch, the administrator allocates hardware interfaces and splits other common resources, such as hardware TCAM for routing tables, access list entries, and NetFlow entries among multiple VDC instances.

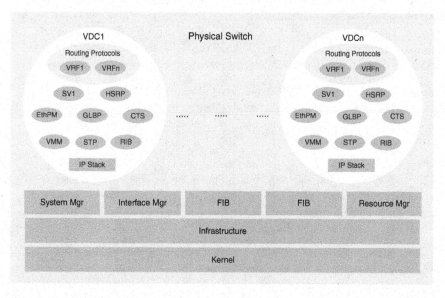

Figure 2-12 *Virtual Device Context (VDC) in Nexus*

Virtualization in Enterprise and Service Provider Environments

This section discusses the evolution of virtualization in enterprise and service provider environments, starting from mainframe days to the 5G era and Wi-Fi 6.

Enterprise

Virtualization in enterprises, especially in the computing segment, started during the mainframe era in the 1960s and later reached PCs when they were widely adopted during the late 1980s. VMware, which is one of the popular virtualization vendors, released its first product during the late 1990s. Virtualization creates an environment that makes underlying hardware efficient by optimizing its usage and makes the infrastructure scalable with utmost security. Virtualization enables enterprises to test and roll out new applications and business policies in a relatively short time, thereby helping the organizations stay agile. Another important benefit that virtualization brings is reduced rack space, power, and cooling requirements compared to legacy nonvirtualized infrastructure.

During this era of clouds, virtualization occurs at each segment of an enterprise—starting from PCs/desktops, servers, storage, and networks all the way to applications—making the journey to digitization easy and seamless.

Network virtualization enables user group segmentation, securing and isolating paths to the services and offering differentiated access control to the services.

Along with their employees, companies must provide network access for their customers, partners, contractors, and guests. To address the needs, enterprises need to build a solution that can control network access and secure that access by segmenting the wired, as well as wireless, users in appropriate groups (referred to as access control). Enterprises need transport paths between remote offices, headquarters/data centers, and the Internet that is isolated through VRFs, MPLS, GRE, and the like. Lastly, the services must be available to different user groups at the right level (control at services edge). The following concepts are shown in Figure 2-13.

- **Access control:** Access control is achieved by assigning VLANs to users based on their 802.1x authentication, physical device identity via MAC-based authentication, and guest SSID for unauthenticated wireless users. It also must make additional SSIDs available for managed users.

- **Path isolation:** Path isolation is achieved through access control lists (ACLs), mapping VLANs' Layer 3 interfaces and tunnel interfaces to specific Virtual Route Forwarding (VRF) instances. Generic routing encapsulation (GRE) tunnels isolated the traffic, and MPLS creates a tunnel mesh across the core network by isolating and routing traffic with label identification.

- **Services edge:** With **access control**, users are categorized with the appropriate groups, and through path isolation, their traffic to the services edge is isolated in a secure manner. Each user group should be given access to the services (such as enterprise business applications and the like) without compromising the security achieved by access control and path isolation. The services edge also provides access to services such as DHCP, DNS, web servers, printers, and shared databases or applications that are common to all user groups.

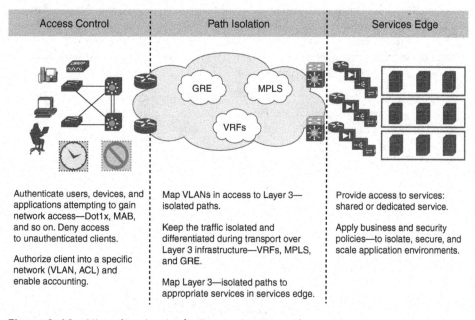

Access Control	Path Isolation	Services Edge
Authenticate users, devices, and applications attempting to gain network access—Dot1x, MAB, and so on. Deny access to unauthenticated clients.	Map VLANs in access to Layer 3—isolated paths.	Provide access to services: shared or dedicated service.
Authorize client into a specific network (VLAN, ACL) and enable accounting.	Keep the traffic isolated and differentiated during transport over Layer 3 infrastructure—VRFs, MPLS, and GRE.	Apply business and security policies—to isolate, secure, and scale application environments.
	Map Layer 3—isolated paths to appropriate services in services edge.	

Figure 2-13 *Virtualization in the Enterprise Network*

Service Provider

Even though virtualization may look like a concept close to data centers and enterprises, it provides significant differences and benefits in the service provider environments.

Virtualization in the service provider networks helps to consolidate multiple layers of routers and multiple networks built to offer different services, such as data and video. In simple terms, virtualization happens at two levels: the networks on which the data is routed and the devices that route the traffic.

Layer 2 and Layer 3 VPN services, VRF instances, and GRE are the technologies that play a key role in virtualizing the transport network between two points. In terms of the devices, Cisco virtual devices such as IOS XRv 9000, CSR 1000v, ASAv, NGFWv, and so on help with virtualizing and consolidating the network resources.

Later chapters discuss concepts, such as software-defined networking and network functions virtualization, that play critical roles in building modern-day service provider networks.

The Era of Software-Defined Networking

From being a legacy platform that handles information, the networking technologies have transitioned to become part of the business strategy and driving outcomes. Yes, it is correct to say one of the key drivers of software-defined networking (SDN) is the business outcome. Businesses need to automate and scale their IT operations, and they need to be agile by making rollouts of new applications and business policies easy and seamless. Because these applications can be provided from an on-premises enterprise data center, private cloud, public cloud, or hybrid cloud, the SDN solution is becoming more and more relevant to achieve those goals.

SDN is a centralized approach to virtualize the network elements, manage them, gain visibility, and automate operations of the network infrastructure (see Figure 2-14). To be specific, it enables the networks to accomplish the following:

■ Automate regular network configuration activities, infrastructure upgrades, and so on

■ Provide visibility into each network component across the infrastructure, including their state of operation, resources usage, and so on

■ Deploy a policy or service and perform specific tasks with high flexibility and agility

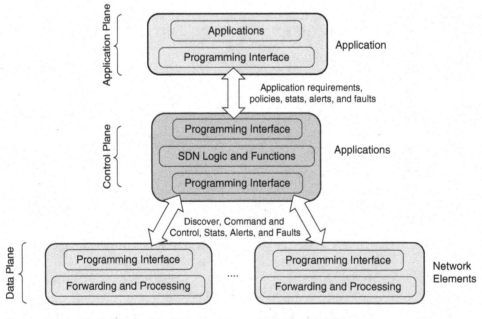

Figure 2-14 *Software-Defined Networking—High-Level Architecture*

With the centralized approach, it becomes relatively easier for enterprises and IT departments to convert the business requirements or policy changes into network policies.

In the era of SDN, the companies and organizations not only must overcome the challenges of digitizing that information, but function as an ecosystem that overcomes the barriers of required process changes, brings the employees' skills up to a specific level, and acquires new talents with new skills, while working within the culture of the working force and seamlessly interoperating with a multivendor infrastructure. Also, while transitioning from standalone/distributed to centralized SDN solutions, enterprises should keep in mind the security and standards compliance.

You can achieve the same things with a standalone devices and distributed solutions approach, but it is going to be time consuming and expensive. In other words, it incurs higher operating expenses (OpEx) and slows down the digitization.

In summary, to achieve the required business outcome, enterprises must be digitized, which can be realized through SDN-based solutions, while realizing numerous operational benefits and minimizing expenditures.

SDN Enablers

To build a software-defined network successfully, the following foundational building blocks are required, which also act as the key SDN enablers.

- **SDN control plane:** Companies and service providers around the world demand and are looking for a premium SDN control plane that is highly available, resilient, and feature-rich.

- **North and south-bound APIs:** SDN has a north-bound interface to automate the interaction with a diverse set of business/management applications and a south-bound interface to run various protocols to control multivendor hardware. It has a rich set of APIs to efficiently communicate with applications (on the north-bound interface) and expose various functions and capabilities of the hardware infrastructure (on the south-bound interface).

- **SDN protocols and data-modeling standards:** These lend support for relevant protocols and data-modeling standards, such as OpenFlow, XML, JSON, YANG, RESTCON, NETCONF, and so on.

The following sections detail these SDN enablers, control plane virtualization, open-source and Cisco proprietary SDN Controllers, APIs, and programmability options.

Control Plane Virtualization

From the perspective of network devices such as routers and switches, the control plane is the portion of the devices' operating system that participates in the protocols such as routing protocols to build neighboring relationships with peers and build required tables or infrastructures. For example, a router configured with the OSPF control plane protocol communicates with neighboring devices, builds relationship, exchanges routes, and updates/builds routing tables. Similarly, numerous control plane protocols exist, such as BGP, OSPF, EIGRP, RSVP, MPLS, LACP, and Spanning Tree Protocol. Engineers and administrators who have worked on these protocols know that the required configurations and troubleshooting commands are vendor specific and demand knowledge and skills specific to platforms, which could vary from one generation of hardware to the next.

Isolating the control plane from the data plane provides a new way for an IT organization to virtualize the network. SDN abstracts the underlying data plane (and any associated vendor/platform-specific commands and configurations) to virtualize the control plane and provide only its logical view to the applications. Those applications intend to automate the day-to-day operations and maintenance of the network. They will also offer insights into the resources that help build an elastic data center, which basically refers to a data center that can quickly respond to business needs by expanding or shrinking resources based on usage and demand.

SDN Controllers

SDN Controllers are usually seen as the "intelligence" of the network because they act as a master control point, managing underlying network devices, its configurations and operations, the applied security policies, and the traffic flow—all by using southbound APIs. Although it manages the underlying hardware, it also provides northbound APIs for business and security applications. The "APIs and Programmability" section, later in this chapter, discusses this further.

Several vendors, including Cisco, ship home-grown SDN Controllers to manage their devices and even ship an ecosystem with multivendor devices. Several open source controllers are also in the marketplace, which manages devices that support open standards.

OpenFlow

OpenFlow is one of the well-known protocols used by SDN Controllers to communicate with networking devices. With OpenFlow, the SDN protocols determine and control the path of the packets through the switches and the whole network. They control the path of the packets by adding or removing, modifying, and manipulating entries in the hardware-forwarding tables. When and where to forward (or not) is determined by the controller, whereas the hardware just follows the controller's decisions and instructions that are communicated through the OpenFlow protocol.

OpenFlow control plane packets between a controller and the devices are TCP-based and use Transport Layer Security (TLS) to secure the control plane traffic.

As you see in Figure 2-15, the flow tables perform the data plane forwarding and processing. These tables are decoupled from the control plane, which is represented by the OpenFlow control module. Here the SDN Controller makes high-level traffic routing and forwarding decisions and securely communicates the instructions to the OpenFlow Control software component in the switch using the OpenFlow protocol. Based on the instructions provided, the control plane in the OpenFlow switch updates the flow table to influence the processing and forwarding functions of the switch ports.

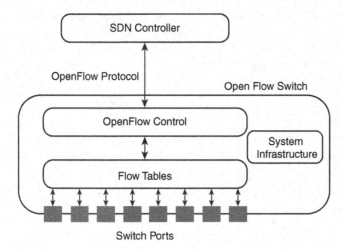

Figure 2-15 *OpenFlow SDN Controller and Switch*

Open Network Foundation (ONF) is an organization dedicated to promoting the adoption of SDN and defining and managing OpenFlow standards and general open-source SDN architecture. Starting with the release of OpenFlow standard 1.0.0 in 2009, ONF continued to develop and approve various versions. The last one announced is version 1.5.1, which was released in 2015.

Several network hardware vendors, including Cisco, are now shipping products that support OpenFlow standards.

Open Source Controllers

Nicira Networks (now part of VMware/EMC) started to develop a controller called NOX that relied on the OpenFlow protocol to communicate with and control underlying network devices. In 2008, Nicira Networks made NOX an open-source solution and opened it to the developer community. NOX, which is basically built on the C++ language, acts as an ecosystem or platform to build network applications on top of it.

There are several open-source SDN Controllers, including POX and Beacon. POX started its life as an OpenFlow controller and now is part of OpenFlow Switch's core function. It is useful for building networking software using the Python programming language.

Since several open-source controllers have been developed, tested, and released by various companies and academia, one of the most popular projects has been Floodlight, an open-source OpenFlow-based controller released by Big Switch Networks in 2012. Floodlight was developed using the Java programming language and is a fork of the Beacon controller.

OpenDaylight is a popular project announced by the Linux Foundation in 2013. It is an open-source framework to bring innovation, create a more transparent approach to software-defined concepts, and promote NFV along with SDN. The OpenDaylight

architecture, illustrated in Figure 2-16, was founded by several companies including
Cisco, Citrix, Ericsson, HP, IBM, Juniper Networks, Microsoft, VMware, Arista
Networks, Big Switch Networks, Brocade NEC, Red Hat, and a few more. Since its incep-
tion in 2013, several versions of OpenDaylight have been released, from Hydrogen in
March 2014, Helium in October 2014, up through Neon in March 2019.

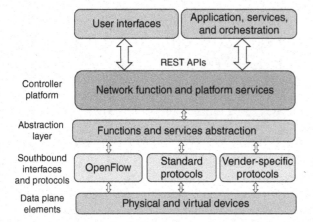

Figure 2-16   *OpenDaylight SDN Controller Architecture*

Cisco Open SDN Controller is a commercial version of OpenDaylight that automates
the network infrastructure and has standards-based devices present in a heterogenous
environment. It is based on the Helium version of OpenDaylight and supports OpenFlow
protocol version 1.0 and 1.2, several embedded applications like OpenFlow Manager,
Inventory Manager, and several network services including Topology Manager, Stats
Manager, Switch Manager, Forwarding Rules Manager, and Host Tracker.

This chapter has touched on some of the key projects in the Open Source SDN Controller
arena, but the list is not exhaustive. Several other controllers exist, including Ryu,
Maestro, OpenTransit, and Open Source Network OS (ONOS).

With several options available in the marketplace, thoroughly research the capabilities of
these controllers, consider the value they bring to your business, and carefully evaluate
them before adopting a specific SDN solution.

APIs and Programmability

This section introduces readers to the fundamentals of API, network programmability,
and various data formats that play a role in programmability and automation.

API

API is a structured routine or standard to access functions, features, or data structures
of an operating system, an application, or even a service. APIs are useful for building

applications, bringing various functions or features of web-based software or tools together to offer a new service.

It is easy to build a table in a spreadsheet and use the data to build a pie chart conveying a simplified message. How effective would it be to send just the data to an API and receive a pie chart in return? To get an idea, access the Google Charts with details provided in the "References in This Chapter" section at the end of this chapter.

APIs like the one mentioned above simply automate processes and help you build applications/services on top. Perhaps you want to build an application or web portal that shows how people in each country or continent spend their time each day. As a developer, you may want to integrate the API in discussion and focus on collecting the data, presenting the visualizations to the users, creating the look-and-feel of the application, creating the customer experience enhancement, and so on, rather than spending time and resources in a monotonous routine of building tables and pie charts. As an added benefit, by integrating the APIs into the application, the data is visualized and presented in real time, removing all the manual process and associated delays. To make use of APIs, you need to understand the service they offer or function they perform, the protocols or standards to follow sending requests, the correct format of data to input, and how to process and consume the results in a programmatic way. Above all, you do not have to know how the service offered by a given API is really achieved. As illustrated in Figure 2-17, it can be a simple black box.

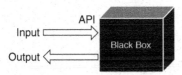

Figure 2-17 *Application Programming Interface—Input/Output*

What is described here is a simple example of how to bring in the perspective of integrating preexisting capabilities and automating the workflow. Imagine what you can achieve by bringing open-source capabilities, systems, and databases together to build a different and new service offering. Have you even wondered how Google Maps knows the timing of public transportation (which is, by the way, not offered by Google) based on your physical location? It is simple. The Google Maps application uses APIs that are supported by the public transportation authority to gather data and report required information. Should Uber develop its own maps or leverage existing maps that focus on the service it is offering? The answer: Uber and other similar companies should focus on their core services and provide the best possible experience to the customers.

Now you will go back to SDN and see how important it is for the underlying physical infrastructure to support APIs and programmability options. In the OpenFlow SDN Controllers example discussed earlier, the OpenFlow switch exposes its functions and capabilities through APIs, which the SDN Controller will use to send instructions to update the flow tables.

Programmability

Network programmability is an evolving market segment, and there is much to learn. To start your programmability journey, first you need to learn programming fundamentals. Today, Python is the most popular programming language for network engineers because of its libraries, its easy-to-learn syntax, its high-level interpretive language, and more. Understanding supported variables, functions, libraries, operations, data structures, and so on is key to becoming proficient in Python programming and performing necessary automation tasks. Python also has some disadvantages when compared to C or C++ programming languages. Python is slower in execution compared to these languages, is less preferred for memory-intensive tasks, and has limitations with database access and interactions.

To communicate with applications, services, or networking devices, you need to learn APIs—specifically, representational state transfer (REST) APIs. As the name suggests, REST APIs transfer the representational state of a device or a service using a client-server architecture. These APIs should conform to six constraints: Uniform Interface, Stateless, Cacheable, Client-Server, Layered System, and Code on Demand. Uniform Interface, a key constraint, suggests that there should be a consistent or uniform way of interacting. Stateless constraint indicates that necessary state information is embedded in the request itself and the server would not store information in reference to the session. Cacheable constraint refers to the response from the server being cacheable or storable on the client side. Client-server constraint means the application should have a client-server architecture and be independent of each other. A Layered System constraint means the client and the server may not be directly interacting and may be interacting through intermediate systems. Through the Code on Demand constraint (optional), a server can transfer an executable code to extend or customize the clients' functionality.

As illustrated in Figure 2-18, applications running on a server can interact and exchange data with networking devices like Cisco switches through HTTP and by making use of APIs supported by these devices. Because the data and the information generated by the devices are different and unstructured, data formats such as JavaScript Object Notation (JSON), XML, and YAML Ain't Markup Language (YAML) bring structure to the data and make it easy to process them programmatically.

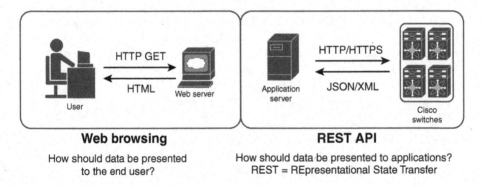

Figure 2-18 *REST APIs and Data Formats*

Standards for data formats alone are not enough to program a networking device. You need to model the data (in other words, a schema for data) and develop associated protocols or standards to install, update, manipulate, or delete the configurations or settings in networking devices. Table 2-1 lists various programming and data modeling elements and the corresponding function each one provides. Yet Another Next Generation (YANG) is one of the most popular data modeling languages in the networking industry. NETwork CONFiguration (NETCONF) and REST CONFiguration Protocol (RESTCONF) are well known and are the most adopted protocols in the industry.

Table 2-1 *Programming and Data Modeling Elements and Their Functions*

Function	Programming and Data Modeling Element
Data Model/Scheme	YANG
Data Modeling Language	YANG Data Model
App Development Environment	YANG SDK, Ansible
Programming Language	Python, C++, Java, Ruby, Erlang
Protocol	NETCONF, RESTCONF
Transport (secure)	SSH, HTTP, TLS
Encoding	XML, JSON, gRPC

Now it is time to bring it all together, starting from the top of Figure 2-19.

Programmers develop applications using different languages including Python, C++, and Java, and they do so in a software development environment such as the YANG Development Kit, Ansible, and a few others.

These applications interact with orchestrators and exchange data, which are essentially built based off the YANG Data Model schema. Data exchanged between elements are different levels, like between Orchestrator and SDN Controllers or between SDN Controllers to network elements, are all built based off YANG Data Model.

The applications, orchestrators, SDN Controllers and network elements communicate among themselves and exchange data using NETCONF or RESTCONF protocols, and they encode the data using XML, JSON, gRPC and the like.

Data requested from the orchestration by these applications (or an Orchestrator requesting data from a controller) is built into the YANG Data Model schema. The applications, orchestrators, SDN Controllers, and network elements use NETCONF, RESTCONF, gRPC, and so on to exchange the data, which is encoded in XML, JSON, and the like.

Figure 2-19 provides a high-level overview of data models used at different levels of communication.

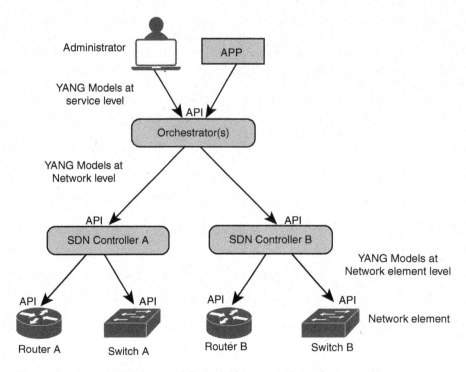

Figure 2-19   *YANG Data Models at Different Levels in the Network*

This section of the chapter would not be complete without looking into a sample YANG Model for a network element. YANG is a language for describing data models. It is a structured and strongly typed language. Following are some aspects of the language:

- Every data model is a **module**, which is a self-contained, top-level hierarchy of nodes.

- Data types can be **imported** from another YANG module or defined within a module.

- YANG uses **containers** to group related nodes.

- YANG uses **lists** to identify nodes that are stored in sequence.

- Each individual attribute of a node is represented by a **leaf**.

- Every leaf must have an associated **type**.

To add further clarity, data models may describe some aspect of a network device or a network service and will be used by network orchestration or management systems to abstract individual device differences. Examples of a device model are interfaces, VLANs, tunnels, and OSPF. Examples of the service model include Network ACL, BGP, VRF, and MPLS.

First you will look at device data models, which is relatively easier. Example 2-1 provides a sample YANG interface data model. Be aware that the model is partial because certain output is omitted for brevity. As you notice, it is an **ietf-interfaces** module. It has an **interfaces** container that uses the **interface** list to group all related nodes. Each node or leaf has a specific attribute of the list. For example, each node or leaf includes the description of an interface, the interface type, or the state of an interface (Boolean: True or False).

Example 2-1   *YANG Interface Data Model*

```
module ietf-interfaces {
    namespace "urn:ietf:params:xml:ns:yang:ietf-interfaces";
    prefix if;
    import ietf-yang-types {
      prefix yang;
    }
    organization
      "IETF NETMOD (NETCONF Data Modeling Language) Working Group";

    <snip>

    typedef interface-state-ref {
      type leafref {
        path "/if:interfaces-state/if:interface/if:name";
      }
      description
        "This type is used by data models that need to reference
         the operationally present interfaces.";
    }

    identity interface-type {
      description
        "Base identity from which specific interface types are
         derived.";
    }

    <snip>

    container interfaces {
      description
        "Interface configuration parameters.";

      list interface {
        key "name";

        leaf name {
          type string;
          description
            "The name of the interface.
        }
```

```
    leaf description {
      type string;
      description
        "A textual description of the interface.
    }

    leaf type {
      type identityref {
        base interface-type;
      }
      mandatory true;
      description
        "The type of the interface.
    }

    leaf enabled {
      type boolean;
      default "true";
      description
        "This leaf contains the configured, desired state of the
         interface.
    }

    <snip>

  }
```

Modeling the data of a network device or the services offered by the device helps to programmatically read the state of the devices or to do a write operation to change its state. A human user can access network devices and use CLI to read its status or modify the configurations. In programmatic terms, this means that you can retrieve or manipulate specific parameters without having to get as text and parse the entire output of a CLI.

Cisco Proprietary SDN Controllers

Cisco Application Policy Infrastructure Controller (Cisco APIC) is the foundational and main component of the Cisco data center SDN solution, which is called the application-centric infrastructure (ACI). For enterprise networks, Cisco Digital Network Architecture (DNA) Center (Cisco DNAC) plays a role similar to APIC but for an Enterprise SDN solution; this is called a software-defined access (SDA). The next section provides a high-level overview of these Cisco SDN solutions.

APIC

Cisco APIC acts as a centralized controller to manage physical as well as virtual elements in a data center infrastructure. Examples of these elements are physical switches (such as Nexus9000), hypervisors and virtual networking, computing servers, storage, devices providing L3-L7 services, Datacenter Interconnect, and so on.

If you take notice, SDN concepts are centered on decoupling the control plane (intelligence) from the data plane (pure processing and forwarding) to address the need for centralized and unified control, stay platform/vendor agnostic, scale and ease service customization, and so on. As you can see in Figure 2-20, ACI takes SDN beyond isolating control and the data plane by providing an end-to-end approach to policies and a relationship between services.

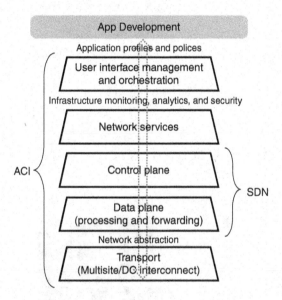

Figure 2-20 *Cisco ACI Approach to Software-Defined Networking*

Attributes of Cisco APIC:

- Built and enforced application-centric unified network policies

- Open framework through rich set of north- and south-bound APIs

- Seamless integration of and interoperability with Layer 4 through Layer 7 services

- Insights into the network, applications, and tenants through intelligent visibility and telemetry

- Uncompromised security for multitenancy and at scale

- Common policy for physical, virtual, and cloud networking

The APIC centrally pushes policies to the underlying infrastructure using an extensible policy protocol designed to exchange abstract policy between a network controller and a set of smart devices capable of rendering a policy called OpFlex. The Cisco APIC policy uses an object-oriented approach, which is based on declarative and scalable control models. With this model, it becomes easy to centrally define a policy and push it all the way to the network nodes and endpoints. Rather than instructing the underlying hardware nodes and endpoints exactly what to do and how to do it, this model just provides the required details (such as provision a network or update the policy). Instructions for how to execute those instructions are not provided.

As you learned earlier in this chapter and as illustrated in Figure 2-21, Cisco APIC offers unified and centralized access to components in the Cisco ACI through an object-oriented RESTful APIs framework with XML and JSON support for northbound applications. These APIs offer full read and write access to the systems in ACI as well as its programmability and automation features. Although Cisco APIC provides a GUI, it also supports user-extensible CLIs. Southbound APIs support extending the policies to virtualized computing resources and devices and appliances providing Layer 4 through Layer 7 services.

Cisco is working to standardize control intelligence in a unified controller instead of a distributed controller architecture for a given ecosystem with Cisco as well as third-party services. To be simple, these efforts are to foster a broader ecosystem by leveraging an open-source version of the Cisco API data model. The Cisco APIC REST API guide is available at the URL shown at the end of this chapter in "References in This Chapter."

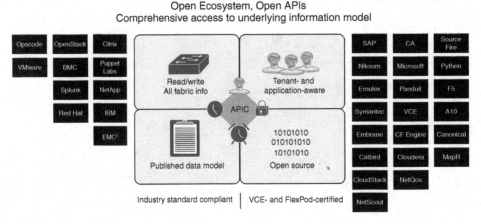

Figure 2-21 *Cisco APIC and Multivendor Ecosystem*

APIC-EM

APIC-EM delivers software-defined networking to the enterprise branch, campus, and WAN. With a simple user interface, it enables customers to automate policy-based application and service profiles. APIC-EM is no longer being sold, and DNA Center is the choice for the next generation of network management, automation, and assurance.

DNA Center

With APIC-EM as a central part, Cisco DNA is built as an intent-based networking system that is constantly learning and adapting and using contextual insights to make sure the network responds to dynamic business needs. As an open, software-driven platform, it takes a software-centric approach that goes beyond automation to providing assurance and security to branches, campuses, and WANs. With advanced analytics and insights, DNA assures network services and detects and mitigates threats in real time.

Cisco DNA Center is the central GUI or dashboard for the DNA Center Appliance managing your network. You can easily discover the network elements, design the network, build policies for the users and devices, provision them, and ensure the best network services with complete visibility. As shown in Figure 2-22, DNA Center controls DNA-C Appliance, which interacts with Identity Services Engine (ISE) for security and Network Data Platform (NDP) for analytics and assurance. The underlying physical as well as virtual infrastructures are DNA-ready, and they are discovered, provisioned, and configured with policies by DNA Center.

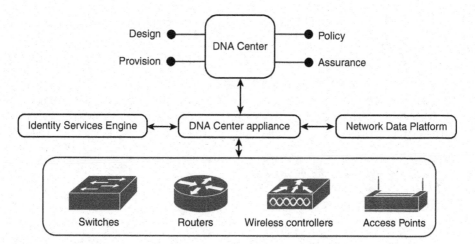

Figure 2-22 *Cisco Digital Network Architecture (DNA)—Software-Defined Access (SDA)*

Next this chapter will examine these four key attributes of DNA Center and see how they help to deliver a software-centric approach.

Design

Design your network using physical maps and logical topologies for a quick visual reference. The direct import feature brings in existing maps, images, and topologies directly from Cisco Prime Infrastructure and APIC-EM, making upgrades easy and quick. Device discovery is automatic and can be done through either the Cisco Discovery Protocol or by simply entering an IP address range.

Policy

Define user and device profiles that facilitate highly secure access and network segmentation. Cisco DNA Center takes the information collected in a policy and translates it into network-specific and device-specific configurations required by the different types, makes and models, operating systems, roles, and resource constraints of your network devices. Using Cisco DNA Center, you can create virtual networks, access control policies, and traffic and application policies.

Provision

After you have created policies in Cisco DNA Center, it can be provisioned by simple drag-and-drop. Categories of identities (users, devices, apps, and so on) in the Cisco DNA Center inventory list are assigned a policy, and this policy will always follow this identity. The process is completely automated and zero touch. New devices added to the network are assigned a policy based on their identity.

Assurance

Cisco DNA Center Assurance provides a comprehensive solution to ensure better and consistent service levels to meet growing business demands. It goes beyond simply doing reactive network monitoring to being proactive and predictive when running the network, ensuring client, application, and service performance.

Being at the heart of intent-based networks, Cisco DNA is an open platform that supports a rich set of APIs, SDKs, and adapters and exposes and extends its capabilities to external applications, systems, and processes, as you see in Figure 2-23.

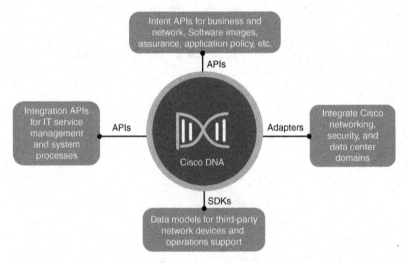

Figure 2-23 *Cisco Digital Network Architecture (DNA)—An Open Platform*

Providing network-centric intelligence helps organizations gather insights into and ensure a positive employee and customer experience, verify compliance to business and security policies, and assist day-to-day network operations to attain the highest possible network availability.

Modern Network Design with SDN and NFV

Business successes are dictated by how quickly they can respond to the changes and bring new products and services to the market. SDN and NFV are enabling the building of networks in new and different ways. SDN and NFV help in the design and offering of new services; significantly reduce CapEx and OpEx; keep the IT organizations agile, nimble, and flexible; and above all, create opportunities to build new services and customize services innovatively.

SDN and NFV are related but different from each other. As you have seen in earlier sections, SDN decouples the "intelligence" or the control plane from the hardware or the data plane and is centralized, which provides a unified view of and control over the network. It abstracts the network devices and hardware-centric elements from the global management view. NFV decouples the specific network functions that can operate independently from the hardware and provides services such as Network Address Translation (NAT), Domain Name System (DNS), and Load Balancers as a software element. Through NFV, various functions independently operate as building blocks, which can then be connected or chained to provide a service. NFV has multiple elements including physical resources, virtualization infrastructure manager, virtual resources, VNFs, and management and orchestration (MANO). The next section discusses various NFV elements in detail.

The concepts and ideas behind SDN can be leveraged for NFV to build and manage the infrastructure. The NFV infrastructure should have a central orchestration and management system (administered by the operators) that accepts requests and tasks, translates them into exact requirements (including computing and storage resources needed), determines the network connections between them, and so on. After the infrastructure is built and activated, the orchestrator offers insights into capacity, utilization, and the health of the resources; the orchestrator also provides insights on where and when to expand or shrink the capacity.

ETSI, the European Telecommunication Standards Institute, is an independent standard organization that was started in 2012. The ETSI Industry Specification Group (ISG) community is intensely engaged to develop, implement, and test various standards for Information and Communication Technology (ICT)-enabled systems, applications, and services.

The ETSI community is working on different industry sectors, such as networks, wireless entities, transportation, and content delivery. If you examine the networks sector, it has standardized Broadband Cable Access, Broadband Wireless Access, Multi-Access Edge Computing, 5G, and, of course, NFV. One of the earliest standards published for NFV details the requirements to virtualize the network functions. Later, the community came up with a framework for NFV. For more details, access the ETSI NFV standards shown in the section "Resources in This Chapter," at the end of this chapter.

Elements in Network Function Virtualization

The next section introduces new concepts and terminologies regarding how virtual network services are built and delivered using Cisco solutions.

First, virtual network functions (VNFs) sound similar to network functions virtualization (NFV). NFV is a concept that isolates the network functions from hardware devices and runs them as independent software elements. VNF refers to a software function or service that is virtualized. NFV Infrastructure (NFVI) has both virtual and physical infrastructure, using the VNFs that can operate. Firewall, load-balancer, and NAT are good examples of VNFs.

In Figure 2-24, notice that NFVI has a virtualization layer called Virtualized Infrastructure Manager (VIM) that abstracts physical (compute, storage, and network) into virtual infrastructure, on top of which VNFs can operate.

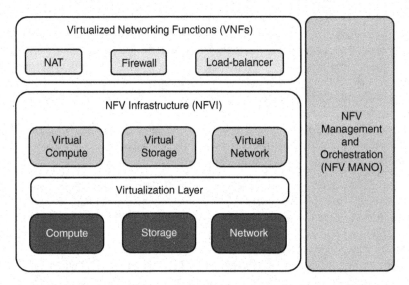

Figure 2-24 *Network Function Virtualization—Architectural Blocks*

Orchestration and Deployment of Virtual Network Services

At this point, you will learn how virtual network services are deployed and how different blocks in the infrastructure are orchestrated.

For example, assume you have endpoints, A and B, and you need to provide a service during transportation of the data between these two endpoints. Figure 2-25 provides a view of the information flowing between them, with virtual service(s) implemented between these two endpoints.

Endpoint A is connected to NFVI PoP1 (point-of-presence 1), and Endpoint B is connected to PoP4. All the virtual services offered are transparent to the endpoints. All the PoP are connected physically, whereas the service offered at each PoP is virtual.

NFV makes it easy to insert services dynamically, as required, and create a chain of services. Assume that a customer requests a specific type of service for Flow-1 between point A and point B, which can be achieved by chaining the services offered by VNF-1, VNF-2, and VNF-4, The traffic in Flow-1 will have physical touchpoints of PoP1, PoP2, and PoP4. Similarly, Flow-2 is serviced by chaining the services offered by VNF-1, VNF-3, and VNF-4 with physical touchpoints of PoP1, PoP2, and PoP3. Figure 2-25 illustrates these flows between the endpoints, the services offered by different VNFs, and the respective physical touchpoints.

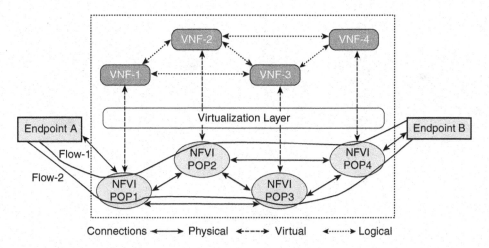

Figure 2-25   *Network Service with VNFs*

Now that you understand NFV standards and concepts and how services can be built dynamically using VNFs, this chapter will look into the solution that Cisco offers—Cisco Elastic Services Controller (ESC) and Network Services Orchestrator (NSO). ESC and NSO help service providers and large enterprises transform their businesses. ESC intends to provide automated lifecycle-management capabilities by combining NSO with the entire NFV and NFVI lifecycle.

The Cisco ESC is the key product in Cisco NFV orchestration products, providing an advanced lifecycle-management platform for NFV. It gives you everything you need to instantiate, monitor, and scale VNFs in an automated fashion. In short, it addresses the expectations of an NFV solution including end-to-end automation, agility, and simplicity.

Cisco ESC offers advanced VNF lifecycle-management capabilities through an open, standards-based platform that conforms to the ETSI NFV MANO reference architecture (see Figure 2-24). By conforming to industry NFV standards and exposing well-defined APIs, it can interoperate with any standards-based NFV orchestration system.

As illustrated in Figure 2-26, key capabilities of NSO include but are not limited to

■ Northbound APIs make integration into existing business tools, processes, and systems seamless.

■ NSO includes Cisco and third-party device abstraction, which is a layer of drivers that mediate access to Cisco as well as third-party physical and virtual devices.

■ NSO is scalable and highly available.

■ NSO is extensible because it supports customer development environment and pre-built function packs. One such pack is Secure Agile Exchange (SAE), which enables enterprises to quickly and securely interconnect users to applications by virtualizing the network edge and even extending it to other colocations and branch offices.

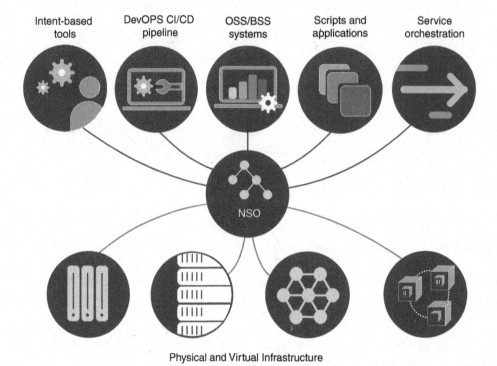

Figure 2-26 *NSO—Connecting an Automation/Orchestration Framework to Physical/Virtual Infrastructure*

For more information on Cisco NFV solutions and offerings, Cisco NFV Infrastructure, ESC, and NSO, see the "Resources in This Chapter" section at the end of this chapter.

To summarize, the modern service provider and enterprise networks are built leveraging SDN and NFV capabilities. Customers are looking for SDN/NFV solutions that can be easily and seamlessly integrated into their business processes, tools, and systems; aid application development with rich software environments and programming languages; and support building a multivendor scalable ecosystem. On the other side, the vendors offering SDN/NFV solutions should not only address these mentioned requirements but provide value-added capabilities and services as market differentiators.

Technology Trends Built on SDN

By now, you know that SDN virtualizes the underlying hardware to automate and expedite network configurations, implements business/security policy changes seamlessly, enhances monitoring capabilities with a rich set of data and intelligence, and above all, makes the network adaptive for any future applications and services. The next section discusses the Internet of Things (IoT) in more detail.

Internet of Things (IoT)

Figure 2-27 depicts an IoT stack, starting with the devices and sensors layer at the bottom and progressing to the business process and systems at the top.

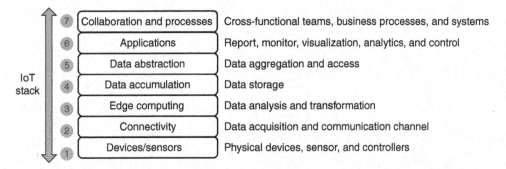

Figure 2-27   *Internet of Things Stack*

The IoT uses many devices and sensors, which generate a massive amount of data. Given the number of devices and the amount of data they generate, the following must be true to realize the IoT vision:

■ The devices and sensors should be plug-and-play for faster provisioning.

■ The devices and sensors should be classified appropriately with the right level of privileges in real time.

■ The devices and sensors need to be connected to and controlled by a centralized controller.

■ The devices and sensors should have complete visibility into the infrastructure.

■ Above all, the data needs to flow securely from end to end.

SDN makes IoT a reality with a centralized controller that enables a seamless plug-and-play provision for hundreds or thousands of devices, classifies them with appropriate privileges and security settings, secures the transport from sensors to the cloud, and above all, virtualizes the underlying hardware. These things make the infrastructure more agile and easier to interoperate with third-party devices and solutions.

The IoT is composed of the devices and sensors that are embedded with basic modules to continuously collect the data and communicate through wireless networks such as Wi-Fi,

Bluetooth, LoRAWAN, Zigbee, Z-Wave, and more. The data generated can be locally processed by the devices, or it can be transmitted through a gateway infrastructure to a centralized controller or to an application in the cloud. To monitor the devices and sensors and generate insights, you need to have an analytics engine that processes a massive amount of data and generates insights. The trending devices and solutions in IoT are more industry focused but consumer driven. For example, IoT devices include connected cars, smart homes (home automation), medical and healthcare automation, manufacturing and retail automations, transportation automation, smart buildings, schools, and cities.

The next section takes a quick look into some of the trending IoT topics.

Cisco's IoT Platform for Industries

Having a platform for connecting the devices and sensors securely at the right time, with the right amount of data, and to the right cloud and applications is critical. The Cisco Kinetic solution securely connects the devices and generated or computed data to the right applications at the right time in a programmatic way to achieve the business outcomes, as illustrated in Figure 2-28.

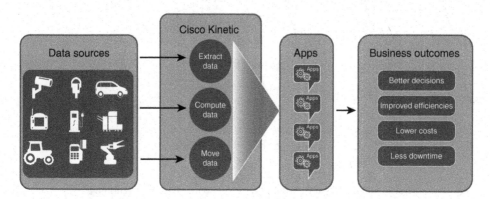

Figure 2-28   *Cisco Kinetic—Data to Business Outcomes*

Cisco Kinetic does this by solving three substantive IoT challenges for companies within a single platform:

■ Manages connections to devices deployed at different geo locations

■ Leverages highly distributed computing capabilities to extract and compute data locally before transporting it to the cloud applications—fog computing

■ Secures transport of the extracted or computed data to application(s), with a focus to derive maximum value

Connection Management

Cisco Kinetic, along with Cisco DNA Center, streamlines and automates the recognition process of devices connected to the local network, authenticates them, applies the right kind of policies, and ensures the data is transported to its intended destination. Given that network devices come and go around the clock, business and security polices change with minimal notice, applications keep evolving, and businesses have new desired outcomes, it is important to provide necessary tools to ensure a complete and successful lifecycle of the products.

Fog Computing

With billions of devices on the network, it is not necessary—and not practical—to send terabytes of data generated to the cloud through each device in between. Cisco Kinetic addresses this challenge by identifying where and how the data needs to be processed, determining which part of the data collected needs to stay local or be sent to the cloud. With fog computing, Kinetic makes it possible to process data at the edge, derive insights, and help to make decisions close to the action.

Data Delivery

Cisco Kinetic securely delivers data from the edge to all the participants of an ecosystem based on rules defined by the data owners. It plays a vital role in enforcing the rules that have been negotiated between parties.

Through Cisco Kinetic, this chapter has discussed an IoT solution that is more enterprise-centric. Now it will cover IoT solutions centered on cellular network service providers.

The Cisco IoT Platform for Service Providers

5G—the 5th Generation—wireless is the latest generation of mobile communications focusing on high data rate (up to 10 Gbps) with low latency (1 millisecond or less) with support for high density of wireless devices. From the recent history of cellular mobile communication starting from 2G all the way to 4G, the key services offered are Internet access and voice services. But the high data rate and support for plentiful devices in 5G is believed to bring new applications and services.

Both 5G and Wi-Fi 6 technologies are engineered to provide more speed, lower latency, and higher device density than previous generations of wireless technology, but they support different use cases. Wi-Fi 6 will be chosen to access indoor networks, whereas 5G suits outdoor networks.

The Cisco Ultra Services Platform, which has end-to-end virtualization, is 5G-ready. It has advanced capabilities for cellular network operators to provide connectivity for wireless devices requiring low power consumption, long range, low cost, and security. It supports the 3GPP Cellular IoT (CIoT) architecture and a range of IoT solutions across multiple market verticals.

As illustrated in Figure 2-29, Cisco Ultra IoT includes core network support for all wireless IoT connectivity, including 2G, 3G, LTE, and unlicensed networks, such as Wi-Fi. With all the wireless networks in discussion, this is about the transport for the data from devices to the edge to the cloud. An application must consume the data and provide a service. One such well-known application is Connected Vehicles.

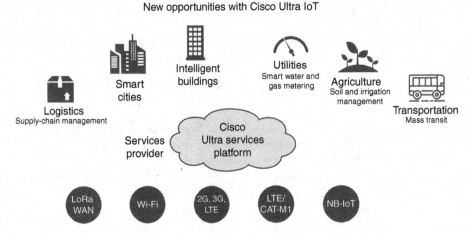

Figure 2-29 *Cisco Ultra Services—Driving IoT and Digitization*

Vehicles are connected in the following ways:

- **Vehicle-to-vehicle (or peer-to-peer):** Each vehicle communicates with peer vehicles about its location, its speed, and the like to know the surroundings and avoid accidents.

- **Vehicle-to-network-infrastructure:** Vehicles stay connected with other vehicles in the same domain or infrastructure and exchange information on mobility, weather conditions, and so on. They also stay connected to the centralized controller or application.

- **Vehicle-to-cloud:** Vehicles communicate with applications or other devices through the cloud to get further information, such as road and traffic conditions, to keep the driver updated and suggest alternative routes and the like.

- **Vehicle-to-mobile-objects:** Vehicles stay connected and communicate with other mobile devices, such as personal mobile devices, wearables, and other devices, to improve safety for pedestrians. Connecting vehicles to their peers and to cloud applications provides services that help the driver avoid accidents, obtain information about the vehicle's surroundings, and learn weather conditions, besides improve pedestrians' safety.

As you know, with vehicles joining and leaving the SDN domain quickly, the domain is going to be dynamic. The underlying SDN capabilities enable these devices to join and leave the domain at the required rate and securely exchange the information. Apart from protecting each device in the domain from malicious attack, these underlying SDN capabilities make rollout of business or security policy updates seamless.

A Use Case for IoT with SDN: Manufacturing

The previous sections discussed various Cisco IoT platforms and their benefits. With IoT solutions available for transportation, automated vehicles, healthcare, and so on, this section will consider the manufacturing sector.

To implement IoT and fully realize its benefits, a manufacturing company's operational technologies (OT) and IT need to be brought together. Typically, the network with IT and OT is segmented and represented by multiple levels, as illustrated in Figure 2-30. In a manufacturing sector such as the one discussed here, SDN and virtualization functions can be brought not only to perform the tasks defined at different levels, but to add further value with service assurance and analytics based on telemetry.

As you may notice, Figure 2-30 shows the Cisco Digital Network Architecture (DNA)/ Software-Defined Access (SDA) as the core SDN solution connecting industrial operational environment with IoT edge devices (level 0–2) to site operations (level 3) and enterprise/data center environments (level 4–5). SDA is the Intent-Based Networking (IBN) solution for the enterprise built on the principles of the Cisco DNA. The DNA Center (DNAC) embraces IoT with the SDA extension for IoT. As a centralized management platform, DNAC enables SDA to make the underlying network more programmable; automate infrastructure deployment; monitor and maintain infrastructure with ease; get visibility into each network component across the infrastructure; and most importantly, deploy or modify a policy to align business needs with a high level of flexibility and agility.

Level 0–2 represents the cell/area zone, which has IoT edge devices such as sensors, machines, equipment, skids, lines, and the like. These IoT edge devices form a heterogenous environment, which is required to be light on all fronts, including weight, memory, CPU consumption, and power consumption. Even the protocols used to communicate are required to be lightweight. These devices—either wired or wireless—are connected to Industrial Ethernet Switches (IES) or access points, and they establish communication and exchange information. Using its profiling technology, the network automatically discovers new endpoints. It also secures and monitors them.

Containers play a major role because they bring a high level of flexibility in virtualization. The containers are deployed in the IE switches to capture and process data as close as possible to the data sources, which is well known as IoT Edge Computing. Real-time computing and processing of data enable customers to make better decisions and achieve higher level of security because there is no need for data to traverse outside the manufacturing space.

Level 3 represents the site operations zone, which has infrastructure including manufacturing service platforms, application servers and storage, and enterprise services such as DNS and DHCP. At this level, the infrastructure can be physical or virtual, as can the services being offered.

The demilitarized zone (DMZ) hosts firewalls and intrusion detection and prevention systems, offers VPN and remote-access services, implements inter-zone security policies and traffic segmentation, and handles inter-site communication as needed.

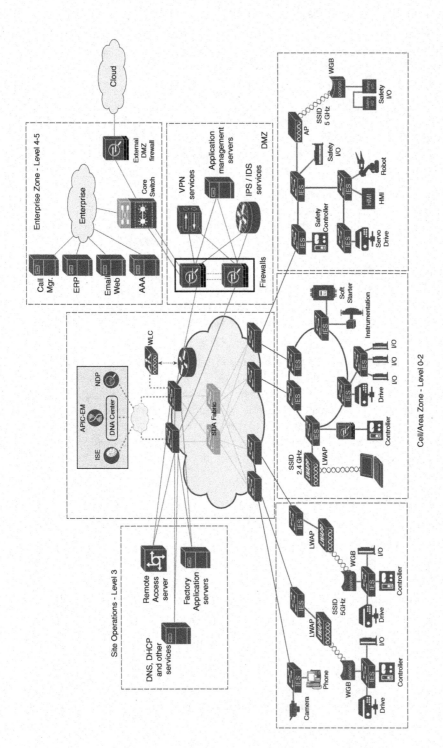

Figure 2-30 *IoT with SDN for Manufacturing*

Level 4–5 represents the enterprise zone, which has application servers; enterprise resource planning (ERP) systems; email and web servers; security services such as Active Directory (AD) and authentication, authorization, and accounting (AAA); and connections to data centers and cloud services.

The preceding use-case discussion highlights only a subset of functions and benefits that DNA/SDA brings to IoT. Please refer to the latest Cisco Kinetic for Manufacturing at Cisco.com to see how unified enterprise and manufacturing are brought together to handle growth and security by constantly adapting to business needs, improving operational efficiency, maintaining compliance, and providing real-time insights.

Intent-Based Networking (IBN)

IBN is built on SDN, transforming the networks that are hardware-centric and manually operated to those that are software-centric and fully automated. The software-centric and automated networks add context, learn continuously and assure intended services. Intent-based networks capture business intents and use analytics, machine learning, and automation to align the network continuously and dynamically to changing business needs. They continuously apply and ensure applications' performance requirements and automate implementing user, security compliance, and IT operations policies across the whole network.

Figure 2-31 illustrates the solution suite that has end-to-end coverage connecting devices, things, and users in a campus environment to applications and services offered from on-premise data center or public cloud solutions. Businesses are looking for a network infrastructure strategy that covers the entire enterprise network. To simplify and streamline IT operations, businesses need a centralized management in which the business intent is defined as policies. With these policies propagated across the WAN, campus/branch, and cloud, IBN enforces and monitors these policies, ensures services, and ensures end-to-end compliance with regulations.

Today, Cisco ACI policy integration maps Cisco ACI application-based micro-segmentation in the data center and Cisco SD-Access policy with user group–based segmentation across the campus and branch. Now security administrators can automate and manage end-to-end segmentation seamlessly with uniform access policies—from the user to the application. With such segmentation, policies can be set that allow IoT devices to access specific applications in the data center or allow only financial executives and auditors to access confidential data. This is just one example of how Cisco solutions are enabling consistent multidomain policy segmentation and assurance for end-to-end alignment to business intent.

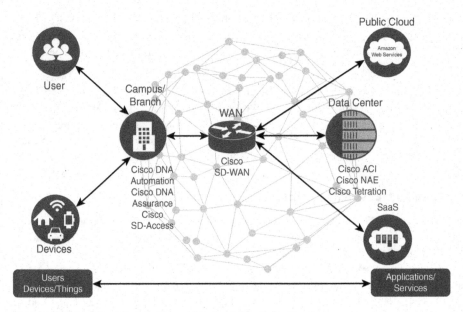

Figure 2-31   *Cisco Intent-Based Networking Solution Suite*

Summary

This chapter started with a detailed discussion of various virtualization techniques including VLANs, Dot1Q trunking, VRFs, GRE, MPLS/VPNs, stacking of switches, VSS, vPC, and VDC that are available in Cisco routing and switching platforms. It discussed how these techniques help to scale the infrastructure for more users and segment the user groups matching security requirements. It moved on to discuss how these techniques and virtual devices such as XRv 9000, CSR 1000v, ASAv, and NGFWv help to realize virtualization in enterprises and service provider networks.

The discussion of virtualization in the networking devices moved to the era of software-defined networking. Starting from high-level SDN architecture and key enablers, the discussion continued with control plane virtualization, SDN Controllers, OpenFlow, and the different open-source SDN Controllers available. After a quick refresher on APIs and programmability elements, the chapter covered the importance of protocols, encoding standards and data modeling standards, and the roles they play in the world of virtualization and SDN.

This chapter continued with a detailed discussion of Cisco proprietary SDN Controllers such as ACI and SDA available for data centers and enterprises, respectively. These compelling solutions are open platforms that support a multivendor ecosystem. These solutions take SDN beyond control plane virtualization to include software developers and become part of the business processes and systems workflow.

The chapter moved into a discussion of how modern-day service provider networks are built deploying NFV capabilities and how the NFV platforms are orchestrated, such as with Cisco NSO/ESC platforms.

The virtualization and SDN/NFV help to realize the vision of IoT. Readers learned about the Cisco Kinetic and Ultra IoT platforms and how they are adopted in various industries and service provider environments.

Figure 2-32 shows the concepts discussed so far.

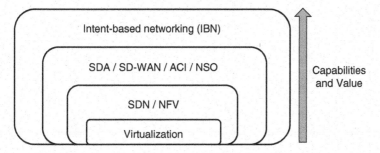

Figure 2-32   *Virtualization as a Foundation and Beyond*

To summarize, virtualization is the foundation on top of which SDN and NFV can be built. Cisco SD-Access, SD-WAN, ACI, and NSO take SDN a few notches up by making the platforms open and programmable. They support the multivendor ecosystem and more importantly bring software developers and business processes and systems into the workflow. Now with the Intent-Based Networking (IBN) architecture, businesses and companies can express intent at a centralized location, apply it across all the domains (Campus, WAN, Data Center, Cloud), enforce and monitor them, and ensure services for the best possible user experience.

References in This Chapter

Google Charts: https://developers.google.com/chart/interactive/docs/gallery/piechart

Cisco APIC REST API Configuration Guide: https://www.cisco.com/c/en/us/td/docs/switches/datacenter/aci/apic/sw/4-x/rest-api-config/Cisco-APIC-REST-API-Configuration-Guide-401/Cisco-APIC-REST-API-Configuration-Guide-401_chapter_00.html

NFV Virtualization Requirements: https://www.etsi.org/deliver/etsi_gs/NFV/001_099/004/01.01.01_60/gs_NFV004v010101p.pdf

NFV Architectural Framework: https://www.etsi.org/deliver/etsi_gs/NFV/001_099/002/01.02.01_60/gs_NFV002v010201p.pdf

Cisco Elastic Services Controller: https://www.cisco.com/c/en/us/products/collateral/cloud-systems-management/network-services-orchestrator/datasheet-c78-734670.pdf

Cisco NFV Solutions for Service Providers: https://www.cisco.com/c/en/us/solutions/service-provider/network-functions-virtualization-nfv/index.html

Overview of Cisco NFV Infrastructure: https://www.cisco.com/c/en/us/td/docs/net_mgmt/network_function_virtualization_Infrastructure/2_0/install_guide/Cisco_VIM_Install_Guide_2_0/b_Cisco_NFVI_Install_Guide_2_0_chapter_00.pdf

Cisco NSO: https://www.cisco.com/c/en/us/solutions/service-provider/solutions-cloud-providers/network-services-orchestrator-solutions.html#~innovation

Chapter 3

Container Orchestration and Management

In this chapter, you will learn the following:

- Basic principles of the cloud-native reference model and the components that guide the development of container applications

- Various virtualization techniques and tools that Cisco products use to host and manage container applications

- Examples of container deployment on Cisco products using supported tools

Introduction to the Cloud-Native Reference Model

The previous chapters elaborated the evolution of virtualization and the impact created by various cloud-based service offerings in different business verticals. To exploit the benefits that are promised by the cloud-based service offerings, the application must support infrastructure-agnostic instantiation and automated lifecycle management. To be more precise, the service or the application must be

- **Infrastructure agnostic:** Capable of being instantiated on the cloud

- **DN ready:** Capable of automated lifecycle management

Migrating an application from a standalone server or virtual machine to the cloud is not a straightforward task. It requires that the application stack be developed based on the cloud-native principles. The cloud-native reference model is shown in Figure 3-1.

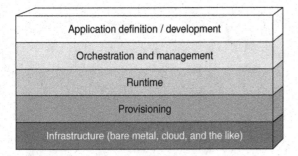

Figure 3-1   *Cloud-Native Reference Model*

Application Development Framework

One of the critical principles of the cloud-native reference model is to follow microservice architecture when developing cloud-native applications. Many benefits are gained by decomposing the full-stack complex application into a loosely coupled stack of small and autonomous functions or microservices:

- **Software agility:** Allows developers to modify an existing microservice or rapidly develop a new microservice with minimal dependency on other processes

- **Environment agnostic portability:** Allows users to deploy the service in testing and producing public or private clouds with ease

- **Reliability:** Allows users to run multiple instances of the relevant process for resiliency

By following the microservice architecture, each microservice is developed as a self-contained, lightweight function with service-level granularity. The computing resources required to run these microservices are satisfied by a container, so it is common to see a stack of microservices being run as containers. Communication between different functions within the application is facilitated by APIs using a new concept called *Service mesh*. Service mesh is a configurable infrastructure layer that provides network-based communication between different functions. Each of the functions also uses northbound APIs and southbound APIs to communicate with other external services, such as Orchestrator, operations support system (OSS), business support system (BSS) services, and the like.

This ability to decompose the application into loosely coupled independent containers enables the users to deploy the workloads in an infrastructure-agnostic manner.

Automated Orchestration and Management

"Software defined" is a buzzword that finds its way into any new technology portfolio. It describes the ability to automate the service orchestration and management functionality based on the business intent. Running the microservice as a container inherently derives the automated lifecycle management capability of the containers. The use of orchestrators to manage the lifecycle of each container allows developers to create, update, or decommission services independently without affecting other services within the same application stack. Kubernetes and Docker Swarm are two well-known orchestration engines that are used in the industry. These container orchestration tools are discussed in more detail later in this chapter.

Container Runtime and Provisioning

Container Runtime is the layer that is responsible for resource management, such as the container image and compute resource. Container Runtime is a collection of API-driven scripts and tools that play a crucial role in executing the container image by requesting the underlying kernel to allocate the required resources for the deployed container.

Container Runtime initializes the container image and sets up the initial configuration and other operational primitives before enabling the container task. **runc** is a lightweight and commonly used container runtime developed as part of the Open Container Initiative (OCI) specifications.

The Container Runtime Interface (CRI) is the interface between the orchestrator and the container runtime.

The Journey from Virtual Network Function (VNF) to Cloud Native Function (CNF)

The principles of the cloud-native reference model mentioned earlier have proven to be an effective way of developing cloud-native applications. Cisco, along with other network vendors and telcos, identified cloud-native principles that could help develop the network functions to realize the full benefits of the cloud.

The next generation of network functions is being built using cloud-native constructs known as cloud-native network functions (CNFs). The CNF deployment model is shown in Figure 3-2.

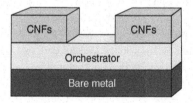

Figure 3-2   *Cloud-Native Network Functions (CNFs)*

Using microservice architecture, CNFs are developed as packages that are instantiated as containers using supported container orchestrators. Parallel efforts are happening both from vendors and from telcos to containerize network functions and applications that span across verticals covering data center, cable, 5G, service provider, and core infrastructure networks.

CNF applications that Cisco has developed typically follow the model shown in Figure 3-3 to ensure consistent deployment and operational characteristics across all the network services and applications.

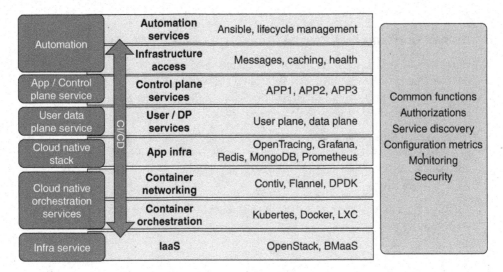

Figure 3-3 *Cisco CNF Framework*

Among the different business verticals, the mobility industry is one of the early adopters of virtualization techniques in the Evolved Packet Core (EPC) network. The 3rd Generation Partnership Project (3GPP) is a standard defining organization that develops protocols and standards for mobility technologies. The 3GPP construct follows a new disaggregated architecture known as the Control Plane and User Plane Separation (CUPS) model that disaggregates the 3GPP control plane and data plane functionalities of Packet Gateway (PGW) and Service Gateway (SGW) components as a virtual control plane (vCP) and a virtual user plane forwarder (vUPF). The vCP is positioned as a virtual entity in the compute node and uses an out-of-band interface to communicate with the vUPF. Although the CUPS model has become the de-facto architecture for 5G deployment, other new 5G features, such as mobile edge computing (MEC), network slicing, and service function chaining (SFC), also heavily leverage virtualization and containerization capability. The deployment velocity of the new architectures such as 5G are directly influenced by the ability of the network infrastructure to adopt and support virtual and container workloads.

As explained in the preceding use case, network services are being migrated from physical (PNF) to virtual (vNF) and now to cloud-native (cNF). Therefore, it is equally important to make the infrastructure and the operational workload ready to embrace the evolution and accelerate the business.

As always, Cisco listens to its customer demands and addresses the requirements with an array of industry-leading solutions. This time, the ask from the industry is this: Can customers have the capability to host the applications directly on the network elements?

The evolution of container-based network services can immensely benefit by leveraging the computing resources directly from the network elements. Moreover, bringing the workload as close as possible to the data is a huge success.

Containers that are developed natively or by using the cloud-native models discussed earlier can be easily deployed on Cisco platforms using a native application-hosting mechanism such as LXC or KVM or by using Docker. Some of the recent versions also come with Kubernetes support that allows the users to deploy containers on Cisco platforms using the Kubernetes orchestration engine. Later, you will read about different container deployment and orchestration capabilities and how to use them to deploy and manage container applications on Cisco platforms.

Container Deployment and Orchestration Overview

The industry is witnessing an evolution in which different network services are decomposed into microservices. Soon, there will be a plethora of services running as containers in an infrastructure-agnostic manner. Cloud-native network functions (CNFs) are built as self-contained container images that are a collection of relevant files packed together as a filesystem bundle. Depending on the type of tools used for container image packaging, various deployment tools are available for container lifecycle management.

Depending on numerous factors, such as business intent, resource availability, and deployment model, the magnitude of applications hosted as containers may vary. On one end of the spectrum, a Cisco Unified Computing System (UCS) platform in a data center may host several thousand containers; on the other end of the spectrum, a couple of open agent applications, such as Puppet and Chef, may be hosted as containers on Cisco Edge Routers.

Running a couple of containers on one edge router is manageable, but running a couple of containers on 1000 such edge routers leads to operational challenges. Soon, medium to large networks may see thousands of containers running. Identifying a failed container in such a large network is like looking for a needle in a haystack. Manually deploying and operating a large number of containers is humanly impossible. The industry has learned from experience that the efficiency of the network and service deployment are significantly improved by automation; this applies to container lifecycle management, too. Automated container orchestration is an essential part of the success of this new CNF architecture.

By definition, orchestration is an automated process of workload lifecycle management that includes scheduling workload and scaling resources based on demand. Many orchestration tools are developed to automate the lifecycle management of the containers that primarily rely on certain basic, yet critical, components. Figure 3-4 highlights these essential components and the interaction between those components to execute the container image and spawn-up containers.

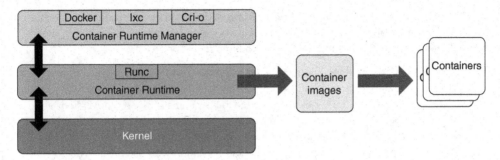

Figure 3-4 *Container Orchestration*

A container image is composed of a base image, executable source code, binaries, libraries, and a manifest file. The binaries and libraries are dependent files required to run the source code, and the manifest file defines the configuration and properties for the containers.

The container runtime manager (also known as "container platforms") is the component that is responsible for fetching the relevant container image from the centralized registry, and it leverages the runtime component to spawn up and manage the container. Upon receiving the instruction from the manager, the container runtime reads the manifest file, which is part of the container image package, and makes relevant resource allocations, such as namespace and cgroup creation, by collaborating with the underlying kernel.

Different types of container runtime managers are evolving, but this book will focus on some of the commonly used runtime managers supported in various Cisco product portfolios.

Linux Containers (LXC)

A Linux container, also known as LXC, is a userspace interface for the Linux kernel that provides a method to run multiple isolated Linux containers on a Linux host. The containers that are deployed using LXC are usually full-stack Linux servers. LXC supports a range of Linux distributions and a variety of 32-bit and 64-bit based processors.

Note: The LXC is specific to the Linux operating system and does not work on other underlying operating systems.

LXC is not primarily used as an enterprise-grade container platform because its applicability is limited to Linux distributions and does not work for other host operating systems. Other container platforms are developed in a host-agnostic manner, and they overtook LXC. Although LXC is not largely deployed in the commercial environment, it plays a crucial role in hosting applications on the Cisco platforms. Cisco IOS-XE, IOS-XR, and NXOS architectures are built on top of Cisco-customized Linux distribution (MontaVista or Wind River Linux). This architecture choice makes the platforms natively capable of instantiating LXC containers.

Extending the native Linux bash shell on Cisco platforms to host service applications is not a viable option because it raises numerous challenges. The service application must be customized or built for the specific Linux distribution. Customizing open-source applications to fit such specific distributions is always a challenge. Providing complete root access to the host kernel is not because it raises serious security concerns. Cisco created application hosting capability support using KVM/LXC by addressing the preceding challenges without compromising the security concerns.

Cisco Service Containers

Virtualization infrastructure support for KVM/LXC was introduced in Cisco routers to support hosting loosely coupled application services. IOS-XE software architecture was extended by including a Virtualization Manager (VMAN) component that leverages libvirt, an open-source virtualization management tool for packaging and installing virtual service packages. The virtual environment hosted using such packages is known as Service Containers. A Cisco Virtual WAN Optimization function such as Virtual Wide Area Application Service (vWAAS) or security functions such as One Firewall (ONEFW) are early service containers instantiated for workload consolidation by running services such as WAAS as a virtual entity on the router.

Service Containers are hosted using virtual service packages that are developed by Cisco or other third parties and signed by Cisco. The service package is an OVA file containing the following components:

- **Disk Image:** One or more disk files comprising the actual source code of the service application. The format of the disk image can be ISO, RAW, or QCOW2.

- **Manifest File:** Text file carrying SHA1 hashing metadata for the other files in the package.

- **YAML/XML Descriptor File:** File describing the resource requirement for the service application.

Example 3-1 shows a sample YAML Descriptor file created for each service container.

Example 3-1 *Sample YAML Descriptor File*

```
manifest-version: <manifest version>
info:
 name: <application name>
 description: <application description string>
 version: <application version>
 author-name: <application author/vendor>
 author-link: <application author/vendor website>
app:
 apptype: <vm/app type>
```

```
resources:
 cpu: <cpu share %>
 memory: <memory in megs>
 vcpu: <no. of vcpus>
 disk:
 - target dev: <disk name>
 file: <image name>
 upgrade-model: <ha-sync | local>
 share-model: <core>
 capacity: <disk capacity in megs>
 - ...
 interfaces:
 - target-dev: <interface name>
 type: <management>
 - ...
 serial:
 - serial
 - console
 - syslog
 - tracelog
 startup:
 runtime: <kvm>
 boot-dev: <boot device>
```

The descriptor file shown in Example 3-1 has the details and the resource settings for the application. The disk image along with the other files and certificates are packaged as an OVA tarball and signed using Cisco internal script. The OVA service package is installed and activated on the Cisco routers using virtual-service, CLI-based commands, as shown in Example 3-2.

Example 3-2 *CLI-Based Commands*

```
csr1000v-1#virtual-service ?
  clear      Clear command
  connect    Connect to an appliance
  install    Install an appliance package
  move       Copy files for an appliance package
  uninstall  Uninstall an appliance package
  upgrade    Upgrade an appliance package

csr1000v-1#
```

See Chapter 5 for details about how to copy and activate service containers using CLI.

The software support matrix for service containers is shown in Table 3-1.

Table 3-1 *Service Container–Supported Version*

IOS-XE	IOS-XR	NXOS	
Cisco IOS-XE running 3.9 release onwards	Cisco IOS-XR running 5.1.1 release onwards	Cisco Nexus 3000 series switches	6.0(2)U1(1) and newer
		Cisco Nexus 5000 series switches	6.0(3) and newer
		Cisco Nexus 6000 series switches	6.0(3) and newer
		Cisco Nexus 7000 series switches	7.x and newer
		Cisco Nexus 9000 series switches	6.x and newer

Cisco Application Hosting Framework

To further expand application hosting and to allow users to build and host applications, Cisco introduced a new SDK framework known as Cisco Application Hosting Framework (CAF) for application lifecycle management. CAF, also referred to as Cisco IOX (IOS + Linux), was initially introduced for IoT spaces to build fog/edge applications for IoT use cases; later, it was extended to other IOS-XE platforms. The framework provides a unified interface for application development and hosting by abstracting the underlying resource complexity. Example 3-3 shows the CLI command options to host the applications using CAF.

Example 3-3 *App-Hosting CLI Command Options*

```
csr1000v-1#app-hosting ?
  activate      Application activate
  connect       Application connect
  deactivate    Application deactivate
  install       Application install
  move          Move File
  start         Application start
  stop          Application stop
  uninstall     Application uninstall
  verification  Application signature verification setting (global)

csr1000v-1#
```

One of the key components of CAF is IOx Client, a CLI-based utility component that controls the lifecycle tasks of the application by allowing users to convert natively built application into OVA files that can be deployed on CAF-supported platforms. The CAF framework is flexible and allows users to package the application by defining the type. The **package.yaml** file used by IOx Client defines the type of application as LXC, virtual machine, or Docker. This informa-tion is embedded in the OVA file during packaging. The information helps the framework to use the appropriate tool, such as LXC or KVM, during application deployment.

> **Note:** An application can be packaged using Docker and can use IOx Client to convert the Docker image into OVA packages that can be hosted in IOx-supported platforms.

See Chapter 5, "Container Orchestration in Cisco IOS-XE Platforms," for more details on using IOx Client to build and deploy applications.

The software support matrix for service containers is shown in Table 3-2.

Table 3-2 *IOx Framework Supported Version*

IOS-XE		IOS-XR	NXOS
ASR 1000 routers	16.3 and newer	NA	7.3 and newer
ISR 4000 routers	16.3 and newer		
Catalyst 9000 series switches	16.11 and newer		

> **Note:** The Docker functionality is natively supported in IOS-XR and Nexus 9000 platforms; therefore, there is little business need to introduce IOx support for these platforms.

Cisco Guest Shell

Cisco Guest Shell, a secure LXC container instantiated on Cisco platforms, provides open Linux environments with user space and resource isolation as shown in Figure 3-5. Cisco Guest Shell is a 64-bit CentOS version 7–based environment with a well-populated repository that allows users to host standard Linux applications, such as Puppet, Chef, and the like. It also allows users to develop and host customized applications. Cisco Guest Shell is an unprivileged container that prevents malicious users from accessing the host kernel or making changes to the host configuration or the processes running on the kernel. Although the Guest Shell container provides root access like any other Linux kernel, it does not offer the same capabilities as the root on the host kernel. This characteristic of the Guest Shell makes it a safe environment to host any application securely.

All recent Cisco operating systems are embedded with the Guest Shell package that is required to instantiate the LXC Guest Shell container. By default, the Guest Shell container package comes with essential libraries along with some applications, such as Python, installed. Any additional libraries or applications can be installed using the *yum install <package>* command.

Some of the MIPS platform-based switches running IOS-XE, such as Cisco Catalyst 3850 and Catalyst 3650, come with a simplified version of Guest Shell known as Guest Shell Lite. As the name says, this is a lighter version of Guest Shell that runs MontaVista Carrier Grade Edition (CGE) version 7.0 and comes with Python 2.7 version. Although users can install and run basic Python-based scripts, Guest Shell Lite does not allow users to install additional packages or enable users to upgrade the Python version or other existing packages. At the time this book was written, Guest Shell 2.4 is the current version.

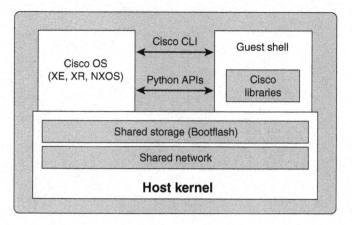

Figure 3-5 *Cisco Guest Shell Container*

Table 3-3 shows a quick comparison between different versions of the Guest Shells.

Table 3-3 *Comparison of Guest Shell Versions*

	Guest Shell Lite	Guest Shell 1.x	Guest Shell 2.x
Platform supported	MIPS	X86	X86
Software supported	IOS-XE	IOS-XE, IOS-XR	IOS-XE, IOS-XER, NXOS
Environment	MontaVista CGE 7	Centos 7 (IOS-XE, IOS-XR) Poky (NXOS)	Centos 7
Python 2.7	Supported	Supported	Supported
Python 3.0	Not supported	Supported	Supported
Python package upgrade (PIP Install)	Not supported	Supported	Supported
RPM package install	Not supported	Supported	Supported

Cisco Open Agent Containers

Although Cisco Guest Shell is available in various Cisco product portfolios, some of the Cisco platform architecture cannot natively support the ability to integrate Guest Shell functionality into the operating system. Cisco Nexus 5xxx, Nexus 6xxx, and Nexus7xxx series switches do not come with Guest Shell integrated with the operating system. To introduce the application hosting capability in such platforms, a customized and secured container environment known as Open Agent Container (OAC) is introduced. The OAC environment is specifically targeted for open-agent applications such as Chef and Puppet. It is also available for download from the CCO, as shown in Figure 3-6.

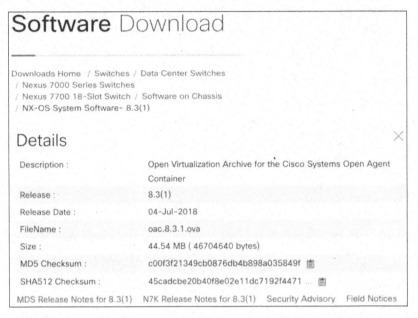

Figure 3-6   *OVA File for Nexus 7700*

Open Agent Container is a 32-bit Cent-OS–based environment that is instantiated as an LXC container on Nexus switches running Cisco 7.3.0 release or later. When this book was written, the OAC OVA files were packaged with Cent-OS version 6.9. Although the OAC environment can provide bash shell, the environment is based on a 32-bit architecture. Applications that may be installed on an OAC environment are limited to the one developed for the 32-bit architecture.

Like other OVA files, the **OAC.OVA** file is a tar file that is composed of the application source, manifest file, and certificate file, as shown in Example 3-4.

Example 3-4   *OAC Tar File Contents*

```
bash-4.3$ tar tvf oac.ova
-rw-r--r-- nxbld/andbld      325 2018-05-04 13:48 oac.cert
-rw-r--r-- nxbld/andbld 46687615 2018-05-04 13:48 oac.iso.bz2
-rw-r--r-- nxbld/andbld      168 2018-05-04 13:48 oac.mf
-rw-r--r-- nxbld/andbld        4 2018-05-04 13:48 oac.ver
-rw-r--r-- nxbld/andbld     1793 2018-05-04 13:48 oac.xml
bash-4.3$
```

The content of the **oac.xml** file that defines the resource requirement is listed in Example 3-5.

Example 3-5 *OAC Manifest File*

```
<ciscodefinition>
  <ciscoservices>
    <ciscodomain>
      <applicationName>OpenAgentContainer</applicationName>
      <applicationVersion>1.0</applicationVersion>
      <applicationDescription>Cisco Systems Open Agent Container
</applicationDescription>
      <applicationVendor>Cisco Systems, Inc.</applicationVendor>
    </ciscodomain>
    <cisconetwork>
      <network stack='host_restricted'/>
    </cisconetwork>
  </ciscoservices>
  <domain type='lxc'>
    <name>oac</name>
    <uuid>uuid</uuid>
    <memory>393216</memory>
    <currentMemory>393216</currentMemory>
    <os>
      <type>exe</type>
      <init>/sbin/init</init>
    </os>
    <clock offset='utc'/>
    <on_poweroff>destroy</on_poweroff>
    <on_reboot>restart</on_reboot>
    <on_crash>destroy</on_crash>
    <devices>
      <emulator>/usr/sbin/libvirt_lxc</emulator>
      <filesystem type='mount' accessmode='passthrough'>
        <source dir='/oac.iso'/>
        <target dir='/'/>
        <cisco capacity='500' initModel='copy'/>
      </filesystem>
      <filesystem type='mount' accessmode='passthrough'>
        <source dir='/core_storage'/>
        <target dir='/cisco/core'/>
        <cisco shareModel='core'/>
      </filesystem>
      <serial type='tcp'>
        <source mode='bind' host='' service='5444'/>
        <target type='serial' port='0'/>
        <protocol type='telnet'/>
      </serial>
```

```
    <serial type='tcp'>
       <source mode='bind' host='' service='5445'/>
       <target type='serial' port='1'/>
       <protocol type='telnet'/>
    </serial>
    <serial type='pty'>
       <source path='syslog'/>
       <target port='2'/>
       <alias name='serial2'/>
    </serial>
    <serial type='pty'>
       <source path='tracelog'/>
       <target port='3'/>
       <alias name='serial3'/>
    </serial>
  </devices>
 </domain>
</ciscodefinition>
```

Just like Cisco Guest Shell containers, open-agent containers cannot be instantiated using native LXC commands. Nexus switches are enabled with **virtual-service** commands that internally use LXC commands to instantiate the Cent-OS–based open-agent container, as here:

```
Nexus7k# virtual-service install name ciscoOAC package bootflash:oac.ova
Nexus7k#
```

Note: Once the **'bootflash:/oac.ova' for virtual service 'ciscoOAC'** package is installed, the virtual machine may be activated. Use the **'show virtual-service list'** command to show the progress.

While native **virsh** commands are available in the bash shell for informational purposes as shown in Example 3-6, the lifecycle of the service container is managed using Cisco CLI.

Example 3-6   *OAC Resource Output*

```
bash-4.3$ sudo virsh -c lxc:/// list
 Id Name                   State
---------------------------------
26206 vdc_1_oacnew         running


bash-4.3$


bash-4.3$ sudo virsh -c lxc:/// nodeinfo
```

```
CPU model:            x86_64
CPU(s):               16
CPU frequency:        2133 MHz
CPU socket(s):        2
Core(s) per socket:   4
Thread(s) per core:   2
NUMA cell(s):         1
Memory size:          32939156 kB


bash-4.3$
```

By default, each instance of open-agent container allocates 1 percent of the system CPU and consumes less than 500 MB of disk space and memory on the Nexus switches. In a dual supervisor environment, the open-agent container does not synchronize the file system to the standby container. That is one of the primary disadvantages of open-agent container compared to the Cisco Guest Shell environment. Chef and Puppet are the only OAC agents that are officially supported by Cisco. This is another disadvantage of open-agent container compared to the Cisco Guest Shell, which serves as a general-purpose container.

More details about the switch configuration and commands to instantiate an open-agent container on Nexus switches are available in Chapter 7.

Note: Beginning with Cisco NX-OS Release 8.4(1), the Open Agent Container support is deprecated.

Docker

Docker is one of the commonly used and widely accepted carrier-grade open source container platforms. It is used to develop, package, ship, and run container applications. Docker is a client-server architecture that can be enabled on various Linux distributions and on a Microsoft Windows–based infrastructure. When Docker was introduced in 2013, it used lxc as the container runtime, but the recent edition of Docker is implemented with runc as the container runtime.

The Docker architecture is made up of the following components:

- Docker daemon (dockerd)
- Docker client
- Docker registry
- RESTful API for communication between the client and daemon

The Docker architecture and the various components are shown in Figure 3-7.

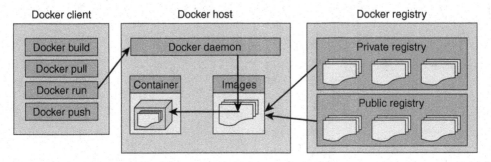

Figure 3-7   *Docker Architecture*

The Docker daemon (dockerd) acts as a server that accepts incoming API requests over different types of sockets, such as UNIX, tcp, and fd. The Docker daemon is responsible for managing objects such as images, containers, networks, and volumes. When the Docker daemon receives a request to instantiate a container, it is responsible for pulling the relevant image from the registry if it is not available in the local repository.

Docker has become the choice packaging model for application packaging and delivery because it shares common layers; therefore, it makes the image thin. It is portable and easy to integrate with devops automation toolchains.

Docker image is built and packaged by following a layered architecture in which each layer represents the essential files and tasks to run the container application. The image layers start from a read-only base image followed by intermediate read-only layers depending on the libraries and binaries that are required to build the container application. The topmost container application layer is a read-write layer that gives users full access. The concept of layering architecture used by Docker makes the image flexible because it can share the base layer. The layering model also makes it easier to modify the image because any changes are required to rebuild the relevant layer without touching the other layers.

Docker uses Dockerfile, which is prepopulated with a set of commands. These commands are executed by the Docker client to build the container image. Figure 3-8 shows a sample Dockerfile to build a container image.

Dockerfile

FROM python:alpine3.7	Base layer
RUN pip install -r requirements.txt COPY ./sbfd WORKDIR /sbfd	Intermediate layer
CMD ["python3", "./sbfd-server_udp.py"]]	Container layer

Figure 3-8   *Sample Dockerfile*

The FROM layer helps build the base layer. Applications developed using Python require a base Linux image. The choice of base image also reduces the overall docker image size. Alpine is one of the Linux distributions that is best suited as the base image for Python applications because it satisfies most of the library requirements and builds a container image smaller than 100 MB. When using Ubuntu as the base image, the same Python application will result in a container image of about 700 MB. Python is one of the most used programming languages, but it is not unusual to see other languages used. Based on the type of programming language used to build the application, the base image may vary. For example, an application built using C can use SCRATCH as a base image, which will result in a container image smaller than 10 MB. The selection of the proper base image plays a key role in optimizing the container image size without compromising the application requirement.

RUN, COPY, and **WORKDIR** are some of the other Dockerfile commands that build the intermediate layer comprising the libraries and binaries that are essential to run the container application.

The container layer is the topmost layer that executes the application-specific commands. **CMD,** at the container layer, executes the relevant command to start the application service upon instantiating the container.

More details about other Dockerfile commands and environment variables are available at https://docs.docker.com/engine/reference/builder/.

The resulting docker image built from the preceding method is made up of the following components:

- **Manifest file:** A JSON-based file that represents the description of the container image

- **Layered file system:** The actual binary image that will be provisioned

- **System Configuration:** The specifications required to run the container

Docker provides rich image-management capabilities and a repository hub that allows users to upload the images to a public registry or to create a private registry. Images in a public registry are accessible by other users, whereas the images in a private registry need credentials to access.

Cisco operating systems are built on the Linux distribution kernel that has made it easy to integrate the support for Docker. As such, Docker is now an integral part of the operating system and is natively available in most of the Cisco platforms that are running IOS-XE, IOS-XR, and NXOS software. By default, the Docker service is not enabled in any of the platforms, and the operators are responsible for enabling the service before hosting applications. The Cisco OS architecture with Docker is shown in Figure 3-9.

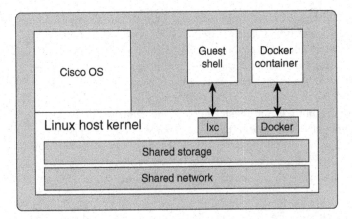

Figure 3-9   *Docker Container Hosting on Cisco Platforms*

Cisco Nexus 3000 and 9000 series switches support the Docker functionality within the bash shell from the 9.2(1) release. Cisco Nexus 3000 series switches with RAM that is less than 8 GB do not support Docker functionality. Cisco IOS-XR supports Docker from the 6.1.2 version. Catalyst 9000 series switches support Docker from the IOS-XE 16.9.1 release. Although Nexus 3000 and 9000 series switches and Cisco IOS-XR platforms natively support Docker, some of the IOS-XE platforms do not.

When the Docker daemon is started from the bash shell on the supported platform, it carves out a storage space from the **bootflash.** In Example 3-7, when the Docker daemon is started on a Nexus series switch, it carves out a fixed-size storage known as **dockerpart** from the device **bootflash.**

Example 3-7   *Dockerpart on NXOS*

```
N9K-C93180YC# dir bootflash:dockerpart
 2000000000    Apr 28 19:51:43 2019  dockerpart

Usage for bootflash://sup-local
 1597718528 bytes used
114994958336 bytes free
116592676864 bytes total
N9K-C93180YC#
```

The software support matrix for Docker is shown in Table 3-4.

Table 3-4   *Docker-Supported Software Versions*

IOS-XE	IOS-XR	NXOS
Cisco 9000 series switches running 16.9.1 and newer	Cisco IOS-XR running 6.1.2 and newer	Cisco Nexus 3000 series switches and Nexus 9000 series switches running 9.2 and newer

Kubernetes

As explained in the preceding sections, the Cisco platform supports the use of proprietary commands to deploy LXC containers and native Docker commands for container deployments. Such deployment models lack dynamic lifecycle management, which means the operator must manage the lifecycle of the container workloads manually. Container orchestration is an automated process that leverages the Container Runtime for scheduling and managing the container applications.

Kubernetes (K8S) has become the de-facto production-grade orchestration engine for container and microservice workload environments. Kubernetes, built on the Go language, was initially developed by Google for internal container deployment and management purposes. It was later adopted by Cloud Native Computing Foundation (CNCF), a vendor-neutral, open-source community. CNCF is one of the active open-source projects, with industry experts from more than 100 companies contributing to develop the tool further.

The Kubernetes architecture is shown in Figure 3-10.

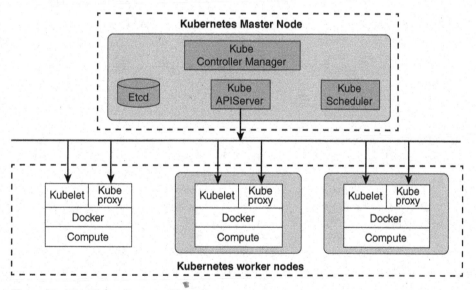

Figure 3-10 *Kubernetes Architecture*

Kubernetes is a client-server–based cluster architecture, with the cluster being a collection of multiple compute resources managed by the master control plane. The cluster concept of Kubernetes is analogous to virtual machine clusters where multiple hypervisors are managed by a cluster manager. The Kubernetes architecture is composed of two main components:

- Kubernetes master node (k8s master)
- Kubernetes worker node (k8s worker)

The Kubernetes master node is the master brain component of the cluster that makes global decisions such as workload scheduling and scaling. Each Kubernetes cluster has a minimum of one k8s master node with one or more k8s worker nodes. The Kubernetes master is a collective set of components that can run on a single node or can spread across different physical nodes. Some of the critical components of master node are explained here:

- **etcd** is one of the master components that plays a key role for critical data storage in the Kubernetes cluster. etcd is a distributed and highly available key-value store that is used to preserve data, such as cluster configuration, workload states, service discovery, and so on. The data stored in etcd is sensitive to the cluster, so it is accessible only by an API server that is another master component. This component uses TCP ports 2379 and 2380 for communication.

- **Kube-apiserver** is another master component that exposes the Kubernetes API to receive and accept commands from the northbound applications and tools. Kube-apiserver acts as the front end for the cluster through which all the other components interact. This component uses TCP port 6443 for communication.

- **Kube Controller Manager** is a daemon that runs and controls various controller processes such as replication controllers.

- **Kube-scheduler** is responsible for scheduling the workload based on the resource requirement requested by the workload. This component monitors new workload requests from Kube-apiserver and selects the relevant worker node based on resource availability. This component uses TCP port 10251 for communication.

The Kubernetes worker node provides the compute resource for the Kubernetes cluster. It can be a physical or a virtual host that is capable of deploying containers. Each cluster must have one or more worker nodes that are registered with the Kubernetes master and can accept any commands to instantiate workloads. By default, the master node will not act as a worker node, so containers cannot be deployed on the physical host where the master components are running. This is because of a node affinity property known as taint that repels the scheduler to run any container on the node. However, you can override this behavior by removing the master node from taint. Some of the critical components of the Kubernetes worker node are listed next:

- **docker** is a mandatory worker node component installed in all the worker nodes. Kubernetes heavily leverages docker for deploying the containers that make it a necessity for all worker nodes. More details about docker were explained in the previous chapter.

- **Kubelet** is the component on the worker node that interacts with kube-apiserver on the master node to get the pod specification and ensures that the pods are running healthy. Kubelet uses a Pod Lifecycle Event Generator (PLEG) function that creates a time series–based list of the state of all containers and compares it with the previous time frame list to detect any failures to redeploy the workload. This component uses TCP port 10255 for communication

■ **Kube-proxy** is another worker node component that acts as a network proxy to reflect services defined by the API.

Some of the key features of Kubernetes that made it a production-grade de-facto orchestration engine are listed here:

■ Service discovery and load balancing

■ Storage orchestration

■ Dynamic workload scaling

■ Automated rollouts

■ Batch execution

■ Self-healing

The workloads in the Kubernetes cluster are deployed as pods. Each pod is an entity capable of running multiple containers with its own control group (cgroup) but with a shared namespace. The network stack is assigned at the Pod level, so all the containers within the same pod will share the same IP address. Each container within the pod will have its own port range and will use interprocess communication (IPC) for intercontainer communication within the pod.

A detailed explanation about each Kubernetes components is available at https://Kubernetes.io/docs/concepts/overview/what-is-Kubernetes/.

Cisco Nexus 9000 series switches running 9.x release or later are capable of running as both Kubernetes master and worker node.

Container Deployment and Orchestration

This section describes the basic procedure to instantiate containers using different deployment tools. The examples provided in this section familiarize the audience with various orchestration tools and the commands used for running the container. A more detailed explanation of the tools on each platform is found in later chapters.

Orchestrating and Managing Containers Using LXC

This section uses Cisco IOS-XE–based platforms to explain how an LXC component is used to deploy Guest Shell. Cisco IOS-XE platforms must be preconfigured with basic commands before enabling the Guest Shell. For example, IOx is the application hosting framework that leverages LXC to host the container, and this feature must be enabled before instantiating the Guest Shell container. More details about the device configuration are covered in Chapter 5.

Example 3-8 shows a sample capture from a CSR1000 virtual router running IOS-XE software. By default, the Guest Shell is not enabled, and it must use the IOx service to enable the same.

Example 3-8 *IOx Service on IOS-XE*

```
CSR-PE3#show iox-service
Virtual Service Global State and Virtualization Limits:

Infrastructure version : 1.7
Total virtual services installed : 0
Total virtual services activated : 0

Machine types supported   : KVM, LXC
Machine types disabled    : none

Maximum VCPUs per virtual service : 0
Resource virtualization limits:
Name                       Quota       Committed    Available
----------------------------------------------------------------
system CPU (%)                 7              0            7
memory (MB)                 1024              0         1024
bootflash (MB)             20000              0         5741

IOx Infrastructure Summary:
---------------------------
IOx service (CAF)     : Running
IOx service (HA)      : Not Running
IOx service (IOxman)  : Running
Libvirtd              : Running

CSR-PE3#
```

As can be noted from Example 3-8, the architecture limits the availability of the system resources, such as CPU and memory for virtualization, and the application hosting cannot exceed this limit. The resource allocation limit is not on a per-application basis, and it can be customized based on the hosted application. Example 3-8 also shows that the platform is capable of supporting KVM- and LXC-based instantiation. Although it is true that the internal components leverage LXC and KVM to instantiate the Guest Shell or other application hosting, Cisco-specific CLI commands are used to execute the KVM and LXC tasks, and Cisco IOS-XE does not support the use of native LXC or KVM commands for container instantiation.

The lifecycle of the Guest Shell container is managed by Guest Shell CLI commands that are executed from the **exec** prompt. Table 3-5 shows the commands and their descriptions.

Table 3-5 *Guest Shell CLI Commands*

CLI	Description
guestshell enable	This CLI pulls the Guest Shell container package from the system image and instantiates the container.
guestshell run [cmd]	This CLI executes the command on the Guest Shell container or takes users to the bash prompt of the Guest Shell container.

CLI	Description
guestshell disable	This CLI stops the Guest Shell container but does not clear the **rootfs**.
guestshell destroy	This CLI destroys the Guest Shell container and clears all the contents related to the container.
guestshell sync	This CLI is used in dual supervisor nodes to sync the Guest Shell content to the standby supervisor.

When the **guestshell enable** command is executed, the IOx service instantiates the CentOS Linux container, as shown in the syslog message in Example 3-9.

Example 3-9   *IOX-Specific syslog Message*

```
csr1000v-2#guest enable
Interface will be selected if configured in app-hosting
Please wait for completion
guestshell activated successfully
Current state is: ACTIVATED
guestshell started successfully
Current state is: RUNNING
Guestshell enabled successfully

csr1000v-2#
*Apr 18 11:26:08.495: %IM-6-IOX_INST_INFO: R0/0: ioxman: IOX SERVICE guestshell
  LOG: Guestshell is up at 03/18/2019 11:26:08
*Apr 18 11:26:12.720: %IM-5-IOX_INST_NOTICE: R0/0: ioxman: IOX SERVICE guestshell
  LOG: CentOS Linux 7 (Core)
csr1000v-2#
```

Upon instantiating the Guest Shell container, IOx will mount the **rootfs** for Guest Shell in the **bootflash**, and this will be used as the storage for Guest Shell contents. Any files and folders created in the Guest Shell are visible from the **bootflash**. Example 3-10 shows a capture of the **rootfs** content of the Guest Shell from the **bootflash**.

Example 3-10   *Guestshell rootfs Content*

```
csr1000v-2#dir bootflash:iox/repo-1xc/guestshell/rootfs_mnt
Directory of bootflash:iox/repo-1xc/guestshell/rootfs_mnt/

  529  drwx       51200000  Jun 21 2018 18:43:19 +00:00  lost+found
 3697  drwx           1024  Jun 10 2014 00:11:46 +00:00  srv
 4225  dr-x           1024  Jun 10 2014 00:11:46 +00:00  sys
 4753  drwx           1024  Jun 21 2018 18:40:52 +00:00  selinux
 5809  drwx           1024  Jun 21 2018 18:40:59 +00:00  run
17425  drwx           1024  Jun 10 2014 00:11:46 +00:00  mnt
17953  drwx           1024  Apr 18 2019 11:26:07 +00:00  var
<removed>
```

```
7897796608 bytes total (6017056768 bytes free)
csr1000v-2#
```

guestshell run [cmd] can be used to execute Linux-specific commands on the Guest
    Shell container or to log in to the **guestshell** bash prompt.

```
csr1000v-2#guestshell run bash
[guestshell@guestshell ~]$ uname -a
Linux guestshell 4.4.119 #1 SMP Thu Jun 7 21:48:52 PDT 2018 x86_64 GNU/Linux
[guestshell@guestshell ~]$
```

More details about the IOx framework and Guest Shell along with the device configuration are explained in the forthcoming chapters. As mentioned in the earlier section, the
Cisco platform does not allow the use of native LXC or KVM commands to instantiate
virtual entities, but most of the Linux distributions natively support nested virtualization.

For various reasons, you may need to use LXC to boot the container in a traditional server-
based setup to check the libraries or packages before instantiating the same on Cisco platforms. This section explains how to use LXC in Ubuntu server. Like other binaries, users
can install an LXC daemon to enable and use it for nested virtualization. Example 3-11
explains the use of LXC to instantiate an Alpine Linux container on an Ubuntu host.

Example 3-11   *Using LXC to Instantiate an Alpine Linux Container on an Ubuntu Host*

```
ubuntu@openconfig:~$ lxc launch images:alpine/3.6 cisco-alpine
Creating cisco-alpine
Starting cisco-alpine
ubuntu@openconfig:~$

ubuntu@openconfig:~$ lxc list --fast
+----------+---------+--------------+------------------+----------+----------+
|NAME      | STATE   | ARCHITECTURE | CREATED AT       | PROFILES |   TYPE   |
+----------+---------+--------------+------------------+----------+----------+
| alpine   | RUNNING | x86_64       |     <date>       | default  |PERSISTENT|
+----------+---------+--------------+------------------+----------+----------+
| alpine1  | RUNNING | x86_64       |     <date>       | default  |PERSISTENT|
+----------+---------+--------------+------------------+----------+----------+
|  puma    | RUNNING | x86_64       |     <date>       | default  |PERSISTENT|
+----------+---------+--------------+------------------+----------+----------+
ubuntu@openconfig:~$
```

A list of free Linux container images is available at https://us.images.linuxcontainers.org/.

Orchestrating and Managing Containers Using Docker

This section explains the basic steps to verify the status of the Docker daemon on Cisco
IOS-XR and the procedure to deploy an Alpine container. The intention of this section

is to provide a high-level overview of how the Docker functions in the IOS-XR platform. A detailed explanation about the architecture and related configuration is available in Chapter 6, "Container Orchestration in Cisco IOS-XR Platforms."

Docker Daemon Status Verification

By default, the Docker daemon is enabled in the Cisco IOS-XR bash shell. Example 3-12 presents the output from a Cisco XR9000v router that shows that the Docker daemon is up and running. The example displays the output collected from the XR bash shell.

Example 3-12 *XR Bash Shell Output*

```
RP0/RP0/CPU0:IOSXR# run
Sat Apr  6 22:51:01.896 UTC


[xr-vm_node0_RP0_CPU0:~]$service docker status
docker start/post-stop, process 22433
[xr-vm_node0_RP0_CPU0:~]$
```

Note: Like any other process, the Docker daemon can be stopped or restarted from the bash shell using the bash native service commands, as shown in Example 3-13. However, the Docker daemon is integrated with the Cisco OS, so the Docker version cannot be upgraded.

Example 3-13 *Docker Daemon Output*

```
[xr-vm_node0_RP0_CPU0:~]$docker version
Client:
 Version:      1.10.0
 API version:  1.22
 Go version:   go1.4.2
 Git commit:   cb6da92
 Built:        Tue Aug  8 22:08:35 2017
 OS/Arch:      linux/amd64


Server:
 Version:      1.10.0
 API version:  1.22
 Go version:   go1.4.2
 Git commit:   cb6da92
 Built:        Tue Aug  8 22:08:35 2017
 OS/Arch:      linux/amd64
[xr-vm_node0_RP0_CPU0:~]$
```

> **Note:**   Docker version numbering followed the 1.X.X format until the 1.13.1 release. Now Docker follows the **YY.MM.XX** format, where **YY** refers to the year of the release, **MM** refers to the month of the release, and **XX** refers to the version number.

The next command is used from the bash shell to control the Docker daemon service.

```
[xr-vm_node0_RP0_CPU0:~]$service docker {start|stop}
[xr-vm_node0_RP0_CPU0:~]$
```

Docker Client

The Docker Client provides the CLI interface, which is the primary mode for users to interact with the Docker daemon. The client receives the command via CLI from the user and leverages RESTful API instructions to communicate the command to the daemon. A Cisco platform running the Docker daemon can use the native docker CLI commands to create or delete the containers, as shown in Example 3-14.

Example 3-14   *Docker Command Options from XR Bash Shell*

```
RP/0/RP0/CPU0:ios#run
Sat Apr  6 22:51:01.896 UTC
[xr-vm_node0_RP0_CPU0:~]$
[xr-vm_node0_RP0_CPU0:~]$docker
Usage: docker [OPTIONS] COMMAND [arg...]
       docker [ --help | -v | --version ]


A self-sufficient runtime for containers.


<removed>


Commands:
    attach    Attach to a running container
    build     Build an image from a Dockerfile
    commit    Create a new image from a container's changes
    cp        Copy files/folders between a container and the local filesystem
    create    Create a new container
    diff      Inspect changes on a container's filesystem
    events    Get real time events from the server
    exec      Run a command in a running container
    export    Export a container's filesystem as a tar archive
    history   Show the history of an image
    images    List images
    import    Import the contents from a tarball to create a filesystem image
```

```
info      Display system-wide information
inspect   Return low-level information on a container or image
kill      Kill a running container
load      Load an image from a tar archive or STDIN
login     Register or log in to a Docker registry
logout    Log out from a Docker registry
logs      Fetch the logs of a container
network   Manage Docker networks
pause     Pause all processes within a container
port      List port mappings or a specific mapping for the CONTAINER
ps        List containers
pull      Pull an image or a repository from a registry
push      Push an image or a repository to a registry
rename    Rename a container
restart   Restart a container
rm        Remove one or more containers
rmi       Remove one or more images
run       Run a command in a new container
save      Save an image(s) to a tar archive
search    Search the Docker Hub for images
start     Start one or more stopped containers
stats     Display a live stream of container(s) resource usage statistics
stop      Stop a running container
tag       Tag an image into a repository
top       Display the running processes of a container
unpause   Unpause all processes within a container
update    Update resources of one or more containers
version   Show the Docker version information
volume    Manage Docker volumes
wait      Block until a container stops, then print its exit code

Run 'docker COMMAND --help' for more information on a command.
[xr-vm_node0_RP0_CPU0:~]
```

Getting Docker Images

Like any other Docker host, IOS-XR is expected to have connectivity to the Docker registry to pull the images from the registry to the local store. By default, the IOS-XR bash shell uses the management interface to reach the Internet; therefore, it is essential to ensure that connectivity is available through the management interface. In scenarios where the IOS-XR does not have direct connectivity to the Internet, the Docker images must be copied manually to the local store before running the container.

In the topology shown in Figure 3-11, the Docker image is initially pulled to the local store in the server and then copied to the IOS-XR bash shell. To accomplish this, it is necessary to pull the Alpine image on the server, save it as a local file, and then use secure copy (**scp**) to push the image to the IOS-XR bash shell. In Example 3-15, the image is copied to the **/disk0:/** location in the bash shell.

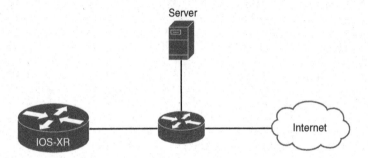

Figure 3-11   *Docker Hosting Topology*

Example 3-15   *Pulling Docker Image*

```
root@server:~# docker pull alpine      /* Pulls the image to local store */
Using default tag: latest
latest: Pulling from library/alpine
743f2d6c1f65: Pull complete
6bfc4ec4420a: Pull complete
688a776db95f: Pull complete
Digest: sha256:1d0dfe527f801c596818da756e01fa0e7af4649b15edc3eb245e8da92c8381f8
Status: Downloaded newer image for alpine:latest
root@server:~# docker save alpine -o /root/alpine/*Save the image locally */
root@server:~# scp /root/alpine cisco@10.0.0.10:/disk0:/    /* Copy the file to
  IOS-XR */
Password:
alpine                                    100%  108MB  80.1KB/s   22:58
root@server:~#
```

Like any other Docker host, the **docker load** command is used to load the local image file to the local Docker store in the host (see Example 3-16).

Example 3-16   *Listing Docker Images*

```
[iosxrv9000-1:~]$ docker load -i /disk0:/alpine
[iosxrv9000-1:~]$ docker images
REPOSITORY          TAG             IMAGE ID          CREATED           SIZE
nginx               latest          53f3fd8007f7      36 hours ago      109.3 MB
ubuntu              latest          d131e0fa2585      12 days ago       101.7 MB
alpine              latest          cdf98d1859c1      4 weeks ago       5.529 MB
[iosxrv9000-1:~]$
```

The Docker images are stored locally in the Docker host using a layered file system from which the Docker daemon pulls the image along with other details while running the container. In Cisco IOS-XR bash shell, Docker images are stored in the /misc/app_host/ docker/image/devicemapper location, as shown in Example 3-17.

Example 3-17 *Docker Image Layers*

```
[iosxrv9000-1:~]$ ls -l /misc/app_host/docker/image/devicemapper/
total 16
drwx------ 2 root root 4096 May  8 19:29 distribution
drwx------ 4 root root 4096 May  8 19:29 imagedb
drwx------ 5 root root 4096 May  8 20:13 layerdb
-rw------- 1 root root  319 May  9 15:51 repositories.json
[iosxrv9000-1:~]$


[iosxrv9000-1:~]$ more /misc/app_host/docker/image/devicemapper/repositories.json

{"Repositories":
  {"alpine":{"alpine:latest":"sha256:<removed>"},
   "nginx":{"nginx:latest":"sha256:<removed>"},
   "ubuntu":{"ubuntu:latest":"sha256:<removed>"}}}
[iosxrv9000-1:~]$
```

Running the Container

When the image is available in the local store for use, the **docker run** command is executed along with the appropriate Docker options to deploy the container on Cisco IOS-XR bash shell, as shown in Example 3-18.

Example 3-18 *Running a Docker Container*

```
[iosxrv9000-1:~]$ docker run -itd --net=host --name alpine  -v /var/run/netns/
  global-vrf:/var/run/netns/global-vrf --cap-add=SYS_ADMIN alpine
c145515a7775161956b7334c3e6c3f2c689c2d541e7559233a3ea6206dbc0e2f
[iosxrv9000-1:~]$
```

In Example 3-18, the following options are used:

- **-it:** This option is required for interactive processes, and it instructs the daemon to allocate a **pseudo-tty** for the container.

- **-d:** This option instructs the daemon to run the container in detached mode.

- **—net:** This option defines the network for the container. The type **host** will attach the host network stack inside the container.

- **-v:** This option defines the volume to be mounted.

- **--cap-add:** This option specifies additional Linux capabilities for the container.

The list of containers that are actively running can be listed using the command as shown in Example 3-19.

Example 3-19 *Listing Active Containers*

```
[iosxrv9000-1:~]$ docker ps
CONTAINER ID      IMAGE        COMMAND         CREATED      STATUS      PORTS      NAMES
c145515a7775      alpine       "/bin/sh"       <time>                              alpine
[iosxrv9000-1:~]$
```

It could be noted that the host network stack is attached to the container and allows the container to access the network. In the output shown in Example 3-20, the interface stack of the host, including the G0/0/0/0 interface, can be seen listed inside the container.

Example 3-20 *Docker Network Stack*

```
[iosxrv9000-1:~]$ docker attach alpine

/ # ifconfig
Gi0_0_0_0 Link encap:Ethernet   HWaddr FA:16:3E:C0:44:28
          inet addr:10.0.0.10  Mask:255.255.255.252
          inet6 addr: fe80::f816:3eff:fec0:4428/64 Scope:Link
          UP RUNNING NOARP MULTICAST  MTU:1500  Metric:1
          RX packets:372143 errors:0 dropped:0 overruns:0 frame:0
          TX packets:147618 errors:0 dropped:0 overruns:0 carrier:0
          collisions:0 txqueuelen:1000
          RX bytes:465914341 (444.3 MiB)  TX bytes:9183508 (8.7 MiB)

fwd_ew    Link encap:Ethernet   HWaddr 00:00:00:00:00:0B
          inet6 addr: fe80::200:ff:fe00:b/64 Scope:Link
          UP RUNNING NOARP MULTICAST  MTU:1500  Metric:1
          RX packets:1 errors:0 dropped:0 overruns:0 frame:0
          TX packets:2 errors:0 dropped:1 overruns:0 carrier:0
          collisions:0 txqueuelen:1000
          RX bytes:110 (110.0 B)  TX bytes:140 (140.0 B)

fwdintf   Link encap:Ethernet   HWaddr 00:00:00:00:00:0A
          inet6 addr: fe80::200:ff:fe00:a/64 Scope:Link
          UP RUNNING NOARP MULTICAST  MTU:1482  Metric:1
          RX packets:0 errors:0 dropped:0 overruns:0 frame:0
          TX packets:38316 errors:0 dropped:1 overruns:0 carrier:0
          collisions:0 txqueuelen:1000
          RX bytes:0 (0.0 B)  TX bytes:2694053 (2.5 MiB)

lo        Link encap:Local Loopback
          inet addr:127.0.0.1  Mask:255.0.0.0
          inet6 addr: ::1/128 Scope:Host
```

```
           UP LOOPBACK RUNNING  MTU:65536  Metric:1
           RX packets:234 errors:0 dropped:0 overruns:0 frame:0
           TX packets:234 errors:0 dropped:0 overruns:0 carrier:0
           collisions:0 txqueuelen:0
           RX bytes:19464 (19.0 KiB)  TX bytes:19464 (19.0 KiB)

lo:0       Link encap:Local Loopback
           inet addr:192.168.0.3  Mask:255.255.255.255
           UP LOOPBACK RUNNING  MTU:65536  Metric:1

/ #
```

Orchestrating and Managing Containers Using Kubernetes

In this section, you learn the basic steps to verify the status of the Docker daemon on Cisco NXOS and the procedure to use Docker CLI to join a Kubernetes cluster. With this approach, the container deployment can be directly orchestrated from the Kubernetes master.

Note: In a traditional Kubernetes environment, the worker node running Ubuntu or CentOS uses the **kubeadm** package command to join the cluster, but this package is available only for selective operating systems. Cisco Nexus switches use **hyperkube** to join the cluster.

Running Docker Daemon

By default, the Docker daemon is not enabled in Cisco NXOS platforms. To enable the Docker daemon, the first step is to enable the bash shell feature to gain access to the NXOS bash shell prompt. When the Docker daemon is started for the first time, a new back-end storage space file of fixed size 2 GB is created in the bootflash. This file is mounted to the /var/lib/docker location in the bash shell and stores any docker-related content, such as images.

In Example 3-21, the Docker daemon service is created from the bash shell. Notice that the **dockerpart** file is created in the **bootflash**.

Example 3-21   *Starting the Docker Daemon*

```
nx-osv9000-1#run bash
bash-4.3$ su - root
root@ nx-osv9000-1#service docker start
Free bootflash: 26808 MB, total bootflash: 51771 MB
Carving docker bootflash storage: 2000 MB
2000+0 records in
2000+0 records out
2000000000 bytes (2.0 GB) copied, 24.9124 s, 80.3 MB/s
mke2fs 1.42.9 (28-Dec-2013)
fs_types for mke2fs.conf resolution: 'ext4'
...
<snip>
```

```
...
Updating certificates in /etc/ssl/certs...
0 added, 0 removed; done.
Running hooks in /etc/ca-certificates/update.d...
done.
Starting dockerd with args '--debug=true':

root@ nx-osv9000-1#
root@nx-osv9000-1#service docker status
dockerd (pid  7279) is running...
root@nx-osv9000-1#
```

Note: Starting the Docker daemon or other Docker functionality requires root access. Non-root users cannot start the daemon or execute Docker functionalities. By using **su – root** in the bash prompt, you can change the user to root.

Enabling Kubernetes Master

In Figure 3-12, the Ubuntu server is used as the Kubernetes master node. Hyperkube is a Docker container image that comprises all the Kubernetes daemons and libraries as one file. Running a hyperkube container installs all the relevant daemons required to function as a Kubernetes master.

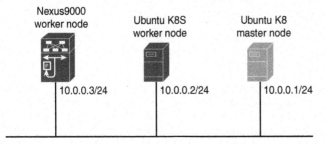

Figure 3-12 *Nexus 9000 Topology*

Following are the services that are enabled by hyperkube:

- API-Server
- Scheduler
- Controller-Manager
- Kubelet

In Example 3-22, the Kubernetes API server is enabled and exposed in port 8080 on the Ubuntu server. Worker nodes must use port 8080 to join the Kubernetes cluster.

Example 3-22   *Kubernetes Master*

```
root@ubuntu:~# kubectl cluster-info
Kubernetes master is running at http://localhost:8080
KubeDNS is running at http://localhost:8080/api/v1/proxy/namespaces/kube-system/
  services/kube-dns
Kubernetes -dashboard is running at http://localhost:8080/api/v1/proxy/namespaces/
  kube-system/services/Kubernetes -dashboard
root@ubuntu:~#
```

Note: Although this example uses Ubuntu server as a Kubernetes master node, Nexus 9000 series switches can act as both Kubernetes Master node and worker node.

Enabling Nexus 9000 Switch as Kubernetes Worker Node

From the bash shell, the hyperkube container is executed using the Docker daemon. This enables all the daemon services required to run the Nexus switch as a worker node. The hyperkube container is executed using Docker with the **api-server** attribute set to the master node's IP address and the port set to 8080.

In Example 3-23, the CLI is executed from the bash shell on the Cisco Nexus switch.

Example 3-23   *Enabling Hypercube in Nexus 9000 Switch*

```
docker run -d --name=ciscok8sn9k \
    --net=host --pid=host --privileged=true \
    --volume=/:/rootfs:ro --volume=/sys:/sys:ro --volume=/dev:/dev \
    --volume=/var/lib/docker/:/var/lib/docker:rw \
    --volume=/var/lib/kubelet/:/var/lib/kubelet:rw \
    --volume=/var/run:/var/run:rw \
 gcr.io/google_containers/hyperkube:v1.2.2 \
 /hyperkube kubelet --allow-privileged=true --containerized \
    --enable-server --cluster_dns=10.0.0.10 \
    --cluster_domain=cluster.local \
    --config=/etc/Kubernetes /manifests-multi \
    --hostname-override="10.0.0.3" \
    --address=0.0.0.0 --api-servers=http://10.0.0.1:8080
```

From the master node, you can see that the Nexus switch is one of the worker nodes. The Nexus switch is now part of the Kubernetes cluster, and it is managed by the Kubernetes master, as shown in Example 3-24.

Example 3-24 *Listing the Kubernetes Worker Nodes*

```
root@ubuntu:~# kubectl get nodes
NAME            STATUS   AGE
127.0.0.1       Ready    1d
10.0.0.3        Ready    1d       /* Nexus 9000 Switch */
root@ubuntu:~#
```

Deploying Workload Using Kubernetes

Now that the Kubernetes cluster is ready to host application containers, simple YAML files are created to deploy the application workloads. Example 3-25 shows a sample YAML file that deploys an Alpine Linux container on the worker node.

Example 3-25 *Pod Configuration YAML File*

```
apiVersion: v1
kind: Pod
metadata:
  name: alpine
  namespace: default
spec:
  containers:
  - image: alpine:latest
    command:
      - /bin/sh
      - "-c"
      - "sleep 60m"
    imagePullPolicy: IfNotPresent
    name: alpine
  restartPolicy: Always
```

Note: Using a YAML file is the human-readable way of defining the Kubernetes object specifications to deploy the container workload. **Kubectl** converts the information in the YAML file to JSON while making the API calls to the server.

From the Kubernetes master node, the workload is deployed using the **kubectl** command and the preceding YAML file as shown in Example 3-26.

Example 3-26 *Creating a Container*

```
root@ubuntu:~# kubectl create -f alpine-pod.yaml
pod "alpine" created
root@ubuntu:~#
```

The Alpine Linux container is now deployed on the Nexus 9000 switch, as shown in Example 3-27.

Example 3-27 *Listing the Containers*

```
root@ubuntu:~# kubectl get pod -o wide
NAME                       READY   STATUS     RESTARTS   AGE    NODE
alpine                     1/1     Running    0          43m    10.0.0.3
k8s-proxy-127.0.0.1        1/1     Running    0          2d     127.0.0.1
k8s-proxy-64.102.242.131   1/1     Running    0          2d     10.0.0.3
root@ubuntu:~#
```

Note: Further details such as the resource used and the network configuration about the container created on the Nexus 9000 worker node are available in /lib/var/docker/containers/.

Summary

This chapter introduced the cloud-native reference model and how it is used to develop cloud-native network functions. It discussed the penetration of containers into the network world, as well as the use cases that benefit by bringing the container workloads on the network elements.

This chapter explained the different container orchestration tools that are available and the applicability of such tools in Cisco platforms to host the applications. Lastly, it provided an overview of how to use different tools to host the applications on different Cisco platforms.

References

Developing Cloud Native Applications: https://www.cncf.io/blog/2017/05/15/developing-cloud-native-applications/

Cloud-Native Network Functions (CNFs): https://www.cisco.com/c/en/us/products/collateral/routers/cloud-native-broadband-router/white-paper-c11-740841.pdf

Docker Overview: https://docs.docker.com/engine/docker-overview/

Kubernetes Documentation: https://kubernetes.io/docs/home/

IOX Resource Downloads: https://developer.cisco.com/docs/iox/#!iox-resource-downloads

Chapter 4

Container Networking Concepts

In this chapter, you will learn the following:

- The basics of container networking and the components involved

- The container networking model and container network interfaces

- The different types of container networking modes

- The container network configuration on Cisco platforms

Container Networking—Introduction and Essentials

Indubitably, networking is an essential infrastructure element for end-to-end service delivery. Typically, the applications hosted in a physical server are identified using a combination of the IP address assigned to the physical server and the transport port to which the application is listening. This is slightly different when virtualization comes into the picture. As shown in Figure 4-1, the virtual entity hosted in a physical server may need to communicate to the external network or to other entity within the same server. The physical server hosting the virtual entity, such as a virtual machine or containers, may not necessarily have IP addresses assigned, and even if assigned, it may not be used for application resources. Instead, each virtual machine or container will have its dedicated IP address that allows intra-host or inter-host communication.

The previous chapter discussed different ways of hosting applications on Cisco platforms. Depending on the type of application hosted, it might require one or more of the communication types discussed in the following sections.

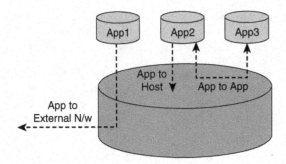

Figure 4-1 *Communication Modes*

Application to Host

In this communication type, the hosted application is required to communicate only with
the host on which the application is deployed. Some applications are developed to collect telemetry data from the local hosted network device and locally process that data for
analytical purposes; the results are then logged locally. Such applications are not required
to communicate with other applications or with the external network.

Application to Application

In this communication type, the hosted application is required to communicate with the
local host and with some or all applications hosted on the same network device. A good
example is a data collection and analytics application that is developed using microservice architecture by splitting the data collection and analytics modules into different
applications.

Application to External Network

In this communication type, the hosted application is required to communicate with
other entities in the external network. A good example is an application that collects and
consolidates the telemetry data from the host or other applications running on the host
and exposes it to the external users or a machine learning agent.

As you learned in Chapter 3, "Container Orchestration and Management," applications
can be hosted as containers on Cisco platforms using native-app hosting capability,
Docker, or Kubernetes orchestration capabilities. To facilitate communications, the following basic container networking requirements must be met:

- **IP Address Assignment and Management (IPAM):** Each hosted application should
  have its unique identity, which can be a dedicated IP address for each container or
  dedicated transport layer port for each container, or it shares the IP address with
  the host. The former is commonly known as "dedicated mode," whereas the latter is
  known as "shared mode." More details about the modes are explained in the latter
  part of this chapter.

- **Network isolation:** Container networking must provide some sort of isolation to control the communication between containers or communication from the containers to the host. Such isolation also addresses security concerns in which compromising one container does not compromise the entire ecosystem.

- **Network connectivity:** For intra-host or inter-host container communication, a network bridge with relevant forwarding instructions populated must be used.

The network stack of the application is abstracted from the container that allows the developers to control and accomplish the preceding network requirements outside the scope of the application being developed. Application developers are not expected to be concerned with developing the application based on the network requirements.

This chapter discusses the container network model and the different types of container networks and interfaces. Then it discusses how these container networks and interfaces can be configured while hosting applications on Cisco platforms using native-app hosting, Docker, or Kubernetes.

Note: Some of the container network interfaces explained in this chapter might not be supported or used while hosting applications on Cisco platforms, but they are discussed here so that you gain a better understanding.

Container Networking

Those who are familiar with the Linux environment might be aware of **namespaces**. A namespace wraps system resources, making them appear to be an isolated instance of the resources to the relevant process. This concept plays a critical role for process isolation that allows users to run multiple services in the same server without concern for the process security. Depending on the type of resources being isolated, there are different types of namespaces, including cgroup, IPC, network, PID, and the like.

A **network namespace** applies the concept of resource isolation for the network stack. It logically provides isolated and different instances of the network stack with its own interfaces and route table, and it forwards rules that operate independently. Virtual Ethernet (veth) is an interconnected pair of veth ports that act as a tunnel that connects different network namespaces. These two play a key role in providing network communication between the processes or containers in different network namespaces.

Now you will learn the basics of network namespaces and the manual procedure for creating and managing namespaces and veth interface pairs.

Note: The outputs displayed in this section are captured from Ubuntu server. The output format may vary depending on the type of Linux distribution.

Namespace to External Network

By default, Linux machines will boot up with a single namespace to which the **init** process with Process ID (PID) **1** is associated. Any new process created with PID 1 as the parent will inherit the network namespace of PID 1. All the physical interfaces are normally positioned in the default namespace. As mentioned, the network namespace provides network resource isolation. Now create a new network namespace using the Linux command shown in Example 4-1.

Example 4-1 *Creating a Network Namespace*

```
root@openconfig:~# ip netns add cisco1        /* Creates a new network namespace */
root@openconfig:~# ip netns list              /* List all the network namespaces */
cisco1
root@openconfig:~#
root@openconfig:~# ip netns exec cisco1 ip link  /* Namespace specific commands */
1: lo: <LOOPBACK> mtu 65536 qdisc noop state DOWN mode DEFAULT group default qlen
  1000
    link/loopback 00:00:00:00:00:00 brd 00:00:00:00:00:00
root@openconfig:~#
```

With the preceding set of commands executed, a new network namespace named **cisco1** is created with a default loopback interface. Now create a veth pair and associate it to the newly created network namespace, as shown in Example 4-2.

Example 4-2 *Creating the veth Interface*

```
root@openconfig:~# ip link add vethcisco01 type veth
root@openconfig:~# ip link set vethcisco01 netns cisco1
root@openconfig:~# ip netns exec cisco1 ip link
1: lo: <LOOPBACK> mtu 65536 qdisc noop state DOWN mode DEFAULT group default qlen
  1000
    link/loopback 00:00:00:00:00:00 brd 00:00:00:00:00:00
26: vethcisco01@if25: <BROADCAST,MULTICAST> mtu 1500 qdisc noop state DOWN mode
  DEFAULT group default qlen 1000
    link/ether c6:5b:4b:04:39:6b brd ff:ff:ff:ff:ff:ff link-netnsid 0
root@openconfig:~#
root@openconfig:~# ip link
<snip>
25: veth0@if26: <BROADCAST,MULTICAST> mtu 1500 qdisc noop state DOWN mode DEFAULT
  group default qlen 1000
    link/ether a2:94:cb:9d:86:4f brd ff:ff:ff:ff:ff:ff link-netnsid 3
root@openconfig:~#
```

With the preceding set of commands executed, a new veth pair named **vethcisco01** is created and associated with the network namespace **cisco1**. Note that the command **ip**

link add vethcisco01 type veth created a pair of veth interfaces in which one end of the pair with **ifindex 26** (in the **cisco1** namespace) is interconnected to the other end with **index 25** in the default network namespace. By default, any newly created veth pair will be in the **DOWN** state. The commands shown in Example 4-3 bring the interfaces to the UP state and assign the relevant IP address, as shown in Figure 4-2.

Example 4-3 *veth Interface Configuration*

```
root@openconfig:~# ip link set veth0 up
root@openconfig:~# ip netns exec cisco1 ip link set vethcisco01 up
root@openconfig:~#
root@openconfig:~# ip addr add 10.0.0.1/24 dev veth0
root@openconfig:~# ip netns exec cisco1 ip addr add 10.0.0.2/24 dev vethcisco01
root@openconfig:~#
```

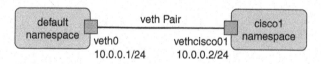

Figure 4-2 *veth Pair Interface*

Now you have the veth pair created with one end connected to the **cisco1** network namespace and the other end connected to the default namespace. The connectivity can be validated using the **ping** command, as shown in Example 4-4.

Example 4-4 *Network Namespace Connectivity*

```
root@openconfig:~# ip netns exec cisco1 ping 10.0.0.1
PING 10.0.0.1 (10.0.0.1) 56(84) bytes of data.
64 bytes from 10.0.0.1: icmp_seq=1 ttl=64 time=0.260 ms
64 bytes from 10.0.0.1: icmp_seq=2 ttl=64 time=0.075 ms
64 bytes from 10.0.0.1: icmp_seq=3 ttl=64 time=0.040 ms
^C
--- 10.0.0.1 ping statistics ---
3 packets transmitted, 3 received, 0% packet loss, time 2045ms
rtt min/avg/max/mdev = 0.040/0.125/0.260/0.096 ms
root@openconfig:~#
```

By configuring the relevant forwarding instructions in the default namespace route table, the **cisco1** network namespace can communicate with the external network. The network namespace can be imagined as a network interface card that provides network connectivity to any container that is associated with the namespace.

Note: Some commands, such as **ip netns list**, can be executed on the Linux bash shell of Cisco platforms. But other commands, such as creating the veth interface, might not be supported.

Namespace to Namespace

What if two containers that are instantiated in the same host are expected to be in the same network subnet? What if they are expected to communicate among themselves?

The veth interface is a pair in which one end is connected to the container network namespaces. By connecting the other end to a virtual bridge and assigning an IP address from the same subnet, you can easily make the containers communicate among themselves.

Example 4-5 looks at creating a network namespace.

Example 4-5 *Creating a Network Namespace*

```
root@openconfig:~# ip netns add cisco1    /* Creates a new network namespace */
root@openconfig:~# ip netns add cisco2    /* Creates a new network namespace */
root@openconfig:~# ip netns list          /* List all created network namespaces */
cisco2
cisco1
root@openconfig:~#
```

With the preceding set of commands executed, two new network namespaces will be created as **cisco1** and **cisco2**. Now you will create a veth pair for each network namespace (see Example 4-6).

Example 4-6 *Creating a veth Interface*

```
root@openconfig:~# ip link add vethcisco01 type veth    /* Creates a new veth pair */
root@openconfig:~# ip link add vethcisco02 type veth    /* Creates a new veth pair */
root@openconfig:~#
root@openconfig:~# ip link set vethcisco01 netns cisco1  /* Assign the veth pair to
   namespace */
root@openconfig:~# ip link set vethcisco02 netns cisco2 /* Assign the veth pair to
   namespace */
root@openconfig:~#
root@openconfig:~# ip netns exec cisco1 ip link set vethcisco01 up
root@openconfig:~# ip netns exec cisco2 ip link set vethcisco02 up
```

With the preceding set of commands, you created two new veth pairs as **vethcisco01** and **vethcisco02**. Each veth device is linked to namespaces **cisco1** and **cisco2**, respectively. One end of the veth pair will be connected to the default network namespace. The veth pairs are listed in Example 4-7.

Example 4-7   *veth Interface Output*

```
root@openconfig:~# ip link
<snip>
27: veth0@if28: <BROADCAST,MULTICAST,UP,LOWER_UP> mtu 1500 qdisc noqueue master
   ciscobridge state UP mode DEFAULT group default qlen 1000
     link/ether ce:bf:68:e5:cd:18 brd ff:ff:ff:ff:ff:ff link-netnsid 3
29: veth1@if30: <BROADCAST,MULTICAST,UP,LOWER_UP> mtu 1500 qdisc noqueue master
   ciscobridge state UP mode DEFAULT group default qlen 1000
     link/ether 4e:ba:79:90:e2:19 brd ff:ff:ff:ff:ff:ff link-netnsid 4
root@openconfig:~#
```

As shown in Example 4-7, **veth0** and **veth1** are the remote ends of veth pairs from the namespaces **cisco1** and **cisco2**, respectively. By creating a virtual bridge and connecting these veth pairs, traffic between the namespaces can be bridged easily (see Figure 4-3).

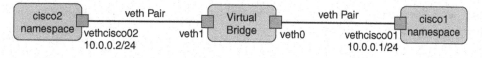

Figure 4-3   *Bridging the Network Namespace*

The configuration required to create a Linux virtual bridge named **ciscobridge** is shown in Example 4-8.

Example 4-8   *Creating and Mapping the Linux Bridge*

```
root@openconfig:~# ip link add ciscobridge type bridge    /* Creates a new virtual
   bridge */
root@openconfig:~# ip link set ciscobridge up             /* Set the bridge status as
   UP */
root@openconfig:~# ip link set veth0 master ciscobridge   /* Connect the veth remote
   end */
root@openconfig:~# ip link set veth1 master ciscobridge   /* Connect the veth remote
   end */
root@openconfig:~# ip link set veth1 up
root@openconfig:~# ip link set veth0 up
```

The configuration required to connect the veth pairs to the virtual bridge created earlier is shown in Example 4-9.

Example 4-9 *veth Interface Configuration*

```
root@openconfig:~# ip netns exec cisco1 ip addr add 10.0.0.1/24 dev vethcisco01
root@openconfig:~# ip netns exec cisco2 ip addr add 10.0.0.2/24 dev vethcisco02
root@openconfig:~# ip netns exec cisco2 ping 10.0.0.1
PING 10.0.0.1 (10.0.0.1) 56(84) bytes of data.
64 bytes from 10.0.0.1: icmp_seq=1 ttl=64 time=0.348 ms
64 bytes from 10.0.0.1: icmp_seq=2 ttl=64 time=0.064 ms
64 bytes from 10.0.0.1: icmp_seq=3 ttl=64 time=0.368 ms
^C
--- 10.0.0.1 ping statistics ---
3 packets transmitted, 3 received, 0% packet loss, time 2025ms
rtt min/avg/max/mdev = 0.064/0.260/0.368/0.138 ms
root@openconfig:~#
```

By simply replacing the virtual bridge in Figure 4-3 with a forwarder that supports Overlay networking, the containers in different physical hosts can be enabled to communicate among themselves.

> **Note:** Don't panic. You don't need to worry about manually creating such virtual interfaces or the forwarder. The intention of the preceding section is to explain the basics of container networking. In most of the container deployment environment, all the relevant components are created and managed dynamically by the container orchestration tools.

Key Points

Following are some of the key takeaways from the detailed explanation on container networking:

- Each container can be instantiated with its own network namespace for network stack isolation.

- Each veth pair is created as a pair, where one end is connected to the default network namespace and the other end is manipulated based on the type of connectivity intended for the container.

    - For intra-host container communication, the remote end is connected to a virtual bridge.

    - For inter-host container communication, the remote end is connected to an overlay bridge or a virtual router.

- Containers sharing the same network namespace will share the same network stack. In other words, all the interfaces created in a namespace will be reflected in all containers sharing the same namespace.

Although the preceding manual procedure of creating and managing a namespace was explained using an Ubuntu server, the same concept is used for Cisco platforms. Example 4-10 is a snapshot from Nexus 9K showing different namespaces that are created. By default, in most Cisco platforms, there are two namespaces created.

Example 4-10 *Cisco NXOS Network Namespace*

```
N9K-C93180YC# run bash
bash-4.3$ sudo -i
root@N9K-C93180YC#
root@N9K-C93180YC#ls /var/run/netns/
default  management
root@N9K-C93180YC#ip netns
management (id: 1)
default (id: 0)
root@N9K-C93180YC#
```

Note: Cisco IOS-XR and some Nexus platforms support Linux bash shell access. Linux commands similar to the ones in Example 4-10 can be executed on the bash shell to check the network namespaces.

Container Network Models and Interfaces

The application hosting capability on Cisco platforms can be categorized into different modes, as explained here:

- Cisco native-app hosting
- Docker containers
- Kubernetes

The previous section explained the characteristics of namespaces and veth pairs and how they can be used to control the communication between different containers. The concept of network namespace–based isolation and veth pairs is the basis for any container networking model. Containers hosted using any of the deployment modes mentioned follow a network model that is derived by leveraging the network namespace and veth concept.

Now you will look into the container network models and interfaces used by different Cisco platforms for each of the supported deployment modes.

Cisco Native App Hosting Network Model

Applications hosted with the IOX framework or with the Guest Shell instantiated on Cisco platforms are identified as Cisco native-app hosting applications. The container network model for Cisco native-app hosting is broadly categorized into two modes:

■ Shared mode

■ Dedicated mode

Shared Network Mode

In shared mode, the containers will share the network namespace of the host device in which the container is instantiated (see Figure 4-4).

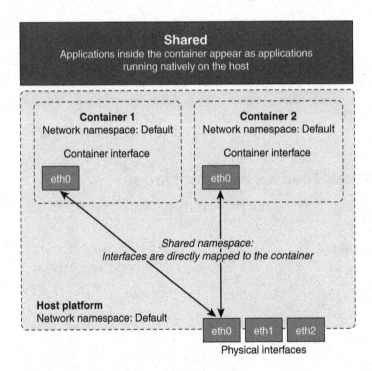

Figure 4-4   *Shared Network Mode*

When the host node boots up, the Linux kernel creates a root namespace, and all the physical interfaces are assigned to that namespace. As shown in Figure 4-4, the host and the containers are using the same network namespace: **Default**. Any container or application hosted in the default network namespace will have all the interfaces listed as part of the application. The application inside the container will appear as an application that is natively running on the host network.

As mentioned in the previous section, sharing the network namespaces means the network stack and the IP address is shared among the containers. Although running more than one container in the same network namespace is supported, care should be taken that the transport layer ports not overlap between the applications sharing the same network namespace.

As shown in Figure 4-5, the host interface G0/0 is assigned with IP address 192.168.1.1/24. Both containers are instantiated in the same network namespace and both are mapped to the same IP address. Note that both containers are assigned the IP address **GigabitEthernet 0/0**. **Container1** listens to port **8080** while **Container2** listens to **port 22**, which helps the host to differentiate the traffic between the containers.

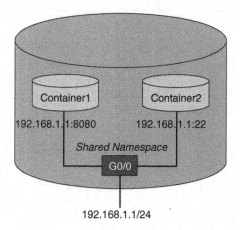

Figure 4-5 *Shared Network Mode*

Cisco Guest Shell containers and the Open Agent containers deployed on Cisco Nexus platforms always use the shared networking model. Dedicated IP address configuration is not required while instantiating these containers on Cisco Nexus Platforms. Example 4-11 shows a snapshot of the network stack from Centos running as Guest Shell on the Cisco Nexus platform.

Example 4-11 *Shared Network Mode Output*

```
N9K-C93180YC# show run int e1/1

!Command: show running-config interface Ethernet1/1
!Running configuration last done at: Tue Jul 30 20:23:42 2019
!Time: Tue Jul 30 20:53:15 2019

version 9.2(2) Bios:version 05.33

interface Ethernet1/1
  ip address 10.1.1.1/24
  no shutdown
```

```
N9K-C93180YC# guestshell
[admin@guestshell ~]$ ifconfig Eth1-1
Eth1-1: flags=4163<UP,BROADCAST,RUNNING,MULTICAST>  mtu 1500
        inet 10.1.1.1  netmask 255.255.255.0  broadcast 10.1.1.255
        ether 00:3a:9c:5a:00:67  txqueuelen 100  (Ethernet)
        RX packets 131959  bytes 23600643 (22.5 MiB)
        RX errors 0  dropped 110814  overruns 0  frame 0
        TX packets 36501  bytes 6656447 (6.3 MiB)
        TX errors 0  dropped 321 overruns 0  carrier 0  collisions 0

[admin@guestshell ~]$
```

Any overlap between the containers or between the container and the host will result in traffic black holes. Assume that the host is configured with a BGP protocol, which makes the host to listen to TCP port 179. If a new container is instantiated with an application listening to 179, the traffic destinated to 192.168.1.1:179 will be consumed by the BGP protocol running on the host, causing application instability.

Note: Some applications allow users to change the transport layer port by using environment settings. For example, the SSH port on a Linux-based application can be modified in the /etc/ssh/ssh_config location. If applications listening to the same transport layer port are required to be instantiated in the same host, the environment settings can be modified as a workaround such that each application listens to different and nonoverlapping ports.

In scenarios involving such overlapping applications, the shared network model is not the right choice because it requires complex environment changes. A better option is to enable a dedicated IP address for each such application. Now you will learn how the dedicated model will handle such scenarios.

Dedicated Network Mode

In the dedicated mode shown in Figure 4-6, the hosted application does not share the network namespace with the host. Instead, each container has its own network namespaces and dedicated IP address. Communication between the containers, between the container and the host, or from the container to external network is achieved by leveraging the host routing table.

Running each container in its own network namespace allows the user to assign different IP addresses and not to worry about overlapping transport layer ports. This reduces the operational challenges and complexities while handling multiple applications with overlapping transport layer ports.

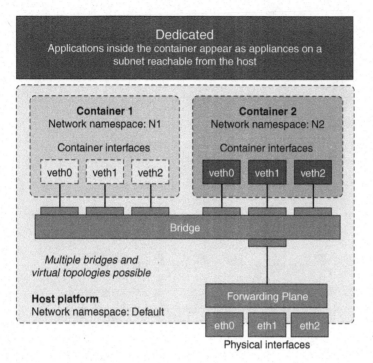

Figure 4-6 *Dedicated Network Mode*

In dedicated mode, the veth pair is created for each container, where one end of the pair is connected to the newly created namespace and the other end is connected to the default namespace. The veth end connected to the default namespace appears as a virtual interface in the host routing table.

> **Note:** Native-app hosting on Cisco NXOS platforms to deploy Cisco Guest Shell or virtual open agent containers does not support a dedicated network mode. Native-app hosting on Cisco IOS XR does not support dedicated network mode.

Cisco Guest Shell containers and the Virtual Service containers deployed on Cisco IOS-XE platforms always use the dedicated networking model. Before deploying the Guest Shell containers, the IP addresses for the veth pair must be configured manually using CLI-specific commands. More details about different configuration options are explained later in this chapter. The virtual interfaces created and attached to the containers are connected to the host routing table (RIB) for external connectivity, as shown in Figure 4-7.

The output of one such container with its own IP address is shown in Example 4-12.

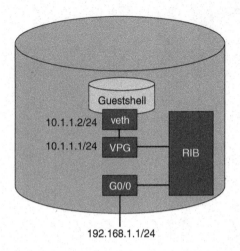

Figure 4-7 *Cisco IOS-XE Guest Shell in Dedicated Network Mode*

Example 4-12 *Dedicated Network Mode Output*

```
csr1000v-1#show app-hosting detail
App id                : Guest Shell
Owner                 : iox
State                 : RUNNING
Application
  Type                : lxc
  Name                : Guest Shell
  Version             : 2.4.1(0.1)
  Description         : Cisco Systems Guest Shell XE for x86
Activated profile name : custom


Resource reservation
  Memory              : 512 MB
  Disk                : 1 MB
  CPU                 : 800 units


Attached devices
  Type            Name              Alias
  --------------------------------------------

  serial/shell    iox_console_shell  serial0
  serial/aux      iox_console_aux    serial1
  serial/syslog   iox_syslog         serial2
  serial/trace    iox_trace          serial3


Network interfaces
  --------------------------------------------
```

```
eth0:
   MAC address          : 52:54:dd:f1:22:f4
   IPv4 address         : 10.1.1.2

Port forwarding
  Table-entry  Service  Source-port  Destination-port
  ---------------------------------------------------

csr1000v-1#
```

Docker Networking—Container Network Model

Docker networking leverages the **libnetwork** package for container networking. Libnetwork is a package that provides the extensions to create network namespaces and allocate the container interfaces to the namespace to satisfy the composable need for container networking. Docker implements the Container Network Model (CNM) specification shown in Figure 4-8.

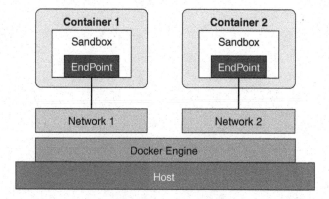

Figure 4-8 *Docker Container Network Model*

Note: Readers who are interested in learning more about libnetwork can visit https://godoc.org/github.com/docker/libnetwork.

Docker uses libnetwork as an interface between the Docker daemon and the network drivers in the host, providing an abstraction; thereby, it supports multiple network drivers. The Docker CNM is composed of the following three components:

- **Network sandbox:** This component provides resource isolation for network configuration. Network sandbox is implemented by leveraging the Linux network namespace concept. Ideally, a network sandbox can be considered the network stack for any single container that manages all the interfaces, iptables, and DNS settings for the container to which it is associated.

■ **Network endpoint:** This component is the veth pair that acts as the interface for the container. As mentioned earlier, the veth interface comes as a pair. One end of the endpoint is connected to the network sandbox, whereas the other end is connected to the network component of CNM. Because the endpoint is a veth, it can be connected to a maximum of one network. If the container requires multiple interfaces or connections to a different network, multiple endpoints are created and attached to the container's network sandbox.

■ **Network:** This component is a collective set of endpoints that enables the containers to communicate with each other. In other words, endpoints connected to the same network can communicate among themselves. The network component is implemented by leveraging the virtual Linux bridge concept. Docker allows the user to create multiple network components and associate different types of network drivers.

Depending on the type of network drivers associated with the network component, Docker networking can be one of the following:

■ None

■ Host networking

■ Bridge networking

■ Overlay networking

■ Macvlan networking

By default, when the Docker daemon is started in Cisco IOS-XR, it creates two types of network mode, as shown in Example 4-13.

Example 4-13 *Docker Network Output*

```
RP/0/RP0/CPU0:XR1#
RP/0/RP0/CPU0:XR1#run bash
Wed Jul 31 21:24:27.397 UTC
[xr-vm_node0_RP0_CPU0:~]$docker network ls
NETWORK ID            NAME               DRIVER
71719bd5efd0          none               null
b6c1adb5b6b2          host               host
[xr-vm_node0_RP0_CPU0:~]$
```

Note: In Nexus platforms, when the Docker daemon is started, three types of network modes are created by default: null, host, and bridge modes.

A new Docker network is created by defining the type of network driver, as shown in Example 4-14.

Example 4-14   *Creating a Docker Network*

```
[xr-vm_node0_RP0_CPU0:~]$docker network create --driver=bridge ciscodocker
7220df9f41603713f88e0c394dc935e118fd42cea398894e0dc6ec36f8cb936d
[xr-vm_node0_RP0_CPU0:~]$docker network ls
NETWORK ID            NAME                DRIVER
71719bd5efd0          none                null
b6c1adb5b6b2          host                host
7220df9f4160          ciscodocker         bridge
[xr-vm_node0_RP0_CPU0:~]$
```

Note: Although a Docker image can be natively instantiated in Cisco IOS XE platforms, those platforms do not support the Docker CLI user interface, so none of the native Docker commands can be executed or used in Cisco IOS XE platforms. In other Cisco platforms running IOS-XR and NXOS, native Docker CLI are supported.

None Networking

The **Docker None** network type does not create veth pairs, and the network stack is disabled on containers that are instantiated with this network type. Only the loopback interface is created within these containers. Because these containers lack a veth interface, they cannot communicate with the host or with the external network.

The None network is normally used when a standalone container is instantiated for testing purposes or when the user wants to set up custom networking. This is one of the networks created by default when the Docker daemon is enabled in any supported platform.

Host Networking

The **Docker Host** network type is similar to shared networking, in which the containers share the network namespace of the host. Containers that are instantiated with the host networking type will have all the host interfaces listed as connected interfaces on the container. The same challenges with the shared network model are applicable here. Running a container in the host network requires transport layer port mapping to differentiate the traffic destined for the host from the traffic destined for the container.

The Docker host network type is used when the involved use cases require the application to appear as a process running on the host. This is one of the networks created by default when the Docker daemon is enabled on a supported platform.

Bridge Networking

The **Docker Bridge** network type is similar to the dedicated network mode that leverages the virtual bridge concept. The Docker daemon creates a virtual bridge (**docker0**) with its own subnet. It creates a veth pair in which one end is connected to the bridge and the other end is connected to the default network namespace of the host. This end acts as the default gateway for containers connected to **docker0**. The bridge **docker0** is the default bridge chosen by Docker if a container is instantiating without defining the network CLI option.

Docker allows users to create more than one bridge, each with its own assigned subnet. The subnet for each bridge can be manually assigned by the operator, or the Docker daemon can automatically assign one from a unique address pool. All the containers connected to a specific bridge will receive the IP address from the respective subnet assigned to the bridge and can communicate among themselves with no routing involved.

Overlay Networking

The **Docker Overlay** network is used for multihost scenarios in which the containers that are instantiated on different physical hosts are required to communicate among themselves. Multihost Docker container instantiation is common when using orchestration tools, such as Docker swarm. This network type uses UDP port 4789–based Virtual Extensible Local Area Network (VxLAN) overlay encapsulation.

The Docker Overlay network is not supported on any Cisco platform.

Note: VxLAN is the primary overlay encapsulation type used for network virtualization that attempts to connect a dispersed Layer 2 network over the IP network. More details about VxLAN are available from IETF RFC at https://tools.ietf.org/html/rfc7348.

Macvlan

The **Docker MACVLAN** network type is used when the container must have a dedicated IP address yet must appear as if it is directly connected to the physical network. The Macvlan driver enables the user to configure multiple logical interfaces with their own IP/MAC addresses and associate them to a physical interface of the host.

Docker Macvlan is not created by default when the Docker daemon is enabled. The user must create it explicitly by defining the IP subnet and the physical interface to which it is associated. Any container enabled with Macvlan will share the broadcast domain of the physical interface.

Kubernetes Container Network Interface (CNI) Model

Kubernetes uses the CNI specification, which is different from the CNM specification Docker uses. The Docker CNM specification uses network drivers that are host-centric.

Kubernetes, on the other hand, uses CNI, which defines a common interface between the network plug-ins and the container runtime, as shown in Figure 4-9.

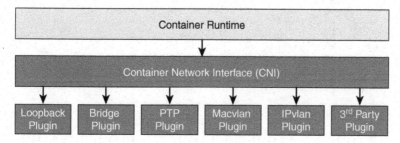

Figure 4-9 *Kubernetes Container Network Interface Model*

CNI has two main components:

- **CNI specification:** API between the container runtime and the network plug-ins
- **Network plug-ins:** Configures and provides network setup

A plethora of network plug-ins are available for Kubernetes implementation, including Weave, Contiv, and Flannel. At the time this book was written, Kubernetes deployment was only supported in Cisco NXOS platforms, and the current deployments that were tested and supported by Cisco used host networking. Work is going into supporting other CNI, so in the future, you might see more CNI support.

Setting Up Container Networking

By now, you likely understand container networking and how the machinery works under the hood. The previous sections also explained the different container network concepts. Now you'll get your hands dirty by playing around with the configuration.

Native App Hosting—Shared Networking Configuration

This section explains the configuration required on the host to instantiate an application using the shared networking concept. To reiterate, when a container is instantiated with shared networking, it shares the network namespace with the host and appears to the external world as a process running on the host.

Cisco IOS-XE Configuration

Native application hosting is possible in Cisco IOS-XE platforms using the legacy VMAN component or the new IOX framework. The service containers that leverage the VMAN component can be hosted in a shared network model, as shown in Figure 4-10.

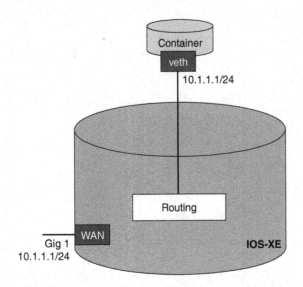

Figure 4-10 *Service Containers with a Shared Network*

The VMAN component allows you to control the interface that should be shared with the container. Although the same host interface can be shared with more than one service container, each container can have a maximum of one interface connected. The host device must be configured by instructing the host interface that should be shared with the container, as shown in Example 4-15.

Example 4-15 *Cisco IOS-XE Shared Network Configuration*

```
!
interface GigabitEthernet 1
 ip address 10.1.1.1 255.255.255.0
!
virtual-service ciscoservice
 ip shared host-interface GigabitEthernet1
!

csr1000v-2#
csr1000v-2# virtual-service install name ciscoservice package flash:ciscoservice.ova
```

In Example 4-15, the **GigabitEthernet1** interface is configured with 10.1.1.1/24 and shared with the service container. The service container does not have its own dedicated IP address, and it has shared the IP and MAC address of the GigabitEthernet1 interface.

When the IOX framework is used for hosting the Cisco Guest Shell or other third-party applications, shared networking is not supported.

Note: The legacy VMAN component and Service Containers are not supported in Cisco Catalyst 9000-series switches. Accordingly, the shared network model is not supported on this platform.

Cisco IOS-XR Configuration

The application-hosting architecture for the IOS-XR platforms offer the ability to host applications natively in the XR Control Plane LXC or as third-party applications in the Third-Party Container. Accordingly, the Linux Kernel of IOS-XR creates the following network namespaces:

- XR network namespace (XRNNS)

- Third-party network namespace (TPNNS)

The different network namespaces, associated interfaces, and user CLI commands used to log in to different network namespaces are represented in Figure 4-11.

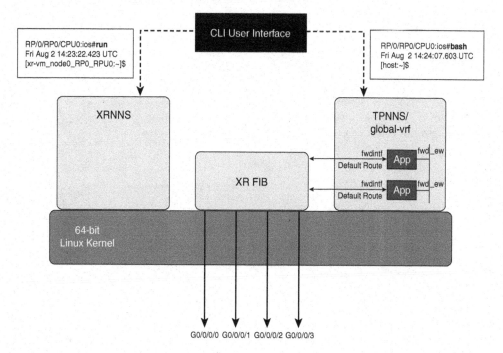

Figure 4-11 *IOS-XR Network Namespaces*

XRNNS is the default network namespace used by any native applications instantiated on the XR Control Plane LXC container space. Many internal interfaces are connected to this network namespace that do not interact with networks outside IOS XR. By default, accessing the XR Linux shell will take the user to XRNNS. In other words, when either the **run** or the **run bash** commands are executed from XR CLI, the user is taken to the default network namespace, XRNNS, as shown in Example 4-16.

Example 4-16   *Cisco IOS-XR XRNNS Output*

```
RP/0/RP0/CPU0:ios#
RP/0/RP0/CPU0:ios#
RP/0/RP0/CPU0:ios#run bash
Thu Aug  1 21:52:25.325 UTC
[xr-vm_node0_RP0_CPU0:~]$
[xr-vm_node0_RP0_CPU0:~]$netns_identify $$
xrnns
[xr-vm_node0_RP0_CPU0:~]$ifconfig
eth0      Link encap:Ethernet  HWaddr 52:46:1a:1a:37:e6
          UP BROADCAST RUNNING MULTICAST  MTU:9596  Metric:1
          RX packets:0 errors:0 dropped:0 overruns:0 frame:0
          TX packets:34 errors:0 dropped:0 overruns:0 carrier:0
          collisions:0 txqueuelen:1000
          RX bytes:0 (0.0 B)  TX bytes:6653 (6.4 KiB)


eth-vf0   Link encap:Ethernet  HWaddr 52:54:00:cd:70:89
          inet addr:10.11.12.14  Bcast:10.11.12.255  Mask:255.255.255.0
          inet6 addr: fe80::5054:ff:fecd:7089/64 Scope:Link
          UP BROADCAST RUNNING MULTICAST  MTU:9000  Metric:1
          RX packets:24 errors:0 dropped:0 overruns:0 frame:0
          TX packets:16 errors:0 dropped:0 overruns:0 carrier:0
          collisions:0 txqueuelen:1000
          RX bytes:1984 (1.9 KiB)  TX bytes:1336 (1.3 KiB)


eth-vf1   Link encap:Ethernet  HWaddr 52:54:00:a8:c7:6c
          inet6 addr: fe80::5054:ff:fea8:c76c/64 Scope:Link
          UP BROADCAST RUNNING MULTICAST  MTU:9600  Metric:1
          RX packets:13560244 errors:0 dropped:8 overruns:0 frame:0
          TX packets:12118343 errors:0 dropped:0 overruns:0 carrier:0
          collisions:0 txqueuelen:10000
          RX bytes:3274087646 (3.0 GiB)  TX bytes:1700002721 (1.5 GiB)


eth-vf1.1794 Link encap:Ethernet  HWaddr 52:54:01:5c:55:8e
          inet6 addr: fe80::5054:1ff:fe5c:558e/64 Scope:Link
          UP BROADCAST RUNNING MULTICAST  MTU:9596  Metric:1
          RX packets:10 errors:0 dropped:0 overruns:0 frame:0
          TX packets:17 errors:0 dropped:0 overruns:0 carrier:0
          collisions:0 txqueuelen:0
          RX bytes:1002 (1002.0 B)  TX bytes:1895 (1.8 KiB)
```

```
eth-vf1.3073 Link encap:Ethernet  HWaddr e2:3a:dd:0a:8e:06
             inet addr:192.0.0.4  Bcast:192.255.255.255  Mask:255.0.0.0
             inet6 addr: fe80::e03a:ddff:fe0a:8e06/64 Scope:Link
             UP BROADCAST RUNNING MULTICAST  MTU:9596  Metric:1
             RX packets:11278199 errors:0 dropped:135325 overruns:0 frame:0
             TX packets:9915314 errors:0 dropped:0 overruns:0 carrier:0
             collisions:0 txqueuelen:0
             RX bytes:1741953147 (1.6 GiB)  TX bytes:770483071 (734.7 MiB)

eth-vf1.3074 Link encap:Ethernet  HWaddr 4e:41:50:00:00:01
             inet addr:172.0.0.1  Bcast:172.255.255.255  Mask:255.0.0.0
             inet6 addr: fe80::4c41:50ff:fe00:1/64 Scope:Link
             UP BROADCAST RUNNING MULTICAST  MTU:9596  Metric:1
             RX packets:2281994 errors:0 dropped:0 overruns:0 frame:0
             TX packets:2202996 errors:0 dropped:0 overruns:0 carrier:0
             collisions:0 txqueuelen:0
             RX bytes:1342286003 (1.2 GiB)  TX bytes:929516419 (886.4 MiB)

lo           Link encap:Local Loopback
             inet addr:127.0.0.1  Mask:255.0.0.0
             inet6 addr: ::1/128 Scope:Host
             UP LOOPBACK RUNNING  MTU:65536  Metric:1
             RX packets:101788908 errors:0 dropped:0 overruns:0 frame:0
             TX packets:101788908 errors:0 dropped:0 overruns:0 carrier:0
             collisions:0 txqueuelen:0
             RX bytes:11521845347 (10.7 GiB)  TX bytes:11521845347 (10.7 GiB)

tap123       Link encap:Ethernet  HWaddr 6a:ae:6c:c5:59:ff
             inet6 addr: fe80::68ae:6cff:fec5:59ff/64 Scope:Link
             UP BROADCAST RUNNING MULTICAST  MTU:1500  Metric:1
             RX packets:2 errors:0 dropped:0 overruns:0 frame:0
             TX packets:10 errors:0 dropped:0 overruns:0 carrier:0
             collisions:0 txqueuelen:500
             RX bytes:196 (196.0 B)  TX bytes:804 (804.0 B)

[xr-vm_node0_RP0_CPU0:~]$
```

TPNNS is the other network namespace created in the XR Linux kernel that is meant for third-party application hosting. TPNNS has been renamed as **global-vrf**, so it is common to see both names while playing around with TPNNS. The remainder of this chapter will continue to define TPNNS as **global-vrf**. When the **bash** command is executed from XR CLI, it takes the user to the **global-vrf** network namespace, as shown in Example 4-17.

Example 4-17 *Cisco-XR Global VRF Network Namespace*

```
RP/0/RP0/CPU0:ios#
RP/0/RP0/CPU0:ios#bash
Thu Aug  1 21:47:56.269 UTC
[host:~]$
[host:~]$ netns_identify $$
tpnns
global-vrf
[host:~]$ ifconfig
Gi0_0_0_0 Link encap:Ethernet  HWaddr 52:46:f8:b8:27:88
          inet addr:10.1.1.1  Mask:255.255.255.0
          inet6 addr: fe80::5046:f8ff:feb8:2788/64 Scope:Link
          UP RUNNING NOARP MULTICAST  MTU:1500  Metric:1
          RX packets:8824 errors:17 dropped:0 overruns:0 frame:17
          TX packets:91 errors:0 dropped:0 overruns:0 carrier:0
          collisions:0 txqueuelen:1000
          RX bytes:2915230 (2.7 MiB)  TX bytes:7089 (6.9 KiB)

fwd_ew    Link encap:Ethernet  HWaddr 00:00:00:00:00:0b
          inet6 addr: fe80::200:ff:fe00:b/64 Scope:Link
          UP RUNNING NOARP MULTICAST  MTU:1500  Metric:1
          RX packets:0 errors:0 dropped:0 overruns:0 frame:0
          TX packets:2 errors:0 dropped:1 overruns:0 carrier:0
          collisions:0 txqueuelen:1000
          RX bytes:0 (0.0 B)  TX bytes:140 (140.0 B)

fwdintf   Link encap:Ethernet  HWaddr 00:00:00:00:00:0a
          inet6 addr: fe80::200:ff:fe00:a/64 Scope:Link
          UP RUNNING NOARP MULTICAST  MTU:1482  Metric:1
          RX packets:0 errors:0 dropped:0 overruns:0 frame:0
          TX packets:9 errors:0 dropped:1 overruns:0 carrier:0
          collisions:0 txqueuelen:1000
          RX bytes:0 (0.0 B)  TX bytes:729 (729.0 B)

lo        Link encap:Local Loopback
          inet addr:127.0.0.1  Mask:255.0.0.0
          inet6 addr: ::1/128 Scope:Host
          UP LOOPBACK RUNNING  MTU:65536  Metric:1
          RX packets:256 errors:0 dropped:0 overruns:0 frame:0
          TX packets:256 errors:0 dropped:0 overruns:0 carrier:0
          collisions:0 txqueuelen:0
          RX bytes:19840 (19.3 KiB)  TX bytes:19840 (19.3 KiB)

[host:~]$
```

TPNNS plays a vital role by providing communication from applications hosted on Cisco IOS-XR platforms. The interfaces listed in Example 4-17 are used for actual traffic forwarding.

- **Gi0_0_0_0** is the physical interface of the IOS XR platform. The IP and MAC address, **GigabitEtehrnet0/0/0/0**, will be used.

- **fwd_ew** is a virtual interface that is used for communication between the applications instantiated in this namespace. **ew** stands for east-west communication.

- **fwdintf** is a virtual interface that is connected to the XR FIB table and used for communication between the application hosted in this namespace and the external network.

- **lo** is a local loopback interface.

The IP route table for the **global-vrf** namespace installs a default route pointing toward the **fwdintf** interface and is shown in Example 4-18.

Example 4-18 *Global VRF Route Table*

```
[host:~]$ route
Kernel IP routing table
Destination      Gateway          Genmask          Flags Metric Ref    Use Iface
default          *                0.0.0.0          U     0      0        0 fwdintf
 [host:~]$
```

Any traffic from a locally hosted application destined to an unknown address will be forwarded over **fwdintf** to the XR FIB table, which then forwards packets outside the hosting IOS-XR router to external destinations.

Now that the network namespaces for Cisco IOS-XR platforms have been introduced, the next section demonstrates how namespaces are used by the hosted applications for communication.

By default, applications hosted in the global-vrf network namespace are programmed to use the default route through the management port. Accordingly, any traffic originated from the application will choose a management port address as the source IP address. This behavior can be overridden so that another interface in the global table is chosen, as shown in Example 4-19.

Example 4-19 *TPA Configuration*

```
!
tpa
 vrf default
  address-family ipv4
   update-source dataports GigabitEthernet0/0/0/0
  !
```

Example 4-20 shows the command to check the routing table from the bash shell prompt.

Example 4-20   *TPNNS Route Table*

```
RP/0/RP0/CPU0:ios#bash
Thu Aug  1 22:50:01.253 UTC
[host:~]$ ip route
default dev fwdintf  scope link  src 10.1.1.1
172.17.0.0/16 dev br-25f690748fd7  proto kernel  scope link  src 172.17.0.1
[host:~]$
```

To choose **global-vrf** as the network namespace, the LXC specification file used to instantiate the application must be configured to use shared networking with **global-vrf** as the network namespace, as shown in Example 4-21.

Example 4-21   *LXC Spec File*

```
<lxc:namespace>
<sharenet type='netns' value='global-vrf'/>
</lxc:namespace>
```

This section provides the essentials required to enable the networking for applications hosted on Cisco IOS-XR platforms. Chapter 6, "Container Orchestration in Cisco IOS-XR Platforms," offers further details about how applications can be hosted with VRF segmentation.

Note: Cisco IOS-XR platforms do not support Guest Shell, and any application hosted in TPNNS will always use shared networking. In other words, the TPA IP will be shared with one of the host interfaces. There is no provision for manually assigning a dedicated address for the hosted application.

Cisco Nexus OS Configuration

The application hosting architecture for Cisco Nexus platforms creates different network namespaces for each Virtual Route Forwarding (VRF) instance. By default, two VRFs are created: **management** and **default**. Accordingly, the Linux kernel creates two network namespaces, as shown in Figure 4-12.

The **management** network namespace contains the mgmt0 interface, along with a set of virtual interfaces. The management VRF and the network namespace are reserved for the mgmt0 interface. Other interfaces cannot be assigned to this namespace. This network namespace is used for management communication for device access and administration.

The **default** network namespace is the namespace for VRF **default** where all the physical interfaces are listed. When a service container or secure Guest Shell is instantiated, the default network namespace is shared.

The network namespaces can be verified by logging in to the bash shell of the Cisco Nexus 9000. As shown in Example 4-22, management and default network namespaces are created.

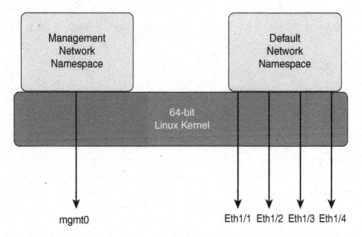

Figure 4-12 *NXOS Network Namespaces*

Example 4-22 *Creating Network Namespace*

```
N9K-C93180YC# run bash
bash-4.3$
bash-4.3$ ip netns list
management (id: 1)
default (id: 0)
bash-4.3$
```

As shown in Example 4-23, the only interface listed in the management network namespace is **eth1**, which is the virtual representation of the **mgmt0** interface.

Example 4-23 *Cisco NXOS Management Network Namespace*

```
N9K-C93180YC# show run int mgmt0
!Command: show running-config interface mgmt0
!Running configuration last done at: Fri Aug  2 20:53:32 2019
!Time: Fri Aug  2 21:09:10 2019

version 9.2(2) Bios:version 05.33

interface mgmt0
  vrf member management
  ip address 172.16.1.1/24

N9K-C93180YC# run bash
bash-4.3$ ip netns exec management ip addr

<removed>
```

```
 8: eth1: <BROADCAST,MULTICAST,UP,LOWER_UP> mtu 1500 qdisc mq state UP group default
    qlen 1000
   link/ether 00:3a:9c:5a:00:60 brd ff:ff:ff:ff:ff:ff
     inet 172.16.1.1/24 brd 172.16.1.255 scope global eth1
        valid_lft forever preferred_lft forever
31: veth1-2@if32: <BROADCAST,MULTICAST,UP,LOWER_UP> mtu 9400 qdisc pfifo_fast state
    UP group default qlen 1000
     link/ether a2:c2:dc:b6:23:c2 brd ff:ff:ff:ff:ff:ff link-netnsid 0
bash-4.3$
```

As shown in Example 4-24, all the physical interfaces are listed as part of default network namespaces.

Example 4-24 *Cisco NXOS Default Network Namespaces*

```
N9K-C93180YC#
N9K-C93180YC# run bash
bash-4.3$
bash-4.3$ ip netns exec default ip link  | grep Eth1
34: Eth1-1: <BROADCAST,MULTICAST,UP,LOWER_UP> mtu 1500 qdisc pfifo_fast state UP
    mode DEFAULT group default qlen 100
35: Eth1-2: <NO-CARRIER,BROADCAST,MULTICAST,UP> mtu 1500 qdisc pfifo_fast state DOWN
    mode DEFAULT group default qlen 100
36: Eth1-3: <NO-CARRIER,BROADCAST,MULTICAST,UP> mtu 1500 qdisc pfifo_fast state DOWN
    mode DEFAULT group default qlen 100
37: Eth1-4: <NO-CARRIER,BROADCAST,MULTICAST,UP> mtu 1500 qdisc pfifo_fast state DOWN
    mode DEFAULT group default qlen 100
38: Eth1-5: <NO-CARRIER,BROADCAST,MULTICAST,UP> mtu 1500 qdisc pfifo_fast state DOWN
    mode DEFAULT group default qlen 100
<Removed>
```

While enabling the secure Guest Shell, the centos environment is hosted by sharing the network namespace with the host. As shown in Example 4-25, all physical interfaces are listed in the Guest Shell, and they use the host IP as the source address for any traffic originating from that shell.

Example 4-25 *Guest Shell with a Shared Network*

```
N9K-C93180YC#
N9K-C93180YC# guestshell
[admin@guestshell ~]$ ifconfig
Eth1-1: flags=4163<UP,BROADCAST,RUNNING,MULTICAST>  mtu 1500
        inet 10.1.1.1  netmask 255.255.255.0  broadcast 10.1.1.255
        ether 00:3a:9c:5a:00:67  txqueuelen 100  (Ethernet)
        RX packets 305673  bytes 53772130 (51.2 MiB)
        RX errors 0  dropped 253670  overruns 0  frame 0
        TX packets 86160  bytes 15568404 (14.8 MiB)
        TX errors 0  dropped 364 overruns 0  carrier 0  collisions 0
```

```
Eth1-2: flags=4099<UP,BROADCAST,MULTICAST>  mtu 1500
        ether 00:3a:9c:5a:00:67  txqueuelen 100  (Ethernet)
        RX packets 0  bytes 0 (0.0 B)
        RX errors 0  dropped 0  overruns 0  frame 0
        TX packets 0  bytes 0 (0.0 B)
        TX errors 0  dropped 0 overruns 0  carrier 0  collisions 0
```

Support Matrix

Table 4-1 consolidates the status of each Cisco platform to support native-app hosting with the shared networking concept.

Table 4-1 *Native App-Hosting Feature Support*

Platform		Feature Support	Configuration
Cisco IOS-XE	VMAN component-based instantiation	Supports shared networking	Specific configuration required.
	CAF-based instantiation	Does not support shared networking	Not applicable.
Cisco IOS-XR		Supports shared networking	Default behavior. No specific configuration required.
Nexus OS		Supports shared networking	Default behavior. No specific configuration required.

Native App Hosting—Dedicated Networking Configuration

This section explains the configuration required on the host to instantiate an application using the dedicated networking concept. To reiterate, when a container is instantiated with dedicated networking, an application-specific network name space is created and attached to the container.

Cisco IOS XE Configuration

In Cisco IOS-XE, when Cisco Application-Hosting Framework (CAF) is used for application hosting, dedicated networking mode is the only mode supported. Following the traditional analogy of container networking, the veth pair is created for each application hosted on the device. One end of the created veth pair will be injected into the container while the other end is attached to the host. Depending on the type of connectivity required for the application and the configuration on the host, the veth pair end connected to the host will be represented as **VirtualPortGroup** interface or **AppGigEthernet** interface, as shown in Figure 4-13.

The VirtualPortGroup interface is a logical Layer 3 interface that connects the hosted application to the routing domain of the host. To be more precise, the VirtualPortGroup interface is connected to the RIB of the host. Each host supports a maximum of 32 VirtualPortGroup interfaces.

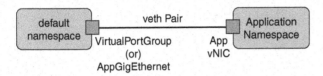

Figure 4-13 *Cisco IOS-XE Dedicated Network*

The AppGigEthernet interface is a logical Layer 2 interface that connects the hosted application to the bridging domain of the host. This interface is used when the host is offering Layer 2 connectivity between the application and the external network. The AppGigEthernet interface is connected to the switching table of the host. This type of interface is supported only on Catalyst 9000 series switches.

App VNIC is the logical Layer 3 interface in the hosted application. This interface is the software construct of the veth pair end that is injected into the application. The vNIC inside the container appears as a standard Ethernet interface.

As part of application hosting, the network configuration involves the following:

- Configure the relevant interface (VirtualPortGroup or AppGigEthernet) on the host side.
- Assign relevant IP addresses for the VirtualPortGroup interface and the vNIC.
- Set the default gateway for the application.

There are three different ways to configure dedicated networking. In this section, you will learn how to configure dedicated networking using each of these ways.

Routing Mode—Numbered

In this mode, each hosted application appears as a stub network with an IP address assigned from a dedicated subnet, as shown in Figure 4-14. For the routing mode, one of the VirtualPortGroup interfaces is chosen as the host interface.

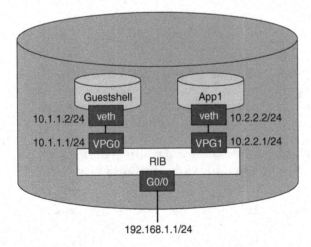

Figure 4-14 *Routing Mode Configuration*

The relevant configuration to enable the VirtualPortGroup is shown in Example 4-26.

Example 4-26   *Cisco IOS-XE VirtualPortGroup Configuration*

```
!
interface VirtualPortGroup0
 ip address 10.1.1.1 255.255.255.0
!
!
interface VirtualPortGroup1
 ip address 10.2.2.1 255.255.255.0
!
app-hosting appid App1
 app-vnic gateway0 virtualportgroup 1 guest-interface 0
  guest-ipaddress 10.2.2.2 netmask 255.255.255.0
 app-default-gateway 10.2.2.1 guest-interface 0
app-hosting appid Guest Shell
 app-vnic gateway0 virtualportgroup 0 guest-interface 0
  guest-ipaddress 10.1.1.2 netmask 255.255.255.0
 app-default-gateway 10.1.1.1 guest-interface 0
!
```

The VirtualPortGroup interfaces are configured like any other interface using Cisco IOS CLI-configuration commands. For each hosted application, including the Guest Shell, a dedicated VirtualPortGroup interface is configured with an IP address.

The app-hosting configuration mode allows the user to associate the VirtualPortGroup to the application and configure the vNIC IP address using the **guest-ipaddress x.x.x.x netmask y.y.y.y** command.

For each hosted application, the default gateway will be set to the respective VirtualPortGroup interface IP address.

The output from the Guest Shell that is instantiated based on this configuration is shown in Example 4-27.

Example 4-27   *Cisco IOS-XE Guest Shell Network Output*

```
C9300#
C9300#guestshell
[guestshell@guestshell ~]$
[guestshell@guestshell ~]$ sudo -i
[root@guestshell ~]# ifconfig
eth0: flags=4163<UP,BROADCAST,RUNNING,MULTICAST>  mtu 1500
        inet 10.1.1.2  netmask 255.255.255.0  broadcast 10.1.1.255
        inet6 fe80::5054:ddff:fee3:f8fe  prefixlen 64  scopeid 0x20<link>
        ether 52:54:dd:e3:f8:fe  txqueuelen 1000  (Ethernet)
```

```
          RX packets 8   bytes 648 (648.0 B)
          RX errors 0   dropped 0   overruns 0   frame 0
          TX packets 8   bytes 648 (648.0 B)
          TX errors 0   dropped 0 overruns 0   carrier 0   collisions 0


lo: flags=73<UP,LOOPBACK,RUNNING>   mtu 65536
          inet 127.0.0.1   netmask 255.0.0.0
          inet6 ::1   prefixlen 128   scopeid 0x10<host>
          loop  txqueuelen 1  (Local Loopback)
          RX packets 960  bytes 133708 (130.5 KiB)
          RX errors 0   dropped 0   overruns 0   frame 0
          TX packets 960  bytes 133708 (130.5 KiB)
          TX errors 0   dropped 0 overruns 0   carrier 0   collisions 0

[root@guestshell ~]# route
Kernel IP routing table
Destination     Gateway        Genmask           Flags Metric Ref      Use Iface
default         gateway        0.0.0.0           UG   1       0        0 eth0
10.1.1.0        0.0.0.0        255.255.255.0     U    0       0        0 eth0
[root@guestshell ~]#
```

Note: As mentioned earlier, the application hosted using the VirtualPortGroup interface configuration will appear as another subnet connected to the host. To provide external connectivity, the subnet must be advertised to the external network, or other features, such as NAT, must be configured on the host.

Routing Mode—Unnumbered

This mode uses the VirtualPortGroup interface as the host interface, and the concept is similar to the numbered routing mode. The only difference between this mode and the numbered routing mode is that the IP address is assigned for the VirtualPortGroup interface. As the name says, the IP address for the VirtualPortGroup interface is shared with other physical interfaces on the host by configuring **ip unnumbered <intf>**. The application hosted using **routed** mode is shown in Figure 4-15.

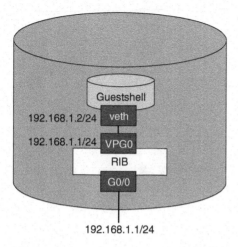

Figure 4-15 *Unnumbered Routing Configuration*

The relevant configuration to enable the VirtualPortGroup is shown in Example 4-28.

Example 4-28 *Unnumbered Routing Mode Configuration*

```
!
interface VirtualPortGroup0
 ip unnumbered GigabitEthernet0/0
!
!
interface GigabitEthernet0/0
 ip address 192.168.1.1 255.255.255.0
!
app-hosting appid guestshell
 app-vnic gateway0 virtualportgroup 0 guest-interface 0
  guest-ipaddress 192.168.1.2 netmask 255.255.255.0
 app-default-gateway 192.168.1.1 guest-interface 0
!
```

Layer 2 Mode

In this mode, the host provides Layer 2 connectivity between the hosted application and the external network. For Layer 2 mode, one of the AppGigEthernet interfaces is chosen as the host interface, as shown in Figure 4-16. Because this is a pure Layer 2 interface, no IP address is assigned for the AppGigEthernet interface.

The AppGigEthernet interface can be configured in access port or trunk mode, depending on the type of traffic expected from the hosted application.

The relevant configuration when the AppGigEthernet interface is configured as an access port is shown in Example 4-29.

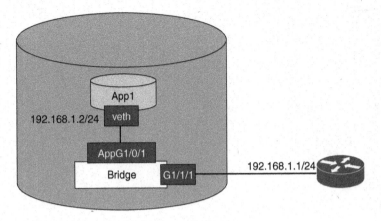

Figure 4-16   *Layer 2 Network Mode*

Example 4-29   *Layer 2 Access Mode Configuration*

```
!
interface GigabitEthernet1/1/1
 switchport access vlan 101
!
app-hosting appid App1
 app-vnic AppGigEthernet vlan-access
  vlan 101 guest-interface 0
   guest-ipaddress 192.168.1.2 netmask 255.255.255.0
 app-default-gateway 192.168.1.1 guest-interface 0
 !
```

The relevant configuration when the AppGigEthernet interface is configured as the trunk port is shown in Example 4-30.

Example 4-30   *Layer 2 Trunk Mode Configuration*

```
!
interface GigabitEthernet1/1/1
 switchport access vlan 101
!
app-hosting appid App2
 app-vnic AppGigEthernet trunk
  guest-interface 0 .
 !
```

Note: Layer 2 mode is supported only in Catalyst 9000 series switches and cannot be configured on other IOS-XE platforms.

Cisco IOS XR and Nexus OS

Neither Cisco IOS-XR nor Nexus OS platforms support dedicated network configuration mode. Applications hosted natively will use shared network mode, and the relevant configuration details are explained in the "Native App Hosting—Shared Network Configuration" section.

Docker Network Configuration

As mentioned earlier, Docker is natively supported in the Cisco IOS XR and Nexus OS platforms. Any native Docker CLI can be executed from the bash shell. Although the CAF framework allows the user to instantiate Docker images as containers in the IOS-XE platform, IOS-XE uses Cisco CLI and does not support native Docker commands.

This section reviews different Docker networking configurations that are supported in Cisco platforms.

None Networking

None networking is one of the default Docker networks created when the Docker daemon is enabled on supported Cisco platforms. Any container deployed with None as the network option will not have a network interface aside from the loopback interface. Example 4-31 shows the command to deploy a Docker container with a None network.

Example 4-31 *Docker None Network Configuration*

```
root@N9K-C93180YC#
root@N9K-C93180YC#docker run -itd --net=none alpine
e4f5c81285032447bc8caa37d8aa6256b7cb533baa3f344e2725df179cbb4a31
root@N9K-C93180YC#
root@N9K-C93180YC#docker ps
CONTAINER ID    IMAGE     COMMAND     CREATED      STATUS    NAMES
e4f5c8128503    alpine    "/bin/sh"   3 seconds ago Up      distracted_goodall
root@N9K-C93180YC#
root@N9K-C93180YC#docker attach distracted_goodall
/ # ifconfig
lo        Link encap:Local Loopback
          inet addr:127.0.0.1  Mask:255.0.0.0
          inet6 addr: ::1/128 Scope:Host
          UP LOOPBACK RUNNING  MTU:65536  Metric:1
          RX packets:0 errors:0 dropped:0 overruns:0 frame:0
          TX packets:0 errors:0 dropped:0 overruns:0 carrier:0
          collisions:0 txqueuelen:0
          RX bytes:0 (0.0 B)  TX bytes:0 (0.0 B)

/ #
```

There is no specific configuration required to enable this network mode. The network driver selected for the None type is "null," and no IPAM is enabled. The output of the Docker None network is shown in Example 4-32.

Example 4-32 *Docker None Network Output*

```
N9K-C93180YC#
N9K-C93180YC# run bash
bash-4.3$ sudo -i
root@N9K-C93180YC#
root@N9K-C93180YC#docker network inspect none
[
    {
        "Name": "none",
        "Id": "6c9d198ffe62a746c1477ed4e2f73d0d9e6183e269014416725eafaf3fc8a597",
        "Created": "2019-05-04T19:09:06.982246544Z",
        "Scope": "local",
        "Driver": "null",
        "EnableIPv6": false,
        "IPAM": {
            "Driver": "default",
            "Options": null,
            "Config": []
        },
        "Internal": false,
        "Attachable": false,
        "Containers": {
            "e4f5c81285032447bc8caa37d8aa6256b7cb533baa3f344e2725df179cbb4a31": {
                "Name": "distracted_goodall",
                "EndpointID": "34996afbac16326fc-
26490c463bd49d4ed2e6e252cbae458ba46949db5043a9d",
                "MacAddress": "",
                "IPv4Address": "",
                "IPv6Address": ""
            }
        },
        "Options": {},
        "Labels": {}
    }
]
root@N9K-C93180YC#
```

Host Network

Host is another default Docker network created when the Docker daemon is enabled on the supported Cisco platforms. The network driver is set to **Host**. Because containers deployed using host networking mode share the IP address with the host, there is no IPAM enabled for this mode.

While instantiating an application using Docker CLI, the **host** network option is selected, as shown in Example 4-33.

Example 4-33   *Docker Host Network Configuration*

```
N9K-C93180YC# run bash
bash-4.3$ sudo -i
root@N9K-C93180YC#
root@N9K-C93180YC#docker run -itd --net=host alpine
6db28efaa8d7cc528433e0c65cbba34e9114e92cdc9eb303ac4dddac0e91d540
root@N9K-C93180YC#
root@N9K-C93180YC#docker ps
CONTAINER ID    IMAGE    COMMAND     CREATED       STATUS     PORTS      NAMES
6db28efaa8d7    alpine   "/bin/sh"   11 seconds ago    Up 10 seconds   stupefied_lamport
root@N9K-C93180YC#
```

The output of the Docker **host** network is shown in Example 4-34.

Example 4-34   *Docker Host Network Output*

```
N9K-C93180YC# run bash
bash-4.3$ sudo -i
root@N9K-C93180YC#
root@N9K-C93180YC#docker network inspect host
[
    {
        "Name": "host",
        "Id": "b20681a5f354e64e241ac7076e39dd557a1f1f01269d012c3e55fb33b60614e5",
        "Created": "2019-05-04T19:09:06.986268554Z",
        "Scope": "local",
        "Driver": "host",
        "EnableIPv6": false,
        "IPAM": {
            "Driver": "default",
            "Options": null,
            "Config": []
        },
        "Internal": false,
        "Attachable": false,
        "Containers": {
            "6db28efaa8d7cc528433e0c65cbba34e9114e92cdc9eb303ac4dddac0e91d540": {
                "Name": "stupefied_lamport",
```

```
            "EndpointID": "f8705dce010205e3ef47a057e0a4901f6bd14407d308bef8d
   7335a23dfff10c8",
            "MacAddress": "",
            "IPv4Address": "",
            "IPv6Address": ""
          }
        },
        "Options": {},
        "Labels": {}
    }
]
root@N9K-C93180YC#
```

Note: Using the **docker attach <container_id>** command, you can log in to the container and check the network stack shared with the host.

Bridge Networking

Bridge is the third default Docker network created when the Docker daemon is enabled on the supported Cisco platforms. The network driver is set to **bridge**. While a default bridge is created, Docker allows the user to create additional user-defined bridges. Each such Docker bridge is assigned a subnet, and the IPAM assigns an IP address from this subnet for each deployed container.

While instantiating any application using Docker CLI, the network option is selected as the bridge, as shown in Example 4-35.

Example 4-35 *Docker Bridge Networking*

```
N9K-C93180YC# run bash
bash-4.3$ sudo -i
root@N9K-C93180YC#
root@N9K-C93180YC#docker run -itd alpine
dab825499f5e8043d302d4d297b5f343d712065d74c0b41f6db81bf7ee11fc77
root@N9K-C93180YC#docker ps
CONTAINER ID    IMAGE     COMMAND      CREATED        STATUS         PORTS        NAMES
dab825499f5e    alpine    "/bin/sh"    3 seconds ago  Up 2 seconds   sharp_noyce
root@N9K-C93180YC#
root@N9K-C93180YC#docker attach sharp_noyce
/ # ifconfig
eth0      Link encap:Ethernet   HWaddr 02:42:AC:11:00:02
          inet addr:172.17.0.2  Bcast:0.0.0.0  Mask:255.255.0.0
          inet6 addr: fe80::42:acff:fe11:2/64 Scope:Link
          UP BROADCAST RUNNING MULTICAST  MTU:1500  Metric:1
```

```
         RX packets:0 errors:0 dropped:0 overruns:0 frame:0
         TX packets:8 errors:0 dropped:0 overruns:0 carrier:0
         collisions:0 txqueuelen:0
         RX bytes:0 (0.0 B)  TX bytes:648 (648.0 B)

lo       Link encap:Local Loopback
         inet addr:127.0.0.1  Mask:255.0.0.0
         inet6 addr: ::1/128 Scope:Host
         UP LOOPBACK RUNNING  MTU:65536  Metric:1
         RX packets:0 errors:0 dropped:0 overruns:0 frame:0
         TX packets:0 errors:0 dropped:0 overruns:0 carrier:0
         collisions:0 txqueuelen:0
         RX bytes:0 (0.0 B)  TX bytes:0 (0.0 B)

/ #
```

The output of the Docker bridge network is shown in Example 4-36.

Example 4-36 *Docker Bridge Network Output*

```
root@N9K-C93180YC#docker network inspect bridge
[
    {
        "Name": "bridge",
        "Id": "b88bf54d35aced529245982ebffd3ae0691e24beeabcaa808505f5ca54156545",
        "Created": "2019-07-28T12:34:48.486323643Z",
        "Scope": "local",
        "Driver": "bridge",
        "EnableIPv6": false,
        "IPAM": {
            "Driver": "default",
            "Options": null,
            "Config": [
                {
                    "Subnet": "172.17.0.0/16",
                    "Gateway": "172.17.0.1"
                }
            ]
        },
        "Internal": false,
        "Attachable": false,
        "Containers": {
            "76414d040b4faa44ead1b40606756b4c705223cca533715a4ba1cb3830773364": {
                "Name": "brave_bell",
```

```
                "EndpointID": "d706e5906466182a6844dec21a4e9c4e8d766539e4880c7e20aad
    4df357c7a95",
                "MacAddress": "02:42:ac:11:00:02",
                "IPv4Address": "172.17.0.2/16",
                "IPv6Address": ""
            }
        },
        "Options": {
            "com.docker.network.bridge.default_bridge": "true",
            "com.docker.network.bridge.enable_icc": "true",
            "com.docker.network.bridge.enable_ip_masquerade": "true",
            "com.docker.network.bridge.host_binding_ipv4": "0.0.0.0",
            "com.docker.network.bridge.name": "docker0",
            "com.docker.network.driver.mtu": "1500"
        },
        "Labels": {}
    }
]
root@N9K-C93180YC#
```

Note: Although all the outputs in this section were collected from the bash shell of a Nexus 9000 switch, the Docker CLI user interface is the same for Cisco IOS-XR, so all the commands are applicable for Cisco IOS XR platforms, too.

Kubernetes

The current Kubernetes deployment on Nexus 9000 series switches leverages host networking. When Nexus 9000 platforms join the Kubernetes cluster as one of the worker nodes, the master will use host networking for containers instantiated on the switches. Other CNI plug-ins are being developed, and you may see other network types supported in future deployments.

Summary

This chapter introduced the basics of container networking by explaining the network namespace and veth pair concept. This chapter further explained how the concepts are used to provide network isolation between applications. You also learned about the shared and dedicated network modes for native application-hosting, along with the relevant device configuration. Finally, you learned about Docker networking and the relevant commands to create different types of Docker networks.

References

Virtual Ethernet: http://man7.org/linux/man-pages/man4/veth.4.html

Linux Namespaces: http://man7.org/linux/man-pages/man7/namespaces.7.html

Application Hosting Configuration for Cisco IOS-XR: https://www.cisco.com/c/en/us/td/docs/iosxr/ncs5500/app-hosting/b-application-hosting-configuration-guide-ncs5500/b-application-hosting-configuration-guide-ncs5500_chapter_00.html

Cisco IOS-XR Network Stack: https://www.cisco.com/c/en/us/td/docs/iosxr/ncs5500/app-hosting/b-application-hosting-configuration-guide-ncs5500/b-application-hosting-configuration-guide-ncs5500_chapter_01.pdf

Virtual Extensible Local Area Network (VxLAN): https://tools.ietf.org/html/rfc7348

Cisco Container Networking: https://www.cisco.com/c/dam/m/en_us/network-intelligence/service-provider/digital-transformation/knowledge-network-webinars/pdfs/1114-dc-ckn.pdf

Docker Networking: https://success.docker.com/article/networking

## Chapter 5

Container Orchestration in Cisco IOS-XE Platforms

In this chapter, you will learn the following:

- The history, key components, and functions of the Cisco IOS-XE Architecture

- Cisco IOS-XE Architecture for application hosting

- Different types of supported applications

- Developing and hosting applications in IOS-XE platforms

Cisco IOS-XE Architecture

IOS-XE, which stands for IOS-eXtended Edition, is one of the key Cisco operating systems and the unified operating system for the Cisco enterprise platforms for switches, aggregate and edge routers, branch routers, industrial routers, industrial Ethernet switches, wireless LAN controllers, and cloud virtual routers.

IOS-XE is built on Linux and provides a distributed software architecture, with many of the operating system's functionalities performed by the Linux kernel itself. Figure 5-1 illustrates the IOS-XE architecture and its components.

The following are the key components of IOS-XE, along with their characteristics and functions:

- IOS-XE uses Linux as the base kernel.

- Linux is responsible for device/chassis management, input/output (I/O) management, process scheduling and management, memory management, handling interrupts, inter-process communication, low-level functions such as On-Board Failure Logging (OBFL), and other functionalities, such as timers.

- IOS runs on top of the Linux kernel as a daemon (or as an application) and is referred to as "IOSd" throughout the remainder of this book.

■ IOSd represents the central management point (control plane), which shares many functions and processes. It also shares CLIs with the legacy IOS.

■ The hosted apps space support infrastructure is needed to host various applications, such as Wireless Client Manager (WCM), Linux Containers (LXC), and Session Manager Daemon (SMD), which manage policies, templates, and so on.

■ A database is used to store operational state and associated data for all operating systems' features consistently.

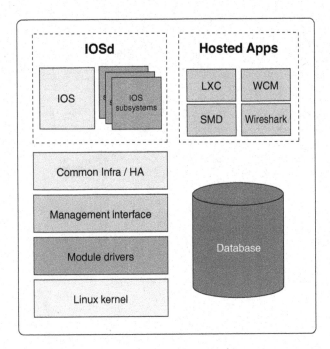

Figure 5-1   *IOS-XE 16.x (Polaris) Architecture*

Brief History of IOS-XE

IOS-XE was introduced with ASR platforms and then later introduced into switching platforms and wireless controllers. Here is a brief history of IOS-XE release up to the latest 16.x releases that support multiple enterprise platforms.

IOS-XE 3S releases:

■ Supported in ASR 9xx/1xxx, ISR4xxx, NCS4200, and CSR1000v

■ Started shipping in May 2008

■ Have gone through several release trains from 3.1S to 3.18S before being merged into the unified release train IOS-XE 16.x

IOS-XE 3E releases:

- Supported in Catalyst 3650/3850 switches, Catalyst 4500, and wireless controllers 5700

- Started shipping in August 2013

- Have gone through several release trains, starting with 3.3E through 3.9E before being merged into the unified release train IOS-XE 16.x

IOS-XE 16 releases (also referred to as Polaris):

- Supports all IOS-XE platforms, as shown in Table 5-1

- Started shipping in October and November 2015

- Have had several release trains from 16.1 to 16.12

Table 5-1   *Platforms Supported by IOS-XE 16.x Releases*

Platform Types	Products Supported
Switches	Cisco Catalyst 9600/9500/9400//9300/9200 and Catalyst 3850/3650 switches
Aggregate/Edge Routers	ASR1013, ASR1009-X, ASR1006-X, ASR1006, ASR1004-X, ASR1002-HX, ASR1001-HX, ASR1002-X, and ASR1001-X Routing platforms
Branch Routers	ISR4451, ISR4431, ISR4351, ISR4331, ISR4321, ISR4221, and ISR1000 routing platforms
Wireless Controllers	Cisco Catalyst 9800 wireless controllers
Industrial Routers and Switches	IR800, IR500 series, and IE3000/4000 series
Cloud/Virtual Routers	CRS 1000v and ISRv

With IOS-XE end-of-life and end-of-sale announced for earlier releases, the remainder of this book will focus on IOS-XE 16.x or future releases.

As illustrated in Figure 5-2, having a unified software stack for enterprise platforms—switches, routers, and wireless—has numerous benefits, including ease of management, a significant reduction in complexity, and the ability to deploy faster.

Architecture Components and Functions

IOS-XE is an operating system with a distributed multiprocess architecture, with each process single-threaded by default. These processes run in an environment that is memory-protected for fault tolerance, restarts or respawns on crash, and supports high-availability services, enabling in-service software upgrade/downgrade (ISSU/ISSD) and the like.

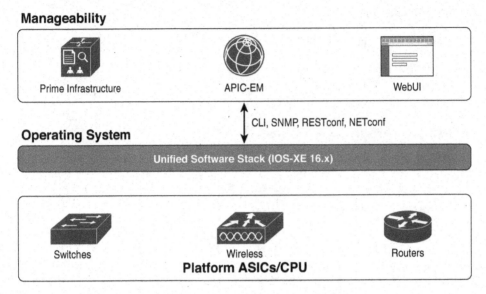

Figure 5-2 *Unified Operating System for Enterprise Platforms*

Because IOS-XE supports multiple underlying hardware platforms that could have different ASICs, interface processors, FPGAs, network modules and associated drivers, and so on, this section provides a high-level overview of the operating system's components and their primary functions, without diving deep into their operation. Even though this chapter discusses the architecture applicable to switching platforms and routing platforms, the concepts shown here are applicable to other IOS-XE platforms.

Switching Platforms

IOSd runs processes dedicated to each control plane function, such as ARP, DHCP, Multicast PIM or IGMP, OSPF, QoS, IP Device Tracking, access lists, and so on. A given process runs only on one CPU core, and in multi-core environments, static pinning of processes to a specific core do not occur. The process scheduler takes advantage of multi-core architecture and can schedule processes in different cores.

See Figure 5-3 to understand the IOS-XE components in switching platforms and interactions between them. IOSd uses shim messaging to interact with the Forwarding Manager (FMAN). FMAN is a key component that programs the hardware ASICs (Doppler in Switching Platforms) through the Forwarding Engine Driver (FED). It validates feature dependencies, and it only downloads via the FED after a validation pass. For example, if a MAC address needs to be programmed in the hardware, you need the interface and VLAN to which to map the MAC address. If a process pushes a MAC address for hardware programming without a VLAN or interface number, the validation fails, and programming is aborted. The FMAN has two parts, which are referred to as the FMAN-RP (Router Processor) and the FMAN-FP (Forwarding Processor). The FMAN-RP interacts with IOSd and pushes information to the FMAN-FP for hardware programming. In turn, the FMAN-FP interacts with ASICs and the driver to program the hardware.

In a redundancy or stacking scenario, the active switch's FMAN-RP interacts with the FMAN-FP in all switches in the stack, including the standby switch and member switches.

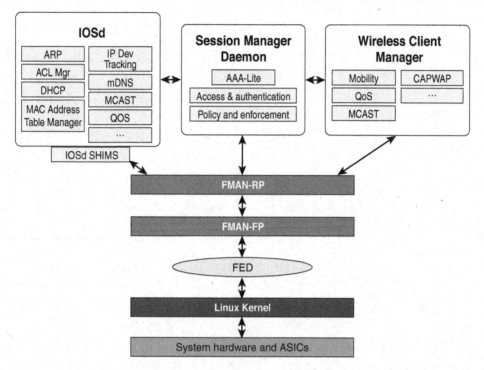

Figure 5-3   *IOS-XE Architecture—Switching Platform*

Session Manager (SMD) is new in Polaris; its functions used to be an integral part of earlier generations of IOS/IOS-XE operating systems. SMD is the new control plane process that handles authentication-type services and network policy enforcement. Isolation of these functions from IOSd significantly speeds up end-user join rates—both in wired and wireless environments—and forms the foundation for scaled deployments.

Wireless Client Manager (WCM) manages wireless access points (WAPs) and all the encapsulation/decapsulation functions needed to communicate with access points (APs).

In a multiprocessor environment (with redundant supervisor engines or stack of switches), it is critical for applications or processes to communicate among themselves reliably, regardless of where they are residing and running. Polaris has different types of interprocess communication (IPC) like the following:

- **Local IPC (LIPC):** LIPC uses UNIX domain sockets and is generally used by the processes residing in the same processor complex.

- **Remote IPC (RIPC):** RIPC uses TCP/IP and is used by the processes residing in different processor complexes, switches, or CPU subsystems.

■ **Message Queue IPC (MQIPC):** MQIPC uses shared memory, is used between control plane processes and FMAN-RP in different processor complexes, and supports persistent storage to achieve process restartability if a process crashes.

In summary, IOS-XE running on switching platforms has several components distributed across dedicated functions, and it is well designed to be resilient and highly available. Because these components play a critical role in communicating with the kernel and with application hosting infrastructure, it is important to become familiar with them.

Routing Platforms

This section looks at IOS-XE components, their functions, and their interactions in IOS-XE routing platforms, such as ASR1000.

As discussed earlier, IOS runs as a Linux process, whereas other processes share the responsibility of running the router. Hardware-specific components have been removed from the IOS process and are handled by separate middleware processes, which can be modified independently without making changes in the IOS process. Figure 5-4 illustrates major components of IOS-XE in the Cisco routing platforms and communication between them.

The major components of IOS-XE in routing platforms are listed here:

■ **Route Processor (RP):** A general-purpose CPU responsible for routing protocols, CLI, network management interfaces, code storage, logging, and chassis management

■ **Embedded Services Processor (ESP):** A forwarding processor that handles the forwarding of control plane traffic and performs packet-processing functions, such as firewall inspection, ACLs, encryption, and QoS

■ **SPA Interface Processor (SIP):** An interface processor that provides the connection between the route processor and the shared port adapters (SPAs)

In IOS-XE router platforms, a separate control processor is embedded on each major component in the control plane, as shown in Figure 5-5.

■ Route Processor (RP)

　　■ Runs the router control plane, including processing network control packets, computing routes, and setting up connections

　　■ Monitors the interface and environmental status, including management ports, LEDs, alarms, and SNMP network management

　　■ Downloads code to other components in the system

　　■ Selects the active RP and ESP and synchronizes the standby RP and ESP

　　■ Manages logging facilities, on-board failure logging (OBFL), statistics aggregation, and the like

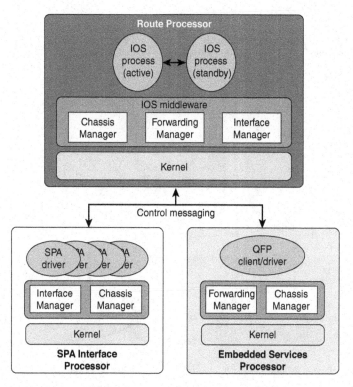

Figure 5-4 *IOS-XE Architecture—Routing Platform*

- Forwarding Engine Control Processor (FECP)

    - Provides direct CPU access to the forwarding engine subsystem—the Cisco Quantum Flow Processor (QFP) subsystem—that is the forwarding processor chipset and resides on the ESP

    - Manages the forwarding engine subsystem and its connection to I/O

    - Manages the forwarding processor chipset

- Input/Output Control Processor (IOCP)

    - Provides and manages direct CPU access to SPAs installed in a SIP

    - Handles SPA Online Insertion and Removal (OIR) events

    - Runs SPA drivers that initialize and configure SPAs

The RP manages and maintains the control plane using a dedicated Gigabit Ethernet Out-of-Band Channel (EOBC). The internal EOBC is used to continuously exchange system state information among the different major components. The inter-integrated circuit (I2C) monitors the health of hardware components. The Enhanced SerDes Interconnect (ESI) is a set of serial links that are the data path links on the midplane connecting the RP, SIPs, and standby ESPs to the active ESP.

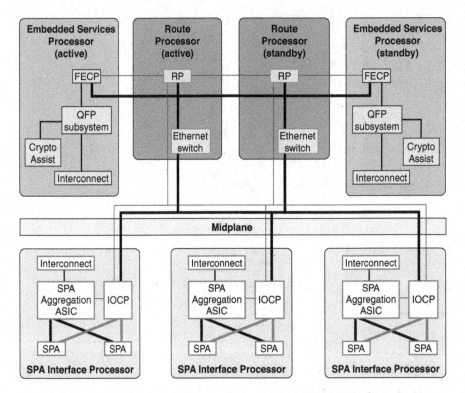

Figure 5-5   *IOS-XE Control Plane Architecture in ASR1000 Platform*

In summary, just like in switching platforms, IOS-XE running on routing platforms has several components distributed across dedicated functions, and it is well designed to offer various services.

With an understanding of IOS-XE software and control plane architecture, you will now look into how the IOS-XE platform enables you to host and manage applications.

IOS-XE Architecture: Application Hosting

Chapter 2 discussed service containers and briefly touched on the application hosting framework available in Cisco IOS-XE. This section examines capabilities and features that enable and support application hosting in IOS-XE. Figure 5-6 provides a high-level overview of application hosting capabilities in IOS-XE.

libvirt and Virtualization Manager

libvirt is an open-source virtualization management tool kit to manage virtualization in a platform. Part of the Linux kernel in IOS-XE, libvirt forms the foundation for application hosting by supporting various hypervisors like Kernel-based Virtual Machine (KVM), Linux Containers (LXC), and emulators like Quick Emulator (QEMU).

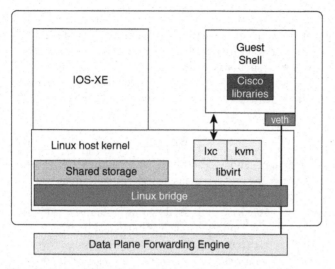

Figure 5-6 *IOS-XE Application Hosting Capabilities*

Linux storage shown in Figure 5-6 is shared among the host, the guest, and the applications, but the file systems and storage allocated to the applications or containers are dedicated. Depending on the requirement of the applications, the Linux kernel provides logical network connectivity to bridge the application(s) to the host or to devices and resources external to the host.

As shown in Figure 5-7, Virtualization Manager (VMAN) is a daemon that runs on top of the Linux kernel. It is the first component introduced in IOS-XE to support application hosting.

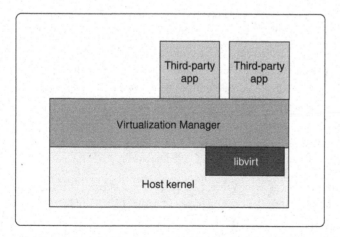

Figure 5-7 *IOS-XE Virtualization Manager*

One limitation with hosting applications with VMAN is that the application should be customized to meet the platform requirements, which poses challenges to third-party application developers because they need to have their applications tested and certified by Cisco. This virtualization manager is supported in some legacy IOS-XE platforms through the installation of a package that introduces *virtual-service* CLI. Because this is a legacy feature supported only in specific platforms, this chapter does not focus on it.

IOx Overview

IOx is an environment that provides application-hosting capabilities in the Cisco enterprise and IoT platforms. IOx facilitates the lifecycle management of applications and associated data exchange by offering a set of services that help developers package prebuilt apps and host them on a target device. IOx is used by various industries, ranging from manufacturing to public sector organizations, such as municipal transportation authorities. IOx allows the customers to execute applications in the Cisco edge devices, which establishes secure and reliable southbound connectivity with sensors and northbound connectivity to the cloud applications. Figure 5-8 offers an overview of the IOx architecture and its various components.

IOx application hosting provides the following features:

■ It hides network heterogeneity because this framework is applicable to different types of edge devices, such as access routers and switches, wireless access points, computing devices like UCS blades, industrial routers and Ethernet (IE) switches, and so on.

■ It supports various types of application hosting, including virtual machine packaged applications, containerized applications packaged for Docker and LXC, and PaaS-style applications written in Python, Java, and other languages.

■ IOx application programming interfaces (APIs) support management applications or controllers to remotely manage the lifecycle of applications hosted on these devices.

■ Lifecycle management of applications can be centralized, for example, via Fog Director or a similar management application. Lifecycle management includes distribution, deployment, hosting, starting, stopping, and monitoring of apps and the data they generate.

■ Developers can integrate third-party applications and controllers or create a customized user interface. It also includes application-distribution and management tools that help users discover and deploy apps to the IOx framework.

The IOx application hosting framework is a Python process that manages virtualized and containerized applications that run on devices. Application hosting offers the following services:

■ Designated applications in containers

■ Available resource checks (memory, CPU, and storage), allocation of those sources, and their management

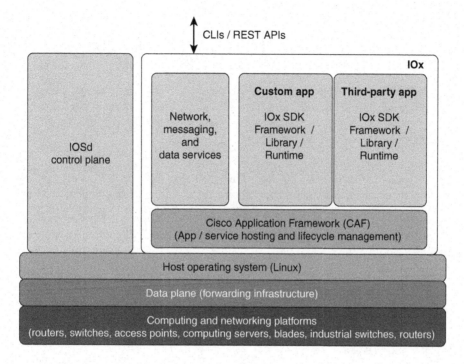

Figure 5-8 *IOx Architecture and Overview*

- Support for console logging.

- Access to services via REST APIs. IOx enables the application lifecycle to be managed externally, perhaps through Fog Director.

- IOx Client, which is a CLI endpoint to manage applications' lifecycles through install/uninstall, activate/deactivate, and start/stop commands.

- An application-hosting infrastructure referred to as Cisco Application Framework (CAF). It is seen as an SDK to develop and run applications in IOS-XE platforms. Also, it allows entities such as IOx Client, Fog Direction, and other web management tools to communicate with and manage the lifecycle of VMs via CAF.

- Setup of platform-specific networking (packet-path) via VirtualPortGroup and management interfaces.

IOx Applications

This section provides details on types of applications that can be deployed with IOx framework, resources required for each type of application, and general workflow to deploy these applications.

Application Types

Broadly, IOx applications can be categorized as shown here, and the associated requirements, rules, and characteristics are discussed in this section.

- **LXC/Container-style apps:** These apps are composed of application code, third-party dependent libraries, and native binaries (and the entire root file system, minus the kernel) and are packaged into one archive. Figure 5-9 represents LXC-style applications and their various components.

  - **Contents:** App Descriptor file (**package.yaml**) and Bootstrap config file (**package_config.ini**). Optional: Root file system that contains code, dependent libraries, binaries, and required language runtime, utilities, daemons, and the like.

  - **Startup:** CAF starts the container's entry point. It must use an init system (such as /sbin/init) so that the environment is automatically configured during system initialization or the boot process.

  - **Network:** CAF sets up networking, but applications should have routines to verify the network configuration (network interfaces, IP addresses through DHCP, and so on).

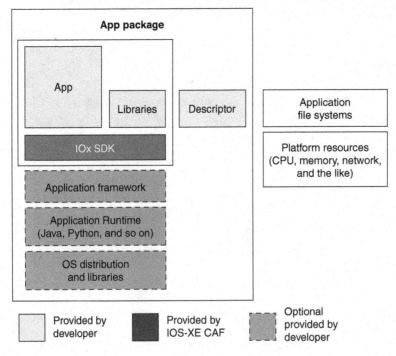

Figure 5-9 *App Hosting—Container-Style Applications*

- **PaaS-style apps:** These applications are more portable; are typically developed using dynamic languages such as Java, Ruby, Python, and the like; and are designed to run in specific PaaS frameworks. Figure 5-10 illustrates PaaS-style applications and their various components.

  - **Contents:** App Descriptor file (**package.yaml**) and Bootstrap config file (package_config.ini). Optional: Application code, dependent libraries, and so on.

  - **Startup:** CAF orchestrates the app. As specified in the startup->target file, CAF provisions applications in a container.

  - **Network:** CAF sets up networking so that an application does not have to do it.

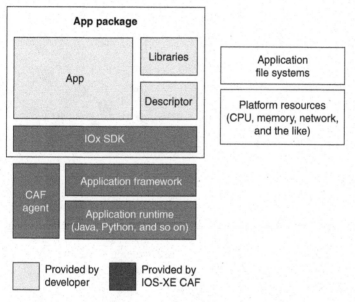

Figure 5-10   *App Hosting—PaaS-Style Applications*

- **Virtual machine packaged apps:** These applications are packaged as virtual machines. They contain a complete OS (kernel + root file system), libraries, and application code packaged into one archive. See Figure 5-11, which illustrates virtual machine–style applications and their various components.

  - **Contents:** App Descriptor file (**package.yaml**) and Bootstrap config file (**package_config.ini**). Optional: Root file system that contains code, dependent libraries, binaries, language runtime, utilities, and daemons.

  - **Startup:** CAF boots up the kernel or the bootup disk as configured.

  - **Network:** CAF sets up networking, but the application should have routines to ensure the network configurations, such as network interfaces, IP addresses through DHCP, and so on, are present and active.

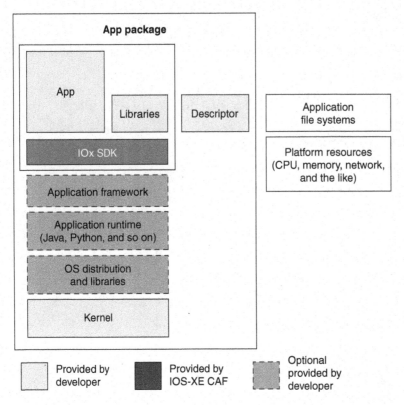

Figure 5-11 *App Hosting—Virtual Machine–Style Applications*

- Docker-style apps: These applications are similar to LXC/container-style applications. The only difference is that at the time of application development, the developer can use Docker tooling to generate the root file system.

  - **Contents:** App Descriptor file (**package.yaml**) and Bootstrap config file (**package_config.ini**). Optional: Root file system that contains code, dependent libraries, binaries, required language runtime, utilities, daemons, and the like.

  - **Startup:** CAF orchestrates the application startup based on the startup--target section in the descriptor file. It must not use an init system.

  - **Network:** CAF sets up networking so that application does not have to do it.

See the "Developing and Hosting Applications" section later in this chapter for a discussion of the steps involved in developing and hosting applications of different styles. Toward the end of this chapter, there is a discussion of hosting Docker applications natively in Catalyst 9000 platforms.

Resource Requirements

In Chapter 3, "Container Orchestration and Management," you learned about different flavors of applications supported in Cisco IOS-XE platforms. Now you will look at the various resource requirements for these applications. To host applications in IOS-XE platforms, memory and storage are required, and you will need to set up network resources to establish connectivity between the host and the external network.

Memory and Storage Requirements

Table 5-2 details the resources required to host applications in enterprise and industrial switching and routing platforms, both physical as well as virtual. The table includes details on the memory and storage required for each of the platform types.

Table 5-2 *Hosting Application—Resource Requirements*

Platforms	Application Type	Memory	Storage
Catalyst 9600/9500 series	Virtual Machine, LXC, Docker	16 GB	120–960 GB HDD/SSD
Catalyst 9300 series	Virtual Machine, LXC, Docker	4 GB+	120–960 GB HDD/SSD
Cat 9400/9200 series	Virtual Machine, LXC, Docker	4 GB+	120–960 GB HDD/SSD
Catalyst 3850/3650	LXC	4 GB	75 MB
ISR 4000 series	LXC	8 GB	20–200 GB HDD/SSD
ASR 1000 series	Virtual Machine, LXC, Docker (16.10)	4 GB+	40–400 GB HDD/SSD
IR 800 / 1000 series	PaaS, LXC, Docker	800 MB	512–1800 MB
CSR 1000v / ISRv	LXC	4 GB	75 MB

Note that at minimum, Catalyst 9000 platforms should be running version 16.12 to natively support the Docker engine.

Now it is time to look at other storage types, such as hard disks, bootflash, and USB storage, that are supported in the Cisco enterprise routing and switching platforms.

- In Cisco ISR 4000 series routers, if Network Interface Module (NIM)-Service Set Identifier (SSID) hard disks are available, there is no option to select bootflash to install Guest Shell.

- For Cisco ASR 1000 routers, you can only do resource resizing if a hard disk (which is optional) is installed in the router and the Guest Shell is installed on that hard disk.

■ During Guest Shell installation, if not enough hard disk space is available, an error message is displayed. The following is a sample error message on an ISR 4000 Series router:

```
% Error:guestshell_setup.sh returned error:255, message:
Not enough storage for installing guestshell.
```

■ Bootflash or hard disk space can be used to store additional data by Guest Shell. On Cisco Catalyst 3850 Series Switches, Guest Shell has 18 MB of storage space available, and on Cisco 4000 Integrated Services Routers, Guest Shell has 800 MB of storage space available. Because Guest Shell accesses the bootflash, it can use the entire space available. Later sections will look into the procedure and associated commands used to enable Guest Shell in an IOS-XE platform.

■ USB 3.0 SSD is enabled on Cisco Catalyst 9300 Series Switches. The USB 3.0 SSD provides an extra 120 GB storage for application hosting. For more information, see the "Configuring USB 3.0 SSD" chapter in the *Interface and Hardware Components Configuration Guide* available at Cisco.com.

■ Starting from Cisco IOS-XE Gibraltar 16.10.1, Cisco Catalyst 9400 Series Switches support application hosting using USB 3.0. Prior to this, the front panel USB was supported for storage but not available for application hosting. This platform also supports M2 Serial Advanced Technology Attachment (SATA) drives that can be plugged into the removable supervisor.

■ Cisco Catalyst 9500 series high-performance switches support back-panel USB 3.0, which is similar to the Cisco Catalyst 9300 Series Switches and Cisco Catalyst 9500 Series switches.

VirtualPortGroup

Besides storage and memory, VirtualPortGroup is another important resource required for application hosting in IOS-XE. As discussed in Chapter 4, "Container Networking Concepts," IOS-XE supports only a dedicated network mode. The VirtualPortGroup is a software construct in Cisco IOS-XE that maps to a Linux bridge IP address. As such, the VirtualPortGroup represents the switch virtual interface (SVI) of the Linux container. Each bridge can contain multiple interfaces, each mapping to a different container. Each container can also have multiple interfaces, as shown in Figure 5-12. Following are the characteristics of the VirtualPortGroup resource.

■ VirtualPortGroup interfaces are configured by using the interface **virtualportgroup** command. After these interfaces are created, IP addresses and other resources are allocated.

■ A maximum of 32 VirtualPortGroup interfaces can be configured. Each of these VirtualPortGroup interfaces will have two forwarding entries.

■ The VirtualPortGroup interface connects the application-hosting network to the IOS routing domain. The Layer 3 interface of the application receives routed traffic from

IOS. The VirtualPortGroup interface connects through the Service (SVC) Bridge to the container/virtual machine interface.

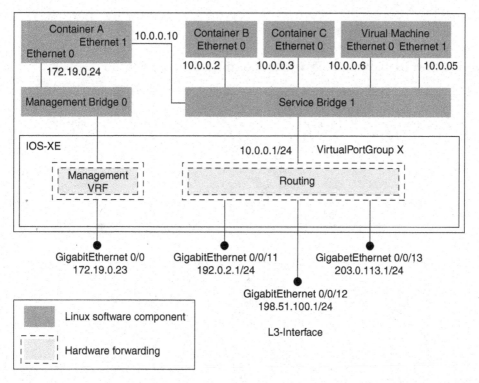

Figure 5-12 *Container Networking—VirtualPortGroup*

Virtual NIC (vNIC)

For the container lifecycle management, the Layer 3 routing model that supports one container per internal logical interface is used. This means that a virtual Ethernet pair is created for each application, and one interface of this pair, called vNIC, is part of the application container. The VirtualPortGroup interface, called vpgX, is part of the host system.

NIC is the standard Ethernet interface inside the container that connects to the platform data plane for sending and receiving of the packets. IOx is responsible for the gateway (VirtualPortGroup interface), IP address, and unique MAC address assignment for each vNIC in the container.

The vNIC inside the container/virtual machine is considered a standard Ethernet interface for network connectivity.

> **Note:** Please refer to the "Native App Hosting—Dedicated Network Configuration" section in Chapter 4 for detailed information on the various container network models and relevant configuration and settings.

Application Deployment Workflow and Operation States

Figure 5-13 provides an overview of application hosting service states and various triggers that transition the service state from the deployed to the activated and to the running and to the stopped states. It also illustrates various activities supported at each state.

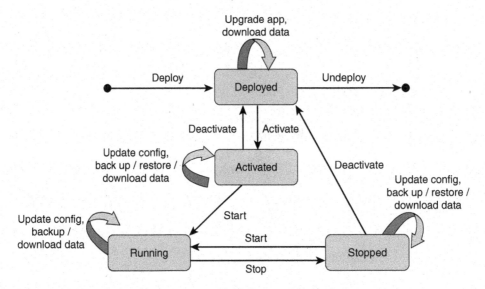

Figure 5-13 *Application Hosting—Workflow and State Transitions*

The first step is to install the application, at which point it transitions to the deployed state. In this state, users can upgrade the application or download necessary supporting data. The platform commits no resources to the application during the deployed state.

The next step is to activate the application, which transitions the application to the activated state. If the resource allocation fails, the system reports the errors, and users can deactivate the application to transition back to the deployed state.

After successful activation, start the application to make sure the intended services are offered. As required, the application can be stopped and restarted.

The next section discusses developing and hosting differently styled applications through various state transitions.

Developing and Hosting Applications

This section teaches readers how to develop applications for different types of containers and host these application in Cisco IOS-XE platforms.

LXC-Based Guest Shell Container

Guest Shell is integrated with IOS-XE. It operates in an isolated user space and uses resources that are completely protected for any memory faults. Guest Shell is a simple but powerful capability with which one can host applications and integrate them into the workflow. It is helpful to develop and prototype scripts and Python-based applications with tighter integration to device-level APIs. The following section explores enabling LXC-type Guest Shell after the activation of IOx.

Activating IOx

Enable IOx in the device with the **iox** command under configuration mode, and make sure the IOx-Service is running. Please make sure the device is installed with a license required to support IOx. For details on the requirements, review the licensing requirements guide for the routing and switching platforms available at Cisco.com.

Example 5-1 shows the command that enables the IOx feature and all associated services including CAF, high availability, IOx Manager (IOxman), and Libvirt Daemon (libvirtd).

Example 5-1 *Activate IOx*

```
Cat9300# config t
Enter configuration commands, one per line. End with CNTL/Z.
Cat9300(config)# iox
Cat9300(config)# end
Cat9300#
Cat9300# show iox-service

IOx Infrastructure Summary:
---------------------------
IOx service (CAF)     : Running
IOx service (HA)      : Running
IOx service (IOxman)  : Running
Libvirtd              : Running
Cat9300#
```

Setting Up Network Configuration

Before enabling Guest Shell, set up the network configuration. As you learned in Chapter 4 and earlier in this chapter, IOS-XE supports dedicated network mode. In Example 5-2, the **VirtualPortGroup** is created and assigned with an IP address/mask.

Example 5-2   *Create VirtualPortGroup for Connectivity*

```
Cat9300# conf t
Cat9300(config)# interface VirtualPortGroup 0
Cat9300(config-if)# ip address 20.1.1.1 255.255.255.0
Cat9300(config-if)# no shut
Cat9300(config-if)# end
```

By executing the commands shown in Example 5-3, the application's virtual guest-interface 0 is connected to VirtualPortGroup 0.

Example 5-3   *Connect Guest Shell to the Host*

```
Cat9300#
Cat9300# conf t
Cat9300(config)# app-hosting appid guestshell
Cat9300(config-app-hosting)# app-vnic gateway0 virtualportgroup 0 guest-interface 0
Cat9300(config-app-hosting-gateway0)# guest-ipaddress 20.1.1.2 netmask 255.255.255.0
Cat9300(config-app-hosting-gateway0)# app-default-gateway 20.1.1.1 guest-interface 0
Cat9300(config-app-hosting)# end
Cat9300#
```

Figure 5-14 logically represents the connectivity between the Guest Shell and the host built by the preceding configurations.

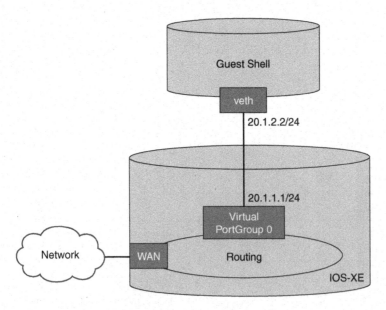

Figure 5-14   *Guest Shell Network Connectivity*

Activating the Guest Shell Container

Enable Guest Shell and make sure it is running. As you can see in Example 5-4, just one command, **guestshell enable**, deploys, activates, and runs the Guest Shell.

Example 5-4   *Deploy, Activate, and Run Guest Shell*

```
Cat9300# guestshell enable
Interface will be selected if configured in app-hosting
Please wait for completion
guestshell installed successfully
Current state is: DEPLOYED
guestshell activated successfully
Current state is: ACTIVATED
guestshell started successfully
Current state is: RUNNING
Guestshell enabled successfully
Cat9300#
Cat9300# show app-hosting list
App id                          State
-----------------------------------------
guestshell                      RUNNING
Cat9300#
```

You can use the **detail** command option, as shown in Example 5-5, to look at the Guest Shell configuration and allocated resources, along with its state.

Example 5-5   *Verify Guest Shell Status and Resource Allocation*

```
Cat9300# show app-hosting detail
App id                 : guestshell
Owner                  : iox
State                  : RUNNING
Application
  Type                 : lxc
  Name                 : GuestShell
  Version              : 2.4.1(0.1)
  Description          : Cisco Systems Guest Shell XE for x86
Activated profile name : custom
Resource reservation
  Memory               : 256 MB
  Disk                 : 1 MB
  CPU                  : 800 units
Attached devices
```

```
  Type              Name                Alias
  ------------------------------------------------
  serial/shell      iox_console_shell   serial0
  serial/aux        iox_console_aux     serial1
  serial/syslog     iox_syslog          serial2
  serial/trace      iox_trace           serial3
Network interfaces
------------------------------------
eth0:
  MAC address        : 52:54:dd:af:64:9f
  IPv4 address       : 20.1.1.2
Port forwarding
  Table-entry  Service  Source-port  Destination-port
  --------------------------------------------------
Cat9300#
```

If the Guest Shell service needs to be disabled, you can use the **guestshell disable** command. If the Guest Shell service needs to be completely uninstalled, use the **guestshell destroy** command.

If a specific program needs to be run in the Guest Shell, you can use the **guestshell run <executable>**. For example, run **guestshell run python.** IOS-XE platforms have Python preinstalled; for example, Python version 2.7.11 is preinstalled in Catalyst 3850/3650 platforms, and version 2.7.5 is installed on ISR 4000 series routers.

Example 5-6 shows the commands used to access Guest Shell.

Example 5-6 *Access Guest Shell*

```
Cat9300# guestshell
[guestshell@guestshell~]$ pwd
/home/guestshell

[guestshell@guestshell~]$ whoami
guestshell
[guestshell@guestshell~]$
[guestshell@guestshell ~]$ dohost "show version"
Cisco IOS Software [Everest], Catalyst L3 Switch Software [CAT3K_CAA-UNIVERSALK9-M],
Experimental Version 16.5.2017200014[v165_throttle-BLD-
 BLD_V165_THROTTLE_LATEST_20170531_192849 132]
```

Note: You can access the Guest Shell to check the network, DNS, and proxy settings, and you can modify these as required.

Developing PaaS-Style Applications and Hosting

Platform as a service (PaaS) refers to a set of services that provide a platform allowing users to develop, run, and manage applications without the challenge of building and maintaining the infrastructure required to develop and launch an app. Typically, the PaaS provider manages language runtimes, the operating system, virtualization, storage, and networking.

IOx PaaS-style applications aim to provide similar development experience in a Fog environment. In PaaS application deployments in IOS-XE platforms, CAF dynamically provides a secure environment and provisions required resources (CPU, memory, storage, language runtimes, and the like) for the application.

Supported Platforms

Hosting PaaS-style applications are one of the legacy-style hosting applications. They are only supported in IoT platforms, such as the Industrial Routers IR800 series and IR500 series.

Setting Up the Development Environment

Before you start setting up the development environment, you need to know the platform on which the application is going to be hosted. Based on the platform, you need to choose the right base image. To make the application development easier, Cisco has built a repository of base images, which are available at the locations listed in Table 5-3.

Table 5-3   *Docker Image Location*

Platforms	Docker Base Image Location
IR8xxx/Cat9k/ ISR4k /ASR1k/ CGR1k	devhub-docker.cisco.com/iox-docker/ir800/base-rootfs, <path>/base-rootfs-dev, <path>/python-2.7.11, <path>/java-8, <path>/base-rootfs-32bit, <path>/base-rootfs-32bit-dev, <path>/python-2.7.11-32bit, and <path>/java-8-32bit.
IR1101	devhub-docker.cisco.com/iox-docker/ir1101/base-rootfs, <path>/base-rootfs-dev, <path>/python-2.7.11
IE4000	devhub-docker.cisco.com/iox-docker/ie4k/base-rootfs, <path>/python-2.7.3

Note: For the Cat9k, ISR4k, ASR1k, and CGR1k platforms, even though the Docker base image location path includes ir800, it is still applicable.

Developing a Python Application

Because the scope of this chapter is to show how to build IOx packages and host applications, it does not focus on developing applications. Instead, it shows a simple Python application in Example 5-7, which prints "helloworld" every 10 seconds when it is activated and running.

Example 5-7 *Simple Python Application*

```
import time
import datetime

while True:
    print format(datetime.datetime.now()), 'helloworld'
     time.sleep(10)
```

Creating a Docker Image

To create a Docker image, start by creating a Docker file and then building a Docker image, as discussed in the following section.

The Docker file shown in Example 5-8 will make the application start as part of the system initialization and utilize a multistage Docker build to keep the overall image size down. A multistage Docker build basically avoids including any building tool in the final image, thereby reducing the overall image size.

Example 5-8 *Docker File*

```
FROM devhub-docker.cisco.com/iox-docker/ir800/base-rootfs:latest
RUN opkg update
RUN mkdir -p /var/helloworld/
COPY helloworld.py /var/helloworld/
```

Building a Docker Image

The command shown in Example 5-9 builds a Docker image named **helloworld** with version 1.0 using a previously created Docker file. Use the **sudo** command option to resolve any permission-related issues.

Example 5-9 *Build a Docker Image*

```
$ docker build -t helloworld:1.0 .
```

Creating an IOx Package Using YAML

To create an IOx package, create an IOx package descriptor file, download IOx Client from Cisco.com, create an IOx Client profile, and then create an IOx package.

Creating an IOx Package Descriptor File

As shown in Example 5-10, an IOx package descriptor file contains metadata about the application, minimum resource requirements for running the application, and runtime requirements.

Example 5-10 *Package.yaml Descriptor File*

```
info:
  name: hello world
  description: "Hello world PaaS type application"
  version: "1.0"
  author-link: "http://www.cisco.com"
  author-name: "Cisco Systems"

app:
  type: paas
  cpuarch: x86_64

  resources:
    profile: custom
    cpu: 200
    memory: 64
    disk: 2


    network:
      -
        interface-name: eth0
# Specify runtime and startup
  startup:
    runtime: python
    runtime-version: 2.7
    target: app.py
```

Creating IOx Package

Before you build the IOx package, download the applicable IOx Client shown in Figure 5-15 from the following location at Cisco.com:

Downloads Home / Cloud and Systems Management / IoT Management and Automation / IOx / IOx Client - 1.8.0

As you can see in Figure 5-15, IOx Client is available for the Windows operating system, macOS, and Linux. Download and install the latest version.

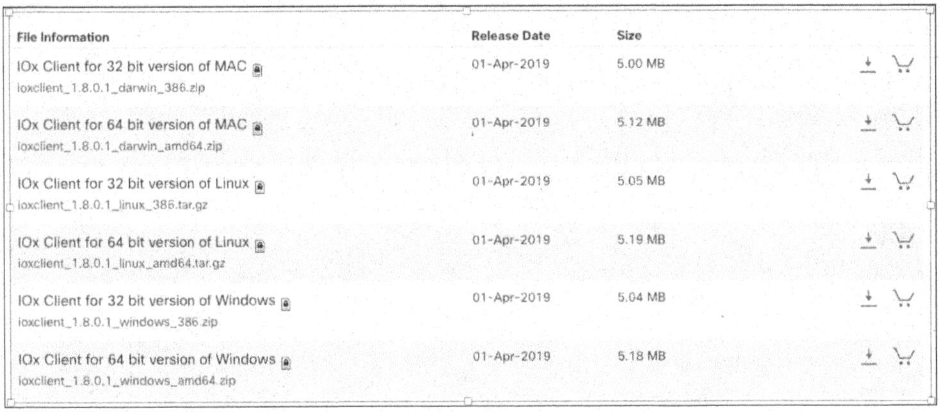

File Information	Release Date	Size		
IOx Client for 32 bit version of MAC 🔒 ioxclient_1.8.0.1_darwin_386.zip	01-Apr-2019	5.00 MB	↓	🛒
IOx Client for 64 bit version of MAC 🔒 ioxclient_1.8.0.1_darwin_amd64.zip	01-Apr-2019	5.12 MB	↓	🛒
IOx Client for 32 bit version of Linux 🔒 ioxclient_1.8.0.1_linux_386.tar.gz	01-Apr-2019	5.05 MB	↓	🛒
IOx Client for 64 bit version of Linux 🔒 ioxclient_1.8.0.1_linux_amd64.tar.gz	01-Apr-2019	5.19 MB	↓	🛒
IOx Client for 32 bit version of Windows 🔒 ioxclient_1.8.0.1_windows_386.zip	01-Apr-2019	5.04 MB	↓	🛒
IOx Client for 64 bit version of Windows 🔒 ioxclient_1.8.0.1_windows_amd64.zip	01-Apr-2019	5.18 MB	↓	🛒

Figure 5-15   *IOx Clients on Cisco.com Downloads*

Set up an IOx Client device profile by configuring the device IP, credentials, and SSH port and using the command, as shown in Example 5-11.

Example 5-11   *Create an IOx Client Profile*

```
bash$ ioxclient profiles create
```

Use the IOx Client command shown in Example 5-12 to build an IOx application package named **package.tar.** You need to pass reference paths to the same Docker image name and version that has been used to build the image in previous steps. Use the **sudo** command option to resolve any permission-related issues.

Example 5-12   *Create an IOx Client Package*

```
bash$ ioxclient docker package helloworld:1.0 .
```

For IR800-series platforms, if the application package needs any cartridges such as Yocto or Java Runtime Environment, you can add them to the package using the command shown in Example 5-13. The available cartridges are listed here.

Example 5-13   *Install IOx Client Cartridges*

```
bash$ ioxclient cartridge install <cartridge>
```

The available cartridges are listed on the Cisco.com downloads page, as shown in Figure 5-16. The applicable cartridges can be downloaded from the following location:

Downloads Home / Routers / Industrial Routers / 800 Series Industrial Integrated Services Routers / 809 Series Industrial Integrated Services Routers / IOx Cartridges-1.2.0

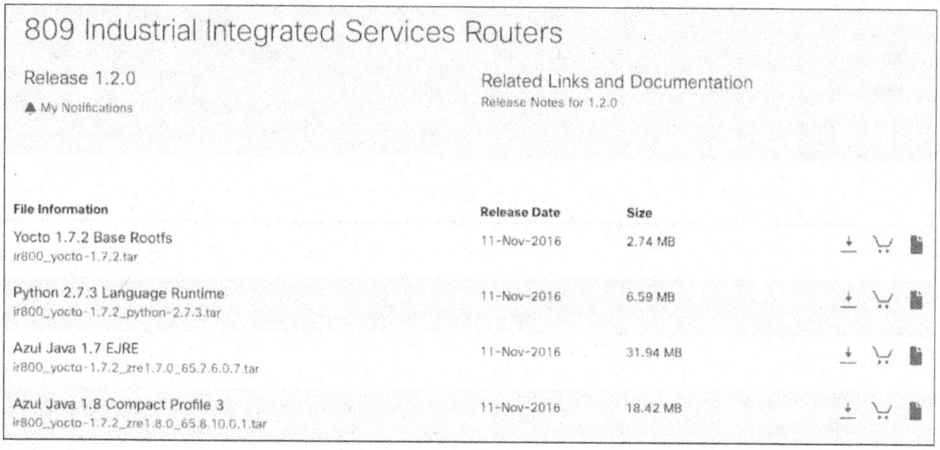

809 Industrial Integrated Services Routers

Release 1.2.0

🔔 My Notifications

Related Links and Documentation

Release Notes for 1.2.0

File Information	Release Date	Size			
Yocto 1.7.2 Base Rootfs ir800_yocto-1.7.2.tar	11-Nov-2016	2.74 MB	⬇	🛒	📄
Python 2.7.3 Language Runtime ir800_yocto-1.7.2_python-2.7.3.tar	11-Nov-2016	6.59 MB	⬇	🛒	📄
Azul Java 1.7 EJRE ir800_yocto-1.7.2_zre1.7.0_65.7.6.0.7.tar	11-Nov-2016	31.94 MB	⬇	🛒	📄
Azul Java 1.8 Compact Profile 3 ir800_yocto-1.7.2_zre1.8.0_65.8.10.0.1.tar	11-Nov-2016	18.42 MB	⬇	🛒	📄

Figure 5-16 *IOx Cartridges at Cisco.com Downloads*

Installing, Activating, and Running the Application

Now you will deploy the application onto a physical or virtual IOS-XE platform using IOx Client. Example 5-14 uses IOx Client to deploy this application to a device and includes commands to install, activate, and start the application.

Example 5-14 *Install, Activate, and Start the Application*

```
$ ioxclient application install hello_world_app ./package.tar
Currently active profile :  h714
Command Name: application-install
Saving current configuration
Installation Successful. App is available at : https://<IOx device IP>:<IOx Port
  Number>/iox/api/v2/hosting/apps/hello_world_app
Successfully deployed
$
$ ioxclient application activate hello_world_app
Currently active profile :  h714
Command Name: application-activate
App hello_world_app is Activated
$
$ ioxclient application start hello_world_app
Currently active profile :  h714
Command Name: application-start
App hello_world_app is Started
$
```

To verify the application is generating **helloworld** messages every 10 seconds, you can access the application directly by logging in through the console using the command shown in Example 5-15 and checking the logs generated by the application.

Example 5-15 *Access the Application via the Console*

```
$ ioxclient application console hello_world_app
Currently active profile :  h714
Command Name: application-console
Console setup is complete…
/#
2019-10-05 18:01:15.733930 helloworld
2019-10-05 18:01:25.738049 helloworld
2019-10-05 18:01:35.741854 helloworld
2019-10-05 18:01:45.742096 helloworld
2019-10-05 18:01:55.745714 helloworld
2019-10-05 18:02:05.748011 helloworld
```

This section discusses how to build a Docker image with a simple Python application, how to convert the Docker image into an IOx package using IOx Client, and how to install, activate, and run the application on the destination platform. The features and capabilities built into the platforms help developers build custom applications and packages that can be installed, activated, and run on an IOS-XE platform.

Developing Virtual Machine–Based Application and Hosting

Figure 5-17 shows the procedure to develop a virtual machine–based application package.

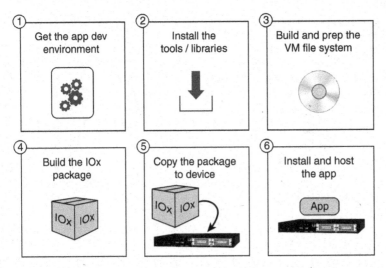

Figure 5-17 *Steps to Develop and Host a Virtual Machine–Based Application*

Setting Up an Application Development Environment

To set up an application development environment, build a virtual machine and then install the required tools and libraries.

Build a Virtual Machine

Start with building a virtual machine with CentOS 6 as the guest operating system. As you see in Example 5-16, a virtual machine is running CentOS release 6.10 and has kernel version 2.6.32-754.e16.x86_64.

Example 5-16 *CentOS Virtual Machine*

```
[root@localhost ~]cat /etc/centos-release
CentOS release 6.10 (Final)
[root@localhost ~]uname -r
2.6.32-754.e16.x86_64
```

Make sure the virtual machine has network connectivity and can resolve the domain names, as shown in Example 5-17.

Example 5-17 *Verify Network Connectivity of a Virtual Machine*

```
[root@localhost ~]
[root@localhost ~]cat /etc/sysconfig/network-scripts/ifcfg-eth0
DEVICE=eth0
HWADDR=00:0C:29:56:C0:6A
TYPE=Ethernet
UUID=3b97eca0-d6ce-469b-b3cd-b7cd851a0da0
ONBOOT=yes
NM_CONTROLLED=yes
BOOTPROTO=dhcp
[root@localhost ~]
[root@localhost ~]cat /etc/resolv.convf
nameserver 8.8.8.8
[root@localhost ~]
[root@localhost ~]ifconfig -a
eth0:     Link encap:Ethernet  HWaddr 00:0C:29:56:C0:6A
          inet addr:192.168.1.17  Bcast:192.168.1.1  Mask:255.255.255.0
          inet6 addr: fe80::20C:29FF:fe1c:185a/64 Scope:Link
          UP BROADCAST RUNNING MULTICAST  MTU:1500  Metric:1
          RX packets:31619 errors:0 dropped:0 overruns:0 frame:0
          TX packets:715 errors:0 dropped:0 overruns:0 carrier:0
          collisions:0 txqueuelen:1000
          RX bytes:26906265 (25.6 MiB)  TX bytes:55379 (54.0 KiB)
          Interrupt:19 Base address:0X2000
[root@localhost ~]
[root@localhost ~]ping 8.8.8.8
```

```
PING 8.8.8.8 (8.8.8.8): 56 data bytes
64 bytes from 8.8.8.8: icmp_seq=0 ttl=52 time=8.926 ms
64 bytes from 8.8.8.8: icmp_seq=1 ttl=52 time=8.970 ms
64 bytes from 8.8.8.8: icmp_seq=2 ttl=52 time=8.764 ms
^C
--- 8.8.8.8 ping statistics ---
3 packets transmitted, 3 packets received, 0.0% packet loss
round-trip min/avg/max/stddev = 8.755/8.829/8.970/0.079 ms
[root@localhost ~]
[root@localhost ~]ping www.cisco.com
PING origin-www.cisco.com (173.37.145.84): 56 data bytes
64 bytes from 173.37.145.84: icmp_seq=0 ttl=243 time=29.163 ms
64 bytes from 173.37.145.84: icmp_seq=1 ttl=243 time=29.033 ms
64 bytes from 173.37.145.84: icmp_seq=2 ttl=243 time=29.050 ms
^C
--- origin-www.cisco.com ping statistics ---
3 packets transmitted, 3 packets received, 0.0% packet loss
round-trip min/avg/max/stddev = 28.968/29.101/29.290/0.114 ms
[root@localhost ~]
```

Install Tools and Libraries

Install the packages, tools, and libraries required for the application using **yum install** commands. For example, install the iPerf package with commands shown in Example 5-18.

Example 5-18 *Install Tools and Libraries*

```
[root@localhost ~]
[root@localhost ~]yum install iperf
Loaded plugins: fastestmirror
Setting up Install Process
Loading mirror speeds from cached hostfile
<snip>
[root@localhost ~]
```

Configure the virtual machine to start the services offered by an application on bootup and to stop or restart the services through the initialization system. The primary purpose of an **init** system, which is also referred to as **systemd**, is to kick off the configured services right after kernel bootup. Along with initialization, **init** system is also used to stop, restart, and manage the services, as shown in Example 5-19.

Example 5-19 *Start or Stop Application Services*

```
[root@localhost ~]
[root@localhost ~] service application.service start
[root@localhost ~] service application.service stop
[root@localhost ~] service application.service restart
[root@localhost ~]
```

In CentOS version 7 or later, you have systemctl commands that are used to enable, start, and manage a service, as shown in Example 5-20.

Example 5-20 *Start or Stop Application Services Using systemctl Commands*

```
[root@localhost ~]
[root@localhost ~] systemctl enable application.service
[root@localhost ~] systemctl start  application.service
[root@localhost ~] systemctl status application.service
[root@localhost ~]
```

Building the Virtual Machine File System

From the host OS, you will prepare and build a virtual machine file system using Quick Emulator (QEMU), as shown in Example 5-21. As you may know, QEMU is one of the popular, free, and open-source emulator tools available to translate disk images to different formats and perform virtualization functions; it supports various hardware architectures such as x86-64 PCs, MIPS64, and the like.

Note: For more information on QEMU and its supported features, visit the QEMU organization's home page provided at https://www.qemu.org.

Example 5-21 *Create Virtual Machine File System*

```
[root@UbuntuServer ~]qemu-img create -f vmdk centosxe.vmdk 4G
Formatting 'centosxe.vmdk', fmt=vmdk size=4294967296 compat6=off zeroed_grain=off
[root@UbuntuServer ~]ls | grep vmdk
centosxe.vmdk
```

Apple Mac users using VMware Fusion to build virtual machines should follow the steps given next to create a virtual machine file system. Once you have finished building the virtual machine with a guest operating system of CentOS and have installed all the packages and libraries, power it off. Under the File menu option, click on Convert to OVF to convert the virtual machine to vmdk/ovf files. Once the conversion is completed, VMware Fusion creates a folder with **vmdk, iso**, and **ovf** files, as shown in Example 5-22.

Example 5-22   *VMware Fusion—Generate the Virtual Machine File System*

```
$ pwd
/Users/TestUser/Virtual-Machines/CentOS6-vmdk
$ ls
CentOS6-vmdk-disk1.vmdk
CentOS6-vmdk-file1.iso
CentOS6-vmdk.mf
CentOS6-vmdk.ovf
```

For the application to be activated in an IOS-XE platform, IOx Client needs a file in qcow2 format. Using the **qemu-img** utility, you will convert the **vmdk** file you created to a **qcow2** file, as shown in Example 5-23.

Example 5-23   *Convert VMDK to QCOW2 Format*

```
[root@UbuntuServer ~]qemu-img convert -f vmdk -O qcow2 centosxe.vmdk centosxe.qcow2
[root@UbuntuServer ~]ls | grep centosxe
centosxe.vmdk
centosxe.qcow2
```

As you saw in previous sections, **centosxe.qcow2** was used to build an IOx package **.tar** file that can be installed on the destination platform.

Build an IOx Package Using YAML

Before you start building the package, download the IOx Client from the Cisco.com software downloads page. As you saw previously in Figure 5-15, IOx Client is available for the Windows operating system, macOS, and Linux. Download and install the latest version on the host device, as shown in Example 5-24.

Example 5-24   *Verify IOx Client Installation*

```
[root@UbuntuServer ~]ls
README.md
ioxclient
[root@UbuntuServer ~]file ioxclient
ioxclient: Mach-O 64-bit executable x86_64
[root@UbuntuServer ~]
```

Now you will build the **package.yaml** descriptor file with the application information, resource requirements, and instructions, as shown in Example 5-25.

Example 5-25 *Description File—Package.yaml*

```
[root@UbuntuServer ~]cat package.yaml
descriptor-schema-version: "2.4"

info:
  name: CentOS-XE-App
  description: "App Hosting Demo for IOS-XE"
  version: "1.0"
  author-link: "http://www.cisco.com"
  author-name: "Cisco Systems"

app:
  type: vm
  cpuarch: x86_64
  resources:
    profile: custom
    cpu: 200
    memory: 64
    disk: 2

    network:
      -
        interface-name: eth0
# Specify runtime and startup
startup:
  disks:
    -
      target-dev: "hdc"
      file: "/Users/TestUser/qemu/centosxe.qcow2"

    qemu-guest-agent: True
[root@UbuntuServer ~]
```

Run IOx Client and build the package. With the command shown in Example 5-26, a tar archive is created at the specified location.

Example 5-26 *Build an IOx Client Package*

```
[root@UbuntuServer ~]ioxclient package -name CentOSXE-App .
[root@UbuntuServer ~]
[root@UbuntuServer ~]ls | grep XE
CentOSXE-App.tar
[root@UbuntuServer ~]
```

Note: To ensure the application package is valid and it is obtained from a trusted source, the package needs to be signed so that it can be deployed on a signature-enabled IOx device such as a Catalyst 9300 switch running IOS-XE releases. For more information on IOx package signature validation, please refer to the IOx Package Signature Validation page provided in the "References" section at the end of this chapter.

Installing, Activating, and Running the Application

Copy the package to IOS-XE platform's USB storage, as shown in Example 5-27.

Example 5-27   *Import the .tar File to the Host*

```
Cat9300# dir usbflash0:CentOSXE-App.tar
Directory of usbflash0:/CentOSXE-App.tar
   115  -rwx       1418270208   Aug 3 2019 11:56:18 +00:00  CentOSXE-App.tar
31963676672 bytes total (18239153254 bytes free)
Cat9300#
```

Activate IOx in the system on which the application is going to be hosted. Enable HTTP and HTTPS servers in the device to have external connectivity and DNS resolution. Make sure to configure a username with a privilege level of 15. See Example 5-28.

Example 5-28   *Activate IOx, Set Up HTTP, and Set the User Privilege*

```
Cat9300#config t
Enter configuration commands, one per line. End with CNTL/Z.
Cat9300(config)# iox
Cat9300(config)#
Cat9300(config)# ip http server
Cat9300(config)# ip http secure-server
Cat9300(config)# username user123 privilege 15 password 0 cisco!123
```

In Example 5-29, **virtualportgroup** is a Layer 3 interface in the host, and it will be part of the IP routing. Interface **gigabitethernet 1/0/1** is the WAN interface connecting to the external network. When IP routing is enabled and the configured IP prefixes are distributed, **virtualportgroup** should be reachable from the external network.

Example 5-29   *Enable Routing and Create VirtualPortGroup for Connectivity*

```
Cat9300# configure terminal
Cat9300(config)# ip routing
Cat9300(config)# interface gigabitethernet 1/0/1
Cat9300(config-if)# no switchport
Cat9300(config-if)# ip address 10.1.1.1 255.255.255.254
```

```
Cat9300(config-if)# exit
Cat9300(config)# interface virtualportgroup 0
Cat9300(config-if)# ip address 10.0.2.1 255.255.255.0
Cat9300(config-if)# end
```

Follow the steps shown in Example 5-30 to install, activate, and start the application. Remember, app-hosting commands as shown in Example 5-4 were used for the LXC-based Guest Shell Containers. In this section, the app-hosting command is used to configure the network connectivity for a specific application identified with **appid** and **guestshell enable** to install, activate, and run the Guest Shell. Here, it is used not only to configure the network but to install, activate, and run the application.

Example 5-30 *Install a Virtual Machine–Based Application*

```
Cat9300# app-hosting install appid CENTOS package usbflash0:CentOSXE-App.tar
Installing package 'usbflash0:CentOSXE-App.tar' for 'CENTOS'. Use 'show app-hosting
  list' for progress.


Cat9300# show app-hosting list
App id                         State
-----------------------------------------------------
CENTOS                         DEPLOYED


Cat9300#show app-hosting det appid CENTOS
App id                  : CENTOS
Owner                   : iox
State                   : DEPLOYED
Application
  Type                  : vm
  Name                  : hello world
  Version               : 1.0
  Description           : Hello world VM type application
  Path                  : usbflash0:CentOSXE-App.tar
Activated profile name  : custom


Resource reservation
  Memory                : 64 MB
  Disk                  : 2 MB
  CPU                   : 200 units


Attached devices
  Type            Name            Alias
  ---------------------------------------------


Network interfaces
  ---------------------------------------------
```

As you can see, the application type is **VM**, and it is in the **DEPLOYED** state.

Before this application can be activated and run, you need to assign a virtual group interface to the interface in the application's container or virtual machine. You also need to assign an IP address to its interface. See Example 5-31 for further details.

Example 5-31 *Configure Network for Virtual Machine–Based Application*

```
Cat9300# config t
Cat9300(config)# app-hosting appid CENTOS
Cat9300(config-app-hosting)# app-vnic gateway0 virtualportgroup 0 guest-interface 0
Cat9300(config-app-hosting-gateway0)# guest-ipaddress 10.0.2.2 netmask 255.255.255.0
Cat9300(config-app-hosting-gateway0)# app-default-gateway 10.0.2.1 guest-interface 0
Cat9300(config-app-hosting-gateway0)# exit
```

Figure 5-18 shows the logical connectivity between the application, host, and external resources.

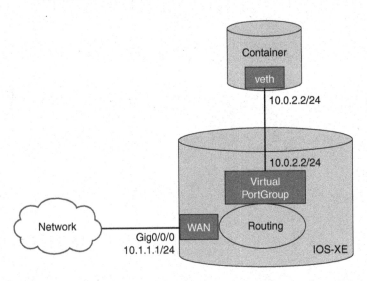

Figure 5-18 *Virtual Machine–Based Application Hosting—Logical Network Connectivity*

Continue the procedure by activating and starting the application with **app-hosting** commands, as shown in Example 5-32.

Example 5-32 *Activate and Run a Virtual Machine–Based Application*

```
Cat9300# app-hosting activate appid CENTOS
CENTOS activated successfully
Current state is: ACTIVATED
Cat9300#
Cat9300# show app-hosting list
```

```
App id                        State
- - - - - - - - - - - - - - - - - - - - - - - - - - - - - - - - - -
CENTOS                        ACTIVATED

Cat9300# app-hosting start appid CENTOS
CENTOS started successfully
Cat9300#
Cat9300# show app-hosting list
App id                        State
- - - - - - - - - - - - - - - - - - - - - - - - - - - - - - - - - -
CENTOS                        RUNNING
```

To summarize what you did in this section of the chapter, you built a CentOS virtual machine, installed the necessary tools and libraries, built a virtual machine package with the guest OS and tools, and using virtual machine package, you built an IOx package to install it in the destination host. As mentioned earlier, the features and capabilities built into the platforms are simple and flexible, and they empower developers to build custom applications and packages that can be installed, activated, and run in an IOS-XE platform.

Developing and Hosting a Docker-Style Application

This section focuses on how to develop and run a Docker-style application, develop a high-level workflow of Docker-style application development, and develop and host the application.

Docker-style applications are similar to container applications from a deployment perspective. The only notable difference is the building process in which the developer uses Docker tooling to create an application root file system.

For Docker, you can use Docker tooling and its ecosystem to develop applications for IOx. A prebuilt virtual machine .ova that has all the necessary IOx development tools, including Docker and IOx Client, is available for downloading at the Cisco Devnet page. This virtual machine .ova file is imported into any VMware hypervisor that emulates the development guest-os.

Note: You can download a prebuilt .ova file containing the necessary IOx development tools, including Docker and IOx Client, at https://developer.cisco.com/docs/iox/#iox-resource-downloads. You can find VMware hypervisor information at https://developer.cisco.com/docs/iox/#tutorial-build-sample-vm-type-iox-app.

Setting Up Docker Toolchain

To set up a Docker toolchain, you need to meet the following prerequisites:

- Docker >= 1.12 (preferred would be 1.26) installed on your development machine
- Latest IOx Client (>=1.4.0) installed on your machine

Caveats and Restrictions

The following restrictions should be noted before starting to develop and host Docker-style applications:

- Developers use existing Docker tooling to create Docker images that can then be packaged into IOx-compatible applications. Only the IOx software development environment is Dockerized.

Note: To check whether your target IOx platform supports Docker-style applications, please refer to the Platform Support Matrix provided at https://developer.cisco.com/docs/iox/#platform-support-matrix.

- The contents of the Docker image are interpreted and composed to create an LXC container root file system on the target environment.

- In general, IOx supports all **build**-specific Docker instructions. However, only a subset of Docker file **run**-specific instructions is supported. See Table 5-4 for a list of supported instructions.

Table 5-4 *IOx-Supported Docker File Instructions*

Docker File Instructions	IOx Support?
FROM, MAINTAINER, RUN, ADD, COPY, ONBUILD, LABEL, CMD, EXPOSE, ENV, ENTRYPOINT, VOLUME, USER*, WORKDIR, HEALTHCHECK	Yes
ARG, STOPSIGNAL	No
SHELL**	Partial

* It is used to set the startup user ID and start point in the Docker image

** Supported only for RUN instruction

- The IOx application created using a Docker image is run using LXC and AUFS on a compatible IOx platform. None of the IOx platforms run the Docker daemon natively.

- The package descriptor file (**package.yaml**) is used to define the IOx application requirements. For Docker-type applications, it is not mandatory to create an application descriptor file. IOx Client creates a default package descriptor file. You can add additional attributes or modify default values using LABEL instruction in the Docker file (Ex. LABEL cisco.cpuarch=x86_64).

- Docker images that are heavily dependent on constructs provided by Docker (for example, Docker file commands) will not run out of the box. Use equivalent attributes in the Docker file or **package.yaml** if available. (For example, the ENV Docker file constructs can be translated to the **package.yaml's app->env** section.)

- Docker apps **must** bring the entire rootfs as part of the application package. The rootfs must be in Docker image format, which is a tar ball that preserves all layers and layer information from the Docker image.

- Docker-style apps cannot use any cartridges that are available on the platform.

- Docker-style apps must not use any init system for container startup. The target command to be run is a user-defined process.

- Although it is possible to run any Docker image, the image size should be compatible with the available resources on the platform.

Development Workflow

Developers are expected to be familiar with the process of working with Docker and creating Docker images.

In addition, they are expected to

- Have an intermediate understanding of Linux, including rootfs, partition, system initialization, and package installation

- Be familiar with how to build a Linux application

- Customize and configure Linux systems

Figure 5-19 shows a high-level workflow for how to create IOx applications using Docker tools and images.

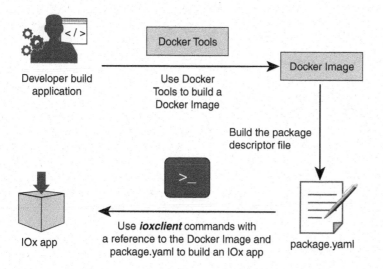

Figure 5-19   *Steps in Developing and Hosting Docker-Based Applications*

Images and Package Repository

Cisco provides Docker base images and prebuilt binary packages to make the IOx application development simple. These base images and binary packages are distributed on the DMZ type of repositories.

Cisco hosted repositories:

- Docker base image repository
- Opkg package repository

The repositories can be accessed in the following two ways:

- **Using Docker daemon and opkg utility:** Use during development to pull the images and to install the packages
- **Using devhub web UI:** Explore the repository and see the contents using a browser

Please refer to the Docker Images and Repository page provided in the "References" section at the end of this chapter to learn about currently available Docker base images, how to pull base images, how to install packages, and how to access the Cisco-hosted repositories via web UI. All the image and package repositories are listed at **devhub-docker. cisco.com/iox-docker/<platform>/<image>:<version>**.

Develop Python Application

Even though you can have a C, C++, or Python-based Docker type IOx application, Example 5-33 uses a simple Python-based application.

Note: If you would like to use sample applications provided by Cisco, you can clone the repository available at the Cisco IOx GitHub page provided at https://github.com/ CiscoIOx/docker-demo-apps.git.

Example 5-33   *Sample Python Code*

```
$ mkdir simple-python-app
$ cd simple-python-app
$ vi poll-temperature.py
#!/usr/bin/python
import time
import os

os.makedirs("/var/volatile/log")
f = open('/var/log/poll-temp.log', 'w')
while (1):
    s = "%s %s polling temperature ...\n" % (time.strftime("%d/%m/%Y"),
time.strftime("%I:%M:%S"))
    f.write(s)
    f.flush()
    time.sleep(5)
```

Build Docker Image

Before starting to build a Docker image, create a Docker file that has command-line instructions to build the image.

In Example 5-34, the rootfs base image used is for an Industrial Router 800 (IR800). However, base images are available for multiple IOS-XE platforms at the repository mentioned in the previous section of this chapter.

Example 5-34 *Create Docker File*

```
$ vi Dockerfile
FROM devhub-docker.cisco.com/iox-docker/ir800/base-rootfs:latest

RUN opkg update && opkg install python
COPY poll-temperature.py /usr/bin/poll-temperature.py
RUN chmod 777 /usr/bin/poll-temperature.py

CMD /usr/bin/poll-temperature.py
```

Once the Docker file built as shown in Example 5-34, use the **docker build** command shown in Example 5-35 to build a Docker image. Please make sure to have the Docker file in the same directory as the Python code.

Example 5-35 *Create Docker Image*

```
$ docker build -t iox-simple-py:1.0 .
Sending build context to Docker daemon 3.072 kB
Step 1/5 : FROM devhub-docker.cisco.com/iox-docker/ir800/base-rootfs:latest
 ---> 4d39f5d04ab4
Step 2/5 : RUN opkg update && opkg install python
 ---> Running in a873629832a2
Downloading https://devhub.cisco.com/artifactory/IOx-Opkg/yocto-1.7.2/ir800/core2-
  64/Packages.gz.
Updated source 'packages'.
<snip>
Step 3/5 : COPY poll-temperature.py /usr/bin/poll-temperature.py
 ---> 6ea51f9ec232
Removing intermediate container 5d82f7b74f2e
Step 4/5 : RUN chmod 777 /usr/bin/poll-temperature.py
 ---> Running in 8c2de53e8534
 ---> d768cf016ade
Removing intermediate container 8c2de53e8534
Step 5/5 : CMD /usr/bin/poll-temperature.py
 ---> Running in ec557654bc50
 ---> 99d1fd944be5
Removing intermediate container ec557654bc50
Successfully built 99d1fd944be5
```

Check the image to ensure you can run the image locally, as shown in Example 5-36.

Example 5-36 *Verify Docker Image*

```
#
# docker images
REPOSITORY      TAG           IMAGE ID          CREATED           SIZE
iox-simple-py  1.0           fc9150946af4      6 seconds ago     17.84 M
#
# docker run -d iox-simple-py:1.0
b5205d87312c4e6f058dcbf6289c3d18299127dd8f211407d581fd07b1092a6d
#
```

Using the commands shown in Example 5-37, access the container and verify whether the application is collecting the logs as intended.

Example 5-37 *Verify the Application*

```
# docker exec -ti
b5205d87312c4e6f058dcbf6289c3d18299127dd8f211407d581fd07b1092a6d /bin/sh
/ # cd /var/log
/var/volatile/log # ls -la
drwxr-xr-x    2 root      root             4096 Nov  2 00:04 .
drwxr-xr-x    5 root      root             4096 Nov  2 00:04 ..
-rw-r--r--    1 root      root              352 Nov  2 00:05 poll-temp.log
/var/volatile/log # tail -F poll-temp.log
02/11/2016 12:04:41 polling temperature ...
02/11/2016 12:04:46 polling temperature ...
02/11/2016 12:04:51 polling temperature ...
```

Building an IOx Application Package Using YAML

For Docker-based applications, it is optional to create a package descriptor file. IOx Client creates a default package descriptor file while creating the IOx Docker application package. If you need to add custom entries in a package descriptor file, you can add those entries using Docker's LABEL directive. IOx Client uses those labels and adds them in a package descriptor file during creation of an IOx Docker application package. Refer to the IOx Client page at Devnet to learn how to use Docker's LABEL and **package.yaml**. Example 5-38 is a sample application descriptor (package.yaml) file.

Example 5-38 *Verify Docker Image*

```
$ vi package.yaml

descriptor-schema-version: "2.2"
```

```
info:
  name: iox_simple_py
  description: "Simple Python based Docker style app"
  version: "1.0"
  author-link: http://www.cisco.com
  author-name: "Cisco Systems"


app:
  # Indicate application type
  cpuarch: "x86_64"
  type: docker
  resources:
    profile: c1.small
    network:

        interface-name: eth0

# Specify runtime and startup
  startup:
    rootfs: rootfs.tar
    target: ["/usr/bin/poll-temperature.py"]
```

Note: If you are using an application descriptor file for non-x86 architecture, refer to the Docker images table at https://developer.cisco.com/docs/iox/#!docker-images-and-packages-repository/overview for the appropriate value of **cpuarch** in the yaml file. For example, for the IE4000 platform, use **'cpuarch'** as **'ppc'** in the descriptor file.

IOx Client (>= 1.4.0) provides a convenient command that generates an IOx application package from a Docker image. First, navigate to the project directory. Create an empty directory—for example, 'app_package'—and execute the IOx Client command in this directory. Make sure the profile for the target platform is created and activated before creating the package. See Example 5-39.

Example 5-39 *Build IOx Package*

```
$ mkdir app_package
$ cd app_package
$ ioxclient docker package -a iox-simple-py:1.0 .
Currently active profile :  ir800
Command Name: docker-package
<snip>
Generated package manifest at  package.mf
Generating IOx Package..
Package docker image iox-simple-py:1.0 at /home/ioxsdk/test_sde/app_package/package.
  tar
$
```

Installing, Activating, and Running the Application

Copy the **package.tar** built to the target IOS-XE platform. In Example 5-40, which uses an Industrial Router (IR) 800 series, you are going to install, activate, and run the package.

Example 5-40   *Install, Activate, and Run the Application*

```
IR800-A#ioxclient application install iox_simple_py ./package.tar
Currently active profile :  h829
Command Name: application-install
Saving current configuration
Installation Successful.
Successfully deployed
IR800-A#
IR800-A#ioxclient application activate iox_simple_py
Currently active profile :  h829
Command Name: application-activate
App iox_simple_py is Activated
IR800-A#
IR800-A#ioxclient application start iox_simple_py
Currently active profile :  h829
Command Name: application-start
App iox_simple_py is Started
IR800-A#
IR800-A#
```

Native Docker Application Hosting in Catalyst 9300

IOS-XE running 16.12 or later supports native Docker container support on Catalyst 9300–series switches. This enables users to build custom applications or pull third-party applications from Docker registries and bring them to the platform without additional packaging. Figure 5-20 illustrates the framework that supports hosting Docker applications natively in Catalyst 9300 platforms.

There are two possible workflows to bring applications to the Catalyst 9300 platforms. One of the options is to build a Docker image with a custom application and save it as a .tar archive, supported by the specified platform. The other option is to pull a Docker image directly from the repositories or registry and save it as a **.tar** archive.

Workflow 1: Building and Exporting a Docker Image

The first step is to create a Docker file, as shown in Example 5-41.

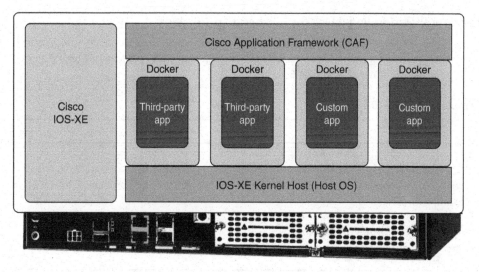

Figure 5-20 *Cisco Application Framework in Catalyst 9300 Platforms*

Example 5-41 *Create Docker File*

```
$ vi Dockerfile
FROM devhub-docker.cisco.com/iox-docker/ir800/base-rootfs:latest

RUN opkg update && opkg install python
COPY poll-temperature.py /usr/bin/poll-temperature.py
RUN chmod 777 /usr/bin/poll-temperature.py

CMD /usr/bin/poll-temperature.py
```

Next, build the Docker image. Once the Docker file and all required config files have been created, you can build a new Docker image with the command shown in Example 5-42.

Example 5-42 *Build the Docker Image*

```
docker build -t <application> .
```

Now export the application. Once you have built the Docker application, the standard Docker save command can be used to export the application as a .tar archive. See Example 5-43.

Example 5-43 *Export Application to .tar Image*

```
docker save MyApp > myapp.tar
```

Workflow 2: Performing a Docker Pull and Export

First, use the **docker pull** command. If you have an existing application repository in the Docker hub or Docker registries, you can use the **docker pull** command and build an application, as shown in Example 5-44.

Example 5-44 *Docker Pull*

```
docker pull MyApp
```

Next, export the application. Once you have built the Docker application, the standard **docker save** command can be used to export the application as a .tar archive, as shown in Example 5-45.

Example 5-45 *Export Application*

```
docker save MyApp > myapp.tar
```

Deploying Native Docker Applications

The application can then be deployed on the Catalyst 9000–series switches. The IOx Client tool discussed in the previous sections is no longer required to package the application. IOx Client is an optional tool for developers who want to define additional parameters for the application.

The application lifecycle on the Cisco Catalyst 9000 series switches consists of the following stages, which are shown in Example 5-46.

- **Install:** Installing the application on the device
- **Activate:** Activating the application by committing the required hardware resources
- **Start:** Starting the application and transitioning to the **running** state

Example 5-46 *Install, Activate, and Run the Application*

```
app-hosting install appid MyApp package usbflash0:myapp.tar
app-hosting activate appid MyApp
app-hosting start appid MyApp
```

The following states are shown in Example 5-47.

- **Stop:** Stop the application to transition back to the **activated** state
- **Deactivate:** Deactivate the application to transition back to the **installed** state and deallocate all the hardware resources committed to the application
- **Uninstall:** Uninstall the application from the system

Example 5-47 *Stop, Deactivate, and Uninstall an Application*

```
app-hosting stop appid MyApp
app-hosting deactivate appid MyApp
app-hosting uninstall appid
```

Docker Container Networking

As you learned in Chapter 4, containers can be connected via the management interface and front panel data ports. The management interface connects to the container interface via the management bridge, and the IP address of the container will be on the same subnet as the management interface. Virtual network interface cards (vNICs) inside containers are seen as standard Ethernet interfaces (veth0, veth1, and so on).

The previous chapter discussed the AppGigabitEthernet interface, which is applicable for the scenario discussed here. It is an internal hardware data port that is hardware-switched to the front panel data ports. The AppGigabitEthernet interface is only available on the Cisco Catalyst 9300–series switches, although other Cisco Catalyst 9000 platforms are expected to support it in future software releases.

Three options are available for assigning an IP address to the container:

- **Linux CLI:** Logging directly into the container and configuring it using Linux commands

- **Dynamic Host Configuration Protocol (DHCP):** Using the DHCP client in the container and configuring a DHCP server or relay

- **Cisco IOS-XE CLI:** Statically assigned via the Cisco IOS-XE CLI

Refer to Chapter 4 for more detailed information on the container network model and the relevant configuration.

Licensing Requirements

For Catalyst 9000 switching platforms, Smart Licensing is required. DNA-Advantage licensing is required to enable the Application Hosting feature. To install the required license for App-Hosting, configure IOS-XE, as shown in Example 5-48.

Example 5-48 *Installing the License*

```
Cat9300# config t
Enter configuration commands, one per line. End with CNTL/Z.
Cat9300(config)# license boot level network-advantage add-on dna-advantage
Cat9300(config)# end
Cat9300# write memory
Cat9300# reload
<after the device comes back up>
Cat9300#
```

```
Cat9300# show version
<snip>
Technology Package License Information:
----------------------------------------------------------
Technology-package                     Technology-package
Current               Type             Next reboot
----------------------------------------------------------
network-advantage     Permanent        network-advantage
dna-advantage         Subscription     dna-advantage
Cat9300# *
```

Note: To learn more about Smart Licensing and creating Smart Licensing Accounts, check out the smart licensing page provided at https://www.cisco.com/c/en/us/products/software/smart-accounts/software-licensing.html.

For Industrial Router and Switch platforms like IR8xx or IE4xxx, users should register their platforms with a valid registration token obtained from the Smart Account at Smart Licensing portals mentioned in the preceding Note. See Example 5-49.

Example 5-49   *IOx Smart Licensing*

```
$ ioxclient license smart register token <token>
```

Note: Refer to the "Smart Licensing Guide for Access and Edge Routers" provided at https://www.cisco.com/c/en/us/td/docs/ios-xml/ios/smart-licensing/qsg/b_Smart_Licensing_QuickStart/b_Smart_Licensing_QuickStart_chapter_01.html.

Summary

This chapter introduced the fundamentals of the IOS-XE architecture, including its history and key internal components and their functions. You learned how key built-in architectural components enable application hosting. You learned about the different types of applications that are supported by and can be hosted in IOS-XE platforms. You learned how to develop, build necessary virtual machine or Docker and IOx packages, install, activate, and run the applications.

The key take-away from this chapter is that Cisco IOS-XE platforms have built-in capabilities that help developers deploy custom applications and bring intelligence closer to the end hosts, nodes, and data they generate. Above all, users can orchestrate and manage the lifecycle of containers and applications by activating or deactivating them, upgrading the applications or packages installed with them, and very importantly, the capabilities that the platforms have for users to automate and achieve scalability.

References

Programmability Configuration Guide, Cisco IOS XE Gibraltar 16.10.x: https://www.cisco.com/c/en/us/td/docs/ios-xml/ios/prog/configuration/1610/b_1610_programmability_cg/guest_shell.html

Programmability Configuration Guide, Cisco IOS XE Gibraltar 16.10.x: https://www.cisco.com/c/en/us/td/docs/ios-xml/ios/prog/configuration/1610/b_1610_programmability_cg/application_hosting.html

The Container Story: Run your apps and tools natively on Cisco boxes: https://www.cisco.com/c/dam/assets/global/DK/seminarer/pdfs/cisco_virtual_update_fog_computing_iox_update.pdf

Getting Started with Service Containers: https://community.cisco.com/t5/networking-blogs/getting-started-with-service-containers/ba-p/3660954

Application Hosting on the Cisco Catalyst 9000 Series Switches: https://www.cisco.com/c/dam/en/us/products/collateral/switches/catalyst-9300-series-switches/white-paper-c87-742415.pdf

Configure IOx Package Signature Validation: https://www.cisco.com/c/en/us/support/docs/cloud-systems-management/iox/212472-configure-iox-package-signature-validati.html

Cisco Devnet, IOx: https://developer.cisco.com/docs/iox/

Docker Images and Packages Repository: https://developer.cisco.com/docs/iox/#!docker-images-and-packages-repository/overview

Wikipedia, Libvirt: https://en.wikipedia.org/wiki/Libvirt

Cisco IOx GitHub Page: Docker Demo Apps: https://github.com/CiscoIOx/docker-demo-apps.git

Cisco Smart Licensing: https://www.cisco.com/c/en/us/products/software/smart-accounts/software-licensing.html

Smart Licensing Guide for Access and Edge Routers: https://www.cisco.com/c/en/us/td/docs/ios-xml/ios/smart-licensing/qsg/b_Smart_Licensing_QuickStart/b_Smart_Licensing_QuickStart_chapter_01.html

## Chapter 6

Container Orchestration in Cisco IOS-XR Platforms

In this chapter, you will learn the following:

- Cisco IOS-XR Architecture and key software components and characteristics

- Platform support and environment readiness for application hosting

- Application hosting workflow—Native hosting, LXC-based, and Docker-based deployments

- Container management considerations

Cisco IOS-XR Architecture

In the 1980s, Cisco introduced the first internetwork operating system (IOS) for multi-protocol routers with limited memory and single-core CPUs with low processing power. Cisco IOS, a monolithic, kernel-based architecture with a centralized infrastructure, uses OS scheduler for scheduling and executing the processes. Each process running in IOS is single threaded, and a priority value is associated to each process to leverage the single core so that processes with higher priority can be executed before treating the low-priority processes. During the IOS days, CPU hogging was one of the common issues that affected network performance and availability. IOS software is compiled as a single file and integrates all the feature sets as a monolithic application stack. Any issue in one module requires a new image with the fix, which causes operational challenges for the network operators because it requires network downtime to upgrade and reload to fix the issues. The market demanded a product and network operating system that was not only more robust but could deliver better scalability and had easier maintenance.

Architecture and Software Evolution

Cisco launched the first generation of the Carrier Routing System (CRS-1) platform in 2004, and it was primarily positioned as a service provider core device that addressed the scale and performance challenges of the monolithic IOS operating system. Multicore CPU and high data rate memory (such as DDR, with a transfer rate of about 3 Gbps) are readily available to boost the performance of the routers. Cisco IOS-XR is a microkernel-based software architecture that is highly scalable, modular, and distributed. IOS-XR software is packaged as Package Installation Envelopes (PIE), which include a combination of mandatory components to boot the router and optional components to enable certain network services, as shown in Figure 6-1.

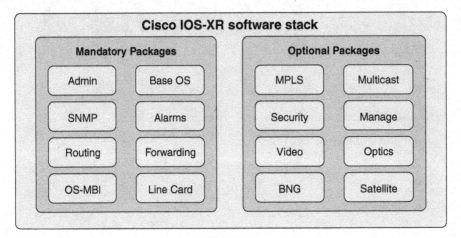

Figure 6-1   *Cisco IOS-XR Software Stack*

The core image includes these mandatory components:

Boot OS with Kernel components such as file system, memory management, and the like

- Base component for interface handling, configuration management, and so on

- Admin components to handle the RP, Fabric, LC, and so on

- Forwarding component

- Routing protocol stack

Other feature sets, such as MPLS, Multicast, and Security features, are available as optional PIE that can be installed and enabled only if those features are required. Such high modularity also allows the network operators to fix any issue in one component by simply upgrading the relevant PIE or component. Software Maintenance Upgrade (SMU) is a software patch PIE with a fix for some defects that can be installed to resolve an issue in a specific component without upgrading the base or core image.

The evolution of Cisco IOS-XR architecture is shown in Figure 6-2.

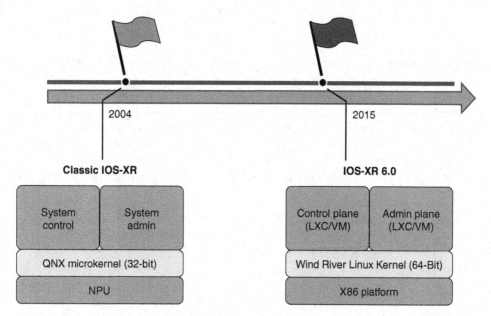

Figure 6-2 *Cisco IOS-XR Architecture Evolution*

The first released Cisco IOS-XR version 2.0 used 32-bit QNX microkernel to provide distributed infrastructure. QNX microkernel is powered with Neutrino, a message-passing operating system that inherited the design of interprocess communication (IPC) and executed the process based on priority. For nearly 10 years, IOS-XR software was built and maintained over QNX microkernel.

Around 2015, Cisco revamped and improved the IOS-XR software architecture by introducing 64-bit Linux-based kernel from version 6.0. IOS-XR Release 6.0 leveraged the virtualization capability of the underlying 64-bit Linux kernel and instantiated the Control and Admin Plane as Linux Containers (LXC) or as virtual machines. This is a huge breakthrough in the architecture that provided an opportunity for the operators to evolve and innovate faster. The new architecture retained the benefits of QNX-based architecture, such as modularity, and introduced additional benefits, such as automation, model-driven telemetry, and application hosting.

To embrace the evolving business opportunities around cloud-scale services, 5G, and programmability, Cisco introduced IOS-XR Release 7.0, which is tailored to fit different form factors with a rich set of features. Although version 7.0 was relatively new during the time of this book authoring, the application-hosting feature is not much different from the earlier versions, so the remaining portion of this chapter focuses on IOS-XR Release 6.5.x.

Application Hosting Architecture

The IOS-XR software architecture is largely classified into two types of deployments that vary based on the platform:

- **LXC deployment model:** NCS5xxx series platforms and virtual XR routers

- **Virtual machine deployment model:** ASR9xxx series platforms

In the LXC deployment model, the components of the software are deployed as Linux containers directly on top of the host Linux kernel. In contrast, the virtual machine deployment model deploys the software components as a virtual machine with its own kernel on top of the host Linux kernel. The LXC deployment model is lightweight and cannot support an in-service software upgrade (ISSU), whereas virtual machine–based deployment can.

With any of the preceding deployment models, the underlying architectural concept is to leverage the **libvirt** daemon in the Linux kernel to instantiate the control and admin plane as LXC/virtual machine on top of the host Linux kernel, as shown in Figure 6-3.

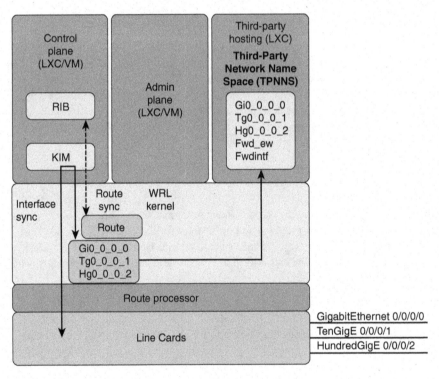

Figure 6-3   *Virtualized Cisco IOS-XR Components*

- **Admin plane:** This is the first virtual instance that will be booted once the host kernel is up. The admin plane is responsible for managing the lifecycle of the other containers, such as the control plane or the third-party hosting space. It runs the processes that are responsible for environment variables, diags, and the like. This is a sensitive container; access to this space is limited for security purposes.

- **XR control plane:** This LXC/virtual machine runs the network control plane processes such as BGP, MPLS, and other standard Linux tools, such as Python and bash. Any native application can be hosted in this space.

- **Third-party hosting plane:** This is an LXC space that is dedicated for hosting third-party applications. It provides network access through the XR dataplane FIB using virtual interfaces connecting this space to the FIB. In a virtual machine–based deployment model, this space is hosted as LXC inside the Control Plane virtual machine.

Kernel Interface Module (KIM)

Kernel Interface Module (KIM) is one of the critical modules that plays a key role in providing the application-hosting service in Cisco IOS-XR software. KIM is a process that runs in the Control Plane LXC/virtual machine. It is responsible for the following:

- **Interface sync:** When a new line card is brought up, the interfaces are mirrored and synchronized with the kernel. KIM communicates with the interface manager component to get the interface details from both the RP and the line card, and they populate the kernel with the same. A sample output from the kernel listing different types of interfaces is shown in Example 6-1.

- **Route sync:** KIM does not synchronize the entire RIB table to the kernel. Instead, it leverages the TPA configuration from the router to populate the default route in the kernel with the relevant egress interface and source address to be used.

- **VRF sync:** By default, there are two network namespaces that are created in the kernel: XRNNS and TPNNS. KIM is responsible for creating network namespaces for each VRF that is configured and enabled under TPA router configuration mode.

- **Transport layer socket sync:** When any native or third-party–hosted application attempts to open a local transport layer port for listening, KIM programs the kernel with the details so that any packet can be interpreted by the LPTS and forwarded to the application for further processing. The netlink messages generated by the application requesting to open or close a port will be used by KIM to program the kernel.

Example 6-1   *Mirrored Interface in IOS-XR Host Kernel*

```
[NCS-540-A:~]$ ifconfig -a | grep ink
BundleEth1 Link encap:Ethernet  HWaddr 00:bc:60:05:04:dd
BundleEth1.100 Link encap:Ethernet  HWaddr 00:bc:60:05:04:dd
Gi0_0_0_3 Link encap:Ethernet  HWaddr 00:bc:60:05:04:0c
Hg0_0_1_0 Link encap:Ethernet  HWaddr 00:bc:60:05:04:80
Tg0_0_0_1 Link encap:Ethernet  HWaddr 00:bc:60:05:04:04
```

Note: In most Linux distributions, the **ifconfig** command will only list the interfaces that are up. Instead, **ifconfig -a** should be used to list all the interfaces, including the ones that are in a down state.

A sample output of the KIM process captured from IOS-XR platform is shown in Example 6-2.

Example 6-2   *Kernel Interface Module Process Output*

```
RP/0/RP0/CPU0:ios#show processes kim
Fri Oct  4 19:17:50.425 UTC
                Job Id: 299
                   PID: 5485
          Process name: kim
        Executable path: /opt/cisco/XR/packages/xrv9k-iosxr-infra-6.0.0.0-r652/rp/
   bin/kim
            Instance #: 1
            Version ID: 00.00.0000
               Respawn: ON
         Respawn count: 1
          Last started: Wed Oct  2 18:51:26 2019
         Process state: Run
         Package state: Normal
                  core: MAINMEM
             Max. core: 0
                 Level: 101
             Placement: None
          startup_path: /opt/cisco/XR/packages/xrv9k-iosxr-infra-6.0.0.0-r652/rp/
   startup/kim.startup
                 Ready: 15.443s
             Available: 15.444s
       Process cpu time: 44.440 user, 29.540 kernel, 73.980 total
JID    TID  Stack  pri  state      NAME           rt_pri
299    5485  0K   20   Sleeping   kim            0
299    5517  0K   20   Sleeping   lwm_debug_threa 0
```

```
299    5518    OK   20    Sleeping    kim               0
299    5519    OK   20    Sleeping    lwm_service_thr   0
299    5520    OK   20    Sleeping    qsm_service_thr   0
299    5531    OK   20    Sleeping    kim               0
299    6144    OK   20    Sleeping    kim               0
299    6150    OK   20    Sleeping    kim               0
299    6499    OK   20    Sleeping    kim               0
299    6500    OK   20    Sleeping    kim               0
299    7111    OK   20    Sleeping    kim               0
299    7112    OK   20    Sleeping    kim               0
299    7114    OK   20    Sleeping    kim               0
-----------------------------------------------------------------------
RP/0/RP0/CPU0:ios#
RP/0/RP0/CPU0:ios#show kim status
Fri Oct  4 18:45:42.414 UTC
Features:
   VRF namespaces                : Enabled
   VLAN interfaces               : Enabled
   VRF dataport interfaces       : Enabled
IM Connection                  : Connected (1 attempts/0 disconnects)
LPTS PA Connection             : Connected (0 disconnects)
Num socket bindings            : 0
Num Interfaces                 : 3
Loopback interfaces            : 0
Mgmt interfaces                : 1
LC interfaces                  : 2
IPv4 RIB routes                : 0
IPv6 RIB routes                : 0
Forwarding LC NPU ID           : 4288
Forwarding i/f MTU             : 1482
IPV4 Source Address            : via Configuration
                    Interface: GigabitEthernet0_0_0_0
            Chosen source IP: 10.1.1.1
IPV6 Source Address            : Not Configured

RP/0/RP0/CPU0:ios#
```

Network Namespaces

The kernel uses the network namespace to isolate the network resources. As explained in Chapter 4, "Container Networking Concepts," two types of namespaces are created by default in the XR platform:

- XR Network Namespace (XRNNS)

- Third-Party Network Namespace (TPNNS)

More detailed explanations about the namespaces are available in Chapter 3, "Container Orchestration and Management." Sample output of the namespaces from the kernel is shown in Example 6-3.

Example 6-3 *Network Namespace Output*

```
[host:~]$ ip netns list
tpnns
xrnns
global-vrf
[host:~]$
[host:~]$ ip netns exec global-vrf ip link
1: lo: <LOOPBACK,UP,LOWER_UP> mtu 65536 qdisc noqueue state UNKNOWN mode DEFAULT
  group default
    link/loopback 00:00:00:00:00:00 brd 00:00:00:00:00:00
6: fwdintf: <MULTICAST,NOARP,UP,LOWER_UP> mtu 1482 qdisc pfifo_fast state UNKNOWN
  mode DEFAULT group default qlen 1000
    link/ether 00:00:00:00:00:0a brd ff:ff:ff:ff:ff:ff
7: fwd_ew: <MULTICAST,NOARP,UP,LOWER_UP> mtu 1500 qdisc pfifo_fast state UNKNOWN
  mode DEFAULT group default qlen 1000
    link/ether 00:00:00:00:00:0b brd ff:ff:ff:ff:ff:ff
8: Mg0_RP0_CPU0_0: <> mtu 1514 qdisc noop state DOWN mode DEFAULT group default
  qlen 1000
    link/ether 52:46:1a:1a:37:e6 brd ff:ff:ff:ff:ff:ff
9: Gi0_0_0_0: <MULTICAST,NOARP,UP,LOWER_UP> mtu 1500 qdisc pfifo_fast state
  UNKNOWN mode DEFAULT group default qlen 1000
    link/ether 52:46:f8:b8:27:88 brd ff:ff:ff:ff:ff:ff
11: Gi0_0_0_2: <> mtu 1514 qdisc noop state DOWN mode DEFAULT group default
  qlen 1000
    link/ether 52:46:11:1d:50:8b brd ff:ff:ff:ff:ff:ff
[host:~]$
```

Docker Hosting Architecture

Like the libvirtd daemon, the Docker daemon is enabled by default in the Linux kernel. The location of the daemon varies depending on the type of architecture. In the LXC deployment model, the Docker daemon is seen running in the host kernel; in the virtual machine deployment model, the Docker daemon is enabled in the kernel of the XR virtual machine. Docker is enabled by default and does not need additional router configuration or a manual procedure to start the service from the kernel. The architecture is shown in Figure 6-4.

While the Docker daemon runs in the kernel, the Docker client is available inside the XR Control Plane LXC. The user uses the Docker client to execute any native Docker commands to orchestrate the container instantiation. Both the Docker client and the daemon are running version 1.10, as shown in Example 6-4.

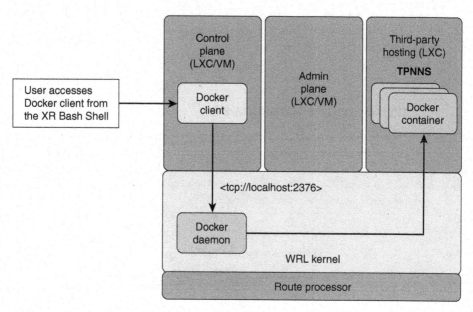

Figure 6-4 *Docker Hosting Architecture*

Example 6-4 *Docker Output*

```
RP/0/RP0/CPU0:ios#
RP/0/RP0/CPU0:ios#bash
Fri Oct  4 20:03:24.922 UTC
[host:~]$ docker version
Client:
 Version:      1.10.0
 API version:  1.22
 Go version:   go1.4.2
 Git commit:   cb6da92
 Built:        Tue Aug  8 22:08:35 2017
 OS/Arch:      linux/amd64

Server:
 Version:      1.10.0
 API version:  1.22
 Go version:   go1.4.2
 Git commit:   cb6da92
 Built:        Tue Aug  8 22:08:35 2017
 OS/Arch:      linux/amd64
[host:~]$
```

Note: Neither the Docker version of the client nor the daemon can be upgraded from the router. However, most of the essential features are available in this version.

Hosting Environment Readiness

This section takes a quick look at the hosting environment readiness for each of the Cisco IOS-XR platforms, along with the software version required to support them. As discussed in the previous section, IOS-XR version 6.0 introduced the 64-bit Linux kernel; prior versions do not support application hosting. The summary of the supported software version for each platform is shown in Table 6-1.

Table 6-1 *Cisco IOS-XR Software Readiness for Application Hosting*

Platform	Minimum Supported Software Version	
	LXC/Native App Hosting	**Docker**
ASR9000	6.0	6.1.2
NCS5x00/NCS5xx	6.0	6.1.2
IOS-XRv9k	6.0	6.1.2

The density of the applications that can be hosted in any computing platform is limited by the availability of the resources, such as vCPU, vMemory, and vStorage. This holds true for the IOS-XR platform as well. The next section discusses the essential resources for application hosting.

Storage

A logical volume of storage **/misc/app_host** is mounted by the underlying host kernel to the XR Control Plane LXC for application hosting. By default, this volume is allocated with a space of about 3.7 GB for NCS5000 and NCS500 series platforms, while the size is about 4 GB for other platforms, including virtual routers. This space is shared by both LXC and Docker-based application hosting. Sample output of the volume is shown in Example 6-5.

Example 6-5 *Application Hosting Volume Output*

```
[host:~]$ df -h
Filesystem                          Size  Used Avail Use% Mounted on
/dev/loop5                          2.9G  1.3G  1.5G  48% /
run                                 9.8G  480K  9.8G   1% /bindmnt_netns
```

```
devfs                                        64K   16K   48K  25% /dev
tmpfs                                        64K    0    64K   0% /dev/cgroup
/dev/mapper/panini_vol_grp-host_lv0         969M  389M  515M  44% /dev/sde
none                                        9.8G  746M  9.0G   8% /dev/shm
none                                        9.8G  746M  9.0G   8% /dev/shm
/dev/mapper/app_vol_grp-app_lv0             3.9G  958M  2.8G  26% /misc/app_host
tmpfs                                       9.8G    0   9.8G   0% /var/volatile
tmpfs                                       9.8G   56K  9.8G   1% /run
tmpfs                                       9.8G    0   9.8G   0% /media/ram
tmpfs                                        64M  152K   64M   1% /tmp
tmpfs                                        64M  152K   64M   1% /tmp
/dev/mapper/panini_vol_grp-ssd_disk1_xr_1   1.5G  8.3M  1.4G   1% /misc/disk1
/dev/mapper/xr-vm_encrypted_log             475M   11M  435M   3% /var/log
/dev/mapper/xr-vm_encrypted_config          475M  2.4M  443M   1% /misc/config
/dev/mapper/xr-vm_encrypted_scratch         989M  6.0M  916M   1% /misc/scratch
none                                        512K    0   512K   0% /mnt
[host:~]$
```

CPU Share

System resources that are shared by containers or virtual machines hosted on a physical host are controlled by the control groups (cgroups). The allocation of vCPU resources is based on CPU shares instead of counts. A CPU share determines the relative amount of CPU time for the tasks to be executed.

The resource allocation for LXC and Docker-based application hosting is governed by cgroup settings in the host kernel. Although most of the IOS-XR platforms are equipped with 4-core CPU processors, 1024 CPU shares are allocated for application hosting, as shown in Example 6-6.

Example 6-6 *CPU Share Output*

```
RP/0/RP0/CPU0:ios#bash
Fri Oct  4 21:43:17.340 UTC
[host:~]$
[host:~]$ cat /dev/cgroup/cpu/cpu.shares
1024
[host:~]$
```

Within a cgroup hierarchy, the CPU share is distributed based on the subgroups at each level. The subgroup sharing the CPU in IOS-XR platform is shown in Example 6-7.

Example 6-7　*cgroup Hierarchy for CPU Shares*

```
[host:~]$ tree -d /dev/cgroup/cpu
/dev/cgroup/cpu
'-- machine
    |-- default-sdr--1.libvirt-lxc
    |-- default-sdr--2.libvirt-lxc
    |   |-- uvfcp
    |   '-- uvfdp
    |-- sysadmin.libvirt-lxc
    '-- tp_app.partition
        |-- docker
        |   |-- 19122794eb3073642bf2181278b2421d39436eb29f249973cb537dabe9961150
        |   '-- 545e5a9a3668dd59f6b3f77022c8ea2116a1ebbef70f3b024f74669913dc780e
        '-- lxc.partition
11 directories
[host:~]$
```

Note:　A detailed output of the CPU shares allocated to different levels requires the user to log in to Admin Plane LXC. This information is not available from the XR bash shell.

Although theoretically each group or subgroup will get the same share of CPU, it is assumed that the processes running are equal on all groups. The CPU share is allocated based on the combination of shares available and the processes running on each group.

Memory

Similar to CPU shares, memory allocation is controlled by cgroup settings. By default, the memory limitation for third-party application hosting is 512 MB, as shown in Example 6-8.

Example 6-8　*cgroup Memory Output*

```
[host:~]$ cat /dev/cgroup/memory/memory.limit_in_bytes
6442450944
[host:~]$
[host:]$ more /dev/cgroup/memory/machine/tp_app.partition/memory.limit_in_bytes
536870912
[host:]$
```

Note:　The preceding limitation is shared by both LXC and Docker-based application hosting. Together, they cannot exceed 512 MB.

The summary of the resource allocation for application hosting in various IOS-XR platforms is shown in Table 6-2.

Table 6-2 *Resource Allocation for Application Hosting*

Platform	Disk Volume	vCPU Shares	Memory
ASR9000	3.9 G	1024	512 MB
NCS5x00/NCS5xx	3.7 G	1024	512 MB
IOS-XRv9k	3.9 G	1024	512 MB

Types of Application Hosting in Cisco XR Platform

Based on the application hosting architecture explained in the previous section, there are different supported ways of hosting an application or container in Cisco IOS-XR:

- Native Application Hosting
- LXC-Based Application Hosting
- Docker-Based Application Hosting

Native Application Hosting

Hosting an application natively is nothing more than installing and enabling the relevant binary packages directly on the operating system. With that said, the resource allocation is limited and will be shared with the operating system. The native application is hosted as a process in a global-VRF network namespace, as shown in Figure 6-5.

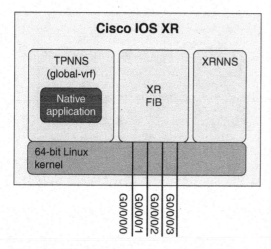

Figure 6-5 *Native Application Hosting*

By now, you know that the Linux OS used in Cisco IOS-XR is WRL version 7, which leverages RedHat Package Manager (RPM), an open-source package management tool for building or installing native applications. To install a native application in WRL, you need to get the relevant application in the RPM binary file format. The RPM binary file can be downloaded from any repository (if one is readily available), or it can be custom-built using SDK.

This section explains how to install the native application in the global-vrf network namespace. You might have noticed that WRL is not as common as other distributions like Ubuntu or Centos, and there may not be many repositories with native RPM files for network applications. To help its customers, Cisco maintains a repository for native network applications for WRL in Cisco devhub. Alternatively, you can build your own RPM file using the SDK that Cisco offers.

Note: Access to https://devhub.cisco.com/artifactory requires Cisco CCO ID.

Native Hosting from an Existing RPM File

Cisco maintains a repository of RPM files that can be readily installed in WRL distribution. The repository is accessible for any users who have Cisco CCO ID using https://devhub.cisco.com/artifactory/. Some of the well-known applications, such as iPerf, tcpdump, and Perl tools, are available as RPM files in the repository. These files can be downloaded and installed natively in the global-vrf network namespace, as shown in Figure 6-6.

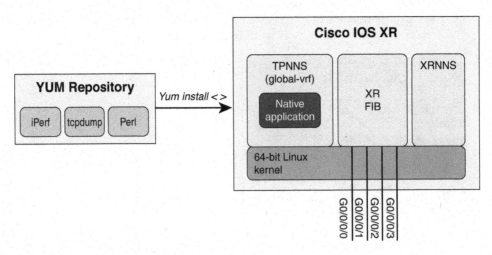

Figure 6-6   *RPM-Based Native Application Hosting*

The native application must be installed in the global-vrf, so the users must log in to the namespace using the **bash** command from the CLI, as shown in Example 6-9.

Example 6-9 *Network Namespace Identity*

```
RP/0/RP0/CPU0:ios#
RP/0/RP0/CPU0:ios#bash
Tue Oct  1 12:30:44.968 UTC
[host:~]$
[host:~]$ netns_identify $$
tpnns
global-vrf
[host:~]$
```

WRL distribution uses YUM to install the binary packages from the defined repository. By default, there is no YUM repository added to the WRL distribution in the Cisco IOS-XR platform, as shown in Example 6-10.

Example 6-10 *YUM Default Repository*

```
[host:~]$ yum repolist all
Loaded plugins: downloadonly, protect-packages, rpm-persistence
repolist: 0
[host:~]$
```

To define a new YUM repository, you can add a repository either by using the **yum-config-manager** command or by editing the **/etc/yum/yum.conf** file. In this example, the command prompt was used to add the repository, as shown in Example 6-11.

Example 6-11 *YUM Repository Configuration*

```
[host:~]$ yum-config-manager  --add-repo https://devhub.cisco.com/artifactory/
  xr600/3rdparty/x86_64/
adding repo from: https://devhub.cisco.com/artifactory/xr600/3rdparty/x86_64/

[devhub.cisco.com_artifactory_xr600_3rdparty_x86_64_]
name=added from: https://devhub.cisco.com/artifactory/xr600/3rdparty/x86_64/
baseurl=https://devhub.cisco.com/artifactory/xr600/3rdparty/x86_64/
enabled=1


[host:~]$
```

Note: As a best practice, it is suggested that you remove the repository using **yum-config-manager --disable <>** after the package is installed. This helps avoid any accidental installations or access to malicious users to install irrelevant packages.

Once the YUM repository is defined, you can install the RPM binary files. Example 6-12 shows an example of how to install iPerf3 from the repository.

Example 6-12 *Installing Native Application Using YUM*

```
[host:~]$ yum install https://devhub.cisco.com/artifactory/xr600/3rdparty/x86_64/iperf3-
  3.0.10+gitr0+de420cc741-r0.0.core2_64.rpm
Loaded plugins: downloadonly, protect-packages, rpm-persistence
Setting up Install Process
iperf3-3.0.10+gitr0+de420cc741-r0.0.core2_64.rpm                      |  55 kB    00:00
Examining /var/tmp/yum-root-v69egx/iperf3-3.0.10+gitr0+de420cc741-r0.0.core2_64.rpm:
  iperf3-3.0.10+gitr0+de420cc741-r0.0.core2_64
Marking /var/tmp/yum-root-v69egx/iperf3-3.0.10+gitr0+de420cc741-r0.0.core2_64.rpm to be
  installed
Resolving Dependencies
--> Running transaction check
---> Package iperf3.core2_64 0:3.0.10+gitr0+de420cc741-r0.0 will be installed
--> Finished Dependency Resolution


Dependencies Resolved


================================================================================
 Package Arch        Version                      Repository              Size
================================================================================
Installing:
 iperf3  core2_64    3.0.10+gitr0+de420cc741-r0.0  /iperf3-3.0.10+gitr0+    121 k
                                                   de420cc741-r0.0.core2_64


Transaction Summary
================================================================================
Install       1 Package

Total size: 121 k
Installed size: 121 k
Is this ok [y/N]: y
Downloading Packages:
Running Transaction Check
Running Transaction Test
Transaction Test Succeeded
Running Transaction
Warning: RPMDB altered outside of yum.
  Installing : iperf3-3.0.10+gitr0+de420cc741-r0.0.core2_64                      1/1


Installed:
  iperf3.core2_64 0:3.0.10+gitr0+de420cc741-r0.0


Complete!
[host:~]$
```

iPerf3 is now installed and ready to be used from the global-vrf network namespace, as shown in Example 6-13.

Example 6-13 *iPerf Application*

```
[host:~]$ iperf3 -v
iperf 3.0.10
Linux host 3.14.23-WR7.0.0.2 _ standard #1 SMP Tue Jun 26 01:02:11 PDT 2018 x86 _ 64 x86 _ 64
  x86 _ 64 GNU/Linux
[host:~]$ iperf3 --help
Usage: iperf [-s|-c host] [options]
       iperf [-h|--help] [-v|--version]


Server or Client:
  -p, --port       #          server port to listen on/connect to
  -f, --format     [kmgKMG]   format to report: Kbits, Mbits, KBytes, MBytes
  -i, --interval   #          seconds between periodic bandwidth reports
  -F, --file name             xmit/recv the specified file
  -A, --affinity n/n,m        set CPU affinity
  -B, --bind       <host>     bind to a specific interface
  -V, --verbose               more detailed output
  -J, --json                  output in JSON format
  -d, --debug                 emit debugging output
  -v, --version               show version information and quit
  -h, --help                  show this message and quit
Server specific:
  -s, --server                run in server mode
  -D, --daemon                run the server as a daemon
Client specific:
  -c, --client     <host>     run in client mode, connecting to <host>
  -u, --udp                   use UDP rather than TCP
  -b, --bandwidth #[KMG][/#]  target bandwidth in bits/sec (0 for unlimited)
                              (default 1 Mbit/sec for UDP, unlimited for TCP)
                              (optional slash and packet count for burst mode)
  -t, --time       #          time in seconds to transmit for (default 10 secs)
  -n, --bytes      #[KMG]     number of bytes to transmit (instead of -t)
  -k, --blockcount #[KMG]     number of blocks (packets) to transmit (instead of -t or -n)
  -l, --len        #[KMG]     length of buffer to read or write
                              (default 128 KB for TCP, 8 KB for UDP)
  -P, --parallel   #          number of parallel client streams to run
  -R, --reverse               run in reverse mode (server sends, client receives)
  -w, --window     #[KMG]     set window size / socket buffer size
  -C, --linux-congestion <algo>  set TCP congestion control algorithm (Linux only)
  -M, --set-mss    #          set TCP maximum segment size (MTU - 40 bytes)
 -N, --nodelay                set TCP no delay, disabling Nagle's Algorithm
  -4, --version4              only use IPv4
  -6, --version6              only use IPv6
```

```
 -S, --tos N                 set the IP 'type of service'
 -L, --flowlabel N           set the IPv6 flow label (only supported on Linux)
 -Z, --zerocopy              use a 'zero copy' method of sending data
 -O, --omit N                omit the first n seconds
 -T, --title str             prefix every output line with this string
 --get-server-output         get results from server


[KMG] indicates options that support a K/M/G suffix for kilo-, mega-, or giga-


iperf3 homepage at: http://software.es.net/iperf/
Report bugs to:     https://github.com/esnet/iperf
[host:~]$
```

When iPerf is enabled, the process starts listening to the relevant port. For example, when iPerf3 is enabled as a server using the **iperf3 -s <>** command, it starts listening to port 5201, as shown in Example 6-14.

Example 6-14 *iPerf Server Command*

```
[host:~]$ iperf3 -s -f K                             .
-----------------------------------------------------------
Server listening on 5201
-----------------------------------------------------------



[host:~]$ netstat -nlp | grep 5201
tcp6     0      0 :::5201                :::*          LISTEN     7762/iperf3
[host:~]$
```

Note: A detailed explanation about the use of the iPerf3 tool is available at https://iperf. fr/iperf-doc.php.

Although this section was explained with iPerf3 as the application that is natively installed, any other application can be installed using a similar mechanism as long as the RPM file is available from any repository.

Building an RPM File for Native Hosting

The management tools used by the operators vary for each network depending on the use case or the specific problem they are trying to solve. It is hard to identify all the RPM files that are readily available in the repository for installation. When the required RPM binary file for any specific application or tool is not available in the repository, you can use the SDK tools to build and convert the application into an RPM file that can be natively installed.

This section discusses the steps to build an RPM package and install it natively in the Cisco IOS-XR platform.

The WRL environment in the Cisco IOS-XR platform is not natively enabled with SDK to build the RPM, so you need to set up an external environment to build the package. Several approaches are possible to set up the build environment as below:

■ Launch a WRL virtual machine from the ISO image using KVM or Virsh.

■ Launch the cross-built SDK from Cisco Devhub.

The cross-built SDK is a package that is readily available in Cisco Devhub with all the libraries and binaries installed to build the package in any Linux environment such as Ubuntu. Accordingly, it is the most preferable option when compared to launching the native WRL virtual machine.

Install the SDK and get the build environment ready, as shown in Example 6-15.

Example 6-15 *Installing the SDK*

```
root@nsoserver:~#
root@nsoserver:~# wget https://devhub.cisco.com/artifactory/xr600/app-dev-sdk/
  x86_64/wrlinux-7.0.0.2-glibc-x86_64-intel_x86_64-wrlinux-image-glibc-std-sdk.sh
--2019-10-05 12:59:41--  https://devhub.cisco.com/artifactory/xr600/app-dev-sdk/
  x86_64/wrlinux-7.0.0.2-glibc-x86_64-intel_x86_64-wrlinux-image-glibc-std-sdk.sh
Resolving devhub.cisco.com (devhub.cisco.com)... 52.73.133.198, 3.225.96.245
Connecting to devhub.cisco.com (devhub.cisco.com)|52.73.133.198|:443... connected.
HTTP request sent, awaiting response... 200 OK
Length: 1430886577 (1.3G) [text/x-script.sh]
Saving to: 'wrlinux-7.0.0.2-glibc-x86_64-intel_x86_64-wrlinux-image-glibc-std-sdk.
  sh'


wrlinux-7.0.0.2-glibc-x86_64-intel_x
  100%[===================================================================>]
  1.33G  2.41MB/s    in 7m 27s


2019-10-05 13:07:08 (3.06 MB/s) - 'wrlinux-7.0.0.2-glibc-x86_64-intel_x86_64-
  wrlinux-image-glibc-std-sdk.sh' saved [1430886577/1430886577]


root@nsoserver:~# ./wrlinux-7.0.0.2-glibc-x86_64-intel_x86_64-wrlinux-image-glibc-
  std-sdk.sh
Enter target directory for SDK (default: /opt/windriver/wrlinux/7.0-intel-x86-64):
  /home/ubuntu/
The directory "/home/ubuntu" already contains a SDK for this architecture.
If you continue, existing files will be overwritten! Proceed[y/N]?y
Extracting SDK...
root@nsoserver:~#
```

With these steps completed, the SDK is installed and ready to be used. Building the RPM package requires the following:

■ **RPM Spec file:** Specifications to build the package

■ **Application file:** The application that should be built as a package

The application can be custom-built by the operator, or it can be downloaded from any public repository. A plethora of network opensource tools can be downloaded and used, or the application can be tailored to fit the operator's requirement.

A sample RPM spec file for the iPerf application is shown in Example 6-16.

Example 6-16 *RPM Spec File*

```
Name: iperf
Version: x.x.x
Release: XR_6.5.2
License: Copyright (c) 2015 Cisco Systems Inc. All rights reserved.
Packager: cisco
SOURCE0 : %{name}-%{version}-source.tar.gz
Group: 3rd party application
Summary: iperf compiled for CiscoPress

%description
This is a compiled version of iPerf for CiscoPress book

%prep

%setup -q -n %{name}-%{version}

%build
./configure
make

%install
mkdir -p %{buildroot}%{_sbindir}
install -m755 src/iperf %{buildroot}%{_sbindir}

%files

%defattr(-,root,root)
%{_sbindir}/iperf

%clean
rm -rf %{buildroot}
```

Note: If you are interested in learning more about RPM spec file creation or if you need any clarity, please refer to http://ftp.rpm.org/max-rpm/s1-rpm-build-creating-spec-file.html.

Build the application as an RPM package by running the following command:

```
root@nsoserver:~# rpmbuild -ba iperf.spec
```

The package is now ready to be transferred to the router and installed natively as any other RPM package.

Note: As you will learn from the remaining part of this chapter, there are easier ways to implement an application as a container, so it is rare to see a need to build an RPM package for native installation.

LXC-Based Application Hosting

The previous section explained how an application is natively implemented on a Cisco IOS-XR router. However, it should be noted that the native hosting is limited to the application that can run directly on the WRL environment. There are good business reasons why any network operator would like to have the liberty to instantiate applications without such environmental limitations.

This section explains the method to build your own isolated environment along with the applications and leverage the LXC capability to instantiate the same on the Cisco IOS-XR platform. A summary of the workflow to build and instantiate the application is shown here.

1. Build an isolated environment such as Ubuntu or Centos virtual machine in an external development environment and install the relevant applications.

2. Identify the root filesystem (rootfs) of the isolated environment and convert the **rootfs** into a tar ball.

3. Copy the **rootfs** tarball to a third-party network namespace (TPNNS) of the Cisco IOS-XR platform.

4. Create an LXC manifest file describing the resource requirement to host the application. The resource definition includes vCPU share, memory, disk capacity, network namespace, and more.

5. Untar the rootfs file and instantiate the application using LXC commands.

This workflow is shown in Figure 6-7.

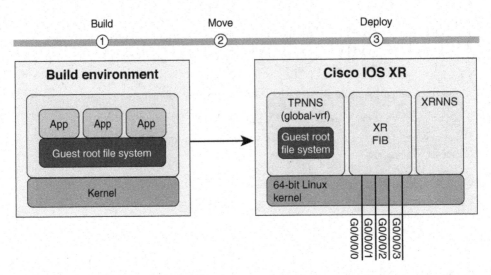

Figure 6-7 *Build Your Own Application*

The workflow starts by building a virtual machine in an external build environment. The choice of the build environment is completely up to the users. It can be a vagrant box or a Linux server that is enabled with LXC. In this section, an LXC-based build environment was used to build a Centos virtual machine and install a couple of applications.

LXC is used to create a Centos 7 virtual machine named **cisco-centos** in a development environment, as shown in Example 6-17.

Example 6-17 *Launching Virtual Machine in Dev Environment*

```
ubuntu@openconfig:~$ lxc launch images:centos/7 cisco-centos
Creating cisco-centos
Starting cisco-centos
ubuntu@openconfig
ubuntu@openconfig:~$ lxc list cisco-centos
+--------------+----------+------+------+------------+-----------+
|     NAME     |  STATE   | IPV4 | IPV6 |    TYPE    | SNAPSHOTS |
+--------------+----------+------+------+------------+-----------+
| cisco-centos | RUNNING  |      |      | PERSISTENT | 0         |
+--------------+----------+------+------+------------+-----------+
ubuntu@openconfig:~$
```

Log in to the bash prompt of the Centos virtual machine and install all the relevant applications. As shown in Example 6-18, tcpdump is installed in the Centos virtual machine; however, depending on the user requirement, additional applications along with the dependent extension modules may need to be installed.

tcpdump is an opensource network analysis tool that captures the raw packet from the specified interface and displays the packet header and payload field for analysis.

Example 6-18 *Installing Applications in the Test Virtual Machine*

```
ubuntu@openconfig:~$ lxc exec cisco-centos -- /bin/bash
[root@cisco-centos ~]#useradd cisco
[root@cisco-centos ~]#passwd cisco
Changing password for user cisco.
New password:
Retype new password:
passwd: all authentication tokens updated successfully.
[root@cisco-centos ~]#
[root@cisco-centos ~]# yum install tcpdump

Failed to set locale, defaulting to C
Loaded plugins: fastestmirror
Determining fastest mirrors
<truncated>
Complete!
[root@cisco-centos ~]#
```

Once all the applications, supporting binaries, and libraries are installed, the root filesystem is now ready for deployment. The root filesystem contains the minimum files that are mandatory for booting the system to mount the other files and applications.

Depending on the type of development environment used, the location of the root file system may vary. When LXC is used, the rootfs for each container is available in **/var/lib/lxd/containers/<container-name>/**, as shown in Example 6-19.

Example 6-19 *LXC Container Root Filesystem*

```
root@openconfig:/var/lib/lxd/containers/cisco-centos/rootfs# ls -l
total 16
lrwxrwxrwx 1 100000 100000    7 Sep 23 07:16 bin -> usr/bin
dr-xr-xr-x 1 100000 100000    0 Apr 11  2018 boot
drwxr-xr-x 1 100000 100000    0 Sep 23 07:22 dev
drwxr-xr-x 1 100000 100000 2310 Sep 23 14:34 etc
drwxr-xr-x 1 100000 100000   10 Sep 23 14:33 home
lrwxrwxrwx 1 100000 100000    7 Sep 23 07:16 lib -> usr/lib
lrwxrwxrwx 1 100000 100000    9 Sep 23 07:16 lib64 -> usr/lib64
drwxr-xr-x 1 100000 100000    0 Apr 11  2018 media
drwxr-xr-x 1 100000 100000    0 Apr 11  2018 mnt
drwxr-xr-x 1 100000 100000    0 Apr 11  2018 opt
dr-xr-xr-x 1 100000 100000    0 Apr 11  2018 proc
dr-xr-x--- 1 100000 100000  116 Sep 23 14:34 root
drwxr-xr-x 1 100000 100000   10 Sep 23 07:16 run
lrwxrwxrwx 1 100000 100000    8 Sep 23 07:16 sbin -> usr/sbin
drwxr-xr-x 1 100000 100000   14 Sep 23 07:18 selinux
```

```
drwxr-xr-x 1 100000 100000     0 Apr 11  2018 srv
dr-xr-xr-x 1 100000 100000     0 Apr 11  2018 sys
drwxrwxrwt 1 100000 100000   176 Sep 23 14:33 tmp
drwxr-xr-x 1 100000 100000   106 Sep 23 07:16 usr
drwxr-xr-x 1 100000 100000   176 Sep 23 14:32 var
root@openconfig:/var/lib/lxd/containers/cisco-centos/rootfs#
```

All the files listed in the rootfs folder are mandatory and should be copied to the Cisco IOS-XR platform. The simple option is to convert the content of the rootfs folder into a tarball. Then copy and untar the file to the router in the respective folder, as shown in Example 6-20.

Example 6-20 *Packing the LXC Container Root File System*

```
root@openconfig:/var/lib/lxd/containers/cisco-centos/rootfs# tar -czf centos.tar.gz *
root@openconfig:/var/lib/lxd/containers/cisco-centos/rootfs#
root@openconfig:/var/lib/lxd/containers/cisco-centos/rootfs# scp cisco@10.1.1.1:/misc/
  app_host/ ./centos.tar.gz
The authenticity of host '10.1.1.1 (10.1.1.1)' can't be established.
RSA key fingerprint is SHA256:n6sl3QYC4UUbeE/VHBT1o9NfS3b+LcOn9cvqDbbVs8k.
Are you sure you want to continue connecting (yes/no)? yes
Warning: Permanently added '10.1.1.1' (RSA) to the list of known hosts.
Password:
root@openconfig:/var/lib/lxd/containers/cisco-centos/rootfs#
```

Note: To access the **/var/lib/lxd/containers** location, the user must be logged in as a root user or have root access. Without root-level access, any content inside **/var/lib/lxd/** cannot be accessed. The root access can be achieved by switching the user to root using the **sudo -i** CLI command.

Note: As mentioned in the "Application Hosting Architecture" section, an isolated Linux environment known as TPNNS is provided to host third-party applications. The **bash** command is used to log in to the TPNNS shell prompt from the router, as shown in Example 6-21.

Example 6-21 *Log In to TPNNS Namespace*

```
RP/0/RP0/CPU0:ios#
RP/0/RP0/CPU0:ios#bash
Tue Sep 24 14:19:04.120 UTC
[host:~]$
 [host:~]$ netns_identify $$
tpnns
global-vrf
[host:~]$
```

Note: Although the **/misc/app_host/** location is also accessible from XRNNS, the namespace is meant for the XR control plane, and it is not advisable to run third-party applications here.

KVM/LXC uses the **virsh** CLI command to create or manage the application workload. When the **virsh** command is used, the resource definition must be declared as an XML file that will be used to allocate the required resources. The sample XML file used to deploy the Centos virtual machine is shown in Example 6-22.

Example 6-22   *LXC Spec File*

```
<domain xmlns:lxc="http://libvirt.org/schemas/domain/lxc/1.0" type="lxc">
<name>centos-vm</name>
<memory>327680</memory>
<os>
<type>exe</type>
<init>/sbin/init</init>
</os>
<lxc:namespace>
<sharenet type="netns" value="global-vrf" />
</lxc:namespace>
<vcpu>1</vcpu>
<clock offset="utc" />
<on_poweroff>destroy</on_poweroff>
<on_reboot>restart</on_reboot>
<on_crash>destroy</on_crash>
<devices>
<emulator>/usr/lib64/libvirt/libvirt_lxc</emulator>
<filesystem type="mount">
<source dir="/misc/app_host/centos/" />
<target dir="/" />
</filesystem>
<console type="pty" />
</devices>
<resource><partition>/machine/tp_app/lxc</partition></resource></domain>
```

Let's dissect the XML file to better understand some of the important elements and attributes that are used to define the resource description for the workload. The **type** attribute in the **<domain>** field specifies the virtualization technology used to instantiate the workload. In this example, LXC is used as the type. The **name** attribute provides a short name for the workload, and the operators are free to use any convenient name. The **memory** attribute defines the amount of memory that should be allocated for the workload during deployment.

The **type** attribute in the **<os>** field specifies the type of operating system. The OS type **exe** specifies the container-based virtualization. The **init** attribute defines the path to the **init** binary that is required to boot the workload.

The **lxc:namespace** attribute is an essential element that defines the network namespace for the workload. As explained in Chapter 5, "Container Orchestration in Cisco IOS-XE Platforms," global-vrf is the network namespace that houses all the interfaces. Third-party applications must use this network namespace. The **vcpu** attribute specifies the CPU share allocated to the workload.

The **on_poweroff, on_reboot**, and **on_crash** attributes specify the action during certain events. For example, the **on_reboot** attribute is configured as a **restart** that specifies the hypervisor to automatically start the workload when the router (and the hypervisor) is rebooted and comes back up.

The **source dir** attribute specifies the location of the root file system. This is where the **rootf** tarball will be copied and extracted.

Note: More details about the XML attributes are available at https://libvirt.org/formatcaps.html.

Create and configure the XML file with the previously mentioned content in the respective location where the **rootfs** content is copied, as shown in Example 6-23.

Example 6-23   *Preparing the Environment*

```
RP/0/RP0/CPU0:ios#bash
Tue Sep 24 15:26:17.795 UTC
 [host:~]$ sudo -i
[host:~]$ cd /misc/app_host/centos/
 [host:/misc/app_host/centos]$ ls centos.xml
centos.xml
[host:/misc/app_host/centos]$
```

The **libvirtd** daemon is used by virsh to launch the containers, and it is enabled by default on Cisco IOS-XR. It does not need special commands or configuration (see Example 6-24).

Example 6-24   *Libvirtd Daemon*

```
[host:/misc/app_host/centos]$ libvirtd --version
libvirtd (libvirt) 1.1.2
[host:/misc/app_host/centos]$
```

Note: To execute **virsh** commands, the user must have root access. Make sure the user has root access for a seamless workflow.

The application workload can be deployed now using the **virsh** command, as shown in Example 6-25.

Example 6-25   *Running the Application Using virsh*

```
[host:/misc/app_host/centos]$ virsh create centos.xml
Domain centos-vm created from centos.xml

 [host:/misc/app_host/centos]$ virsh list
 Id    Name                          State
 --------------------------------------------------
 1917  centos-vm                     running
 4166  default-sdr--2                running
 8303  sysadmin                      running
 21353 default-sdr--1                running

[host:/misc/app_host/centos]$
```

The workload is now up and running with the installed applications. The users are free to enable any of the installed applications by logging in to the workload console using SSH or the **virsh console** command, as shown in Example 6-26.

Example 6-26   *Log In to the Hosted Application*

```
[host:/misc/app_host/centos]$ virsh console centos-vm
Connected to domain centos-vm
Escape character is ^]
systemd 219 running in system mode. (+PAM +AUDIT +SELINUX +IMA -APPARMOR +SMACK
  +SYSVINIT +UTMP +LIBCRYPTSETUP +GCRYPT +GNUTLS +ACL +XZ +LZ4 -SECCOMP +BLKID +ELF-
  UTILS +KMOD +IDN)
Detected virtualization lxc-libvirt.
Detected architecture x86-64.

Welcome to CentOS Linux 7 (Core)!
<truncated>
host login: cisco
Password:
Last login: Mon Sep 23 15:53:25 on pts/0
-bash-4.2$
```

Note: The username and password must be created while building the virtual machine in the built environment.

Network Configuration and Verification

As explained in Chapter 4, the native application hosting on Cisco IOS-XR always uses shared networking, where the physical interfaces of the router are shared with the hosted application, as shown in Example 6-27.

Example 6-27   *Shared Network Output*

```
-bash-4.2$ ip addr
1: lo: <LOOPBACK,UP,LOWER_UP> mtu 65536 qdisc noqueue state UNKNOWN group default
    link/loopback 00:00:00:00:00:00 brd 00:00:00:00:00:00
    inet 127.0.0.1/8 scope host lo
       valid_lft forever preferred_lft forever
    inet6 ::1/128 scope host
       valid_lft forever preferred_lft forever
6: fwdintf: <MULTICAST,NOARP,UP,LOWER_UP> mtu 1482 qdisc pfifo_fast state UNKNOWN
  group default qlen 1000
    link/ether 00:00:00:00:00:0a brd ff:ff:ff:ff:ff:ff
    inet6 fe80::200:ff:fe00:a/64 scope link
       valid_lft forever preferred_lft forever
7: fwd_ew: <MULTICAST,NOARP,UP,LOWER_UP> mtu 1500 qdisc pfifo_fast state UNKNOWN
  group default qlen 1000
    link/ether 00:00:00:00:00:0b brd ff:ff:ff:ff:ff:ff
    inet6 fe80::200:ff:fe00:b/64 scope link
       valid_lft forever preferred_lft forever
8: Mg0_RP0_CPU0_0: <> mtu 1514 qdisc noop state DOWN group default qlen 1000
    link/ether 52:46:1a:1a:37:e6 brd ff:ff:ff:ff:ff:ff
9: Gi0_0_0_0: <MULTICAST,NOARP,UP,LOWER_UP> mtu 1500 qdisc pfifo_fast state UNKNOWN
  group default qlen 1000
    link/ether 52:46:f8:b8:27:88 brd ff:ff:ff:ff:ff:ff
    inet 10.1.1.1/24 scope global Gi0_0_0_0
       valid_lft forever preferred_lft forever
    inet6 fe80::5046:f8ff:feb8:2788/64 scope link
       valid_lft forever preferred_lft forever
10: Gi0_0_0_1: <> mtu 1514 qdisc noop state DOWN group default qlen 1000
    link/ether 52:46:c4:09:b0:ed brd ff:ff:ff:ff:ff:ff
11: Gi0_0_0_2: <> mtu 1514 qdisc noop state DOWN group default qlen 1000
    link/ether 52:46:11:1d:50:8b brd ff:ff:ff:ff:ff:ff
-bash-4.2$
```

Note: Further details about each of the preceding interfaces are clearly explained in Chapter 4.

By default, any traffic originated from the hosted application will use the management port address as the source address. This may not be suitable based on the network deployment. This default behavior can be overridden by manually defining the source port in the router configuration, as shown in Example 6-28.

Example 6-28   *TPA Configuration*

```
!
tpa
 vrf default
  address-family ipv4
   update-source dataports GigabitEthernet0/0/0/0
   !
```

Because the interfaces and IP addresses are shared between the host and the application, care must be taken to avoid any transport layer port overlaps. For example, SSH is one of the common protocols that is enabled on the hosting router. Therefore, the router will be listening to {**<IP-addr>:22**} already, and the same port number cannot be used by the SSH daemon in the hosted application.

When SSH is expected to be used to access the hosted application, it is mandatory to change the port number of the SSH daemon from 22 to some other value before instantiating the application.

Note: The port number of the SSH daemon can be changed in **/etc/ssh/sshd_config.**

Docker-Based Application Hosting

Some of the notable characteristics of Docker, such as its being a lightweight and open-source platform, make it one of the most widely accepted and deployed platforms for container orchestration and management. A detailed explanation of the Docker architecture and the essential components are available in Chapter 3. This section discusses the different platforms and the architecture to support Docker natively on Cisco IOS-XR.

As highlighted earlier, Docker runs as a daemon in the Linux kernel and is enabled by default, as shown in Example 6-29.

Example 6-29   *Docker Daemon Output*

```
RP/0/RP0/CPU0:ios#bash
Wed Oct  2 19:27:21.292 UTC
[host:~]$
[host:~]$ docker version
```

```
Client:
 Version:       1.10.0
 API version:   1.22
 Go version:    go1.4.2
 Git commit:    cb6da92
 Built:         Tue Aug  8 22:08:35 2017
 OS/Arch:       linux/amd64

Server:
 Version:       1.10.0
 API version:   1.22
 Go version:    go1.4.2
 Git commit:    cb6da92
 Built:         Tue Aug  8 22:08:35 2017
 OS/Arch:       linux/amd64
[host:~]$
```

Docker Images and Registry

The Docker image that is required to instantiate the container can be custom-built from scratch or can be obtained from any existing repository. The Docker daemon running in the Cisco IOS-XR Linux kernel must have access to the image to instantiate the container. There are different ways to obtain the Docker image, as listed here:

- Loading from Public Registry

- Loading from Local Registry

- Loading manually to local storage

Loading from Public Registry

By far, this option is the simplest way to pull the Docker image from the public Docker hub registry using the Docker user CLI. The Docker hub public registry is a service Docker offers to share container images among the users. Any images available in the public registry are freely accessible to download.

To pull the container image from the public registry, the device must be able to access the Internet from the Linux kernel prompt with name resolution, as shown in Figure 6-8.

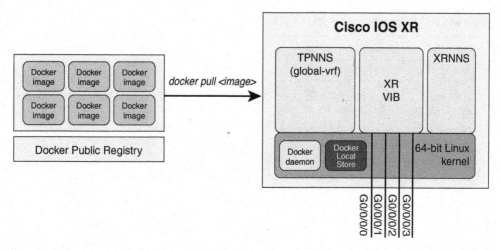

Figure 6-8   *Docker Public Registry*

Provided that Internet access and name resolution services are available, the Docker daemon can execute the standard Docker commands to pull the image from the public registry to the local image store, as shown in Example 6-30.

Example 6-30   *Pulling the Image from Public Registry*

```
RP/0/RP0/CPU0:ios#
RP/0/RP0/CPU0:ios#bash
Wed Oct  2 22:27:06.108 UTC
[host:~]$
 [host:~]$ docker pull ubuntu
Using default tag: latest
latest: Pulling from library/ubuntu
5667fdb72017: Pull complete
d83811f270d5: Pull complete
ee671aafb583: Pull complete
7fc152dfb3a6: Pull complete
Digest: sha256:b88f8848e9a1a4e4558ba7cfc4acc5879e1d0e7ac06401409062ad2627e6fb58
Status: Downloaded newer image for ubuntu:latest
[host:~]$
```

The Docker daemon stores the images locally in the **/misc/app_host/docker/images** location, as shown in Example 6-31.

Example 6-31 *Docker Local Image Store*

```
[host:~]$ docker images
REPOSITORY          TAG              IMAGE ID        CREATED         SIZE
ubuntu              latest           2ca708c1c9cc    13 days ago     64.18 MB
alpine              latest           961769676411    6 weeks ago     5.577 MB
[host:~]$
[host:~]$ ls /misc/app_host/docker/image/devicemapper/
distribution  imagedb  layerdb  repositories.json
[host:~]$
[host:~]$ more /misc/app_host/docker/image/devicemapper/repositories.json
{"Repositories":{"alpine":{"alpine:latest":"sha256:961769676411f082461f9ef46626dd7a2
  d1e2b2a38e6a44364bcbecf51e66dd4"},"ubuntu":{"ubu
ntu:latest":"sha256:2ca708c1c9ccc509b070f226d6e4712604e0c48b55d7d8f5adc9be4a4d360
  29a"}}}
[host:~]$
```

Note: By default, the traffic from the global-vrf (tpnns) network namespace is steered over the data ports in the line card. In some deployments, the Internet connection is provided through the management port. In such cases, you should configure the router and instruct the traffic to be steered over the mgmt port. More details about the configuration are explained in the networking section of this chapter.

To avoid encountering storage issues, it is advisable to clear container images that are no longer required. Alternatively, these images can be moved to a local registry or a server within the network domain and loaded back to the device when they are needed.

Loading from Local Registry

There are many reasons why an operator might not choose to use a public registry. One of the challenges is providing Internet access to all the transit nodes. It is not a best design practice because it exposes the network to security threats. Therefore, it is highly unlikely to have Internet access from all the transit devices. Although it is possible with careful firewall and access control configuration, it raises operational challenges. To address this, a docker image can be provided using a private registry. A network operator can also develop network applications that are not ready to be posted in the Docker hub for various business reasons.

To address such challenges, Docker allows the user to have a private registry within the network domain. The private registry is a docker container that is instantiated within the network domain and is expected to have Internet access to the public registry. A docker registry container is instantiated using a registry image, as shown in Example 6-32. This will create a Docker proxy server listening to port 5000.

Example 6-32 *Creating a Container Using Docker*

```
root@openconfig:~# docker run -d -p 5000:5000 --restart=always --name registry registry:2
Unable to find image 'registry:2' locally
2: Pulling from library/registry
c87736221ed0: Pull complete
1cc8e0bb44df: Pull complete
54d33bcb37f5: Pull complete
e8afc091c171: Pull complete
b4541f6d3db6: Pull complete
Digest: sha256:8004747f1e8cd820a148fb7499d71a76d45ff66bac6a29129bfdbfdc0154d146
Status: Downloaded newer image for registry:2
2af5183e58646bcce7a54668e8f0bea779525e023f73bfbabfcd4746b0b29d36
root@openconfig:~# docker ps
CONTAINER ID IMAGE      COMMAND            CREATED       STATUS            PORTS  NAMES
2af5183e5864  registry:2 "/entrypoint.sh --ne…" 4 seconds ago  Restarting (0) Less        registry
                                                        than a second ago
root@openconfig:~#
```

Any Docker image that is downloaded from the public registry or the image built using Dockerfile locally can be pushed to the local registry, as shown in Example 6-33.

Example 6-33 *Docker Local Registry Example*

```
root@openconfig:~# docker pull ubuntu
Using default tag: latest
latest: Pulling from library/ubuntu
5667fdb72017: Pull complete
d83811f270d5: Pull complete
ee671aafb583: Pull complete
7fc152dfb3a6: Pull complete
Digest: sha256:b88f8848e9a1a4e4558ba7cfc4acc5879e1d0e7ac06401409062ad2627e6fb58
Status: Downloaded newer image for ubuntu:latest
root@openconfig:~# docker tag ubuntu:latest localhost:5000/local-ubuntu
root@openconfig:~# docker push localhost:5000/local-ubuntu
The push refers to repository [localhost:5000/local-ubuntu]
e80c789bc6ac: Pushed
6c3332381368: Pushed
ef1a1ec5bba9: Pushed
a1aa3da2a80a: Pushed
latest: digest: sha256:1bbdea4846231d91cce6c7ff3907d26fca444fd6b7e3c282b90c7fe4251f9f86
   size: 1152
root@openconfig:~# netstat -nlp | grep 5000
tcp6      0      0 :::5000              :::*         LISTEN      27162/docker-proxy
root@openconfig:~#
```

The Docker daemon running in the Cisco IOS-XR device must be enabled to use this local registry server. This is done by modifying the Docker daemon options in the **config** file, as shown in Example 6-34.

Example 6-34   *Docker Local Registry Configuration*

```
[ios:~]$ more /etc/sysconfig/docker
# DOCKER_OPTS can be used to add insecure private registries to be supported
# by the docker daemon
# eg : DOCKER_OPTS="--insecure-registry foo --insecure-registry bar"

# Following are the valid configs
# DOCKER_OPTS="<space>--insecure-registry<space>foo"
# DOCKER_OPTS+="<space>--insecure-registry<space>bar"

DOCKER_OPTS=" -insecure-registry 10.1.1.2:5000"
[ios:~]$
```

In Example 6-34, 10.1.1.2 is the registry proxy server address. With this option, the transit devices are not required to have Internet access. Instead, they should be able to reach the proxy server to fetch the Docker images.

Note: Additional details about deploying a registry server can be found at https://docs. docker.com/registry/deploying/.

Loading Manually to Local Store

This option is explained in Chapter 3 (see Example 3-14), but it is included here for your convenience.

In the preceding topology, the Docker image is initially pulled to the local store in the server and then copied to the IOS-XR bash shell. To do so, you must pull the Alpine image on the server, save it as a local file, and then use secure copy (scp) to push the image to the IOS-XR bash shell. In Example 6-35, the image is copied to the **/disk0:/** location in the bash shell.

Example 6-35   *Loading a Docker Image Manually*

```
root@server-1:~# docker pull alpine        /* Pulls the image to local store */
Using default tag: latest
latest: Pulling from library/alpine
743f2d6c1f65: Pull complete
6bfc4ec4420a: Pull complete
688a776db95f: Pull complete
Digest: sha256:1d0dfe527f801c596818da756e01fa0e7af4649b15edc3eb245e8da92c8381f8
Status: Downloaded newer image for alpine:latest
root@server-1:~# docker save alpine -o /root/alpine/*Save the image locally */
```

```
root@server-1:~# scp /root/alpine cisco@10.0.0.10:/disk0:/    /* Copy the file to
  IOS-XR */
Password:
alpine                                      100%  108MB  80.1KB/s   22:58
root@server-1:~#
```

Like any other Docker host, the **docker load** command is used to load the local image file to the local Docker store in the host, as shown in Example 6-36.

Example 6-36 *Docker Local Image Store*

```
[iosxrv9000-1:~]$ docker load -i /disk0:/alpine
[iosxrv9000-1:~]$ docker images
REPOSITORY            TAG            IMAGE ID         CREATED         SIZE
nginx                 latest         53f3fd8007f7     36 hours ago    109.3 MB
ubuntu                latest         d131e0fa2585     12 days ago     101.7 MB
alpine                latest         cdf98d1859c1     4 weeks ago     5.529 MB
[iosxrv9000-1:~]$
```

Container Deployment Workflow

Once the container image is available, you can deploy the application as a Docker container. The standard Docker client is used in Cisco IOS-XR platforms to communicate with the Docker daemon for sending the commands or instructions, so there is not much difference in handling the same compared to the Docker deployment in other Linux distributions. The command used to deploy an Alpine container is shown in Example 6-37.

Example 6-37 *Deploying an Alpine Container*

```
[host:~]$ docker run -itd --name alpine --net=host --cap-add NET_ADMIN --cap-
  add=SYS_ADMIN alpine
4649bffb6524a9677471a1a0734eef5e8e8502bb214ba77b58b1bee2ae803b10
[host:~]$ docker ps
CONTAINER ID    IMAGE      COMMAND      CREATED        STATUS    PORTS        NAMES
4649bffb6524    alpine     "/bin/sh"    3 seconds ago  Up        2 seconds    alpine
[host:~]$
[host:~]$ docker exec -it alpine ash
/ # ls
bin    dev    etc    home   lib    media  mnt    opt    proc   root   run    sbin
  srv    sys    tmp    usr    var
/ #
```

Using the standard Docker commands, you can attach to the container and execute the applications or other workflows.

Network Configuration and Verification

This section discusses the network configuration required to provide external access for the applications hosted on Cisco IOS-XR devices.

Network Reachability Configuration

Network connectivity and name resolution are essential for any of the preceding options to pull the Docker image from the external registry to a local image store. Third-party applications are hosted as containers in the global-vrf namespace; therefore, this is where the discussion is focused in this section.

As explained in Chapter 3, the global-vrf namespace is connected to the XR FIB table using the fwdintf interface, and a default route is installed with fwdintf as the egress interface, as shown in Example 6-38.

Example 6-38   *Kernel Route*

```
[host:~]$ route
Kernel IP routing table
Destination     Gateway         Genmask         Flags Metric Ref    Use Iface
default         *               0.0.0.0         U     0      0        0 fwdintf
[host:~]$
```

It is essential to configure the TPA before deploying the containers. Without TPA configuration, the containers can be deployed, but without network interfaces attached to the container. The TPA configuration is common for both Docker- and LXC-based container hosting, as shown in Example 6-39.

Example 6-39   *TPA Configuration*

```
!
tpa
 vrf default
  address-family ipv4
   update-source dataports GigabitEthernet0/0/0/0
  !
```

The Docker daemon in the Cisco IOS-XR platform uses host networking by mounting the global-vrf namespace volume while instantiating the container.

Name Resolution Configuration

Docker heavily relies on name resolution to communicate with the external registry, which makes the name server configuration essential for a seamless Docker deployment.

The name server in the TPNNS **resolv.conf** file is dynamically populated by using the configuration from the router. When the domain name-server is not configured in the router, the **resolv.conf** file is empty, as shown in Example 6-40.

Example 6-40 *Default TPNNS Name Service*

```
[iosxrv9000-2:~]$ more /etc/resolv.conf

[iosxrv9000-2:~]$
[iosxrv9000-2:~]$ more /etc/netns/global-vrf/resolv.conf

[iosxrv9000-2:~]$
```

Now when the domain name-server is configured in the router, it automatically populates the same in the relevant files, as shown in Example 6-41.

Example 6-41 *TTPNNS Name Service Configuration*

```
RP/0/RP0/CPU0:iosxrv9000-2(config)#domain name-server 8.8.8.8
RP/0/RP0/CPU0:iosxrv9000-2(config)#commit
Thu Oct  3 01:31:00.946 UTC
RP/0/RP0/CPU0:iosxrv9000-2(config)#end
RP/0/RP0/CPU0:iosxrv9000-2#bash
Thu Oct  3 01:31:05.337 UTC
[iosxrv9000-2:~]$ more /etc/resolv.conf

nameserver 8.8.8.8
[iosxrv9000-2:~]$ more /etc/netns/global-vrf/resolv.conf

nameserver 8.8.8.8
[iosxrv9000-2:~]$
```

Network Proxy Configuration

Although Example 6-41 uses a public DNS server, it is common to see an internal DNS server with a proxy enabled. In such a case, the proxy server and the related configuration must be enabled. A sample configuration is shown in Example 6-42.

Example 6-42 *Proxy Configuration*

```
bash-4.3$ cat /etc/sysconfig/docker | grep http
export http_proxy=<IP>:8080
export https_proxy=<IP>:8080
bash-4.3$
```

Application Hosting in VRF Namespace

So far, this chapter has discussed the various ways of hosting an application in a Cisco IOS-XR router. Hosting the application containers using LXC or Docker in the global-vrf network namespace attaches all the physical interfaces in the global routing table to the container. However, what if you do not want the container to use an interface in the global routing table? What if you need the container to communicate to other applications in a specific VRF?

There are various reasons for an operator wanting to host an application in a specific VRF. For example, the hosted application may be in testing phase and does not need to be in the production network, or it can be done for security purposes. This section discusses hosting the containers and attaching interfaces from a specific VRF.

VRF Namespace

As has been discussed throughout this chapter, two namespaces—global-vrf and xrnns—are created by default in the Linux kernel of the Cisco IOS-XR device. For each VRF configured in the router, a new network namespace is created in the Linux kernel with the list of physical interfaces that are associated with the VRF (see Figure 6-9).

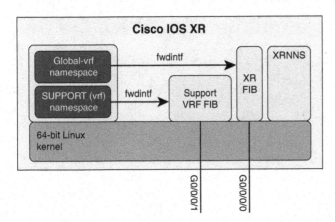

Figure 6-9 *VRF Namespace*

As shown in the figure, G0/0/0/0 is part of the global routing table, whereas the G0/0/0/1 interface is associated with VRF SUPPORT. A sample router configuration is shown in Example 6-43.

Example 6-43 *Router VRF Configuration*

```
!
vrf SUPPORT
!
interface GigabitEthernet0/0/0/1
 vrf SUPPORT
 ipv4 address 192.168.1.1 255.255.255.0
 !
```

To instruct the kernel to create a new network namespace, the TPA router configuration must be enabled with the VRF, as shown in Example 6-44.

Example 6-44 *VRF TPA Configuration*

```
!
tpa
 vrf SUPPORT
  address-family ipv4
   update-source dataports GigabitEthernet0/0/0/1
  !
 !
 vrf default
  address-family ipv4
   update-source dataports GigabitEthernet0/0/0/0
  !
```

Note: TPA must be enabled on a per address-family basis for each VRF. When the container is expected to use an IPv6 address for a specific VRF, the address-family must be enabled for the VRF under TPA configuration mode.

Once the configuration shown in Example 6-44 is committed, a new network namespace with the VRF name will be created in the Linux kernel. In this example, a new network namespace named **SUPPORT** will be created in the Linux kernel, as shown in Example 6-45.

Example 6-45 *VRF Namespace in the Kernel*

```
RP/0/RP0/CPU0:ios#bash
Thu Oct  3 18:02:03.883 UTC
[host:~]$ ip netns list
SUPPORT
tpnns
xrnns
global-vrf
[host:~]$
```

This newly created network namespace will have all the interfaces listed that are configured as part of VRF SUPPORT. In this example, the G0/0/0/1 interface is configured as part of VRF SUPPORT with an IP address of 192.168.1.1/24. This interface is listed as part of the SUPPORT network namespace, as shown in Example 6-46.

Example 6-46   *VRF Namespace Interfaces Output*

```
[host:~]$ ip netns exec SUPPORT bash
 [host:~]$ ifconfig
Gi0_0_0_1 Link encap:Ethernet  HWaddr 52:46:c4:09:b0:ed
          inet addr:192.168.1.1  Mask:255.255.255.0
          inet6 addr: fe80::5046:c4ff:fe09:b0ed/64 Scope:Link
          UP RUNNING NOARP MULTICAST  MTU:1500  Metric:1
          RX packets:18 errors:0 dropped:0 overruns:0 frame:0
          TX packets:2 errors:0 dropped:0 overruns:0 carrier:0
          collisions:0 txqueuelen:1000
          RX bytes:1998 (1.9 KiB)  TX bytes:84 (84.0 B)


fwd_ew    Link encap:Ethernet  HWaddr 00:00:00:00:00:0b
          inet6 addr: fe80::200:ff:fe00:b/64 Scope:Link
          UP RUNNING NOARP MULTICAST  MTU:1500  Metric:1
          RX packets:0 errors:0 dropped:0 overruns:0 frame:0
          TX packets:3 errors:0 dropped:0 overruns:0 carrier:0
          collisions:0 txqueuelen:1000
          RX bytes:0 (0.0 B)  TX bytes:210 (210.0 B)


fwdintf   Link encap:Ethernet  HWaddr 00:00:00:00:00:0a
          inet6 addr: fe80::200:ff:fe00:a/64 Scope:Link
          UP RUNNING NOARP MULTICAST  MTU:1482  Metric:1
          RX packets:0 errors:0 dropped:0 overruns:0 frame:0
          TX packets:6 errors:0 dropped:0 overruns:0 carrier:0
          collisions:0 txqueuelen:1000
          RX bytes:0 (0.0 B)  TX bytes:504 (504.0 B)


lo        Link encap:Local Loopback
          inet addr:127.0.0.1  Mask:255.0.0
          inet6 addr: ::1/128 Scope:Host
          UP LOOPBACK RUNNING  MTU:65536  Metric:1
          RX packets:0 errors:0 dropped:0 overruns:0 frame:0
          TX packets:0 errors:0 dropped:0 overruns:0 carrier:0
          collisions:0 txqueuelen:0
          RX bytes:0 (0.0 B)  TX bytes:0 (0.0 B)


[host:~]$
```

For each VRF namespaces created, the **fwdintf** is created to connect the network namespace to the VRF FIB for packet forwarding. A default route is installed with **fwdintf** as the egress interface, as shown in Example 6-47.

Example 6-47 *VRF Namespace Routes*

```
[host:~]$ route
Kernel IP routing table
Destination     Gateway          Genmask          Flags Metric Ref    Use Iface
default         *                0.0.0.0          U     0      0        0 fwdintf
[host:~]$
```

Application Hosting in VRF Namespace Using LXC

When LXC is used to host the application as a virtual machine, the LXC namespace configuration must be set to the VRF namespace, as shown in Example 6-48.

Example 6-48 *LXC Spec File with VRF Namespace Configuration*

```
<domain xmlns:lxc="http://libvirt.org/schemas/domain/lxc/1.0" type="lxc">
<name>centosvrf-vm</name>
<memory>327680</memory>
<os>
<type>exe</type>
<init>/sbin/init</init>
</os>
<lxc:namespace>
<sharenet type="netns" value="SUPPORT" />
</lxc:namespace>
<vcpu>1</vcpu>
<clock offset="utc" />
<on_poweroff>destroy</on_poweroff>
<on_reboot>restart</on_reboot>
<on_crash>destroy</on_crash>
<devices>
<emulator>/usr/lib64/libvirt/libvirt_lxc</emulator>
<filesystem type="mount">
<source dir="/misc/app_host/centosvrf/" />
<target dir="/" />
</filesystem>
<console type="pty" />
</devices>
<resource><partition>/machine/tp_app/lxc</partition></resource></domain>
```

Note: The specification file is used on a per-workload basis, so it is possible to instantiate a different workload with different namespaces.

By setting the **lxc:namespace** attribute to SUPPORT, LXC injects the interfaces from VRF SUPPORT while deploying the workload, as shown in Example 6-49.

Example 6-49 *Containers with VRF Namespace Interfaces*

```
[host:/misc/app_host/centosvrf]$ virsh console centosvrf-vm
Connected to domain centosvrf-vm
Escape character is ^]
systemd 219 running in system mode. (+PAM +AUDIT +SELINUX +IMA -APPARMOR +SMACK
  +SYSVINIT +UTMP +LIBCRYPTSETUP +GCRYPT +GNUTLS +ACL +XZ +LZ4 -SECCOMP +BLKID +ELF-
  UTILS +KMOD +IDN)
Detected virtualization lxc-libvirt.
Detected architecture x86-64.


Welcome to CentOS Linux 7 (Core)!


-bash-4.2$ ip addr
1: lo: <LOOPBACK,UP,LOWER_UP> mtu 65536 qdisc noqueue state UNKNOWN group default
    link/loopback 00:00:00:00:00:00 brd 00:00:00:00:00:00
    inet 127.0.0.1/8 scope host lo
      valid_lft forever preferred_lft forever
    inet6 ::1/128 scope host
      valid_lft forever preferred_lft forever
12: fwdintf: <MULTICAST,NOARP,UP,LOWER_UP> mtu 1482 qdisc pfifo_fast state UNKNOWN
  group default qlen 1000
    link/ether 00:00:00:00:00:0a brd ff:ff:ff:ff:ff:ff
    inet6 fe80::200:ff:fe00:a/64 scope link
      valid_lft forever preferred_lft forever
13: fwd_ew: <MULTICAST,NOARP,UP,LOWER_UP> mtu 1500 qdisc pfifo_fast state UNKNOWN
  group default qlen 1000
    link/ether 00:00:00:00:00:0b brd ff:ff:ff:ff:ff:ff
    inet6 fe80::200:ff:fe00:b/64 scope link
      valid_lft forever preferred_lft forever
14: Gi0_0_0_1: <MULTICAST,NOARP,UP,LOWER_UP> mtu 1500 qdisc pfifo_fast state UNKNOWN
  group default qlen 1000
    link/ether 52:46:c4:09:b0:ed brd ff:ff:ff:ff:ff:ff
    inet 192.168.1.1/24 scope global Gi0_0_0_1
      valid_lft forever preferred_lft forever
    inet6 fe80::5046:c4ff:fe09:b0ed/64 scope link
      valid_lft forever preferred_lft forever
-bash-4.2$


Application Hosting in VRF namespace using Docker
```

When Docker is used to deploy the application, the respective network namespace should be mounted instead of the global-vrf, as shown in Example 6-50.

Example 6-50   *Docker Container with VRF Mount*

```
[host:~]$ docker run -itd  --name alpine -v /var/run/netns/SUPPORT:/var/run/netns/
   SUPPORT --cap-add NET_ADMIN --cap-add=SYS_ADMIN alpine-iproute2
6e73fb0fa518451778bbd688a0ef344294074d9e116bb6777786b9ccbcf9c33b
[host:~]$
```

The command in Example 6-50 instantiates the Alpine container and mounts the
SUPPORT network namespace into the container, thereby injecting all the interfaces that
are part of the SUPPORT network namespace. Any process hosted in the namespace
within the container uses the relevant VRF interfaces. This can be verified by accessing
the container namespace, as shown in Example 6-51.

Example 6-51   *Container Hosted in VRF Verification*

```
RP/0/RP0/CPU0:ios#bash
Thu Oct  3 18:26:46.349 UTC
[host:~]$ docker exec -it alpine /bin/sh
/ # ip addr
1: lo: <LOOPBACK> mtu 65536 qdisc noop state DOWN group default
    link/loopback 00:00:00:00:00:00 brd 00:00:00:00:00:00
/ #
/ # ip netns exec SUPPORT sh
/ #
/ # ip addr
1: lo: <LOOPBACK,UP,LOWER_UP> mtu 65536 qdisc noqueue state UNKNOWN group default
    link/loopback 00:00:00:00:00:00 brd 00:00:00:00:00:00
    inet 127.0.0.1/8 scope host lo
      valid_lft forever preferred_lft forever
    inet6 ::1/128 scope host
      valid_lft forever preferred_lft forever
12: fwdintf: <MULTICAST,NOARP,UP,LOWER_UP> mtu 1482 qdisc pfifo_fast state UNKNOWN
  group default qlen 1000
    link/ether 00:00:00:00:00:0a brd ff:ff:ff:ff:ff:ff
    inet6 fe80::200:ff:fe00:a/64 scope link
      valid_lft forever preferred_lft forever
13: fwd_ew: <MULTICAST,NOARP,UP,LOWER_UP> mtu 1500 qdisc pfifo_fast state UNKNOWN
  group default qlen 1000
    link/ether 00:00:00:00:00:0b brd ff:ff:ff:ff:ff:ff
    inet6 fe80::200:ff:fe00:b/64 scope link
      valid_lft forever preferred_lft forever
14: Gi0_0_0_1: <MULTICAST,NOARP,UP,LOWER_UP> mtu 1500 qdisc pfifo_fast state UNKNOWN
  group default qlen 1000
    link/ether 52:46:c4:09:b0:ed brd ff:ff:ff:ff:ff:ff
    inet 192.168.1.1/24 scope global Gi0_0_0_1
      valid_lft forever preferred_lft forever
    inet6 fe80::5046:c4ff:fe09:b0ed/64 scope link
      valid_lft forever preferred_lft forever
/ #
```

> **Note:** The default Alpine image does not come with the iproute2 package. This is required to execute any **ip netns <>** commands. This example used a custom Alpine image that has the iproute2 package preinstalled.

Container Management

In the previous sections, you learned how to deploy and run an application using different orchestration tools. Now you will check some of the basic management functionalities.

Persistent Application Deployment

By now, you know applications are hosted by leveraging the Linux Kernel on the route processor (RP). When a router reload or switchover occurs, it is cumbersome to expect users to start all the application containers again. This can be handled simply by deploying the containers in persistent mode.

When LXC-based application hosting is used, the **virsh** commands can deploy the application in the persistent mode. By default, the Admin Plane and third-party hosting space LXC are in persistent mode to survive any switchover or reload. This can be confirmed using the output shown in Example 6-52.

Example 6-52 *Default Application Persistence*

```
RP/0/RP0/CPU0:ios#bash
Sat Oct  5 14:16:28.493 UTC

[host:~]$
[host:~]$ virsh list --all --persistent
 Id    Name                           State
---------------------------------------------------
 3652  default-sdr--1                 running
 23818 default-sdr--2                 running

[host:~]$
```

You can add any new LXC application to this persistence list by defining the application using **virsh** commands, as shown in Example 6-53.

Example 6-53 *virsh Persistence Configuration*

```
[host:/misc/app_host]$ virsh define centosvrf.xml
Domain centosvrf-vm defined from centosvrf.xml

[host:/misc/app_host]$
```

```
[host:/misc/app_host]$ virsh start centosvrf-vm
[host:/misc/app_host]$ virsh dominfo centosvrf-vm
Id:              7314
Name:            centosvrf-vm
UUID:            4810e1ab-03a2-4dea-9eec-1134cdf715d4
OS Type:         exe
State:           running
CPU(s):          1
CPU time:        1.3s
Max memory:      327680 KiB
Used memory:     1460 KiB
Persistent:      yes
Autostart:       disable
Managed save:    unknown
Security model: none
Security DOI:    0

[host:/misc/app_host]$
[host:/misc/app_host]$
```

The **define** command registers the guest domain as persistent and reloads it upon failure. The output shown in Example 6-54 confirms that the guest application centosvrf-vm is added to the persistent list in addition the Admin Plane LXC.

Example 6-54   *Verifying the Persistence Configuration*

```
[host:/misc/app_host]$ virsh list --all --persistent
 Id    Name                          State
-----------------------------------------------------
 3652  default-sdr--1                running
 7314  centosvrf-vm                  running
 23818 default-sdr--2                running

[host:/misc/app_host]$
```

When the router suffers a reload, the user is not required to intervene to bring the application back up. The persistence can be removed by undefining the domain, as shown in Example 6-55.

Example 6-55   *Clearing the Persistence*

```
[host:/misc/app_host]$ virsh undefine centosvrf-vm
Domain centosvrf-vm has been undefined

[host:/misc/app_host]$ virsh list --all --persistent
```

```
Id     Name                      State
----------------------------------------------------
3652   default-sdr--1            running
23818  default-sdr--2            running

[host:/misc/app_host]$
```

By default, when Docker instantiates the container, the container file system persists, although this can be overridden by using the following Docker attribute:

```
[host:/misc/app_host]$ docker run -it --rm alpine-iproute2
```

Summary

This chapter introduced the evolution of software architecture from IOS to IOS-XR, highlighting the primary differences and benefits. It then covered the development of new features introduced as part of XR software Release 6.0. It introduced the application-hosting architecture and the basic components, resource readiness, and environmental setup before discussing the application hosting concept on IOS-XR platforms.

The chapter then moved to natively installing applications in the XR bash shell using YUM commands and building applications as an RPM package to install natively in the bash shell. From there, it presented building a virtual machine in an external environment and deploying the same in the XR platform. It also covered the Docker architecture and how it can be used to deploy containers in the XR platform. The chapter concluded with some basic management aspects of the hosted application.

References

Introduction to Cisco IOS-XR Software: https://www.cisco.com/c/en/us/td/docs/routers/crs/software/crs_r4-1/getting_started/configuration/guide/gs41crs/gs41over.pdf

Application Hosting on Cisco IOS-XR Platform: https://www.cisco.com/c/en/us/td/docs/iosxr/ncs5000/app-hosting/b-application-hosting-configuration-guide-ncs5000/b-application-hosting-configuration-guide-ncs5000_chapter_011.html

Virtual Extensible Local Area Network (VXLAN): https://tools.ietf.org/html/rfc7348

Running WRL7 on Cisco IOS-XR Platform: https://xrdocs.io/application-hosting/tutorials/2016-06-17-xr-toolbox-part-5-running-a-native-wrl7-app/

LXC Container on Cisco IOS-XR Platform: https://xrdocs.io/application-hosting/tutorials/2016-06-16-xr-toolbox-part-4-bring-your-own-container-lxc-app/

## Chapter 7

Container Orchestration in Cisco NX-OS Platforms

In this chapter, you will learn the following:

- Cisco NX-OS architecture—key characteristics and benefits

- Environment readiness to host containers and applications

- Container infrastructure instantiation, network and access configuration, orchestration and application hosting—LXC-based Guest Shell, Bash, Docker and LXC-based Open Agent Container.

Cisco NX-OS Software Architecture

Cisco NX-OS is designed to meet the needs of modern data centers, which demand products, applications, and services that are high performance, highly available, resilient, secure, scalable, and modular in architecture. These criteria are met by all the platforms—Nexus 3000, 5000, 6000, 7000, and 9000—that support and run Cisco NX-OS. These characteristics provide the solid foundation of resilience and robustness necessary for network device OSes powering the mission-critical environment of today's enterprise-class data centers.

NX-OS Foundation

Cisco NX-OS finds its roots in the Cisco SAN-OS operating system used in lossless SAN networks. As a direct result of having been deployed and evolving from nearly a decade in the extremely critical storage area networking space, NX-OS can deliver the performance, reliability, and lifecycle expected in the data center.

Cisco NX-OS is built on a Linux kernel. By using Linux kernel as its foundation, Cisco NX-OS has the following characteristics and benefits:

- An open-source and community development model, which leads to real-world field testing and rapid defect identification and resolution

- Proven stability and maturity, with advanced capabilities

- A near-real-time OS kernel, which is suitable to scale real-time applications

- An architecture leveraging multiple run-queues for handling multicore and multiple-CPU system configurations

- A multithreaded, preemptive multitasking capability that provides protected fair access to kernel and CPU resources because it employs a highly scalable processor queue and process-management architecture

These characteristics and benefits ensure system stability and fair access to the system resources for software functions such as routing protocols, the spanning tree, and internal services and processes. By its inherent nature, NX-OS supports multiprocessor and multicore hardware platforms, which help to simplify scalability by supporting not only current hardware or software features but also future software features.

NX-OS Modular Software Architecture

NX-OS software components are modular and built on top of the Linux kernel, as illustrated in Figure 7-1. These modular components can be described as such:

- Hardware drivers, which are hardware-related and highly dependent on the platform

- Infrastructure modules to manage the system

- Software features or control-plane functions

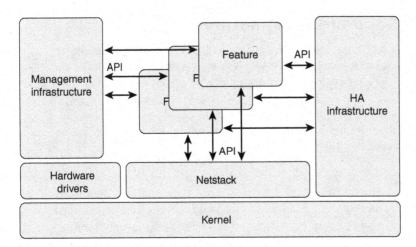

Figure 7-1 *NX-OS Software Architecture*

The platform-dependent modules consist of hardware-related subsystems, such as hardware and chipset drivers specific to a particular hardware model on which Cisco NX-OS runs. These modules typically provide standardized APIs and messaging capabilities to upper-layer subsystems. The modules essentially constitute a hardware abstraction layer to enable consistent development at higher layers in the OS, improving overall OS portability. The code base for these hardware-dependent modules reduces the overall code that needs to be ported to support future NX-OS releases and for other hardware platforms.

The Netstack module runs in user space and is a complete TCP/IP stack with components L2 Packet Manager, ARP, Adjacency Manager, IPv4, Internet Control Message Protocol v4 (ICMPv4), IPv6, ICMPv6, TCP/UDP, and socket library. The Netstack is built and used to handle the traffic sent to and from the CPU. A user can debug Netstack to uncover the process(es) that are triggering a high CPU utilization condition.

The system infrastructure modules such as management infrastructure and high-availability infrastructure provide essential base system services that enable process management, fault detection and recovery, and interservice communication. High-availability infrastructure provides subsecond recovery of a fault, enabling stateful recovery of a process. During the recovery, it preserves the runtime state of the feature, increasing the overall network and services availability. The Persistent Storage System (PSS) and Message Transmission Services (MTS), the core parts of the high-availability infrastructure, enable the subsecond recovery of a fault, resulting in overall higher system uptime.

The feature modules consist of the actual underlying services responsible for delivering a feature or running a protocol at the control plane level. Open Shortest Path First (OSPF), Border Gateway Protocol (BGP), Spanning Tree Protocol, Overlay Transport Virtualization (OTV), and NetFlow export are all examples of modularized system-level features or protocols. Each feature is implemented as an independent, memory-protected process that is spawned as needed based on the overall system configuration.

This approach differs from that of legacy network operating systems in that only the specific features that are configured are automatically loaded and started. This highly granular approach to modularity enables benefits such as these:

- Compartmentalization of fault domains, resulting in overall system resiliency and stability

- Simplified portability for cross-platform consistency

- More efficient defect isolation, resulting in rapid defect resolution

- Easy integration of new feature modules into the OS

- Support of conditional services, resulting in efficient use of memory, CPU and CLI resources, and improved security as lesser OS functions are exposed

Fault Detection and Recovery

In addition to the resiliency gained from architectural improvements, Cisco NX-OS provides internal hierarchical and multilayered system fault detection and recovery mechanisms. No software system is completely immune to problems, so it is important to have an effective strategy for detecting and recovering from faults quickly, with as little effect as possible. Cisco NX-OS is designed from the start to provide this capability.

Individual service and feature processes are monitored and managed by the Cisco NX-OS System Manager, an intelligent monitoring service with integrated high-availability logic. The system manager can detect and correct a failure or lockup of any feature service within the system. The system manager is, in turn, monitored and managed for health by the Cisco NX-OS kernel. A specialized portion of the kernel is designed to detect failures and lockups of the Cisco NX-OS System Manager. The kernel itself is monitored through hardware. A hardware process constantly monitors the kernel health and activity. Any fault, failure, or lockup at the kernel level is detected by hardware and triggers a supervisor switchover. Figure 7-2 illustrates the components involved in the fault detection and recovery process.

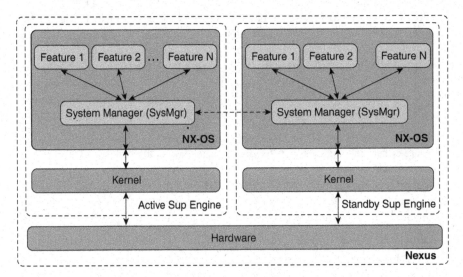

Figure 7-2 *NX-OS Fault Detection and Recovery*

The combination of these multilevel detection and health monitoring systems creates a robust and resilient operating environment that can reduce the overall effect of internal faults and, more importantly, preserve the stability of the overall network by internalizing these types of events.

More Benefits of NX-OS

Following are some of the key but nonexhaustive benefits that this chapter will briefly discuss:

- **Familiar usability and operation:** Cisco NX-OS maintains the familiarity of the Cisco IOS CLI. Users comfortable with the Cisco IOS CLI will find themselves equally comfortable with Cisco NX-OS, which has numerous user interface enhancements.

■ **Virtualization capability:** Cisco NX-OS offers the capability to virtualize the platform on which it is running. Using Cisco NX-OS virtual device contexts (VDCs), a single physical device can be virtualized into many logical devices, each operating independently. And it supports virtualization of overlay transport, which addresses the need to scale Layer 2 by extending the domain across different data centers.

■ **Enhanced security:** NX-OS supports features and tools to secure the platform and its functions. Some of the more advanced security features supported are Cisco TrustSec (CTS), IP Source Guard, DHCP snooping, Unicast Reverse Path Forwarding (uRPF), access control lists (ACLs), and 802.1x.

■ **Unified I/O and unified fabric:** Cisco Unified Fabric includes the flexibility to run Fiber Channel; IP-based storage, such as network-attached storage (NAS) and Small Computer System Interface over IP (iSCSI), or FCoE; or a combination of these technologies on a converged network.

■ **Support of standalone fabric:** NX-OS supports features to build standalone fabrics such as FabricPath, Dynamic Fabric Automation (DFA), and VXLAN/EVPN to scale the Layer 2 domains and meet the demands of today's virtualized computing environments and applications.

■ **Advanced system management:** NX-OS supports SNMP (v1, v2c, and v3) to enable traditional ways of managing systems. NETCONF and XML are integrated to NX-OS, which make it IETF-compliant to transact XML through secure connections. With the support of configuration checkpoint and rollback, managing devices through its software lifecycle is easier.

Hosting Environment Readiness

This section discusses the various shells and containers supported in Nexus switching platforms and the OS version and resources required to support them.

Guest Shell

Guest Shell is an execution environment isolated from the host operating system's kernel space and running within a Linux Container (LXC). As with OAC, having a decoupled execution space allows customization of the Linux environment to suit the needs of the applications without affecting the host system or applications running in other Linux Containers.

Platforms Support

Guest Shell is supported in Nexus 3000/9000 platforms. Table 7-1 provides the minimum NX-OS version required for each platform to run the Guest Shell environment.

Table 7-1 *Nexus Switches and NX-OS Versions Supporting Guest Shell*

Platforms	Minimum Version
Nexus 3000 series	7.0(3)I2(1)
Nexus 9000 series	7.0(3)I2(1)

Platform Resource Requirements

The Guest Shell reserves a specific amount of memory in Bootflash. Upon activation, it reserves dynamic RAM and CPU resources, as shown in Table 7-2.

Table 7-2 *Nexus Resource Requirement for Guest Shell*

Platforms	DRAM Reservation	Bootflash Reservation	CPU reservation
Nexus 3000 series	256 MB	200 MB	1%
Nexus 9000 series	256 MB	200 MB	1%

By default, Nexus switches with 4 GB of RAM will not enable Guest Shell. Use the **guestshell enable** command to install and enable Guest Shell.

Bash

In addition to Guest Shell, Cisco Nexus9000 Series devices support access to the Bourne-Again Shell (Bash). Bash interprets commands that you enter or commands that are read from a shell script. The following sections discuss how Bash enables access to the underlying Linux system on the device and how it manages the system. Bash shell is supported on both Cisco Nexus 3000 series as well as 9000-series platforms, as shown in Table 7-3.

Table 7-3 *Nexus Switches and NX-OS Versions Supporting Bash*

Platforms	Minimum Version
Nexus 3000 series	6.1(2)I2(2)
Nexus 9000 series	6.1(2)I2(2)

The coming sections discuss how Bash enables direct and root access to the underlying kernel and how it instantiates the Docker service and containers.

LXC-based Open Agent Container (OAC)

OAC is a 32-bit, CentOS 6.7-based container that is built specifically to support open agents like Puppet and Chef to manage Nexus switching platforms.

With the current architecture, Open Agents cannot be directly installed and run on Nexus platforms. To overcome this challenge, a special environment is built, which is a decoupled execution space within an LXC called as the Open Agent Container (OAC). Having an execution space that is decoupled from the native host system enables customization of the environment to meet the applications' requirements without affecting the host systems' applications or any other containers.

Platforms Supported

Open Agent Container is one of the earliest container environments supported in Nexus platforms, and it is supported only in Nexus 5600, Nexus 6000, and Nexus 7000/7700 series platforms. Table 7-4 shows the minimum NX-OS release required for each platform supporting OAC.

Table 7-4 *Nexus Switches and NX-OS Versions Supporting OAC*

Platforms	Minimum Version
Nexus 5600 series	7.3(0)N1(1)
Nexus 6000 series	7.3(0)N1(1)
Nexus 7000/7700	7.3(0)D1(1)

Platform Resource Requirements

As the file required to instantiate and for associated data storage, OAC occupies up to a specific memory size in bootflash. Upon activation, it requires dynamic RAM and CPU resources, as shown in Table 7-5.

Table 7-5 *Nexus Resource Requirement for OAC*

Platforms	DRAM Reservation	Bootflash Reservation	CPU Reservation
Nexus 5600 series	256 MB	400 MB	1%
Nexus 6000 series	256 MB	400 MB	1%
Nexus 7000/7700	256 MB	400 MB	1%

Note: The OAC functionality will no longer be supported on the Nexus 7000 from 8.4.1 release onward. When executing the commands to enable OAC, users will be notified about the deprecation. Even though the feature is deprecated, this book covers OAC as a significant install base of Nexus 7000 that still runs pre-8.4.1 releases.

Container Infrastructure Configuration and Instantiation

This section explains and provides procedures to instantiate different types of containers and to access, configure, manage, and orchestrate them. It also provides detailed steps to deploy and manage applications in the containers.

Guest Shell

Just as with OAC, Cisco Nexus 3000/9000 Series devices support access to an isolated execution environment, called the Guest Shell, which is running within a secure Linux Container (sLXC), as illustrated in Figure 7-3. Under the hood, the Guest Shell is just a libvirt-managed LXC container. This Guest Shell is based on CentOS 7 and can be managed using traditional Linux commands.

The Guest Shell has various functions and offers key benefits that aid developers in building and hosting applications in Nexus platforms, such as providing access to the network, NX-OS CLI, bootflash filesystem, and above all, the ability to install Python scripts and Linux applications.

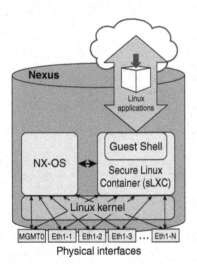

Figure 7-3 *Guest Shell in NX-OS*

Guest Shell OVA File

In Nexus 3000 and 9000 switches, the .ova file for the default version of Guest Shell is integrated with the NX-OS image, and as previously discussed, you do not have to download and install an .ova to enable it.

Deployment Model and Workflow

It is simple to activate Guest Shell in supported platforms, and it can be done with one command, as shown in Example 7-1. The Guest Shell needs to be explicitly activated only in the first generation of the Nexus 3000 platform that came with 4 GB RAM. In later generations of Nexus 3000 and Nexus 9000 platforms, Guest Shell is enabled by default.

This **guestshell enable** command does the following:

1. Creates a virtual service instance

2. Extracts the .ova file built into NX-OS

3. Validates the contents in the file

4. Creates a virtual environment in the device

5. Instantiates the Guest Shell container

Example 7-1   *Enable Guest Shell in NX-OS*

```
N3K-C3548P# guestshell enable
2019 Sep 12 02:04:00 N3K-C3548P %$ VDC-1 %$ %VMAN-2-INSTALL_STATE: Installing
  virtual service 'guestshell+'
N3K-C3548P#
N3K-C3548P# show virtual-service list
Virtual Service List:

Name                    Status              Package Name
--------------------------------------------------------------------------
guestshell+             Activating          guestshell.ova
N3K-C3548P#
2019 Sep 12 02:04:55 N3K-C3548P %$ VDC-1 %$ %VMAN-2-ACTIVATION_STATE: Successfully
  activated virtual service 'guestshell+'
N3K-C3548P# show virtual-service list
Virtual Service List:

Name                    Status              Package Name
--------------------------------------------------------------------------
guestshell+             Activated           guestshell.ova
N3K-C3548P#
```

To know the resources allocated to the shell, use the **show guestshell** command. As you can see in Example 7-2, it reports the operational state of the shell, disk, memory, and CPU resource reservation, and it reports the **filesystems/devices** mounted in the shell. The utilization command shown next shows usage of memory, CPU, and storage resources in real time.

Example 7-2   *Guest Shell Status and Resource Allocation*

```
N3K-C3548P#
N3K-C3548P# show guestshell
Virtual service guestshell+ detail
  State                 : Activated
  Package information
    Name                : guestshell.ova
    Path                : /isanboot/bin/guestshell.ova
    Application
      Name              : GuestShell
      Installed version : 2.4(0.0)
      Description       : Cisco Systems Guest Shell
    Signing
      Key type          : Cisco release key
      Method            : SHA-1
    Licensing
      Name              : None
      Version           : None
  Resource reservation
    Disk                : 250 MB
    Memory              : 256 MB
    CPU                 : 1% system CPU

  Attached devices
    Type              Name          Alias
    ----------------------------------------------
    Disk              _rootfs
    Disk              /cisco/core
    Serial/shell
    Serial/aux
    Serial/Syslog                   serial2
    Serial/Trace                    serial3
N3K-C3548P#
N3K-C3548P# show virtual-service utilization name guestshell+
Virtual-Service Utilization:

CPU Utilization:
  Requested Application Utilization:  1 %
  Actual Application Utilization:  0 % (30 second average)
  CPU State: R : Running

Memory Utilization:
  Memory Allocation: 262144 KB
  Memory Used:       13444 KB
```

```
Storage Utilization:
  Name: _rootfs, Alias:
    Capacity(1K blocks):   243823    Used(1K blocks): 156896
    Available(1K blocks): 82331      Usage: 66 %


  Name: /cisco/core, Alias:
    Capacity(1K blocks):   2097152   Used(1K blocks): 0
    Available(1K blocks): 2097152    Usage: 0  %
N3K-C3548P#
```

By default, the resources allocated to the Guest Shell are small compared to the total resources available in a switch. An administrator can change the size of the CPU, memory, and root filesystem (rootfs) resources allocated to the Guest Shell by using **guestshell resize** commands in the configuration mode. Note that after changing resource allocations, a Guest Shell reboot is required. This can be achieved by using the **guestshell reboot** command, which basically deactivates and reactivates the Guest Shell.

Accessing Guest Shell

By default, the Guest Shell starts with an open-ssh service as soon as it is enabled. The server listens to TCP port 17700 on the local host loopback IP interface 127.0.0.1. This provides password-less access to the Guest Shell from the NX-OS, as shown in Example 7-3.

Example 7-3 *Access Guest Shell*

```
N3K-C3548P#
N3K-C3548P# guestshell
[admin@guestshell ~]$
[admin@guestshell ~]$ whoami
admin
[admin@guestshell ~]$ hostnamectl
   Static hostname: guestshell
         Icon name: computer-container
           Chassis: container
        Machine ID: 2a79cdc74cdc45659ad7788742da0599
           Boot ID: 295a7ceda3684f3caa2d5597de8ae1e0
    Virtualization: lxc-libvirt
  Operating System: CentOS Linux 7 (Core)
       CPE OS Name: cpe:/o:centos:centos:7
            Kernel: Linux 4.1.21-WR8.0.0.25-standard
      Architecture: x86-64
[admin@guestshell ~]$
[admin@guestshell ~]$
[admin@guestshell ~]$ ps -ef | grep 17700
```

```
UID          PID  PPID  C STIME TTY        TIME    CMD
root          91     1  0 Aug30 ?      00:00:00 /usr/sbin/sshd -D -f /etc/ssh/
  sshd_config-cisco -p 17700 -o ListenAddress=localhost
admin       1515  1495  0 18:40 pts/4   00:00:00 grep --color=auto 17700
[admin@guestshell ~]$
```

Notice that the file used to spawn the default SSH process is **/etc/ssh/sshd_config-cisco**. If this file is altered, the **guestshell** command might not function properly. If that occurs, it is recommended that you destroy and re-enable the Guest Shell.

Accessing Guest Shell via SSH

To access the Guest Shell, you need to be in the switch first and then access the shell using the **guestshell** command mentioned earlier in this chapter in "Accessing Guest Shell." This access can be slow, and it is highly preferable to have a direct SSH access.

As you see in Example 7-4, after logging into the Guest Shell, check the SSH configuration—the TCP port it is listening to and the IPv4/v6 addresses associated to the SSH service. Because NX-OS has allocated TCP port number 22 to the SSH process running in the switch, configure an unused and different TCP port number for the Guest Shell's SSH daemon. As you see in Example 7-4, **/etc/ssh/sshd_config** has Port 2222 assigned to the service, and it is listening for connections at 10.102.242.131, which is the IP address assigned to the Ethernet1/1 interface of the switch. Make sure to configure the DNS server for name resolution and domain information for the Guest Shell and the applications installed in it to resolve domain names.

Example 7-4 *Guest Shell Networking*

```
[admin@guestshell ~]$ more /etc/ssh/sshd_config
<snip>
Port 2222
#AddressFamily any
ListenAddress 10.102.242.131
#ListenAddress ::
<snip>
[admin@guestshell ~]$
[admin@guestshell ~]$ cat /etc/resolv.conf
nameserver 8.8.8.8
search example.com
[admin@guestshell ~]$
```

In any CentOS-based Linux platform, Guest Shell uses **systemd** as its service manager. Therefore, **systemctl** commands can be used to start, stop, restart, reload, or check the status of the SSH service, as shown in Example 7-5. Check the status of the SSH service before starting it.

Example 7-5 *Activate SSH Service*

```
[admin@guestshell etc]$ systemctl start sshd
[admin@guestshell ~]$
[admin@guestshell ~]$ systemctl status sshd.service
sshd.service - OpenSSH server daemon
Loaded: loaded (/usr/lib/systemd/system/sshd.service; disabled; vendor preset:
  enabled)
Active: inactive (dead)
<snip>
[admin@guestshell ~]$
[admin@guestshell ~]$ systemctl start sshd.service -l
[admin@guestshell ~]$
[admin@guestshell ~]$ systemctl status sshd.service -l
sshd.service - OpenSSH server daemon
Loaded: loaded (/usr/lib/systemd/system/sshd.service; disabled; vendor preset:
  enabled)
Active: active (running) since Sat 2019-08-31 15:33:52 UTC; 4s ago
Main PID: 886 (sshd)
 CGroup: /system.slice/sshd.service
         └─886 /usr/sbin/sshd -D
Aug 31 15:33:52 guestshell sshd[886]: Executing: /usr/sbin/sshd -D
Aug 31 15:33:52 guestshell sshd[886]: Server listening on 10.102.242.131 port 2222.
[admin@guestshell ~]$
```

As shown in Example 7-6, make sure the TCP socket assigned to Guest Shell's SSH service is open and in the listening state. Because Guest Shell uses **kstack** networking implementation, a Kernel Socket is allocated for TCP port 2222, as shown in Example 7-6.

Example 7-6 *Open Kernel Sockets in Nexus Switch*

```
N3K-C3548P#
N3K-C3548P# show sockets connection
Total number of netstack tcp sockets: 3
Active connections (including servers)
        Protocol State/      Recv-Q/    Local Address(port)/
                 Context     Send-Q     Remote Address(port)
[host]: tcp(4/6) LISTEN      0          *(22)
                 Wildcard    0          *(*)

[host]: tcp      LISTEN      0          *(161)
                 Wildcard    0          *(*)

[host]: tcp(4/6) LISTEN      0          *(161)
                 Wildcard    0          *(*)
```

```
<snip>
Kernel Socket Connection:
Netid    State    Recv-Q   Send-Q   Local Address:Port    Peer Address:Port
tcp      LISTEN   0        128      10.102.242.131:2222   *:*
<snip>
```

Once the SSH service is up and running and all the configured sockets are in the listening state, users can access Guest Shell via SSH from an external device, as shown in Example 7-7.

Example 7-7 *SSH Access to Guest Shell*

```
root@Ubuntu-Server1$ ssh -p 2222 admin@10.102.242.131
admin@10.102.242.131's password:
Last login: Sat Aug 31 11:42:26 2019
[admin@guestshell ~]$
```

It is possible to run multiple instances of SSH Server daemons and associate them to any VRF active in the switch. In other words, the Guest Shell can be accessed via SSH through two sockets associated to different namespaces or VRFs, hence from different networks. Example 7-8 shows that the switch has two sockets open: one for **management** VRF and the other one for **default** VRF. The socket allocated for the SSH service in the **default** VRF is (172.16.1.1:5123) and is (10.102.242.131:2222) for the **management** VRF.

Example 7-8 *SSH Service per Namespace*

```
[admin@guestshell ~]$ chvrf default
[admin@guestshell ~]$
[admin@guestshell ~]$ /usr/sbin/sshd -p 5123 -o ListenAddress=172.16.1.1
[admin@guestshell ~]$
[admin@guestshell ~]$ exit
N3K-C3548P#
N3K-C3548P# show sockets connection | include Netid|2222|5123
Netid    State    Recv-Q   Send-Q  Local Address:Port    Peer Address:Port
tcp      LISTEN   0        128     172.16.1.1:5123       *:*
tcp      LISTEN   0        128     10.102.242.131:2222   *:*
N3K-C3548P#
```

Guest Shell Networking Setup and Verification

Guest Shell is a powerful container and application hosting environment because it provides access to every front-panel port, VLAN SVIs, and port-channels in the device. Using the Cisco **kstack** implementation, all these interfaces are represented and available as network devices in the Linux kernel.

With the command shown in Example 7-9, check the VRFs that are visible to the Guest Shell container, where each VRF is a Kernel Network Namespace, as represented in the Linux kernel.

Example 7-9 *Guest Shell Namespaces*

```
[admin@guestshell ~]$ ip netns list
management
default
[admin@guestshell ~]$
```

Figure 7-4 illustrates that namespaces created for each of the VRFs and shows the interfaces associated to each of these VRFs.

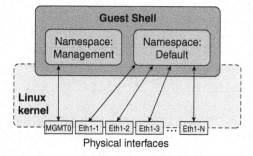

Figure 7-4 *Guest Shell Namespaces*

Because the physical and logical interfaces are accessible through network namespaces, the container can access network elements directly. As shown in Example 7-10, the **chvrf** command switches the context to a specific VRF, and **ifconfig -a** is used to list the interfaces associated to the current context.

The **chvrf** command is a helper utility that uses the **ip netns exec** command under the hood to switch the VRF context. Apart from the **ifconfig** command provided in this example, you can also use the **ip link show** command to obtain a list of interfaces associated to the specific context.

Example 7-10 *Guest Shell Namespaces and Network Devices*

```
[admin@guestshell ~]$ chvrf default
[admin@guestshell ~]$
[admin@guestshell ~]$ ifconfig -a
Eth1-1: flags=4163<UP,BROADCAST,RUNNING,MULTICAST>  mtu 1500
        inet 10.102.242.131 netmask 255.255.255.240 broadcast 10.102.242.143
        ether 00:3a:9c:5a:00:67  txqueuelen 100  (Ethernet)
        RX packets 2045299  bytes 469647600 (447.8 MiB)
        RX errors 0  dropped 1615524  overruns 0  frame 0
```

```
           TX packets 556549  bytes 95536394 (91.1 MiB)
           TX errors 0  dropped 892 overruns 0  carrier 0  collisions 0


Eth1-2: flags=4099<UP,BROADCAST,MULTICAST>  mtu 1500
           ether 00:3a:9c:5a:00:67  txqueuelen 100  (Ethernet)
           RX packets 0  bytes 0 (0.0 B)
          RX errors 0  dropped 0  overruns 0  frame 0
           TX packets 0  bytes 0 (0.0 B)
           TX errors 0  dropped 0 overruns 0  carrier 0  collisions 0


Eth1-3: flags=4099<UP,BROADCAST,MULTICAST>  mtu 1500
           ether 00:3a:9c:5a:00:67  txqueuelen 100  (Ethernet)
           RX packets 0  bytes 0 (0.0 B)
<snip>
Eth1-48: flags=4099<UP,BROADCAST,MULTICAST>  mtu 1500
           ether 00:3a:9c:5a:00:67  txqueuelen 100  (Ethernet)
           RX packets 0  bytes 0 (0.0 B)
           RX errors 0  dropped 0  overruns 0  frame 0
           TX packets 0  bytes 0 (0.0 B)
           TX errors 0  dropped 0 overruns 0  carrier 0  collisions 0


Lo100: flags=65<UP,RUNNING>  mtu 1500
           inet 10.1.1.1  netmask 255.255.255.0
           ether 00:3a:9c:5a:00:60  txqueuelen 100  (Ethernet)
           RX packets 0  bytes 0 (0.0 B)
           RX errors 0  dropped 0  overruns 0  frame 0
           TX packets 0  bytes 0 (0.0 B)
           TX errors 0  dropped 0 overruns 0  carrier 0  collisions 0
<snip>
veobc: flags=67<UP,BROADCAST,RUNNING>  mtu 1494
           inet 127.1.2.1  netmask 255.255.255.0  broadcast 127.1.2.255
           ether 00:00:00:00:01:01  txqueuelen 0  (Ethernet)
           RX packets 0  bytes 0 (0.0 B)
           RX errors 0  dropped 0  overruns 0  frame 0
           TX packets 134  bytes 57112 (55.7 KiB)
           TX errors 0  dropped 0 overruns 0  carrier 0  collisions 0
<snip>
[admin@guestshell ~]$
```

All the software data structures, including ARP tables, routing tables, and prefixes, are synchronized between NX-OS and the Linux kernel by the NetBroker process, as illustrated in Figure 7-5. Because the Guest Shell uses the Linux **kstack**, the data structures synchronization is automatic.

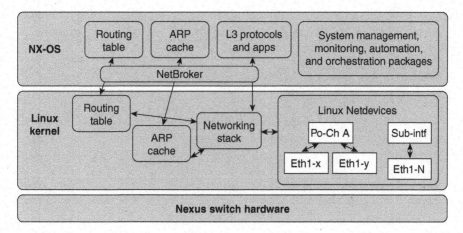

Figure 7-5 *NetBroker—Synchronize NX-OS and the Linux Kernel*

The commands provided in Example 7-11 show the routing table, interface configuration, and statistics as well as the ARP cache in a specific context.

Example 7-11 *Guest Shell Routing and ARP Tables—Default Namespace*

```
[admin@guestshell ~]$
[admin@guestshell ~]$ chvrf default route -vn
Kernel IP routing table
Destination     Gateway         Genmask         Flags Metric Ref   Use Iface
0.0.0.0         10.102.242.129  0.0.0.0         UG    51     0      0 Eth1-1
10.1.1.0        0.0.0.0         255.255.255.0   U     0      0      0 Lo100
10.102.242.128  0.0.0.0         255.255.255.240 U     0      0      0 Eth1-1
10.102.242.129  0.0.0.0         255.255.255.255 UH    51     0      0 Eth1-1
127.1.0.0       0.0.0.0         255.255.0.0     U     0      0      0 veobc
127.1.2.0       0.0.0.0         255.255.255.0   U     0      0      0 veobc
[admin@guestshell ~]$
[admin@guestshell ~]$ ifconfig -a Eth1-1
Eth1-1: flags=4163<UP,BROADCAST,RUNNING,MULTICAST>  mtu 1500
        inet 10.102.242.131 netmask 255.255.255.240 broadcast 10.102.242.143
        ether 00:3a:9c:5a:00:67  txqueuelen 100  (Ethernet)
        RX packets 2044610  bytes 469523762 (447.7 MiB)
        RX errors 0  dropped 1614879  overruns 0  frame 0
        TX packets 556415  bytes 95505736 (91.0 MiB)
        TX errors 0  dropped 892 overruns 0  carrier 0  collisions 0
[admin@guestshell ~]$
[admin@guestshell ~]$ arp 10.102.242.129
Address         HWtype  HWaddress           Flags Mask        Iface
10.102.242.129  ether   00:1e:f7:be:70:c2   CM                Eth1-1
[admin@guestshell ~]$
```

Make sure the new route added in the default VRF context is synchronized to the global routing table. As shown in Example 7-12, a /16 route is added in the NX-OS, which has synchronized to the Guest Shell.

Example 7-12 *NX-OS and Guest Shell Synchronization*

```
N3K-C3548P#(config)# config t
Enter configuration commands, one per line. End with CNTL/Z.
N3K-C3548P(config)# ip route 192.168.0.0/16 10.102.242.129
N3K-C3548P(config)# end
N3K-C3548P# guestshell
[admin@guestshell ~]$
[admin@guestshell ~]$ chvrf default route -nv
Kernel IP routing table
Destination     Gateway         Genmask         Flags Metric Ref   Use Iface
0.0.0.0         10.102.242.129  0.0.0.0         UG    51     0       0 Eth1-1
10.1.1.0        0.0.0.0         255.255.255.0   U     0      0       0 Lo100
10.102.242.128  0.0.0.0         255.255.255.240 U     0      0       0 Eth1-1
10.102.242.129  0.0.0.0         255.255.255.255 UH    51     0       0 Eth1-1
127.1.0.0       0.0.0.0         255.255.0.0     U     0      0       0 veobc
127.1.2.0       0.0.0.0         255.255.255.0   U     0      0       0 veobc
192.168.0.0     10.102.242.129  255.255.0.0     UG    51     0       0 Eth1-1
[admin@guestshell ~]$
```

The NetBroker module synchronizes the ARP, routes, and other Layer 3 configuration to every kernel namespace available. Now you will switch to the Management namespace and verify the routes and ARP cache there (see Example 7-13).

Example 7-13 *Guest Shell Routing and ARP Tables—Management Namespace*

```
[admin@guestshell ~]$
[admin@guestshell ~]$ chvrf management
[admin@guestshell ~]$
[admin@guestshell ~]$ ifconfig -a
eth1: flags=4099<UP,BROADCAST,RUNNING,MULTICAST>  mtu 1500
        inet 172.16.31.5  netmask 255.255.255.0  broadcast 172.16.31.255
        ether 00:3a:9c:5a:00:60  txqueuelen 1000  (Ethernet)
        RX packets 656019  bytes 48111417 (45.8 MiB)
        RX errors 0  dropped 0  overruns 0  frame 0
        TX packets 118874  bytes 31380645 (29.9 MiB)
        TX errors 0  dropped 0 overruns 0  carrier 0  collisions 0
<snip>
[admin@guestshell ~]$ chvrf management route -vn
Kernel IP routing table
```

```
Destination      Gateway        Genmask         Flags Metric Ref  Use Iface
0.0.0.0          172.16.31.1    0.0.0.0         UG    51     0      0 eth1
<snip>
[admin@guestshell ~]$
[admin@guestshell ~]$ arp 172.16.31.1
Address          HWtype  HWaddress          Flags Mask          Iface
172.16.31.1      ether   00:1e:f7:a3:81:c6  CM                  eth1
[admin@guestshell ~]$
```

Installation and Verification of Applications

As you see in Example 7-14, the Guest Shell in Cisco Nexus 9000 Series devices supports Python version 2.7.5 in both interactive and noninteractive (script) modes.

The Python scripting capability in Nexus 9000 gives programmatic access to the device's command-line interface (CLI) to perform various tasks like Power On Auto Provisioning (POAP) and Embedded Event Manager (EEM).

Example 7-14 *Python in Guest Shell*

```
[admin@guestshell ~]$
[admin@guestshell ~]$ python
Python 2.7.5 (default, Jun 17 2014, 18:11:42)
[GCC 4.8.2 20140120 (Red Hat 4.8.2-16)] on linux2
Type "help", "copyright", "credits" or "license" for more information.
>>> print "Hello"
Hello
>>> quit()
[admin@guestshell ~]$
```

You will start with developing and running a Python application in the Guest Shell.

Custom Python Application

Python applications can be run from NX-OS using the **run guestshell python** command, or they can be natively run in the shell itself. As you see in Example 7-15, the Python application hello.py runs natively from NX-OS using the **run guestshell python** command and from the Guest Shell using the **python** command.

Example 7-15 *Run Python Application in Guest Shell*

```
N3K-C3548P#
N3K-C3548P# show file bootflash:hello.py
#!/usr/bin/env python
```

```
import sys

print "Hello, World!"
list = ['one', 'two', 'three']
for item in list:
      print item
N3K-C3548P#
N3K-C3548P# run guestshell python /bootflash/hello.py
Hello, World!
one
two
three
N3K-C3548P#
N3K-C3548P# guestshell
[admin@guestshell ~]$
[admin@guestshell ~]$ python /bootflash/hello.py
Hello, World!
one
two
three
[admin@guestshell ~]$ exit
N3K-C3548P#
```

Python API–Based Application

Cisco NX-OS has a built-in package providing API access to CLIs at the exec level as well
as configuration commands, referred to as Python APIs. As you learned previously, Guest
Shell also has access to Python APIs. As you see in Example 7-16, an NX-OS CLI **show
clock** is accessed using the Python API available in the Guest Shell.

Example 7-16 *Python API–Based Application*

```
N3K-C3548P#
N3K-C3548P# guestshell
[admin@guestshell ~]$
[admin@guestshell ~]$ python
Python 2.7.5 (default, Jun 17 2014, 18:11:42)
[GCC 4.8.2 20140120 (Red Hat 4.8.2-16)] on linux2
Type "help", "copyright", "credits" or "license" for more information.
>>>
>>> from cli import *
>>> cli('show clock')
'02:24:50.130 UTC Sun Sep 01 2019\nTime source is NTP\n'
>>> exit()
[admin@guestshell ~]$
```

Example 7-17 shows a sample custom Python application that leverages Python APIs. In this example, **cli** returns the raw format of the CLI output, including control and special characters. **clid** returns a dictionary of attribute names and values for the given CLI commands, which makes it easier to process the data programmatically and automate.

Example 7-17 *Python API–Based Application: JSON*

```
[admin@guestshell ~]$ more PY-API2.py


#!/usr/bin/python
from cli import *
import json

print("STANDARD CLI OUTPUT ...")
print (cli('show interface eth1/1 brief'))

print("JSON FORMAT CLI OUTPUT ...")
print (clid('show interface eth1/1 brief'))

[admin@guestshell ~]$
[admin@guestshell ~]$
[admin@guestshell ~]$ python PY-API2.py
STANDARD CLI OUTPUT ...
--------------------------------------------------------------------------
Ethernet    VLAN    Type Mode    Status  Reason      Speed     Port
Interface                                                      Ch #
--------------------------------------------------------------------------
Eth1/1      --      eth  routed up        none       1000(D)   --

JSON FORMAT CLI OUTPUT ...
{"TABLE_interface": {"ROW_interface": {"interface": "Ethernet1/1", "vlan": "--",
  "type": "eth", "portmode": "routed", "state": "up", "state_rsn_desc": "none",
  "speed": "1000", "ratemode": "D"}}}
[admin@guestshell ~]$
```

To learn more about Python APIs and the Software Development Kit (SDK) supported in Nexus 9000 platforms, refer to the *Cisco Nexus 9000 Series SDK User Guide* provided in the "References" section.

The **dohost** command shown in Example 7-18 is a Python wrapper script using NX-API functions. Make sure to have the NX-API feature enabled to leverage this capability. Using **dohost** capability, application developers can perform **show** commands as well as configuration commands.

Example 7-18   *Run NX-OS CLIs in Guest Shell with dohost*

```
[admin@guestshell ~]$
[admin@guestshell ~]$ dohost "show clock"
02:23:41.492 UTC Sun Sep 01 2019
Time source is NTP
```

As you learned in the previous section, the Guest Shell with CentOS 7 also can install software packages using Yum utility. The Guest Shell is prepopulated with many of the common tools that would naturally be expected on a networking device, including net-tools, iproute, tcpdump, OpenSSH, and the PIP for installing additional Python packages. As you have just learned, Python 2.7.5 is included by default.

Leveraging high-end capabilities and features in Guest Shell, it is easy to integrate it into your day-to-day automation workflow. With the support of device-level API integration and support for scripting with languages like Python, Ruby, and so on, it is easier now to do on-box prototyping of applications or scripts. Guest Shell has its user space and resources isolated from the host and other containers and any faults/failures seen in those container spaces. All the capabilities make Guest Shell a powerful environment to develop and host applications.

Bash

In addition to the NX-OS CLI, Cisco Nexus 9000 Series devices support access to Bash. Bash interprets commands that you enter or commands that are read from a shell script. It enables access to the underlying Linux kernel on the device and to manage the system.

As you learned in the previous sections, Bash is supported in Nexus 3000 and 9000 switching platforms, but it is disabled by default.

Enabling Bash

In the supported platforms, under configuration mode, the **feature bash-shell** command enables this feature with no special license required. Use the **show bash-shell** command to learn the current state of the feature, as shown in Example 7-19.

Example 7-19   *Check Status and Enable Bash*

```
N9K-C93180YC# show bash-shell
Bash shell is disabled
N9K-C93180YC#
N9K-C93180YC# conf t
Enter configuration commands, one per line. End with CNTL/Z.
N9K-C93180YC(config)# feature bash-shell
N9K-C93180YC(config)# end
```

```
N9K-C93180YC#
N9K-C93180YC# show bash-shell
Bash shell is enabled
N9K-C93180YC#
```

Accessing Bash from NX-OS

In Cisco NX-OS, Bash is accessible for users whose role is set to network-admin or dev-ops; through Bash, a user can change system settings or parameters that could impact devices' operation and stability.

You can execute Bash commands with the **run bash** command, as shown in Example 7-20.

Example 7-20   *Run Bash Commands from NX-OS*

```
N9K-C93180YC#
N9K-C93180YC# run bash pwd
/bootflash/home/admin
N9K-C93180YC#
N9K-C93180YC# run bash ls
N9K-C93180YC# run bash uname -r
4.1.21-WR8.0.0.25-standard
N9K-C93180YC#
N9K-C93180YC# run bash more /proc/version
Linux version 4.1.21-WR8.0.0.25-standard (divvenka@ins-ucs-bld8) (gcc version 4.6.3
   (Wind River Linux Sourcery CodeBench 4.6-60) ) #1 SMP Sun Nov 4 19:44:18 PST 2018
N9K-C93180YC#
N9K-C93180YC#
```

The **run bash** command loads Bash and begins at the home directory for the user. Example 7-21 shows how to load and run Bash as an admin user.

Example 7-21   *Access Bash Through Console*

```
N9K-C93180YC#
N9K-C93180YC# run bash
bash-4.3$
bash-4.3$ pwd
/bootflash/home/admin
bash-4.3$
bash-4.3$ whoami
admin
bash-4.3$
bash-4.3$ id
```

```
uid=2002(admin) gid=503(network-admin) groups=503(network-admin),504(network-
  operator)
bash-4.3$
bash-4.3$ more /proc/version
Linux version 4.1.21-WR8.0.0.25-standard (divvenka@ins-ucs-bld8) (gcc version 4.
6.3 (Wind River Linux Sourcery CodeBench 4.6-60) ) #1 SMP Sun Nov 4 19:44:18 PST
 2018
bash-4.3$
```

For users without network-admin or dev-ops level privileges, the **run bash** command
will not be parsed, and when executed, the system will report that permission has been
denied. As you see in Example 7-22, the **testuser** with the privilege level not set to
network-admin or dev-ops has its permission to execute the **run bash** command denied.

Example 7-22 *Access Bash Privileges*

```
User Access Verification
N9K-C93180YC login: testuser
Password:
Cisco Nexus Operating System (NX-OS) Software
TAC support: http://www.cisco.com/tac
Copyright (C) 2002-2018, Cisco and/or its affiliates.
All rights reserved.
<snip>
N9K-C93180YC# run bash
% Permission denied for the role
N9K-C93180YC#
```

Accessing Bash via SSH

Before accessing Bash via SSH, make sure the SSH service is enabled (see Example 7-23).

Example 7-23 *Access Bash Privileges*

```
bash-4.3$ service /etc/init.d/sshd status
openssh-daemon (pid 14190) is running…
bash-4.3$
bash-4.3$ ps -ef | grep sshd
UID         PID  PPID  C STIME TTY          TIME CMD
admin      5619  5584  0 01:26 ttyS0    00:00:00 grep sshd
root      14190     1  0 Sep12 ?        00:00:00 /usr/sbin/sshd
bash-4.3$
bash-4.3$ ps --pid 1
  PID TTY          TIME CMD
    1 ?        00:00:28 init
bash-4.3$
```

An NX-OS admin user can configure a user with privileges to directly log in to the Bash. Example 7-24 demonstrates user **bashuser** with a default shelltype access.

Example 7-24 *Access Bash Privileges: shelltype*

```
N9K-C93180YC#
N9K-C93180YC# conf t
Enter configuration commands, one per line. End with CNTL/Z.
N9K-C93180YC(config)#
N9K-C93180YC(config)# username bashuser password 0 Cisco!123
N9K-C93180YC(config)# username bashuser shelltype bash
N9K-C93180YC(config)# end
N9K-C93180YC#
```

Log in to Bash directly from an external device with username **bashuser**, as shown in Example 7-25.

Example 7-25 *Access Bash—Shelltype User*

```
Ubuntu-Server$ ssh -l bashuser 172.16.28.5
User Access Verification
Password:
-bash-4.3$
-bash-4.3$ pwd
/var/home/bashuser
-bash-4.3$
-bash-4.3$ id
uid=2003(bashuser) gid=504(network-operator) groups=504(network-operator)
-bash-4.3$
-bash-4.3$ whoami
bashuser
-bash-4.3$
-bash-4.3$ exit
logout
Connection to 10.102.242.131 closed.
Ubuntu-Server$
```

Following are the guidelines for elevating the privileges of an existing user.

■ Bash must be enabled before elevating user privileges.

■ Only an admin user can escalate privileges of a user to root.

■ Escalation to root is password protected.

If you SSH to the switch using the **root** username through a nonmanagement interface, it will default to Linux Bash shell-type access for the root user. If a user has established

an SSH connection directly to Bash and needs to access NX-OS, use **vsh** commands, as
shown in Example 7-26.

Example 7-26 *Access NX-OS from Bash*

```
bash-4.3$
bash-4.3$ vsh -c "show clock"
21:17:24:136 UTC Fri Sep 13 2019
Time source is NTP
bash-4.3$
bash-4.3$ su - root
Password:
root@N9K-C93180YC#
root@N9K-C93180YC# id
uid=0(root) gid=0(root) groups=0(root)
root@N9K-C93180YC# whoami
root
root@N9K-C93180YC#
root@N9K-C93180YC# vsh
Cisco Nexus Operating System (NX-OS) Software
TAC support: http://www.cisco.com/tac
Copyright (C) 2002-2018, Cisco and/or its affiliates.
All rights reserved.
<snip>
root@N9K-C93180YC#
root@N9K-C93180YC# show clock
21:18:53.903 UTC Fri Sep 13 2019
Time source is NTP
root@N9K-C93180YC#
```

Based on what you have learned this section, Bash interprets the instructions and commands
that a user or application provides and executes. With direct access to the underlying infrastructure, file systems, and network interfaces, it enables developers to build and host applications to monitor and manage the devices. However, users should exercise extreme caution
when accessing, configuring, or making changes to the underlying infrastructure because
doing so could affect the host system's operation and performance. Remember that Bash
directly accesses the Wind River Linux (WRL) on which NX-OS is running in a user space,
and unlike Guest Shell or OAC, it is not isolated from the host system.

Docker Containers

Docker provides a way to securely run applications in an isolated environment, with
all dependencies and libraries packaged. If you want to know more about Docker, its
usage, and functionalities, refer to the *Docker Documentation* page provided in the
"References" section.

Beginning with Release 9.2(1), support has been included for using Docker within the Cisco NX-OS switch. The version of Docker that is included on the switch is 1.13.1. By default, the Docker service or daemon is not enabled. You must start it manually or set it up to automatically restart when the switch boots up.

Even though the scope of this book does not intend to cover Docker in detail, it is good to take a quick look at the key components in the Docker architecture and their functions, as illustrated in Figure 7-6.

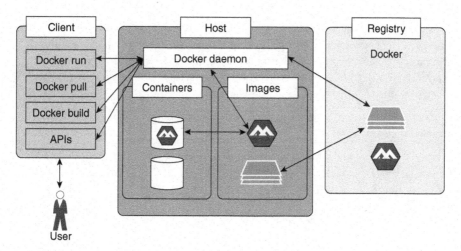

Figure 7-6 *Docker Architecture*

Docker Client

The Docker client enables end users to interact with the Docker host and the daemons running on it. The Docker client can be on a dedicated device or can reside on the same device as a host. A Docker client can communicate with multiple daemons running on multiple host devices. The Docker client provides a CLI and REST APIs that allow users to issue build, run, and stop application commands to a Docker daemon. The main purpose of the Docker client is to provide a means to direct pulling images from a registry and having them run on a Docker host.

Docker Host

The Docker host provides an environment dedicated to executing and running applications. The key component is a Docker daemon that interacts with the client as well as the registry and with containers, images, the network, and storage. This daemon is responsible for all container-related activities and carrying out the tasks received via CLIs or APIs. The Docker daemon pulls the requested image and builds containers as requested by the client, following the instructions provided in a build file.

Images

Images are read-only templates providing instructions to create a Docker container. The images contain metadata that describe the container's capabilities and needs. The necessary Docker images can be pulled from the Docker Hub or a local registry. Users can create their own and customized images by adding elements to extend the capabilities, using Dockerfile.

Containers

As has been discussed in previous chapters, containers are self-contained environments in which you run applications. The container is defined by the image and any additional configuration parameters provided during its instantiation. These configuration parameters are used to identify the file systems and partitions to mount, to set specific network mode, and so on.

Now you will learn how to enable and use Docker in the context of the Cisco Nexus switch environment.

Bash is a prerequisite to enable and activate Docker. Example 7-27 provides the detailed procedure to activate Docker. Before activating Docker, follow these steps.

1. Enable Bash.

2. Configure the domain name and name servers appropriately for the network.

3. If the switch is in a network that uses an HTTP proxy server, set up the **http_proxy** and **https_proxy** environment variables in the **/etc/sysconfig/docker** file.

Example 7-27   *Enable Bash to Activate Docker Service*

```
N9K-C93180YC# conf t
N9K-C93180YC(config)# feature bash-shell
N9K-C93180YC(config)# vrf context management
N9K-C93180YC(config-vrf)# ip domain-name cisco.com
N9K-C93180YC(config-vrf)# ip name-server 208.67.222.222
N9K-C93180YC(config-vrf)# ip name-server 208.67.220.220
N9K-C93180YC(config-vrf)# end
N9K-C93180YC# run bash
bash-4.3$
bash-4.3$ cat /etc/resolv.conf
domain cisco.com
nameserver 208.67.222.222
nameserver 208.67.220.220
bash-4.3$
bash-4.3$ cat /etc/sysconfig/docker | grep http
export http_proxy=http://192.168.21.150:8080
export https_proxy=http://192.168.21.150:8080
bash-4.3$
```

Starting Docker Daemon

Please be aware that when the Docker daemon is started for the first time, 2 GB of storage space is carved out for a file called **dockerpart** in the bootflash filesystem. This file will be mounted as **/var/lib/docker**. If needed, the default size of this space reservation can be changed by editing **/etc/sysconfig/docker** before you start the Docker daemon for the first time.

Start the Docker daemon by following Example 7-28.

Example 7-28 *Enable Docker Service*

```
bash-4.3$
bash-4.3$ service docker start
bash-4.3$
bash-4.3$ service docker status
dockerd (pid  5334) is running...
bash-4.3$
bash-4.3$ ps -ef | grep docker
UID    PID    PPID   C STIME TTY    TIME    CMD
root   16532     1   0 03:15 ttyS0  00:00:00 /usr/bin/dockerd --debug=true
root   16548 16532   0 03:15 ?      00:00:00 docker-containerd -l unix:///var
admin 16949 12789   0 03:18 ttyS0  00:00:00 grep docker
bash-4.3$
bash-4.3$
```

Instantiating a Docker Container with Alpine Image

As you can see in Example 7-29, the host device has various Docker images, including Alpine, Ubuntu, and nginx. Alpine Linux is a lightweight Linux distribution based on musl libc and Busybox, and it is security-oriented. Musl (read as, "muscle") libc is a standard library of Linux-based devices focused on standards-conformance and safety. Busybox brings many UNIX/Linux utilities together into a single and small executable; because it is modular, it is easy to customize and integrate it into embedded systems. For more information, see the references provided for Alpine Linux, musl libc, and Busybox, in the "References" section at the end of this chapter.

Example 7-29 shows instantiating an Alpine Linux Docker container on the switch, which is, by default, launched in the host network mode. The Docker containers instantiated in the **bridged** networking mode have external network connectivity but do not necessarily care about the visibility into or access to ports in the host. Note that the containers operating in **bridged** networking mode are far more secure than the ones operating in **host** networking mode.

Example 7-29   *Container with Alpine Image*

```
bash-4.3$
bash-4.3$ docker images
REPOSITORY        TAG        IMAGE ID        CREATED        SIZE
docker            dind       12adad4e12e2    3 months ago   183 MB
ubuntu            latest     d131e0fa2585    4 months ago   102 MB
nginx             latest     27a188018e18    5 months ago   109 MB
alpine            latest     cdf98d1859c1    5 months ago   5.53 MB
centos            latest     9f38484d220f    6 months ago   202 MB
alpine            3.2        98f5f2d17bd1    7 months ago   5.27 MB
hello-world       latest     fce289e99eb9    8 months ago   1.84 kB
bash-4.3$
bash-4.3$
bash-4.3$ docker run --name=myalpine  -v /var/run/netns:/var/run/netns:ro,rslave
  --rm --network host --cap-add SYS_ADMIN -it alpine
/ #
/ # whoami
root
/ # id
uid=0(root) gid=0(root) groups=0(root),1(bin),2(daemon),3(sys), 4(adm),6(disk),10(wh
  eel),11(floppy),20(dialout),26(tape),27(video)
/ #
/ #  ip route
default via 10.102.242.129 dev Eth1-1  metric 51 onlink
10.1.1.0/24 dev Lo100 scope link
10.102.242.128/28 dev Eth1-1 scope link
10.102.242.129 dev Eth1-1 scope link  metric 51
127.1.0.0/16 dev veobc scope link  src 127.1.1.1
127.1.2.0/24 dev veobc scope link  src 127.1.2.1
172.17.0.0/16 dev docker0 scope link  src 172.17.0.1
172.18.0.0/16 dev br-b96ec30eb010 scope link  src 172.18.0.1
172.16.0.0/16 via 10.102.242.129 dev Eth1-1  metric 51 onlink
/ #
/ # ifconfig Eth1-1
Eth1-1    Link encap:Ethernet  Hwaddr 00:3A:9C:5A:00:67
          inet addr:10.102.242.131 Bcast:10.102.242.143 Mask:255.255.255.240
          UP BROADCAST RUNNING MULTICAST  MTU:1500  Metric:1
          RX packets:2873124 errors:0 dropped:2299051 overruns:0 frame:0
          TX packets:797153 errors:0 dropped:1230 overruns:0 carrier:0
          collisions:0 txqueuelen:100
          RX bytes:622065894 (593.2 MiB)  TX bytes:135952384 (129.6 MiB)
/ #
```

Figure 7-7 illustrates a Docker container running an Alpine image that was instantiated from Bash by the commands provided in Example 7-29.

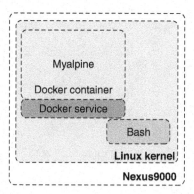

Figure 7-7   *Alpine Docker Container*

The **–rm** option used to launch the Docker container in Example 7-29 removes it automatically when the user exits the container with the **exit** command. Press Ctrl+Q to detach from the container without deinstantiating it and get back to Bash. Use the **docker attach <container-id>** command to reattach to the container that is still up and running, as shown in Example 7-30.

Example 7-30   *Docker Processes—Attach to Container*

```
bash-4.3$
bash-4.3$ docker ps
CONTAINER ID   IMAGE    COMMAND    CREATED         STATUS         PORTS     NAMES
6469af028115   alpine   "/bin/sh"  3 minutes ago   Up 3 minutes             myalpine
bash-4.3$
bash-4.3$ docker attach 6469af028115
/ #
/ #
```

If you want to mount a specific file system or partitions, use the **-v** option, as shown in Example 7-31, when you launch the container. The Bootflash file system will be mounted into and accessible only from the **myalpine1** container; it will not be available from **myalpine**, which was instantiated without mounting the Bootflash file system.

Example 7-31   *Docker Container—File System Mount*

```
bash-4.3$
bash-4.3$ docker run --name=myalpine1  -v /var/run/netns:/var/run/netns:ro,rslave -v
  /bootflash:/bootflash --rm --network host --cap-add SYS_ADMIN -it alpine
/ #
```

```
/ # ls
bin        etc        media      proc       sbin       tmp
bootflash  home       mnt        root       srv        usr
dev        lib        opt        run        sys        var
/ # / # ifconfig
Eth1-1     Link encap:Ethernet  Hwaddr 00:3A:9C:5A:00:67
           inet addr:10.102.242.131 Bcast:10.102.242.143 Mask:255.255.255.240
           UP BROADCAST RUNNING MULTICAST  MTU:1500  Metric:1
           RX packets:2848104 errors:0 dropped:2282704 overruns:0 frame:0
           TX packets:786971 errors:0 dropped:1209 overruns:0 carrier:0
           collisions:0 txqueuelen:100
      /    RX bytes:618092996 (589.4 MiB)  TX bytes:134371507 (128.1 MiB)

Eth1-10    Link encap:Ethernet  Hwaddr 00:3A:9C:5A:00:67
           UP BROADCAST MULTICAST  MTU:1500  Metric:1
<snip>
```

The Alpine Docker containers instantiated in the past few examples were done in the default host namespace. To instantiate a Docker container in a specific network namespace, use the **docker** run command with the **–network <namespace>** option.

Managing Docker Container

Beyond instantiating and activating containers with applications installed, you need to know how to manage the containers. Container management becomes critical when containers are deployed at scale. This section discusses managing containers deployed in the Nexus switches, and associated techniques.

Container Persistence Through Switchover

To have Docker container persisting through the manual supervisor engine switchover, make sure to copy the dockerpart file from the active supervisor engine's bootflash to the standby supervisor engine's bootflash before the switchover of supervisor engines in applicable platforms like Nexus 9500. Be aware that the Docker containers will not be running continuously and will be disrupted during the switchover.

You will start an Alpine container and configure it to always restart unless it is explicitly stopped or the Docker service is restarted. Please note that this command uses the **–restart** option instead of the **–rm** option, which restarts the container right after the user exits. See Example 7-32.

Example 7-32 *Docker Container—Persistent Restart*

```
bash-4.3$
bash-4.3$ docker run -dit --name=myalpine2 --restart unless-stopped --network host
  --cap-add SYS_ADMIN -it alpine
da28182a03c4032f263789ec997eea314130a95e6e6e6a0574e49dfcba5f2776
```

```
bash-4.3$
bash-4.3$ docker ps
CONTAINER ID  IMAGE   COMMAND     CREATED          STATUS          PORTS   NAMES
0355f5ba1fd6  alpine  "/bin/sh"   18 minutes ago   Up 5 minutes            myalpine2
bash-4.3$
bash-4.3$ docker attach 0355f5ba1fd6
/#
/# exit
bash-4.3$
bash-4.3$ docker ps
CONTAINER ID  IMAGE   COMMAND     CREATED          STATUS          PORTS   NAMES
0355f5ba1fd6  alpine  "/bin/sh"   19 minutes ago   Up 2 seconds            myalpine2
bash-4.3$
```

With the previous commands, you have made the Alpine Linux container restart. As shown in Example 7-33, use the **chkconfig** utility to make the service persistent, before the supervisor engine switchover. Then copy the dockerpart file created in the active supervisor engine to standby.

Example 7-33 *Docker Container—Restart on Supervisor Engine Failover*

```
bash-4.3$
bash-4.3$ chkconfig | grep docker
bash-4.3$
bash-4.3$ chkconfig --add docker
bash-4.3$
bash-4.3$ chkconfig | grep docker
docker          0:off   1:off   2:on    3:on    4:on    5:on    6:off
bash-4.3$
bash-4.3$ service docker stop
Stopping dockerd: dockerd shutdown
bash-4.3$
bash-4.3$ cp /bootflash/dockerpart /bootflash_sup-remote/
bash-4.3$
bash-4.3$ service docker start
bash-4.3$
```

Stopping the Docker Container and Service

If a specific container needs to be stopped, use the **docker stop** command, as shown in Example 7-34. To learn more Docker command options, use the **docker –help** and **docker run –help** commands.

When a specific container is stopped, all the applications, along with their packages and libraries, will cease to function, and any file system mounted will be unmounted.

Example 7-34 *Stopping the Docker Container*

```
bash-4.3$ docker ps
CONTAINER ID  IMAGE   COMMAND    CREATED        STATUS         PORTS   NAMES
0355f5ba1fd6  alpine  "/bin/sh"  36 minutes ago Up 13 minutes          myalpine2
bash-4.3$
bash-4.3$ docker stop 0355f5ba1fd6
0355f5ba1fd6
bash-4.3$
```

If a Docker service needs to be stopped altogether, follow the procedure as given in Example 7-35. As you have learned, if a Docker service is not up and running, containers will cease to exist in Nexus switches. Make sure to delete the dockerpart file from the active supervisor engine's bootflash as well as the standby's bootflash in applicable deployment scenarios.

Example 7-35 *Stopping the Docker Service*

```
bash-4.3$
bash-4.3$ service docker stop
Stopping dockerd: dockerd shutdown
bash-4.3$
bash-4.3$ service docker status
dockerd is stopped
bash-4.3$ exit
N9K-C93180YC#
N9K-C93180YC# delete bootflash:dockerpart
Do you want to delete "/dockerpart" ? (yes/no/abort) y
N9K-C93180YC#
```

Orchestrating Docker Containers Using Kubernetes

Kubernetes is an open-source platform for automating, deploying, scaling, and operating containers. Kubernetes was first created by Google and then donated to Cloud Native Compute Foundation (open source). Since Kubernetes became open source, there have been several projects to increase its scope and improve it to enable networking, storage, and more, which allows users to focus on developing and testing applications rather than spending resources to gain expertise in and maintain container infrastructure.

Kubernetes Architecture

Following is a brief discussion on the Kubernetes architecture, which will help you follow the procedures and examples provided later.

In a Kubernetes (or K8s) cluster functionally, there are two major blocks—Master and Node—as illustrated in Figure 7-8.

Master components provide the cluster's control plane. Master components make global decisions about the cluster (for example, scheduling) and detect and respond to cluster events (for example, starting up a new pod). Master components are kube-apiserver, etcd, kube-scheduler, kube-controller-manager, and cloud-controller-manager. Master components can be run on any machine in the cluster, and it is highly recommended that you have all master components running in the same machine, where no containers are instantiated.

Node components run on every host or a virtual machine, maintaining pods deployed and providing the Kubernetes runtime environment. Node components are kubelet, kube-proxy, and container runtime.

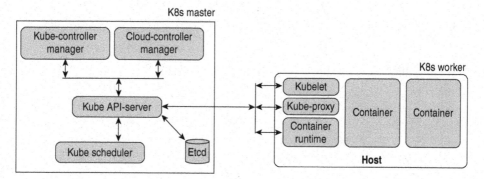

Figure 7-8   *Kubernetes Architecture*

The Cloud controller manager is a daemon that has the cloud-specific control loops. The Kubernetes controller manager is a daemon that has the core control loops. In K8s, a controller is a control loop that monitors the state of the cluster through the API server and makes necessary changes to move the current state toward the desired state. Examples of controllers that ship with Kubernetes are the replication controller, endpoints controller, namespace controller, and service accounts controller.

You will take a quick look at the common terminologies used in the Docker containers and Kubernetes world.

Pod

A pod is a group of containers sharing resources such as volumes, file systems, storage, and networks. It also is a specification on how these containers are run and operated. In a simple view, a pod is synonymous to an application-centric logical host, which contains one or more tightly coupled containers. In a given pod, the containers share an IP address and Layer 4 port space and can communicate with each other using standard interprocess communication.

Controllers

Kubernetes contains many higher-level abstractions called controllers. Controllers build upon the basic objects and provide additional functionality and convenience features, such as ReplicaSet, StatefulSet, and DaemonSet.

The objective of a ReplicaSet is to maintain a set of replica pods running at any given time, guaranteeing the availability of a specified number of identical pods.

StatefulSet is the workload API object used to manage stateful applications. It manages the deployment and scaling of a set of pods **and guarantees the ordering and uniqueness** of these pods.

A DaemonSet is an object that ensures that all or some of the nodes run a copy of a pod. As a cluster expands by adding more nodes, DaemonSet makes sure that pods are added to the new added nodes. When nodes are removed from the cluster, those pods are removed, and the garbage is collected.

If you need more information on Kubernetes, please see the Kubernetes page at https://kubernetes.io/.

Building Kubernetes Master

You are going to build a K8s Master in an Ubuntu server, as shown in Example 7-36.

A K8s Master can be run natively in a Linux environment such as Ubuntu. But for convenience, you will run the K8s Master as a Docker container. The command provided in the example enables the Docker service to prepare the Ubuntu server for running Kubernetes Master components. Note that the following example uses Kubernetes version 1.2.2.

Example 7-36 *Building K8s Master—Docker Service*

```
root@Ubuntu-Server1$
root@Ubuntu-Server1$ service docker start
root@Ubuntu-Server1$
root@Ubuntu-Server1$ service docker status
dockerd (pid  17362) is running…
root@Ubuntu-Server1$
```

etcd is a highly available database of the K8s Master, which has all cluster data in a key-value pair format. As shown in Example 7-37, the **docker run** command starts the etcd component. The IP address and TCP port it is listening to are 10.0.0.6 and 4001, respectively.

Example 7-37 *Building K8s Master—etcd*

```
root@Ubuntu-Server1$ docker run -d \
    --net=host \
 gcr.io/google_containers/etcd:2.2.1 \
 /usr/local/bin/etcd --listen-client-urls=http://10.0.0.6:4001 \
    --advertise-client-urls=http://10.0.0.6:4001 --data-dir=/var/etcd/data
```

As you notice in Example 7-38, the K8s Master components API server is started, and it is listening to the same IP address and TCP port as **etcd.**

Example 7-38 *Building K8s Master—API Server*

```
root@Ubuntu-Server1$ docker run -d --name=api \
    --net=host --pid=host --privileged=true \
  gcr.io/google_containers/hyperkrs/hyperkubeube:v1.2.2 \
/hyperkube apiserver --insecure-bind-address=10.0.0.6 \
      --allow-privileged=true \
      --service-cluster-ip-range=172.16.1.0/24 \
      --etcd_servers=http://10.0.0.6:4001 --v=2
```

The next step is to start the kubelet of the K8s Master components. The kubelet is listening to the same IP address as the **etcd** or the API server, but the TCP port is 8080. Please follow the steps provided in Example 7-39 to start the kubelet.

Example 7-39 *Building K8s Master—Kubelet*

```
root@Ubuntu-Server1$ docker run -d --name=kubs \
    --volume=/:/rootfs:ro --volume=/sys:/sys:ro --volume=/dev:/dev \
    --volume=/var/lib/docker/:/var/lib/docker:rw \
    --volume=/var/lib/kubelet/:/var/lib/kubelet:rw \
    --volume=/var/run:/var/run:rw --net=host --pid=host \
    --privileged=true \
  gcr.io/google_containers/hyperkube:v1.2.2 \
/hyperkube kubelet --allow-privileged=true \
    --hostname-override="10.0.0.6" \
    --address="10.0.0.6 --api-servers=http://10.0.0.6:8080 \
    --cluster_dns=10.0.0.10 \
    --cluster_domain=cluster.local --config=/etc/kubernetes/manifests-multi
```

The last step you need to do in the Master is to enable kube-proxy. It is a network proxy that runs on each node in your cluster, and it maintains the network rules on nodes. These network rules allow network communication to your pods from network sessions inside or outside your cluster. kube-proxy uses the operating system packet filtering layer if it is available. Enable kube-proxy as shown in Example 7-40.

Example 7-40 *Building K8s Master—Kube Proxy*

```
root@Ubuntu-Server1$ docker run -d --name=proxy --net=host –privileged gcr.io/
  google_containers/hyperkube:v1.2.2/hyperkube proxy --master=http://10.0.0.6:8080
  --v=2
```

Figure 7-9 illustrates the K8s Master running in an Ubuntu server and various components in the K8s Master.

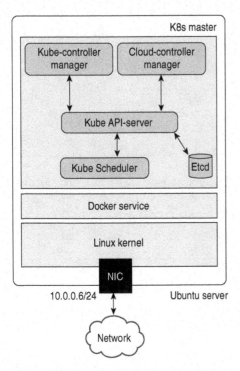

Figure 7-9   *Kubernetes Master—Ubuntu Server*

Now that you have a K8s Master service running, register Nexus 9000 as a node to the K8s Master. As you see in Example 7-41, the **docker run** commands register to the Master and the socket to which the kube-apiserver and other Master components are listening.

Example 7-41   *Register Nexus Switch as K8s Node to Master*

```
N9K-C93180YC# run bash
bash-4.3$
bash-4.3$ docker run -d --name=kubs --net=host --pid=host --privileged=true
  --volume=/:/rootfs:ro --volume=/sys:/sys:ro --volume=/dev:/dev --volume=/var/
  lib/docker/:/var/lib/docker:rw --volume=/var/lib/kubelet/:/var/lib/kubelet:rw
  --volume=/var/run:/var/run:rw \ gcr.io/google_containers/hyperkube:v1.2.2/
  hyperkube kubelet –allow-privileged=true --containerized --enable-server
  --cluster_dns=10.0.0.10 \--cluster_domain=cluster.local --config=/etc/
  kubernetes/manifests-multi \--hostname-override="10.0.0.6" --address=0.0.0.0
  --api-servers=http://10.0.0.6:4001
bash-4.3$
bash-4.3$ docker run  --name=proxy \--net=host --privileged=true gcr.io/google_
  containers/hyperkube:v1.2.2 /hyperkube proxy --master=http://10.0.0.6:4001 --v=2
bash-4.3$
```

Once the Nexus 9000 successfully registers as a K8s Node to the Master, it should begin to communicate with the Master. Figure 7-10 shows a Kubernetes Cluster, with an Ubuntu server acting as a K8s Master and a Nexus 9000 acting as a K8s Node.

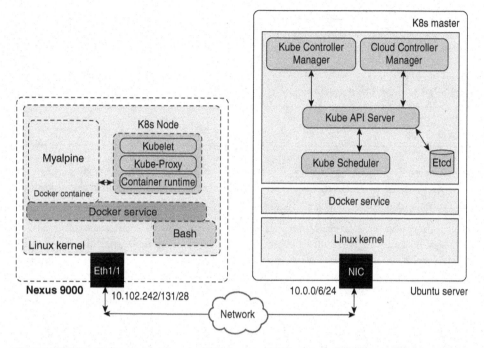

Figure 7-10 *Kubernetes Cluster*

The certificate exchange must happen between the Master and Node to establish a secure connection between them, so all the data and control message communication happens securely.

Orchestrating Docker Containers in a Node from the K8s Master

Now you will look into orchestration of Docker containers in a pod from the K8s Master and how you can manage them through their lifecycles. Kubectl is a critical component in managing and orchestrating containers.

Kubectl is a set of CLI commands to manage Kubernetes clusters. It can deploy applications and inspect and manage cluster resources, among other tasks.

Download and install kubectl packages in an Ubuntu server in which you have already instantiated the K8s Master. Example 7-42 shows using the **curl** command to download a specific version—in this case, it is v1.15.2. If you want to download a different version, replace v1.15.2 with the preferred version.

Example 7-42 *Install Kubectl in K8s Master*

```
root@Ubuntu-Server1$ curl -o ~/.bin/kubectl http://storage.googleapis.com/
  kubernetes-release/release/v1.15.2/bin/linux/amd64/kubectl
root@Ubuntu-Server1$
```

Change the permissions to make the binary executable, and move it into the executable path, as shown in Example 7-43.

Example 7-43 *Make Kubectl Executable*

```
root@Ubuntu-Server1$ chmod u+x ./kubectl
root@Ubuntu-Server1$ mv ./kubectl /usr/local/bin/kubectl
```

By default, kubectl configuration is located in the **~/.kube/config** file. For kubectl to discover and access a Kubernetes cluster, it looks for the **kubeconfig** file in the **~/.kube** directory, which is created automatically when your cluster is created.

This **kubeconfig** file organizes information about clusters, users, namespaces, and authentication mechanisms. The kubectl command uses **kubeconfig** files to find the information it needs to choose a cluster and communicate with the API server of a cluster. If required, you can use the **–kubeconfig** flag to specify other **kubeconfig** files.

To learn how to install kubectl on different operating systems like Microsoft Windows or Apple macOS, please refer to the Install and Setup Kubectl Guide provided in the References section. Table 7-6 shows the kubectl syntax for common operations with examples, such as **apply, get, describe,** and **delete.** Note that the filenames used in the following table are for illustrative purposes only.

Table 7-6 *Kubectl Operations and Commands*

Operations	Commands
Create a service using the definition in the example-service.yaml file	**kubectl apply -f example-service.yaml**
Create a replication controller using the definition in a YAML file	**kubectl apply -f example-controller.yaml**
Create the objects that are defined in any .yaml, .yml, or .json files in a specific directory	**kubectl apply -f <directory>**
List all pods in plain-text output format	**kubectl get pods <pod-name>**
Get a list of all pods in plain-text output format and include additional information (node name, etc.)	**kubectl get pods -o wide**
Get a list of pods sorted by name	**kubectl get pods --sort-by=.metadata.name**

Operations	Commands
Get a list of all pods running on node by name	**kubectl get pods --field-selector=spec. nodeName=<node-name>**
Display the details of the node with node name	**kubectl describe nodes <node-name>**
Display the details of the pod with pod name	**kubectl describe pods/<pod-name>**
Delete a pod using the label	**Kubectl delete pods -l name=<label>**
Delete a pod using the type and name specified in a YAML file	**kubectl delete -f pod.yaml**
Delete all pods—initialized as well as uninitialized ones	**kubectl delete pods --all**

For details about each operation command, including all the supported flags and subcommands, see the Kubectl Overview document provided in the "References" section.

Now that you have learned about kubectl, you will see how to use it to manage clusters and nodes. In this case, the Kubernetes clusters have the Ubuntu server as K8s Master, the Nexus 9000 as Node, and an application named Alpine deployed. Example 7-44 shows kubectl commands to get the nodes, deployment, and pods from the K8s Master. The command results indicate that an application is running as container **myalpine** in the K8s pods.

Example 7-44   *Use Kubectl to Get Nodes, Deployments, and Pods*

```
root@Ubuntu-Server1$
root@Ubuntu-Server1$ kubectl get nodes
NAME             STATUS    ROLES     AGE      VERSION
Ubuntu-Server1   Ready     master    11m      v1.2.2
N9K-C93180YC     Ready     <none>    18m      v1.2.2
root@Ubuntu-Server1$
root@Ubuntu-Server1$ kubectl get deployments
NAME             READY     UP-TO-DATE    AVAILABLE    AGE
alpine           1/1       1             1            16m
root@Ubuntu-Server1$
root@Ubuntu-Server1$ kubectl get pods
NAME             READY     STATUS        RESTARTS     AGE
myalpine         1/1       RUNNING       0            12m
root@Ubuntu-Server1$
```

If you need to delete a specific container, you can orchestrate it from the Master using the command given in Example 7-45. If the pod is using labels, it can also be deleted using the **kubectl delete pods -l** command, as provided in Table 7-6.

Example 7-45 *Use Kubectl to Delete Nodes, Deployments, and Pods*

```
root@Ubuntu-Server1$
root@Ubuntu-Server1$ kubectl delete pods myalpine
pod "myalpine" deleted
root@Ubuntu-Server1$
root@Ubuntu-Server1$ kubectl get pods myalpine
Error from server (NotFound): pods "myalpine" not found
root@Ubuntu-Server1$
root@Ubuntu-Server1$ kubectl delete deployments alpine
deployment.extensios "alpine" deleted
root@Ubuntu-Server1$
root@Ubuntu-Server1$ kubectl get deployments
Error from server (NotFound): deployment.extensions "alpine" not found
root@Ubuntu-Server1$
```

To automate the instantiation, management, and deletion of pods and deployments, kubectl supports YAML, which plays a key role in deploying either a single instance of the objects or at scale. Chapter 8, "Application Developers' Tools and Resources," discusses the usage of JSON/XML and YAML.

Open Agent Container (OAC)

To support network device automation and management, Nexus switches can be enabled with Puppet and Chef agents. However, open agents cannot be directly installed on these platforms. To support these agents and similar applications, an isolated execution space within an LXC called the OAC was built.

As you see in Figure 7-11, the Open Agent Container (OAC) application is packaged into an **.ova** image and hosted at the same location where NX-OS images are published on Cisco.com.

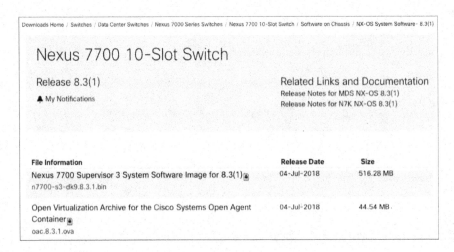

Figure 7-11 *Open Agent Container OVA Download*

First copy the .ova image to the Nexus switch. In Example 7-46, the file is copied to the bootflash file system in a Nexus 7700 switch.

OAC Deployment Model and Workflow

To install and activate OAC on your device, use the commands shown in Example 7-46. The virtual-service install command creates a virtual service instance, extracts the .ova file, validates the contents packaged into the file, validates the virtual machine definition, creates a virtual environment in the device, and instantiates a container.

Example 7-46 *Install OAC*

```
Nexus7700# virtual-service install name oac package bootflash:oac.8.3.1.ova
Note: Installing package 'bootflash:/oac.8.3.1.ova' for virtual service 'oac'. Once
   the install has finished, the VM may be activated. Use 'show virtual-service list'
   for progress
Nexus7000#
2019 Aug 28 10:22:59 Nexus7700 %VMAN-2-INSTALL_FAILURE: Virtual Service
   [oac]::Install::Unpacking error::Unsupported OVA Compression/Packing format
2019 Aug 28 11:20:27 Nexus7700 %VMAN-5-PACKAGE_SIGNING_LEVEL_ON_INSTALL: Pack-
   age 'oac.8.3.1.ova' for service container 'oac' is 'Cisco signed', signing level
   allowed is 'Cisco signed'
2019 Aug 28 11:20:30 Nexus7700 %VMAN-2-INSTALL_STATE: Successfully installed virtual
   service 'oac'
Nexus7700#
Nexus7700# show virtual-service list
Virtual Service List:

Name                     Status               Package Name
-----------------------------------------------------------
oac                      Installed            oac.8.3.1.ova
Nexus7700#
```

Using the **show virtual-service list** command, you can check the status of the container and make sure the installation is successful and the status is reported as **installed**. Then follow the steps given in Example 7-47 to activate the container. The NX-API feature is enabled, which will be used by OAC to perform the NX-OS CLIs directly from the container. As you see in the example, once the OAC is activated successfully, the **show virtual-service list** command shows the status of the container as **activating** and then **activated**.

Example 7-47 *Activate OAC*

```
Nexus7700# configure terminal
Nexus7700(config)# feature nxapi
Nexus7700(config)# virtual-service oac
Nexus7700(config-virt-serv)# activate
Nexus7700(config-virt-serv)# end
```

```
Note: Activating virtual-service 'oac', this might take a few minutes. Use 'show
  virtual-service list' for progress.
Nexus7700#
Nexus7700# show virtual-service list
Virtual Service List:

Name                    Status             Package Name
oac                     Activating         oac.8.3.1.ova

Nexus7700#
2019 Aug 28 11:23:06 Nexus7000 %$ VDC-1 %$ %VMAN-2-ACTIVATION_STATE: Successfully
  activated virtual service 'oac'
Nexus7700#
Nexus7700# show virtual-service list
Virtual Service List:

Name                    Status             Package Name
oac                     Activated          oac.8.3.1.ova

Nexus7700#
Nexus7700# 2019 Aug 28 11:23:06 Nexus7000 %$ VDC-1 %$ %VMAN-2-ACTIVATION_STATE:
  Successfully activated virtual service 'oac'
```

As shown in Example 7-48, you can verify that the OAC is instantiated and actively running on the device with the **show virtual-service detail** command. The command supplies
details of the resources allocated to the container, such as disk space, CPU, and memory.

Example 7-48 *Verify OAC Installation and Activation*

```
Nexus7000# show virtual-service detail
Virtual service oac detail
  State                 : Activated
  Package information
    Name                : oac.8.3.1.ova
    Path                : bootflash:/oac.8.3.1.ova
    Application
      Name              : OpenAgentContainer
      Installed version : 1.0
      Description       : Cisco Systems Open Agent Container
    Signing
      Key type          : Cisco release key
      Method            : SHA1
    Licensing
      Name              : None
      Version           : None
  Resource reservation
    Disk                : 500 MB
    Memory              : 384 MB
    CPU                 : 1% system CPU
```

```
Attached devices
  Type            Name        Alias
  -----------------------------------------------
  Disk            _rootfs
  Disk            /cisco/core
  Serial/shell
  Serial/aux
  Serial/Syslog               serial2
  Serial/Trace                serial3
```

Successful OAC activation depends on the availability of the required resources for OAC. If a failure occurs, the output of the **show virtual-service list** command will show the status as **Activate Failed** (see Example 7-49).

Example 7-49   *OAC Activation Failure*

```
Nexus7700# show virtual-service list
 Virtual Service List:
 Name                  Status             Package Name
 -----------------------------------------------------------------
 oac                   Activate Failed    oac.8.3.1.ova
Nexus7700#
```

To obtain additional information on the failure, you can use the **show system internal virtual-service event-history debug** command. As shown in Example 7-50, the reason for failure is clearly reported as insufficient disk space.

Example 7-50   *System Internal Event History*

```
Nexus7700# show system internal virtual-service event-history debug
243) Event:E_VMAN_MSG, length:124, at 47795 usecs after Wed Aug 28 09:23:52 2019
    (info): Response handle (nil), string Disk storage request (500 MB) exceeds
    remaining disk space (344 MB) on storage
244) Event:E_VMAN_MSG, length:74, at 47763 usecs after Wed Aug 28 09:23:52 2019
    (debug): Sending Response Message: Virtual-instance: oac - Response: FAIL
```

Instantiation of the OAC is persistent across the reload of the switch or supervisor engine. It means that the OAC will be instantiated upon supervisor engine reset or reload, but it will not be activated. It is not necessary to save the configurations with "copy running-config startup-config" to have the OAC instantiated and activated, without manual intervention, upon supervisor engine reset or reload. Because the OAC does not have high-availability support, the instantiation of the OAC is not replicated automatically to the standby supervisor engine. In other words, if you need to have OAC instantiated and activated for switchover, copy and save either the same .ova file or a different file in the standby supervisor engine's bootflash.

Accessing OAC via the Console

To connect to the virtual service environment from the host Nexus switch, use the
virtual-service connect command, as shown in Example 7-51.

Example 7-51 *Accessing OAC via the Console*

```
Nexus7700# virtual-service connect name oac console
Connecting to virtual-service.  Exit using ^c^c^c
Trying 127.1.1.3...
Connected to 127.1.1.3.
Escape character is '^]'.

CentOS release 6.9 (Final)
Kernel 3.14.39ltsi+ on an x86_64

Nexus7700 login:
Password:
You are required to change your password immediately (root enforced)
Changing password for root.
(current) UNIX password:
New password:
Retype new password:
[root@Nexus7700 ~]#
[root@Nexus7700 ~]#whoami
root
[root@Nexus7700 ~]#
```

The default credentials to attach to the containers' console are **root/oac or oac/oac.** You
must change the root password upon logging in. Just like in any other Linux environment,
you can use Sudo to **root** after logging in as user **oac.**

Because you are accessing through console needs, you need to be on the switch first.
The access can be slow, so many users prefer to access OAC via SSH. Before OAC can be
accessed via SSH, the SSH service should be enabled and the container networking set
up. The following section tells you how to enable this access method.

OAC Networking Setup and Verification

By default, networking in the OAC is done in the default routing table instance. Any additional route that is required (for example, a default route) must be configured natively in
the host device and should not be configured in the container.

As you can see in Example 7-52, the **chvrf management** command is used to access
a different routing instance (for example, the management VRF). After logging in
to the container through the console, enable **SSH process/daemon** (sshd) in the
management VRF.

Every VRF in the system has a numerical value assigned to it, so you need to make sure the sshd context matches the number assigned to the management VRF to confirm that the SSH process is active on the right VRF context. As shown in Example 7-52, the number assigned to VRF management is 2, which matches with the **DCOS_CONTEXT** assigned to the SSHD process.

Example 7-52   *Verify Container Networking*

```
[root@Nexus7700 ~]# chvrf management
[root@Nexus7700 ~]#
[root@Nexus7700 ~]# getvrf
management
[root@Nexus7700 ~]#
[root@Nexus7700 ~]# /etc/init.d/sshd start
Starting sshd:
[  OK  ]
[root@Nexus7700 ~]#
[root@Nexus7700 ~]# more /etc/init.d/sshd | grep DCOS
export DCOS_CONTEXT=2
[root@Nexus7700 ~]#
[root@Nexus7700 ~]# vrf2num management
2
[root@Nexus7700 ~]# /etc/init.d/sshd status
openssh-daemon (pid 315) is running…
[root@Nexus7700 ~]#
```

Because NX-OS has allocated TCP port number 22 to the SSH process running in the host, configure an unused and different TCP port number for the OAC's SSH daemon. As demonstrated in Example 7-53, the **/etc/sshd_config** file has been edited to assign Port 2222 to OAC's SSH service, and the SSH service is listening for connections at 10.122.140.94, which is the Mgmt0 interface of the Nexus switch.

Example 7-53   *Configure TCP Port for SSH*

```
[root@Nexus7700 ~]# cat /etc/ssh/sshd_config
<snip>
Port 2222
#AddressFamily any
ListenAddress 10.122.140.94
#ListenAddress ::
<snip>
[root@Nexus7700 ~]#

 [root@Nexus7700 ~]#
```

Make sure to configure the DNS server and domain information so that OAC and agents installed in it can resolve domain names, as shown in Example 7-54.

Example 7-54   *Verify DNS Configuration*

```
[root@Nexus7700 ~]#
[root@Nexus7700 ~]# cat /etc/resolv.conf
nameserver 208.67.222.222
nameserver 208.67.220.220
[root@Nexus7700 ~]#
```

The command shown in Example 7-55 is performed in the host device, which confirms that a socket is open for OAC for the SSH connections at the IP address of the management port and TCP port 2222.

Example 7-55   *Verify Open Sockets*

```
Nexus7700# show sockets connection
Total number of netstack tcp sockets: 5
Active connections (including servers)
         Protocol State/      Recv-Q/    Local Address(port)/
                  Context     Send-Q     Remote Address(port)
<snip>
[slxc]: tcp      LISTEN      0          10.122.140.94(2222)
                 default     0          *(*)
<snip>
Nexus7700#
```

Access the container to verify SSH accessibility, as shown in Example 7-56.

Example 7-56   *Verify SSH Access for OAC*

```
Ubuntu-Server1$
Ubuntu-Server1$ ssh -p 2222 root@10.122.140.94
CentOS release 6.9 (Final)
Kernel 3.14.39ltsi+ on an x86_64

Nexus7700 login: root
Password:
Last login: Tue Sep 10 10:26:46 on pts/0
#
```

If you are making changes to SSH parameters and settings in OAC, it is recommended that you restart the SSH service and check the status with **service sshd** commands. Now you have an active OAC that can be accessed via console or SSH. Next you will learn how the kernel and OAC handles the packet from and to the front-panel ports in the host device, as illustrated in Figure 7-12.

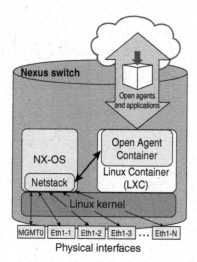

Figure 7-12 *Packet Handling in OAC*

As far as the containers are concerned, it all comes back to its namespace and the sockets and file descriptors associated to each container.

Once a socket is listening on a port, the kernel tracks those structures by namespace. As a result, the kernel knows how to direct traffic to the correct container socket. Here is a brief look at how traffic received by a Nexus switch's front-panel port is forwarded to a specific container:

1. OAC implements a Message Transmission Service (MTS) tunnel to redirect container IP traffic to an NX-OS Netstack for forwarding lookup and packet processing to the front-panel port. This requires **libmts** and **libns** extensions, which are already included and set up in the **oac.ova**. Nexus 7000 has Netstack, which is a complete IP stack implementation in the user space of NX-OS. Netstack handles any traffic sent to the CPU for software processing.

2. The modified stack looks for the **DCOS_CONTEXT** environment variable, as mentioned in Example 7-56, to tag the correct VRF ID before sending the MTS message to Netstack.

3. The OAC is VDC aware because the implementation forwards traffic to the correct Netstack instance in which the OAC is installed.

Example 7-56 helped you verify that the OAC is accessible through SSH from an external device. In other words, the container should also be able to connect to the external network. Verify the reachability to the external network by sending ICMP pings to an external device, as shown in Example 7-57.

Example 7-57 *OAC Reachability to External Network*

```
[root@Nexus7700 ~]# chvrf management ping 10.122.140.65
PING 10.122.140.65 (10.122.140.65): 56 data bytes
64 bytes from 10.122.140.65: icmp_seq=0 ttl=254 time=2.495 ms
64 bytes from 10.122.140.65: icmp_seq=1 ttl=254 time=3.083 ms
64 bytes from 10.122.140.65: icmp_seq=2 ttl=254 time=2.394 ms^C
--- 10.122.140.65 ping statistics ---
3 packets transmitted, 3 packets received, 0.0% packet loss
round-trip min/avg/max/stddev = 1.221/2.444/3.962/1.138 ms
[root@Nexus7700 ~]#
```

From within the OAC, in addition to accessing the network, the network administrator can access the device CLI using the **dohost** command, access the Cisco NX-API infrastructure, and more importantly, install and run Python scripts as well as 32-bit Linux applications.

Management and Orchestration of OAC

If there is a new version of OVA available for OAC, you can upgrade the currently active container using virtual-service commands, as shown in the following example. To upgrade, you need to deactivate the currently active container, as shown in Example 7-58.

Example 7-58 *Upgrade OAC*

```
Nexus7700(config)# virtual-service oac
Nexus7700(config-virt-serv)# no activate
Nexus7700(config-virt-serv)# end
2019 Sep  9 22:46:46 N77-A-Admin %$ VDC-1 %$ %VMAN-2-ACTIVATION_STATE: Successfully
  deactivated virtual service 'oac'
Nexus7700#
Nexus7700# show virtual-service list
Virtual Service List:

Name                    Status              Package Name
-------------------------------------------------------------------------
oac                     Deactivated         oac.8.3.1.ova
Nexus7700#
Nexus7700# virtual-serv install name oac package bootflash:oac.8.3.1-v2.ova
Nexus7700#
Nexus7700# show virtual-service list
Virtual Service List:

Name                    Status              Package Name
--------------------------------------------------------------
oac                     Installed           oac.8.3.1-v2.ova
Nexus7700#
```

```
Nexus7700# config t
Nexus7700(config)# feature nxapi
Nexus7700(config)# virtual-service oac
Nexus7700(config-virt-serv)# activate
Nexus7700(config-virt-serv)# end
Nexus7700# show virtual-service list
Virtual Service List:

Name                      Status              Package Name
-------------------------------------------------------------
oac                       Activated           oac.8.3.1-v2.ova
Nexus7700#
```

To deactivate the container and uninstall the package, follow the steps as depicted in Example 7-59.

Example 7-59 *Deactivate OAC*

```
Nexus7700#
Nexus7700# config t
Nexus7700(config)# virtual-service oac
Nexus7700(config-virt-serv)# no activate
Nexus7700(config-virt-serv)# end
Nexus7700# show virtual-service list
Virtual Service List:

Name                      Status              Package Name
-------------------------------------------------------------
oac                       Deactivated         oac.8.3.1-v2.ova
Nexus7700#
Nexus7700# config t
Nexus7700(config)# no virtual service oac
Nexus7700(config)# exit
Nexus7700# virtual-service uninstall name oac
```

Installation and Verification of Applications

Open Agent Container, as the name suggests, is specifically developed to run open agents that cannot be natively run on NX-OS, such as Puppet agents and Chef agents.

Custom Python Application

To demonstrate the capability, you will look into a simple Python application. The Python file in Example 7-60 prints the system date and time every 10 seconds until the user stops the application by pressing Ctrl+C.

Example 7-60   *OAC—Sample Python Application*

```
[root@Nexus7700 ~]# more datetime.py

#!/usr/bin/python
import datetime
import time

while True:
    print("Time now is ... ")
    DateTime = datetime.datetime.now()
    print (str(DateTime))
    time.sleep(10)

[root@Nexus7700 ~]#
```

Check the file permissions and make sure the user **root** has permission to execute the file. Execute the Python file, as shown in Example 7-61.

Example 7-6   *Run Python Application in OAC*

```
[root@Nexus7700 ~]#
[root@Nexus7700 ~]# ls -l datetime.py
-rwxr--r-- 1 root root 194 Sep 10 23:16 datetime.py
[root@Nexus7700 ~]#
[root@Nexus7700 ~]# ./datetime.py
Time now is ...
2019-09-10 23:16:09.563576
Time now is ...
2019-09-10 23:16:19.573776
Time now is ...
2019-09-10 23:16:29.584028
^CTraceback (most recent call last):
  File "./ datetime.py", line 8, in <module>
    time.sleep(10)
KeyboardInterrupt
[root@Nexus7700 ~]#
```

Now that you know how to run a simple Python application in an OAC, you will see how to use Python APIs that are built-in and available in Nexus platforms. You can use these Python APIs to develop and run customized applications to monitor device health, track events, or generate alerts.

Application Using Python APIs

Cisco NX-OS has a built-in package providing API access to CLIs, both at the exec level as well as configuration commands, referred to as Python APIs. Example 7-62 is a simple Python script that leverages Python APIs that are natively available in the Nexus switches.

Example 7-62 *Application Using Python APIs*

```
[root@Nexus7700 ~]# more PY-API.py

#!/usr/bin/python
from cli import *
import json

print("STANDARD CLI OUTPUT ...")
print (cli('show interface brief'))

print("JSON FORMAT CLI OUTPUT ...")
print (clid('show interface brief'))

[root@Nexus7700 ~]#
```

Example 7-63 demonstrates the outputs generated by the application. As you notice, **cli** returns the raw format of the CLI results, including control and special characters. **clid** returns a dictionary of attribute names and values for the given CLI command.

Example 7-63 *Run Python API Application in OAC*

```
[root@Nexus7700 ~]# ls -l PY-API.py
-rwxr--r-- 1 root root 194 Sep 10 23:37 PY-API.py
[root@N77-A-Admin ~]#
[root@N77-A-Admin ~]# ./PY-API.py
STANDARD CLI OUTPUT ...
--------------------------------------------------------------------
Port   VRF         Status IP Address            Speed    MTU
--------------------------------------------------------------------
mgmt0  --          up     10.122.140.94         1000     1500

JSON FORMAT CLI OUTPUT ...
{"TABLE_interface": {"ROW_interface": {"interface": "mgmt0", "state": "up", "ip_
  addr": "10.122.140.94", "speed": "1000", "mtu": "1500"}}}
[root@Nexus7700 ~]#
```

The **dohost** command in Example 7-64 is a Python wrapper script using NX-API functions and Linux domain sockets back to NX-OS. Using **dohost** capability, a user can perform **show** commands and configuration commands within the VDC in which the container is created.

Example 7-64 *Run NX-OS CLIs in OAC with dohost*

```
[root@N77-A-Admin ~]#
[root@N77-A-Admin ~]# dohost "show clock"
Time source is NTP
23:38:15.692 EST Tue Sep 10 2019
[root@N77-A-Admin ~]#
```

Package Management

As shown in Example 7-65, you can install packages in OAC using **yum install <package-name>** commands, just like in any CentOS Linux environment. Before installing packages, make sure to install them in the right VRF context. The namespace or VRF should have network connectivity and have the configurations required to resolve domain names.

Example 7-65 *OAC Package Management*

```
[root@Nexus7700 ~]# chvrf management yum install -y vim
Setting up Install Process
Resolving Dependencies
<snip>
```

Use **yum repolist** commands to verify the installed packages and repositories.

From OAC, you can run Open Agents, 32-bit Linux applications, and custom Python applications leveraging Python APIs, NX-APIs, or simple **dohost** commands to run CLIs and analyze the data. Chapter 9, "Container Deployment Use Cases," will discuss the various use cases for packages and applications.

Summary

This chapter introduced the fundamentals of the NX-OS architecture—its key components and benefits. It presented the key built-in capabilities that enable application hosting and containers in Nexus switching platforms. It discussed various popular features such as Open Agent Containers (OAC), Guest Shell, Bash, and Docker containers—how to enable or instantiate them; how to configure them to communicate with external networks; how to enable console as well as SSH access; how to install simple Python or Python API-based applications and run those applications; how to instantiate Docker containers in supported platforms; and how to orchestrate them using Kubernetes.

Cisco NX-OS platforms have built-in capabilities helping developers deploy custom applications in the networking devices connected to the end hosts. These applications become more effective as they are brought closer to the data generated at the network edge, which can be processed in real time to gain insights. Above all, users can orchestrate and manage the lifecycle of containers and applications by activating or deactivating them, upgrading the applications or packages installed, and leveraging the abilities the platforms provide for automation and scalability.

References

Cisco Nexus 7000 series Switches–NX-OS Architecture and Features: https://www.cisco.com/c/en/us/products/collateral/switches/nexus-7000-series-switches/white_paper_c11-622511.html

Open NX-OS and Linux–Developer Guide: https://developer.cisco.com/docs/nx-os/

Cisco Nexus 9000 series Python SDK User Guide and API Reference: https://developer.cisco.com/docs/nx-os/#!cisco-nexus-9000-series-python-sdk-user-guide-and-api-reference

Docker Documentation: https://docs.docker.com/

Alpine Linux–Home Page: https://alpinelinux.org/

Musl libc–Home Page: http://musl.libc.org/

Busybox–Home Page: https://busybox.net/about.html

Install and Setup Kubectl Guide: https://kubernetes.io/docs/tasks/tools/install-kubectl/

Kubectl Overview: https://kubernetes.io/docs/reference/kubectl/overview/

## Chapter 8

Application Developers' Tools and Resources

In this chapter, you will learn the following:

■ Various tools and resources available for application developers in Cisco IOS-XE, IOS-XR, and NX-OS platforms.

■ How to leverage these tools and resources in developing and hosting applications in the above-mentioned platforms.

Cisco Development Tool Kits and Resources

This section introduces readers to different tool kits and resources available in the Cisco routing and switching platforms. These tools and resources help application developers with developing and testing applications and deploying them at scale.

Nexus Software Development Kit (NX-SDK)

Cisco NX-SDK offers a simple, flexible, modernized, and powerful tool for third-party custom application development. Cisco NX-SDK helps application developers access the Nexus infrastructure functionalities, which when run inside or outside the Nexus switches, allow custom applications to run natively just like any other Cisco-native Nexus applications. It is appropriate to develop custom applications to fit your automation needs, thereby decoupling the application development from Nexus releases. NX-SDK offers various functionalities, such as the ability to generate custom CLIs, Syslog, Event Manager, high-availability, Route Manager, Streaming Telemetry, and much more.

NX-SDK has an abstraction/plug-in library layer that decouples the application from the underlying infrastructure. Therefore, it is easy to change infrastructure without affecting the applications, which means NX-SDK is being used to develop native Cisco Applications, too.

NX-SDK is built using the C++ language. Because other language bindings (for Python, Go, and Ruby) are provided for NX-SDK, custom applications can be developed and built in any language of the users' choice. Starting from NX-SDK v2.0.0, NX-SDK applications can run inside or outside of NX-OS. As illustrated in Figure 8-1, for the custom applications development environment, the NX-SDK Abstraction Layer Library gives access to the NX-OS infrastructure, including CLIs, Syslog, and Event Managers.

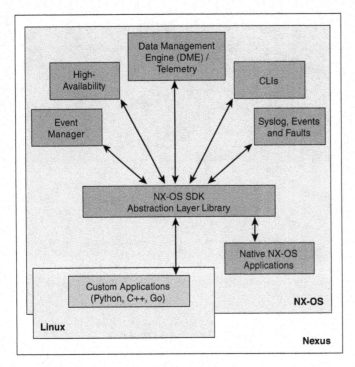

Figure 8-1   *Cisco NX SDK Framework*

This Cisco DevNet NX-SDK GitHub page, which is included at the end of the chapter in the "References" section, includes the NX-SDK toolkit for custom application development. You can use this toolkit in your favorite Linux environment to gain access to the NX-OS infrastructure.

NX-SDK Release Versions

Table 8-1 includes details of the NX-SDK release available in specific NX-OS releases, as well as the programming languages supported in each NX-SDK release.

Table 8-1   *NX-OS and SDK Release Matrix*

Platforms	NX-OS Versions	NX-SDK Release	Languages Supported
Nexus 3000/9000	7.0(3)I6(1) / I7(1) or later	1.0.0	C++, Python
Nexus 3000/9000	7.0(3)I7(3) or later	1.5.0	C++, Python
Nexus 3000/9000	9.2(x) releases	1.7.5	C++, Python, Go
Nexus 3000/9000	9.3(x) releases	2.0.0	C++, Python, Go

NX-SDK Deployment Modes

Starting with NX-SDK V2.0.0, NX-SDK applications can be deployed either inside or outside NX-OS, depending on the use case and where you want to have the application deployed.

NX-SDK Installation and Activation

At a high level, Figure 8-2 illustrates the key steps that are followed when developing and running an application using NX-SDK. The steps are shown here:

1. Build a Linux environment (Ubuntu or CentOS) with the Docker service enabled, issue the docker pull NX-SDK command, and activate the NX-SDK Container.

2. Develop applications in the C++, Python, or Go programming languages.

3. Package the application built into an RPM image.

4. Copy the RPM package to the Nexus switch, and then install and activate it.

5. Run the application.

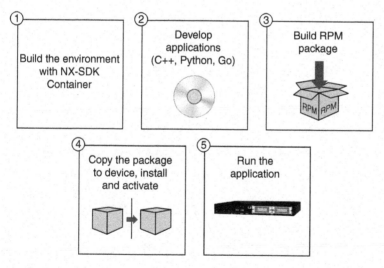

Figure 8-2 *Developing and Hosting Applications Using NX-SDK*

The following section instructs you how to develop and host the application.

Step 1: Build the Linux Environment

In Ubuntu version 14.04+ or Centos version 6.7+, use the **docker pull dockercisco/nxsdk** command to download the Cisco NX-SDK from the Docker Hub page at https://hub. docker.com/r/dockercisco/nxsdk.

Example 8-1 shows the steps for installing Docker in a Linux environment, the Docker pull NX-SDK, and updates with the **git** command.

Example 8-1 *Installing Docker*

```
[root@Ubuntu-Server2 ~]# yum -y install docker
[root@Ubuntu-Server2 ~]# docker pull dockercisco/nxsdk:v1
[root@Ubuntu-Server2 ~]# docker run -it dockercisco/nxsdk:v1 /bin/bash
root@b7d33ce8a7b8:/# cd /NX-SDK
root@b7d33ce8a7b8:/NX-SDK# git pull
root@b7d33ce8a7b8:/NX-SDK#
```

Step 2: Develop a Custom Application

The application that will be developed here is a custom CLI added to the NX-OS, which on execution provides the history of specific end-host or IP address movement in a network. Python was used to develop this application, but it is not the only option.

Typically, tracking an end-host's movement in a data center with Nexus switching platforms involves three steps:

1. **show ip arp:** Do this to make sure the IP address is valid and active on the network and to map it to a mac-address.

2. **show mac address-table <address>:** Do this to determine the current interface and VLAN from which the MAC address is being learned.

3. **show system internal L2FM L2dbg macdb address <address>:** This provides information on end-host movement.

In the preceding commands, L2FM stands for Layer 2 Feature Manager. It retains the Layer 2 debugs in a MAC address database for each MAC address the system learns.

Example 8-2 shows a portion of Python code that performs the **show ip arp** command to obtain the MAC address for a given IP address.

Example 8-2 *Python Code for show ip arp*

```
def get_mac_from_arp(cli_parser, clicmd, target_ip):
    exec_cmd = "show ip arp {}".format(target_ip)
    arp_cmd = cli_parser.execShowCmd(exec_cmd, nx_sdk_py.R_JSON)
    if arp_cmd:
        try:
            arp_json = json.loads(arp_cmd)
        except ValueError as exc:
            return None
        count = int(arp_json["TABLE_vrf"]["ROW_vrf"]["cnt-total"])
        if count:
            intf =arp_json["TABLE_vrf"]["ROW_vrf"]["TABLE_adj"]["ROW_adj"]
            if intf.get("ip-addr-out") == target_ip:
                target_mac = intf["mac"]
```

You can download the **IP_Move.py** application with complete Python code at the *Cisco DevNet GitHub NX-SDK IP_Move Application* page in the "References" section at the end of this chapter.

Step 3: Package the Application

The next step is to package the application, as shown in Example 8-3. Create a folder directory in the root directory to copy the downloaded **IP_Move** application. Execute **rpm_gen.py** to build the RPM package.

Example 8-3 *Packaging the Application*

```
root@b7d33ce8a7b8:/#
root@b7d33ce8a7b8:/# cd /root
root@b7d33ce8a7b8:~# mkdir nxsdk-scripts
root@b7d33ce8a7b8:~# cd nxsdk-scripts/
root@b7d33ce8a7b8:~# cp /tmp/ip_move.py .
root@b7d33ce8a7b8:~/nxsdk-scripts# python /NX-SDK/scripts/rpm_gen.py ip_move.py —s /
  root/nxsdk-scripts —u
<snip>
RPM package has been built
```

Once the application is packaged, the Spec and RPM files are at the locations shown in Example 8-4.

Example 8-4 *SPEC and RPM Files*

```
/nxsdk/rpm/SPECS/ip_move.py.spec
/nxsdk/rpm/RPMS/ip_move.1.0-1.5.0.x86_64.rpm
```

Note: To package custom-built C++ applications, follow the instructions provided at https://www.cisco.com/c/en/us/td/docs/switches/datacenter/nexus9000/sw/92x/programmability/guide/b-cisco-nexus-9000-series-nx-os-programmability-guide-92x/b-cisco-nexus-9000-series-nx-os-programmability-guide-92x_chapter_010001.html#id_50768.

Step 4: Copy the RPM to Nexus and Activate the Application

Move the RPM file built in a Linux environment to a Nexus switch, install it, and activate it, as shown in Example 8-5.

Example 8-5 *Install and Activate RPM in NX-OS*

```
N93180# copy ftp://10.64.11.76/ip_move.1.0-1.5.0.x86_64.rpm bootflash: vrf management
N93180# install add bootflash:ip_move.1.0-1.5.0.x86_64.rpm
N93180# install activate ip_move.1.0-1.5.0.x86_64
```

Enable the NX-SDK feature in the Nexus switch, activate it, and verify it, as shown in Example 8-6.

Example 8-6   *Enable NX-SDK and Activate IP_Move App*

```
N93180(config)# feature nxsdk
N93180(config)# nxsdk service-name ip_move.py
N93180(config)# exit
N93180# show nxsdk internal service
NXSDK Started/Temp unavailable/Max services : 0/0/32
NXSDK Default App Path        : /isan/bin/nxsdk
NXSDK Supported Versions      : 1.0
Service-name          Base App        Started(PID) Version RPM Package
--------------------- --------------- ------------ ------- ------------
/isan/bin/ip_move.py  nxsdk_app1      VSH(28161)   1.0     ip_move.py-1.0-1.5.0.x86_64
```

As you can see in Example 8-6, the **nxsdk_app1** base application is actively running in the Nexus 9300 switch. Now test the custom CLI built by the IP_Move application to track simple movement of an end host, as shown in Example 8-7.

Step 5: Run the Application

Example 8-7   *Run IP_Move App*

```
N93180# show ip_move.py 20.20.20.3
20.20.20.3 is currently present in ARP table, MAC address 0010.9400.0002
0010.9400.0002 is currently present in MAC address table on interface Ethernet1/3,
  VLAN 20
0010.9400.0002 has been moving between the following interfaces, from most recent to
  least recent:
Fri Sep 27 12:05:17 2019 - Ethernet1/3 (Current interface)
Fri Sep 27 12:04:13 2019 - Ethernet1/5
Fri Sep 27 12:04:13 2019 - Ethernet1/4
Fri Sep 27 12:03:50 2019 - Ethernet1/5
Fri Sep 27 12:03:50 2019 - Ethernet1/4
Fri Sep 27 12:03:26 2019 - Ethernet1/5
```

The results indicate that the specific end host with IPv4 address 20.20.20.3 is present in VLAN 20 with the physical mac-address of 0010.9400.0002, and it is reachable via the interface Ethernet1/3. The command reports various interfaces to which this end host has moved, starting with the current interface on the top and reporting in the reverse chronological order.

As you have seen, with a few simple steps, a developer can develop an application and host it on a Cisco Nexus switching platform, taking the intelligence all the way to the edge, analyzing the data right where it is generated. You can automate a complex multistep workflow or sequence of commands by creating a single command. Developers can also design the applications to create data that is easily understandable and consumable, even by those who may not have knowledge of the platform.

Python APIs—IOS-XE / NX-OS

Python is an easy-to-learn, powerful programming language. It has efficient high-level data structures and a simple but effective approach to object-oriented programming. Python's elegant syntax and dynamic typing, together with its interpreted nature, make it an ideal language for scripting and rapid application development.

The Python interpreter and the extensive standard library are freely available in source as well as in binary form for all major platforms from the Python website provided at https://www.python.org/. The same site also contains distributions of and pointers to many free third-party Python modules, programs and tools, and additional documentation.

Python API in NX-OS

The Cisco Nexus 9000 Series devices support Python v2.7.5 in both interactive and noninteractive (script) modes and are available in the Guest Shell as well as in Bash. If needed, users can upgrade Guest Shell Python.

The Python scripting capability gives programmatic access to the device's command-line interface (CLI) to perform various tasks and Power On Auto Provisioning (POAP) or Embedded Event Manager (EEM) actions.

The Python interpreter is also available in the Cisco NX-OS and can be accessed via CLIs.

Python API Package

Cisco NX-OS has a Cisco Python package that enables access to many core network-device modules, such as interfaces, VLANs, VRFs, ACLs, and routes. You can display the details of the Cisco Python package by entering the **help(<package>)** command. To obtain additional information about the classes and methods in a module, you can run the help command for a specific module. For example, **help(cisco.interface)** displays the properties of the **cisco.interface** module.

For more Python modules, you can install **python-modules-nxos RPM (python-modules-nxos-1.0.0-9.2.1.lib32_x86.rpm)** from the package repository available at https://devhub.cisco.com/artifactory/open-nxos/.

Example 8-8 shows how to display information about the OS as well as Cisco packages.

Example 8-8   *Displaying Python Packages*

```
N9K-C93180YC# run bash
bash-4.3$
bash-4.3$
bash-4.3$ python
Python 2.7.9 (default, Aug 12 2018, 23:56:37)
[GCC 5.2.0] on linux2
```

```
Type "help", "copyright", "credits" or "license" for more information.
>>>
>>> import os
>>> os.name
'posix'
>>>
>>> os.system('whoami')
admin
0
>>>
>>> import cisco
>>> help(cisco)
Help on package cisco:
NAME
    cisco
FILE
    /isan/python/scripts/cisco/__init__.py

PACKAGE CONTENTS
    acl
    bgp
    cisco_secret
    cisco_socket
    feature
    interface
    key
    line_parser
    md5sum
    nxcli
    ospf
    routemap
    routes
    section_parser
    ssh
    system
    tacacs
    vrf

CLASSES
    __builtin__.object
        cisco.cisco_secret.CiscoSecret
        cisco.interface.Interface
        cisco.key.Key
>>>
```

As you might have noticed at the previously mentioned RPM repository, packages are available for major NX-OS releases starting from 7.0(2). For example, for 9.2(3), more than 380 different packages are available.

Using CLI APIs and Display Formats

The Python programming language uses three APIs that can execute CLI commands. The APIs are available from the Python CLI module. You must enable the APIs with the **cli import *** command. The arguments for these APIs are strings of CLI commands. To execute a CLI command through the Python interpreter, you enter the CLI command as an argument string of one of the following three APIs:

- **cli('<command>'):** Returns the command's result in a raw format

- **clid('<command>'):** Returns the command's result in JSON format

- **clip('<command>'):** Returns the command's result directly to stdout and not to the Python interpreter

In Example 8-9, the cli Python API passes three commands together to NX-OS and brings up an interface.

Example 8-9 *Python API—Passing Commands*

```
>>> import json
>>> import cli
>>> from cli import *
>>>
>>> cli('configure terminal ; interface mgmt0 ; no shut')
>>>
```

The operational state from one command does not persist for the next command. In other words, the second command in Example 8-10 fails.

Example 8-10 *Python API—Sequential Command Persistence*

```
>>>
>>> cli('configure terminal')
>>> cli('interface mgmt0')
>>>
```

As discussed in Chapter 7, "Container Orchestration in Cisco NX-OS Platforms," in the "Open Agent Container (OAC)" section, the **clid** option returns the command results in JSON, as shown in Example 8-11, which makes it easier to process the results and automate as needed. The example also shows sample results from the **clip** command, which prints the output of the CLI directly to **stdout** and returns nothing to Python.

Example 8-11   *Python API—JSON Results*

```
>>>
>>> clid('show interface brief')
'{"TABLE_interface": {"ROW_interface": {"interface": "mgmt0", "state": "up",
 "ip_addr": "172.16.28.5", "speed": "1000", "mtu": "1500"}}}'
>>>
>>> cli('configure terminal ; interface mgmt0')
>>> clip('where detail')
   mode:
   username:            admin
   vdc:                 Nexus9500-A-Default
   routing-context vrf: default
>>>
```

Now you will learn how to easily process results in JSON format and programmatically find the ports that are up. Example 8-12 shows some sample results. **json.loads(clid('show interface brief'))** prints the interface list in JSON format. The result is processed by matching the **state** attribute to check the interface state and print the interface name only if the **state** is **up**.

Example 8-12   *Python API Automation with JSON Results*

```
>>>
>>> intflist=json.loads(clid('show interface brief'))
>>> i=0
>>> while i < len(intflist['TABLE_interface']['ROW_interface']):
...     intf=intflist['TABLE_interface']['ROW_interface'][i]
...     i=i+1
...     if intf['state'] == 'up':
...       print intf['interface']
...
mgmt0
Ethernet1/1
Ethernet1/2
loopback0
loopback1
>>>
```

Using Python APIs in Noninteractive Mode

A Python script can run in noninteractive mode if you provide the Python script name as an argument to the **Python** command. Python scripts must be placed under the bootflash file system. A maximum of 32 command-line arguments for the Python script is allowed with the **Python** command. Example 8-13 shows a script and how to run it.

Example 8-13   *Python API—Noninteractive Mode*

```
N9K-A# show file bootflash:deltaCounters.py
#!/isan/bin/python

from cli import *
import sys, time

ifName = sys.argv[1]
delay = float(sys.argv[2])
count = int(sys.argv[3])
cmd = 'show interface ' + ifName + ' counters'

out = json.loads(clid(cmd))
rxuc = int(out['TABLE_rx_counters']['ROW_rx_counters'][0]['eth_inucast'])
rxmc = int(out['TABLE_rx_counters']['ROW_rx_counters'][1]['eth_inmcast'])
rxbc = int(out['TABLE_rx_counters']['ROW_rx_counters'][1]['eth_inbcast'])
txuc = int(out['TABLE_tx_counters']['ROW_tx_counters'][0]['eth_outucast'])
txmc = int(out['TABLE_tx_counters']['ROW_tx_counters'][1]['eth_outmcast'])
txbc = int(out['TABLE_tx_counters']['ROW_tx_counters'][1]['eth_outbcast'])
print 'row rx_ucast rx_mcast rx_bcast tx_ucast tx_mcast tx_bcast'
print '========================================================='
print '    %8d %8d %8d %8d %8d %8d' % (rxuc, rxmc, rxbc, txuc, txmc, txbc)
print '========================================================='

i = 0
while (i < count):
  time.sleep(delay)
  out = json.loads(clid(cmd))
  rxucNew = int(out['TABLE_rx_counters']['ROW_rx_counters'][0]['eth_inucast'])
  rxmcNew = int(out['TABLE_rx_counters']['ROW_rx_counters'][1]['eth_inmcast'])
  rxbcNew = int(out['TABLE_rx_counters']['ROW_rx_counters'][1]['eth_inbcast'])
  txucNew = int(out['TABLE_tx_counters']['ROW_tx_counters'][0]['eth_outucast'])
  txmcNew = int(out['TABLE_tx_counters']['ROW_tx_counters'][1]['eth_outmcast'])
  txbcNew = int(out['TABLE_tx_counters']['ROW_tx_counters'][1]['eth_outbcast'])
  i += 1
  print '%-3d %8d %8d %8d %8d %8d %8d' % \
    (i, rxucNew - rxuc, rxmcNew - rxmc, rxbcNew - rxbc, txucNew - txuc, txmcNew -
  txmc, txbcNew - txbc)
N9K-A#
N9K-A#
N9K-A# python bootflash:deltaCounters.py Ethernet1/1 1 5
```

```
row rx_ucast rx_mcast rx_bcast tx_ucast tx_mcast tx_bcast
==========================================================
         0       791        1        0   212739        0
==========================================================
1        0         0        0        0       26        0
2        0         0        0        0       27        0
3        0         1        0        0       54        0
4        0         1        0        0       55        0
5        0         1        0        0       81        0
N9K-A#
```

NX-OS Python API—More Benefits

As listed next, NX-OS Python APIs have more benefits than those discussed in earlier sections.

- Noninteractive execution of Python modules can be integrated into EEM to automate system monitoring, diagnosis, and troubleshooting activities.

- Python is integrated with the underlying Cisco NX-OS network interfaces. Users can switch from one virtual routing context to another by setting up a context through the cisco.vrf.set_global_vrf() API.

- Cisco NX-OS resources are protected by the Cisco NX-OS Sandbox layer of software and by the CLI role-based access control (RBAC). All users who are associated with a Cisco NX-OS network-admin or dev-ops role are privileged. Users who are granted access to Python with a custom role are regarded as nonprivileged. Nonprivileged users have limited access to Cisco NX-OS resources, such as the file system, guest shell, and Bash commands. Privileged users have greater access to all the resources of Cisco NX-OS.

Python API in IOS-XE

Cisco IOS-XE has a built-in Python module that provides access to execute EXEC and configuration commands. The Cisco IOS-XE devices support Python v2.7.5 and are available in the Guest Shell. The Guest Shell Python module can be accessed with a simple **guestshell run python** command, as shown in Example 8-14.

Example 8-14 *Accessing Guestshell Python in IOS-XE*

```
Cat9300# guestshell run python
Python 2.7.5 (default, Jun 17 2014, 18:11:42)
[GCC 4.8.2 20140120 (Red Hat 4.8.2-16)] on linux2
Type "help", "copyright", "credits" or "license" for more information.
>>>
```

You can display the details and properties of the Cisco Python modules by entering the **help()** command. Example 8-15 displays information about the **cli** Python module.

Example 8-15 *Displaying CLI Python Module*

```
>>> from cli import cli, clip, configure, configurep, execute, executep
>>>
>>> help(cli)
Help on function cli in module cli:

cli(command)
    Execute Cisco IOS CLI command(s) and return the result.

    A single command or a delimited batch of commands may be run. The
    delimiter is a space and a semicolon, " ;". Configuration commands must be
    in fully qualified form.

    output = cli("show version")
    output = cli("show version ; show ip interface brief")
    output = cli("configure terminal ; interface gigabitEthernet 0/0 ; no shutdown")

    Args:
        command (str): The exec or config CLI command(s) to be run.

    Returns:
        string: CLI output for show commands and an empty string for
            configuration commands.

    Raises:
        errors.cli_syntax_error: if the command is not valid.
        errors.cli_exec_error: if the execution of command is not successful.
>>>
```

Like **cli**, the Python API supports different modules including **configure**, **configurep**, **execute**, **executep**, and **clip**. Arguments for these functions are strings of CLI commands. To execute a CLI command through the Python interpreter, enter the CLI command as an argument string of one of those functions.

cli and clip

Command syntax:

```
cli(command) or clip(command)
```

- **cli.cli(command):** This function takes an IOS command as an argument, runs the command through the IOS parser, and returns the resulting text. If this command is malformed, a Python exception is raised.

■ **cli.clip(command):** This function works the same as the **cli.cli(command)** function, except that it prints the resulting text to stdout rather than returning it.

Example 8-16 shows the usage of **cli.cli** and **cli.clip** commands and sample results.

Example 8-16   *cli and clip Python API Modules in IOS-XE*

```
>>>
>>> cli.clip('show clock')
'\n*21:16:51.313 UTC Thu Oct 31 2019\n'
>>>
>>> cli.cli('show clock')
>>> output=cli.cli('show clock')
>>> print (output)
*21:17:14.612 UTC Thu Oct 31 2019
>>>
```

configure and configurep

Command syntax:

```
configure(command) or configurep(command)
```

cli.configure(command): This function configures the device with the configuration available in commands. It returns a list of named tuples that contain the command and its result. The command parameters can be in multiple lines and in the same format that is displayed in the output of the show running-config command.

cli.configurep(command): This function works the same as the cli.configure(command) function, except that it prints the resulting text to **stdout** rather than returning it.

Example 8-17 shows the usage of the **configure** and **configurep** commands, and sample results.

Example 8-17   *configure and configurep Python API Modules in IOS-XE*

```
>>>
>>> cli.configure(["interface GigabitEthernet1/0/7", "no shutdown", "end"])
[ConfigResult(success=True, command='interface GigabitEthernet1/0/7',
line=1, output='', notes=None), ConfigResult(success=True, command='no shutdown',
line=2, output='', notes=None), ConfigResult(success=True, command='end',
line=3, output='', notes=None)]
>>>
>>> cli.configurep(["interface GigabitEthernet1/0/7", "no shutdown", "end"])
Line 1 SUCCESS: interface GigabitEthernet1/0/7
Line 2 SUCCESS: no shut
Line 3 SUCCESS: end
>>>
```

execute and executep

Command syntax:

```
configure(command) or configurep(command)
```

cli.execute(command): This function executes a single **EXEC** command and returns the output; however, it does not print the resulting text. No semicolons or newlines are allowed as part of this command. To execute multiple commands, use a **for-loop** to iterate over the commands and execute them one by one in the given order.

cli.executep(command): This function executes a single command and prints the resulting text to **stdout** rather than returning it, as shown in Example 8-18.

Example 8-18 *execute and executep Python API Modules in IOS-XE*

```
>>>
>>> cli.execute("show clock")
'22:43:26.916 UTC Thu Oct 31 2019'
>>>
>>> cli.executep('show clock')
*22:43:26.916 UTC Thu Oct 31 2019
>>
```

The Python API capability in IOS-XE platforms makes it powerful because it can be integrated into EEM to automate system monitoring, diagnosis, and troubleshooting activities.

Nexus API (NX-API)

NX-API is an enhancement to the NX-OS CLI system, which supports XML and JSON outputs. On Cisco Nexus devices, CLIs are run only on the device. NX-API improves the accessibility of these CLIs—which are traditionally run on the devices directly—by making them available outside the switch using HTTP/HTTPS.

NX-API is composed of three major components: Transport, Message Format, and Security. Figure 8-3 gives an overview of NX-API components.

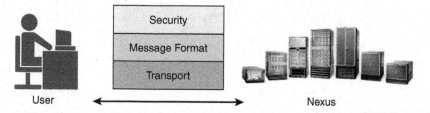

Figure 8-3 *Nexus API (NX-API) Overview*

Transport

The TNX-API feature is not enabled by default in Nexus platforms. Once it is enabled, by default, it uses HTTPS port 443 and has HTTP port 80 disabled. NX-API is also supported through UNIX Domain Sockets for applications running natively on the host or within Guest Shell. The NX-API back end uses the Nginx HTTP server. The Nginx process and all its children processes are under the Linux cgroup protection where the CPU and memory usage are capped. If the Nginx memory usage exceeds the cgroup limitations, the Nginx process is restarted and the NX-API configuration (the VRF, port, and certificate configurations) is restored.

Message Formats

NX-API is an enhancement to the NX-OS CLI system that supports XML output. NX-API also supports the JSON output format for specific commands. The NX-API uses HTTP functions such as GET, PUT, POST, and DELETE to programmatically interact with the device to obtain configurations or to make changes. NX-API XML output presents data in a user-friendly format, which can also be converted into JSON.

Security

NX-API supports HTTPS. All communication to the device is encrypted when you use HTTPS. NX-API does not support insecure HTTP or TLSv1 protocols by default. NX-API is integrated into the role-based authentication control (RBAC) on the device. Users must have appropriate accounts to access the device through NX-API.

NX-API provides a session-based cookie, nxapi_auth, when users first successfully authenticate. With the session cookie, the username and password are included in all subsequent NX-API requests that are sent to the device. The username and password are used with the session cookie to bypass performing the full authentication multiple times, in a repeated fashion. Avoiding unnecessary use of the authentication process reduces the workload on the device. If the session cookie is not included with subsequent requests, another session cookie is required and is provided by the authentication process. NX-API performs authentication through a Programmable Authentication Module (PAM) on the switch. Use of cookies reduces the number of PAM authentications, which in turn reduces the load on the PAM.

Note: A nxapi_auth cookie expires in 600 seconds. This value is fixed and cannot be adjusted through CLIs.

Enabling NX-API

By default, NX-API is not enabled, but it can be enabled using the commands shown in Example 8-19. The **feature nxapi** command given in the example enables the NX-API feature and Data Management Engine (DME) that manages objects, which will be discussed later.

Example 8-19   *Enabling NX-API*

```
Nexus7000#
Nexus7000# config t
Nexus7000(config)# feature nxapi
Nexus7000(config)# nxapi http port 80
Nexus7000(config)# nxapi https port 443
Nexus7000(config)# nxapi use-vrf management
Nexus7000(config)# nxapi sandbox
Nexus7000(config)# exit
Nexus7000#
Nexus7000# show nxapi
NX-API:      Enabled        Sandbox:      Enabled
HTTP Port:   80             HTTPS Port:   443


Certificate Information:
    Issuer:
    Expires:  Oct  3 20:03:11 2019 GMT
    Content:  -----BEGIN CERTIFICATE-----
MIIC0zCCAbugAwIBAgIJAIoeQ1+1dy6sMA0GCSqGSIb3DQEBCwUAMAAwHhcNMTkx
MDAyMjAwMzExWhcNMTkxMDAzMjAwMzExWjAAMIIBIjANBgkqhkiG9w0BAQEFAAOC
AQ8AMIIBCgKCAQEAqxB/TN0ZnXsOkuDwG/21BlCIxNzR3q7HZRRfdhp3OBG/fz1S
ZR6rluzHeeSCTGW3+MFM5wis+g/PAyXoxNxcgQRhb/0jg0JYa2Gwp9Y7ApFogi62
3z4/0MhZgMdFgnOusxTTm6SnpitJeRyMaFg5qXgRyfOH7Qkrpmrjzmim88ocPdY/
iX2ZvvItS3X3q3Hm33HncMXkmxrUjaTM8ogSYP8Ji4aUa5hjdwOsoQr4WoerYTmb
MsZmQRdFPezNPjXN/KY88ifszs8eMnLOGmraWWVMenbNeQ379VYticEPj2guDdVP
F9zBFGDTQtMFra+ZxCn4sfnsd11XYAxpIfAIrwIDAQABolAwTjAdBgNVHQ4EFgQU
mdwgy4D/Cw25RVYvPelNtNeW9WQwHwYDVR0jBBgwFoAUmdwgy4D/Cw25RVYvPelN
tNeW9WQwDAYDVR0TBAUwAwEB/zANBgkqhkiG9w0BAQsFAAOCAQEAlfBFIlReuZJ3
0CAAIkDGgUsQgIe6rcjGGfCXPK/NAgUdiEsIoJdmJweNt/Ydub3jSHq06B5LYHH1
aqfRqigZ8JM4kufUJq4CWQY+XQWuj06QcFcjNotxwKVwvLwdKtOQI3R+mvUzFuFK
IU26SoeajymocXZPfA8PIPzLaOxJRCgj8P087LMD+HdICvh7U1KmMid18MM8gvUo
RunLEW0hBEM2AxUtYKDyOEaSByxgc0vicCfsdM+CzR/08P6WdsKF5NCOmpJ/dnGC
JENQXTvE9asymQQ24K8/HzbPWav0bLzhHoLfYmvj6JWI/A+8GkOrwOdPfJvQI0B5
WIIvUB7+bA==
-----END CERTIFICATE-----
Nexus7000#
```

If you want to have a self-signed certificate and associated key, generate them using **openssl** commands in a Linux server and copy the certificate to the switch bootflash before you enable the NX-API feature.

Example 8-20 walks you through generating a self-signed certificate for HTTPS operations.

Example 8-20 *Generating Self-Signed Certificate for HTTPS*

```
root@Ubuntu-Server1$ openssl req -x509 -newkey rsa:4096 -keyout nxapi-key.pem -out
  nxapi-cert.pem -days 365
Generating a 4096 bit RSA private key
.......................................................................................
    .....................................................................................
    .............................................................................
    ..............................................++
......................................++
writing new private key to 'nxapi-key.pem'
Enter PEM pass phrase:
Verifying - Enter PEM pass phrase:
-----
You are about to be asked to enter information that will be incorporated
into your certificate request.
What you are about to enter is what is called a Distinguished Name or a DN.
There are quite a few fields but you can leave some blank
For some fields there will be a default value,
If you enter '.', the field will be left blank.
-----
Country Name (2 letter code) []:US
State or Province Name (full name) []:DC
Locality Name (eg, city) []:Washington
Organization Name (eg, company) []:Cisco
Organizational Unit Name (eg, section) []:CX
Common Name (eg, fully qualified host name) []:TEST
Email Address []:testuser@example.com
root@Ubuntu-Server1$
root@Ubuntu-Server1$ ls -l | grep pem
-rw-r--r--   1 yramdoss  staff       1939 Oct  2 22:03 nxapi-cert.pem
-rw-r--r--   1 yramdoss  staff       3418 Oct  2 22:03 nxapi-key.pem
root@Ubuntu-Server1$
root@Ubuntu-Server1$
```

As shown in Example 8-21, export the certificate and key generated to the switch and apply them.

Example 8-21 *NX-API—Exporting Certificate and Key*

```
Nexus7000# mkdir bootflash:nxapi
Nexus7000# copy ftp:root@Ubuntu-Server1 bootflash:/nxapi
<snip>
Nexus7000#
Nexus7000# dir bootflash:nxapi
       1939    Oct 02 22:03:31 2019  nxapi-cert.pem
       3418    Oct 02 22:03:36 2019  nxapi-key.pem
```

```
Nexus7000#
Nexus7000# config t
Nexus7000(config)# feature nxapi
Nexus7000(config)# no nxapi http port 80
Nexus7000(config)# nxapi https port 443
Nexus7000(config)# nxapi use-vrf management
Nexus7000(config)# nxapi certificate httpscrt certfile bootflash:nxapi/
  nxapi-cert.pem
Upload done. Please enable. Note cert and key must match.
Nexus7000(config)# nxapi certificate httpskey keyfile bootflash:nxapi/nxapi-key.pem
Upload done. Please enable. Note cert and key must match.
Nexus7000(config)# nxapi certificate enable
Nexus7000(config)# exit
Nexus7000#
```

You can use NX-API via CLIs local to the device or use NX-API REST from a remote device or from an NX-API client. NX-APIs can be scripted to offer access to NX-OS CLIs through Python using HTTP and JSON/XML libraries.

Data Management Engine and Managed Objects

In Nexus switches, configuration and state information of the switch are stored in a hierarchical inverted tree structure known as the management information tree (MIT), which can be accessed through the API. You can make changes on a single object or on an object subtree. Each node in the MIT represents a managed object or group of objects. These objects are organized in a hierarchical way, creating logical object containers. Figure 8-4 illustrates the logical hierarchy of the MIT object model.

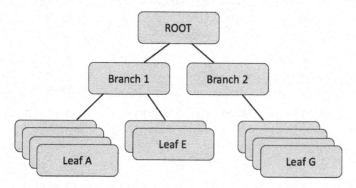

Figure 8-4 *MIT Object Model—Logical Hierarchy*

Here is a quick look at these managed objects and their characteristics.

Every managed object in the system can be identified by a unique distinguished name (DN). This approach allows the object to be referred to globally.

In addition to its distinguished name, each object can be referred to by its relative name (RN). The relative name identifies an object relative to its parent object. Any given object's distinguished name is derived from its own relative name appended to its parent object's distinguished name. Distinguished names are directly mapped to URLs. Either the relative name or the distinguished name can be used to access an object, depending on the current location in the MIT. The relationship among managed objects, relative names, and distinguished names is shown in Figure 8-5.

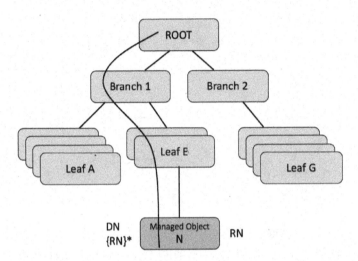

Figure 8-5 *MIT Objects, Relative Names, and Distinguished Names*

Because of the hierarchical nature of the tree and the attribute system that identifies object classes, the tree can be queried in several ways for managed object information. Queries can be performed on an object itself through its distinguished name, on a class of objects, or on a tree level, discovering all members of an object. For all MIT queries, you can optionally return the entire subtree or a partial subtree. Additionally, the RBAC mechanism in the system dictates which objects are returned; only the objects that the user has rights to view will be returned.

To browse the data models supported in the Nexus platform, refer to the DevNet Data Model reference provided at https://www.getpostman.com/downloads/.

Through a web browser, you can explore the Managed Objects store by accessing the device at the URL http://<device-ip-address-or-DNS>/visore.html, where <device-ip-address> is the management IP address of the device.

NX-API REST

NX-API REST is available for use with all Cisco Nexus 9000 and Cisco Nexus 3000 switches, except Nexus 3016, 3046, 3064, 3132 non-XL, 3172 non-XL, and 3500 non-XL switches. It is also available in Nexus 7000 platforms starting from 8.x releases.

NX-API REST (REpresentational State Transfer) brings model-driven programmability to standalone Nexus switches. The model referenced here is nothing but an explicit representation of the administrative and operational state of the system's components, completely maintained by system software. This model of managed objects (MOs) is a formal specification understood by the programmers and application developers. It is made available through standard REST interfaces, making it easier to access and manipulate the object model.

Cisco NX-API REST interfaces enable programmatic access to these managed objects in the Nexus switches, which is done by HTTP or HTTPS operations, as shown in Figure 8-6. The operations supported using HTTP/S methods are GET, PUT, POST, and DELETE. The object-based information model makes it a good fit for REST interfaces; URLs and URIs map directly to distinguished names identifying objects on the tree, and any data on the MIT can be described as a self-contained structured text tree document encoded in XML or JavaScript Object Notation (JSON).

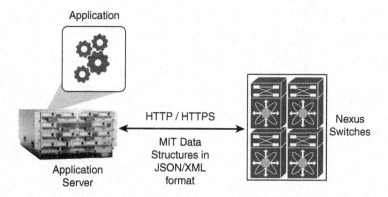

Figure 8-6 *NX-API REST—Logical View*

The URL format used can be represented as follows: <system>/api/[mo|class]/[dn|class] [:method].[xml|json]?{options}

- **System:** System identifier; an IP address or DNS-resolvable host name

- **mo | class:** Indication of whether this is a managed object (**MO**), a tree (**MIT**), or a class-level query

- **class:** Managed-object class (as specified in the information model) of the objects queried

- **dn:** Distinguished name—unique hierarchical name of the object in the MIT tree—of the object queried

- **method:** Optional indication of the method being invoked on the object; applies only to POST requests

- **xml | json:** Encoding format

- **options:** Query options, filters, and arguments

Following is a query made through Google Postman, which is a developer utility commonly used as a REST client. Google Postman can be downloaded from https://www.getpostman.com/downloads/.

Now you will learn how to gain API access to get the **running-configuration of Ethernet 1/1** interface from a Nexus 9000 switch. The API request sent is http://10.102.242.131/api/mo/sys/intf/phys-[eth1/1].json, and the response obtained is shown in Example 8-22.

Example 8-22 *Response to REST API Request*

```json
{
  "totalCount": "1",
  "imdata": [
    {
      "l1PhysIf": {
        "attributes": {
          "FECMode": "auto",
          "accessVlan": "vlan-1",
          "adminSt": "up",
          "autoNeg": "on",
          "beacon": "off",
          "bw": "default",
          "childAction": "",
          "controllerId": "",
          "delay": "1",
          "descr": "",
          "dn": "sys/intf/phys-[eth1/1]",
          "dot1qEtherType": "0x8100",
          "duplex": "auto",
          "ethpmCfgFailedBmp": "",
          "ethpmCfgFailedTs": "00:00:00:00.000",
          "ethpmCfgState": "0",
          "id": "eth1/1",
          "inhBw": "4294967295",
          "layer": "Layer3",
          "linkDebounce": "100",
          "linkDebounceLinkUp": "0",
          "linkLog": "default",
          "linkTransmitReset": "enable",
          "mdix": "auto",
          "medium": "broadcast",
          "modTs": "2019-07-30T20:20:35.975+00:00",
          "mode": "access",
          "mtu": "1500",
          "name": "",
```

```
        "nativeVlan": "vlan-1",
        "packetTimestampEgressSourceId": "0",
        "packetTimestampIngressSourceId": "0",
        "packetTimestampState": "disable",
        "persistentOnReload": "true",
        "portT": "leaf",
        "routerMac": "not-applicable",
        "snmpTrapSt": "enable",
        "spanMode": "not-a-span-dest",
        "speed": "auto",
        "speedGroup": "auto",
        "status": "",
        "switchingSt": "disabled",
        "trunkLog": "default",
        "trunkVlans": "1-4094",
        "usage": "discovery",
        "userCfgdFlags": "admin_layer,admin_state",
        "vlanmgrCfgFailedBmp": "",
        "vlanmgrCfgFailedTs": "00:00:00:00.000",
        "vlanmgrCfgState": "0",
        "voicePortCos": "none",
        "voicePortTrust": "disable",
        "voiceVlanId": "none",
        "voiceVlanType": "none"
      }
    }
   }
  ]
}
```

Figure 8-7 puts all the things discussed—NX-API, NX-API REST, DME, and Managed Objects—in perspective.

Here is a brief look at the NX-API Sandbox and how to leverage it to develop simple Python codes. Before using NX-API Sandbox, enable it with the **nxapi sandbox** command at the configuration mode in the Nexus switches.

You can access NX-API Developer Sandbox by entering **http://<device-ip-address-or-DNS-name>** in your web browser, with the same credentials used for SSH access to the device.

Figure 8-8 depicts the GUI of the NX-API Developer Sandbox, with the device model and NX-OS version listed on the top.

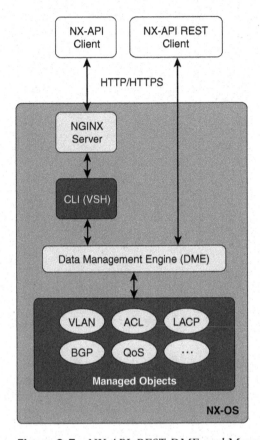

Figure 8-7 *NX-API, REST, DME, and Managed Objects*

On the right side of the screen, you can see various drop-down menu options available to choose Method, Message Format, Input Type, and Error Action.

The sample options are as follows:

- **Method:** NX-API CLI, NX-API REST (DME), RESTCONF (Yang)

- **Message Format:** JSON-RPC, XML, JSON

- **Input Type:** cli, cli_ascii, cli_array, cli_show, cli_show_ascii, cli_conf, bash

- **Error Action:** stop_on_error, continue_on_error, rollback_on_error

- **Chunk Mode:** Enable Chunk Mode option for specific input types, with a box to provide the session ID.

Note: Not all variables are available for a given option. For example, Chunk Mode is available only for the NXAPI-CLI method, XML message format, and **cli_show** or **cli_show_ascii** input types. It is highly recommended that you enable the NX-API Sandbox and access it to explore further.

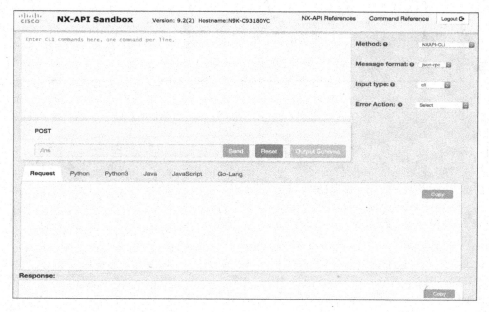

Figure 8-8 *NX-API Sandbox*

Following is a sample use case of NX-API Sandbox using the REST option discussed earlier.

1. From the Managed Objects repository list, pick a specific MO to explore, such as SNMP. The MIT path is /api/mo/sys/snmp.json.

2. Enter the details in the Developer Sandbox by choosing the following option and entering the details given here for the pull-down menu:

   Method: NXAPI-REST (DME)

   Input Type: CLI

3. Select the operation GET (from the POST, GET, PUT, or DELETE options available) and enter the MIT path /api/mo/sys/snmp.json. Then press Send. Figure 8-9 illustrates the options that are chosen for this example.

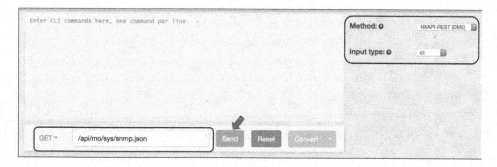

Figure 8-9 *NX-API Sandbox—Sending GET Request*

In the Response box at the bottom of the Sandbox page, you should see the results shown in Example 8-23 in response to the REST API request sent.

Example 8-23 *Response to NX-API GET Request*

```
{
  "totalCount": "1",
  "imdata": [
    {
      "snmpEntity": {
        "attributes": {
          "adminSt": "enabled",
          "childAction": "",
          "dn": "sys/snmp",
          "modTs": "2019-04-19T15:18:20.507+00:00",
          "name": "",
          "operErr": "",
          "operSt": "enabled",
          "persistentOnReload": "true",
          "status": ""
        }
      }
    }
  ]
}
```

In the Request box (above the Response box), you should see multiple options to convert the NX-API request into Python, Python v3, Java, JavaScript, or Go-Lang codes. Figure 8-10 shows that the Python v3 option has been chosen.

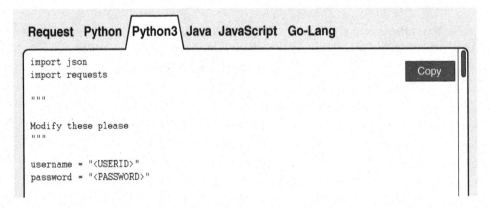

Figure 8-10 *NX-API—Convert Request to Code in Programming Languages*

For the specific NX-API REST GET request of SNMP, the Python v3 code looks like the one shown in Example 8-24.

Example 8-24 *NX-API GET Request in Python v3 Code*

```
import json
import requests


"""
Modify these please
"""
username = "<USERID>"
password = "<PASSWORD>"

ip_addr =  "10.102.242.131"
endpoints = "/api/mo/sys/snmp/inst/traps/aaa.json"
payload = None
def aaa_login(username, password, ip_addr):
    payload = {
        'aaaUser' : {
            'attributes' : {
                'name' : username,
                'pwd' : password
                }
            }
        }
    url = "http://" + ip_addr + "/api/aaaLogin.json"
    auth_cookie = {}

    response = requests.request("POST", url, data=json.dumps(payload))
    if response.status_code == requests.codes.ok:
        data = json.loads(response.text)['imdata'][0]
        token = str(data['aaaLogin']['attributes']['token'])
        auth_cookie = {"APIC-cookie" : token}

    print ()
    print ("aaaLogin RESPONSE:")
    print (json.dumps(json.loads(response.text), indent=2))

    return response.status_code, auth_cookie

def aaa_logout(username, ip_addr, auth_cookie):
    payload = {
        'aaaUser' : {
            'attributes' : {
```

```
                        'name' : username
                       }
                 }
           }
     url = "http://" + ip_addr + "/api/aaaLogout.json"

     response = requests.request("POST", url, data=json.dumps(payload),
                                   cookies=auth_cookie)

     print ()
     print ("aaaLogout RESPONSE:")
     print (json.dumps(json.loads(response.text), indent=2))
     print ()

def get(ip_addr, auth_cookie, url, payload):
     response = requests.request("GET", url, data=json.dumps(payload),
                                   cookies=auth_cookie)

     print ()
     print ("GET RESPONSE:")
     print (json.dumps(json.loads(response.text), indent=2))

if __name__ == '__main__':
     status, auth_cookie = aaa_login(username, password, ip_addr)
     if status == requests.codes.ok:
         url = "http://" + ip_addr + endpoints
         get(ip_addr, auth_cookie, url, payload)
         aaa_logout(username, ip_addr, auth_cookie)

   ]
}
```

The NX-API Developer Sandbox is helpful for developers at the beginner level, to whom it acts as a stepping-stone to leverage API capabilities available in Nexus platforms and to develop simple Python, Java scripts that can be part of the normal workflow.

RESTCONF, NETCONF, and YANG

RESTCONF (REST CONFiguration) and NETCONF (NETwork CONFiguration) are the network management protocols that are alternative to each other and used to send data defined by a data modeling language such as YANG (Yet Another Next Generation). As you may remember, Chapter 2, "Virtualization and Cisco," discussed YANG and how it helps to model the data at different levels in the network. The following section focuses on RESTCONF and NETCONF and how they can be used to implement model-based network configuration management. Figure 8-11 illustrates the RESTCONF and NETCONF implementation in Cisco platforms.

NETCONF (RFC 6241) provides mechanisms to install, manipulate, and delete the configuration of network devices. These operations are realized as remote-procedure calls (RPCs) and use an XML-based data encoding for the operations data as well as the protocol messages.

NETCONF Agent is a client-facing interface that provides secure transport to send requests and get responses with data in the form of a YANG model, encoded in XML. These agents support a datastore that temporarily holds the candidate configuration and any changes the user makes. During the NETCONF session of updating configuration in the temporary datastore, the devices running configuration are not updated unless and until the user chooses to commit the updated candidate configuration.

RESTCONF is a protocol based on HTTP methods to provide Create, Read, Update, and Delete (CRUD) operations on a datastore containing YANG-defined data. The RESTCONF protocol supports both XML and JSON payload encodings. User authentication is done through the basic HTTP authentication.

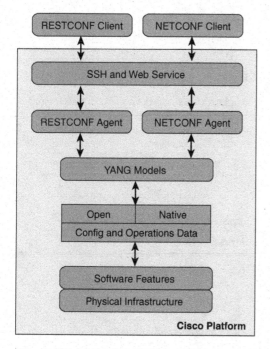

Figure 8-11   *RESTCONF and NETCONF in Cisco Platforms*

NETCONF and RESTCONF are alternative protocols for performing operations on YANG data models. Network management systems and SDN controllers use NETCONF to integrate with network devices. RESTCONF is used for more ad-hoc network device integration.

Table 8-2 shows how RESTCONF operations relate to NETCONF protocol operations.

Table 8-2   *RESTCONF and NETCONF Protocol Operations*

RESTCONF	NETCONF
OPTIONS	None
HEAD	<get-config>, <get>
GET	<get-config>, <get>
POST	<edit-config> (nc:operation="create")
POST	Invoke an RPC operation
PUT	<copy-config> (PUT on datastore)
PUT	<edit-config> (nc:operation="create/replace")
PATCH	<edit-config> (nc:operation depends on PATCH content)
DELETE	<edit-config> (nc:operation="delete")

The following sections discuss RESTCONF and NETCONF Agents that are supported in the Cisco IOS-XE, IOX-XR, and NX-OS platforms, and steps to enable them in detail.

Enabling RESTCONF Agent in IOS-XE

The RESTCONF Agent is supported in various platforms running IOS-XE release 16.6.x or later. The https-based RESTCONF protocol uses secure HTTP methods to provide CREATE, READ, UPDATE, and DELETE (CRUD) operations on a conceptual datastore that contains YANG-based data.

Table 8-3 shows different HTTP/HTTPS options and corresponding methods available for RESTCONF.

Table 8-3   *RESTCONF HTTP Options and Supported Methods*

Option	Supported Method
GET	Read
PATCH	Update
PUT	Create or Replace
POST	Create or Operations (reload, default)
DELETE	Deletes the targeted resource
HEAD	Header metadata (no response body)

RESTCONF sessions must be authenticated using authentication, authorization, and accounting (AAA). A user for these sessions must be authenticated via RADIUS or

TACACS+ protocols and authorized to a privilege level of 15. Make sure to enable HTTP secure server service because RESTCONF Agent runs over HTTPS.

In Example 8-25, a test user cisco has been created with a privilege level set to 15. AAA has been enabled and configured to use the local database for authentication and authorization. To configure AAA with the authentication server, refer to *Programmability Configuration Guide—Cisco IOS-XE Everest 16.6.x* provided in the "References" section.

Example 8-25   *Enabling RESTCONF and Configuring User Authentication*

```
Cat9300# conf t
Cat9300(config)# ip http secure-server
Cat9300(config)# username cisco privilege 15 password 0 cisco123
Cat9300(config)# aaa new-model
Cat9300(config)# aaa authentication login default local
Cat9300(config)# aaa authorization config-commands
Cat9300(config)# aaa authorization exec default local
Cat9300(config)# RESTCONF
Cat9300(config)#
```

Verify and check the state of the RESTCONF Agent by executing the command provided in Example 8-26, which shows that the **nginx** process is running. NGINX is an internal process that acts as a proxy webserver that provides Transport Layer Security (TLS)-based HTTPS. A RESTCONF request sent via HTTPS is received and processed further by the NGINX proxy webserver; it is responsible for building and transmitting responses.

Example 8-26   *RESTCONF and nginx Processes*

```
Cat9300#
Cat9300# show platform software yang-management process monitor
COMMAND     PID S    VSZ    RSS %CPU %MEM      ELAPSED
nginx     26403 S 337764 18216  0.0  0.2  6-17:01:21
nginx     27685 S 343864 12868  0.0  0.1  6-17:00:50
Cat9300#
```

Once RESTCONF is enabled, all supported operations can be governed through model interfaces, including optional settings for RESTCONF configuration and operational data settings.

Using a RESTCONF Agent in IOS-XE

A RESTCONF device determines the root of the RESTCONF API through the link element **/.well-known/host-meta resource**, which contains the RESTCONF attribute. The RESTCONF device uses the RESTCONF API root resource as the initial part of the path in the request URI.

A sample URI for GigabitEthernet0/0 is https://10.105.221.229/restconf/data/ Cisco-IOS-XE-native:native/interface/GigabitEthernet=0%2F0.

Example 8-27 shows the response from a Catalyst 9300 switch to a GET request for the URI just mentioned.

Example 8-27   *Response to GET Request for Gig0/0 URI*

```
<GigabitEthernet xmlns="http://cisco.com/ns/yang/Cisco-IOS-XE-native"
  xmlns:ios="http://cisco.com/ns/yang/Cisco-IOS-XE-native">
  <name>0/0</name>
  <vrf>
    <forwarding>Mgmt-vrf</forwarding>
  </vrf>
  <ip>
  <address>
  <primary>
    <address>10.105.221.229</address>
    <mask>255.255.255.224</mask>
  </primary>
</address>
</ip>
<negotiation xmlns="http://cisco.com/ns/yang/Cisco-IOS-XE-ethernet">
  <auto>true</auto>
</negotiation>
<speed xmlns="http://cisco.com/ns/yang/Cisco-IOS-XE-ethernet">
  <value-1000/>
</speed>
</GigabitEthernet>
```

The same request can be sent through the Linux **Curl** command, as shown in Example 8-28.

Example 8-28   *GET Request Through Curl Command*

```
Ubuntu$ curl -i -k -X "GET" "https://10.105.221.229/restconf/data/Cisco-IOS-
  XE-native:native/interface/GigabitEthernet=0%2F0" -H 'Accept: application/
  yang-data+json' -u 'cisco:cisco123'
HTTP/1.1 200 OK
Server: nginx
Date: Fri, 25 Oct 2019 03:38:26 GMT
Content-Type: application/yang-data+json
Transfer-Encoding: chunked
Connection: keep-alive
Cache-Control: private, no-cache, must-revalidate, proxy-revalidate
Pragma: no-cache
```

```
{
  "Cisco-IOS-XE-native:GigabitEthernet": {
    "name": "0/0",
    "vrf": {
      "forwarding": "Mgmt-vrf"
    },
    "ip": {
      "address": {
        "primary": {
          "address": "10.105.221.229",
          "mask": "255.255.255.224"
        }
      }
    },
    "Cisco-IOS-XE-ethernet:negotiation": {
      "auto": true
    },
    "Cisco-IOS-XE-ethernet:speed": {
      "value-1000": [null]
    }
  }
}
Ubuntu$
```

Note: For detailed information on features supported in different platforms and versions, refer to the Programmability Configuration Guide—Cisco IOS-XE Everest 16.6.x provided at https://www.cisco.com/c/en/us/td/docs/ios-xml/ios/prog/configuration/166/b_166_programmability_cg/configuring_yang_datamodel.html#id_44510. There are no plans to add RESTCONF support to Cisco Catalyst platforms other than the ones mentioned in the support guide.

Enabling RESTCONF Agent in NX-OS

The RESTCONF Agent is supported in Nexus 3000 and 9000 platforms, starting with the 7.x releases. Following are the protocol operations that the Cisco NX-OS RESTCONF Agent supports: OPTIONS, HEAD, GET, POST, PUT, PATCH, and DELETE.

This agent can be enabled, as shown in Example 8-29. Please make sure to enable NX-API and the associated HTTP/HTTPS access before enabling the RESTCONF Agent.

Example 8-29 *Enabling RESTCONF Agent in NX-OS*

```
SW-N9K# config t
SW-N9K(config)# feature nxapi
SW-N9K(config)# nxapi http port 80
SW-N9K(config)# nxapi https port 443
SW-N9K(config)# feature restconf
SW-N9K(config)#
```

Once RESTCONF is enabled, you can check its state using the command in Example 8-30.

Example 8-30 *Verify RESTCONF Agent Status in NX-OS*

```
SW-N9K# show restconf nxsdk state

Custom App State information
--------------------------------
App Name                  : RESTCONF(RESTCONF Agent Service App)
Nexus Mapped App Name     : RESTCONF
Uuid                      : 2625 (VSH)
Environment               : Python
App Priority              : No Priority
Sup State                 : Active
Start Reason              : configuration
Start State               : Stateless


Custom CLI Cmd State information
--------------------------------

Name                      : RESTCONF_show_tech_support_cmd
Syntax                    : show  tech-support RESTCONF
Mode                      : Show
State                     : ADDED_TO_PARSER

CLI Parser Init           : Yes
CLI Parser Err            : Registered with NX CLI Parser
CLI Callback Handler      : Registered


Custom HA information
--------------------------------
Hot Standby               : Down
Recovery                  : Done
```

```
    DB                              | Status    | Record#
    ----------------------------------------------------------
    runtime_data                    | In-Use    | 0
    runtime_config                  | In-Use    | 0
    startup_config                  | In-Use    | 0
SW-N9K#
```

Using the RESTCONF Agent in NX-OS

As has been discussed in earlier chapters, with the HTTP/HTTPS secure communication channel set up to a device, you should be able to perform general operations such as GET and POST by exchanging appropriate HTTP/HTTPS requests.

Example 8-31 shows the response from the Nexus 9000 switch to the HTTP GET request sent with URL http://10.102.242.131/restconf/data/Cisco-NX-OS-device:System/intf-items/phys-items/PhysIf-list, where 10.102.243.131 is the management IP address of the device.

Example 8-31   *Response to RESTCONF GET Request*

```
    <PhysIf-list>
        <id>eth1/39</id>
        <FECMode>auto</FECMode>
        <accessVlan>vlan-1</accessVlan>
        <adminSt>down</adminSt>
        <aggrmbrif-items>
            <bdlPortNum>0</bdlPortNum>
            <channelingSt>unknown</channelingSt>
            <flags/>
            <ltlProgrammed>false</ltlProgrammed>
            <name/>
            <operSt>down</operSt>
            <summOperSt>down</summOperSt>
            <uptime>00:00:00:00.000</uptime>
        </aggrmbrif-items>
        <autoNeg>on</autoNeg>
        <beacon>off</beacon>
        <bw>0</bw>
        <controllerId/>
        <dbgDot3Stats-items>
            <alignmentErrors>0</alignmentErrors>
            <babble>0</babble>
            <carrierSenseErrors>0</carrierSenseErrors>
            <controlInUnknownOpcodes>0</controlInUnknownOpcodes>
            <deferredTransmissions>0</deferredTransmissions>
            <excessiveCollisions>0</excessiveCollisions>
            <fCSErrors>0</fCSErrors>
<snip>
```

The request sent is to get the list of physical interfaces, their configuration, and their operational states and statistics. As shown in Example 8-31, the list shows interface Eth1/39, which is in Vlan 1.

The same request can be sent through the Linux **Curl** command, as shown in Example 8-32.

Example 8-32 *RESTCONF GET Request Through the Curl Command*

```
Ubuntu$ curl -X GET -u admin "http://10.102.242.131/restconf/data/
  Cisco-NX-OS-device:System/intf-items/phys-items/PhysIf-list" -i
Enter host password for user 'admin':


HTTP/1.1 200 OK
Server: nginx/1.7.10
Date: Wed, 23 Oct 2019 21:40:53 GMT
Set-Cookie: nxapi_auth=admin:8EeFQtDF3nTDd/hMPDS5e/53aok=; Secure; HttpOnly;
Status: 200 OK
Access-Control-Allow-Headers: Origin, X-Requested-With, Content-Type, Accept,
  devcookie
Access-Control-Allow-Origin: http://127.0.0.1:8000
Access-Control-Allow-Methods: POST,GET,OPTIONS
Content-Length: 14208
Content-Type: application/yang.data+xml
Via: 1.1 rtp1-dmz-wsa-3.cisco.com:80 (Cisco-WSA/X)
Connection: keep-alive

    <PhysIf-list>
        <id>eth1/39</id>
        <FECMode>auto</FECMode>
        <accessVlan>vlan-1</accessVlan>
        <adminSt>down</adminSt>
        <aggrmbrif-items>
            <bdlPortNum>0</bdlPortNum>
            <channelingSt>unknown</channelingSt>
            <flags/>
            <ltlProgrammed>false</ltlProgrammed>
            <name/>
            <operSt>down</operSt>
            <summOperSt>down</summOperSt>
            <uptime>00:00:00:00.000</uptime>
        </aggrmbrif-items>
        <autoNeg>on</autoNeg>
        <beacon>off</beacon>
<snip>
```

Enabling NETCONF Agent in IOS-XE

The NETCONF Agent is supported in various platforms with IOS-XE release 16.3.x or later.

NETCONF sessions must be authenticated using AAA. Just like for RESTCONF, a user for these sessions must be authenticated via RADIUS or TACACS+ protocols and authorized to a privilege level of 15.

In Example 8-33, AAA has been enabled and configured to use the local database for authentication and authorization. A local test user cisco with a privilege level set to 15 has been created and used. NETCONF is enabled with one simple command: **NETCONF-yang.**

Example 8-33 *Enabling NETCONF in IOS-XE*

```
Cat9300-A# config t
Cat9300-A(config)# aaa new-model
Cat9300-A(config)# aaa authentication login default local
Cat9300-A(config)# aaa authorization config-commands
Cat9300-A(config)# aaa authorization exec default local
Cat9300-A(config)# username cisco privilege 15 password 0 cisco123
Cat9300-A(config)# netconf-yang
Cat9300-A(config)#
```

To configure the AAA server for centralized authentication, refer to the Programmability Configuration Guide—Configuring NETCONF-YANG at https://www.cisco.com/c/en/us/td/docs/routers/asr9000/software/data-models/guide/b-programmability-cg-asr9000-62x/b-data-odels-config-guide-asr9000_chapter_010.html#id_20896.

There are multiple optional configurations that can be enabled with NETCONF, such as SNMP. The snmp-server configurations must be present to enable the generation of NETCONF notifications (RFC 5277 for Syslog messages and for any configured SNMP traps to generate NETCONF notifications).

Example 8-34 shows the command to verify the status of NETCONF. As you notice, the command result provides the status of various software processes including **confd** and **syncfd**, which are required to support the Data Model Interface (DMI) of NETCONF.

Example 8-34 *Verifying NETCONF Status in IOS-XE*

```
C9300-A# show NETCONF-yang datastores
Device# show NETCONF-yang datastores
Datastore Name : running
Globally Locked By Session : 16
Globally Locked Time : 2019-10-15T14:21:17-05:00

C9300-A# show NETCONF-yang sessions detail
R: Global-lock on running datastore
C: Global-lock on candidate datastore
S: Global-lock on startup datastore
```

```
Number of sessions      : 1

session-id              : 16
transport               : NETCONF-ssh
username                : admin
source-host             : 2001:db8::1
login-time              : 2019-10-15T14:21:17-05:00
in-rpcs                 : 0
in-bad-rpcs             : 0
out-rpc-errors          : 0
out-notifications       : 0
global-lock             : None


C9300-A# show platform software yang-management process
confd           : Running
nesd            : Running
syncfd          : Running
ncsshd          : Running
dmiauthd        : Running
vtyserverutild  : Running
opdatamgrd      : Running
nginx           : Running
ndbmand         : Running
pubd            : Running
```

Table 8-4 provides a basic description of each process reported in the preceding command.

Table 8-4   *NETCONF-Yang Processes in IOS-XE*

Process	Description
confd	Configuration daemon
nesd	Network element synchronizer daemon
syncfd	Sync from daemon
ncsshd	NETCONF Secure Shell (SSH) daemon
dmiauthd	Device management interface (DMI) authentication daemon
vtyserverutild	VTY server utility daemon
opdatamgrd	Operational data manager daemon
nginx	NGINX web server
ndbmand	NETCONF database manager

Note: The process **nginx** runs **if ip http secure-server** or **ip http server** is configured on the device. This process is not required to be in the **running** state for NETCONF to function properly. However, the **nginx** process is required for RESTCONF.

Using the NETCONF Agent in IOS-XE

As you might have read in earlier sections, the NETCONF protocol has a set of operations to manage device configurations and retrieve device state information. NETCONF supports a global lock and can kill nonresponsive sessions.

To ensure consistency and prevent conflicting configurations, the owner of the session can lock the NETCONF session. The NETCONF locks the configuration parser and the running configuration database; therefore, other NETCONF sessions cannot perform edit operations but can perform read operations. These locks are intended to be short-lived and allow the owner to make changes without interaction with other NETCONF clients, non-NETCONF clients (such as SNMP and CLI scripts), and human users.

A global lock held by an active session is revoked when the associated session is killed. The lock gives the session holding the lock exclusive write access to the configuration. When a configuration change is denied due to a global lock, the error message will specify that a NETCONF global lock is the reason the configuration change has been denied.

The **<lock>** operation takes a mandatory parameter, **<target>**, which is the name of the configuration datastore that is to be locked. When a lock is active, the **<edit-config>** and **<copy-config>** operations are not allowed.

If the clear configuration lock command is specified while a NETCONF global lock is being held, a full synchronization of the configuration is scheduled, and a warning syslog message is produced. This command clears only the parser configuration lock.

Example 8-35 shows a sample RPC that shows the **<lock>** operation of the running configuration datastore.

Example 8-35   *RPC Showing Lock Operation*

```
<rpc message-id="101"
        xmlns="urn:ietf:params:xml:ns:NETCONF:base:1.0">
     <lock>
       <target>
         <running/>
       </target>
     </lock>
</rpc>
```

During a session conflict or client misuse of the global lock, NETCONF sessions can be monitored via the **show NETCONF-yang sessions** command, as shown in one of the examples, and nonresponsive sessions can be cleared using the **clear NETCONF-yang session** command, which clears both the NETCONF lock and the configuration lock.

A **\<kill-session\>** request forces a NETCONF session to terminate. When a NETCONF entity receives a **\<kill-session\>** request for an open session, it stops all operations in process, releases all locks and resources associated with the session, and closes any associated connections.

A **\<kill-session\>** request requires the session ID of the NETCONF session that is to be terminated. If the value of the session ID is equal to the current session ID, an invalid-value error is returned. If a NETCONF session is terminated while its transaction is still in progress, the data model infrastructure requests a rollback, applies it to the network element, and triggers a synchronization of all YANG models.

If a session kill fails and a global lock is held, enter the **clear configuration lock** command via the console or SSH. At this point, the data models can be stopped and restarted.

Example 8-36 shows how to send RPC messages to edit the SNMP traps configuration.

Example 8-36　*NETCONF—Editing SNMP Configuration*

```xml
<?xml version="1.0" encoding="utf-8"?>
<rpc xmlns="urn:ietf:params:xml:ns:NETCONF:base:1.0" message-id="">
  <edit-config>
    <target>
      <running/>
    </target>
    <config>
      <NETCONF-yang xmlns="http://cisco.com/yang/cisco-self-mgmt">
        <cisco-ia xmlns="http://cisco.com/yang/cisco-ia">
          <snmp-trap-control>
            <trap-list>
              <trap-oid>1.3.6.1.4.1.9.9.41.2.0.1</trap-oid>
            </trap-list>
            <trap-list>
              <trap-oid>1.3.6.1.6.3.1.1.5.3</trap-oid>
            </trap-list>
            <trap-list>
              <trap-oid>1.3.6.1.6.3.1.1.5.4</trap-oid>
            </trap-list>
          </snmp-trap-control>
        </cisco-ia>
      </NETCONF-yang>
    </config>
  </edit-config>
</rpc>
```

To learn more YANG data models, refer to the GitHub: YANG Models for Cisco IOS-XE repository at https://github.com/ChristopherJHart/floodlight/blob/master/Dockerfile.

Note: For detailed information on features supported in different platforms and versions, refer to the Programmability Configuration Guide—NETCONF Feature Information at https://www.cisco.com/c/en/us/td/docs/ios-xml/ios/sec_usr_ssh/configuration/xe-16-6/sec-usr-ssh-xe-16-6-book/sec-ssh-config-auth.html. There are no plans to add NETCONF support to Cisco Catalyst platforms other than the ones mentioned in the guide.

Enabling NETCONF Agent in IOS-XR

As discussed earlier, NETCONF is an XML-based protocol used over Secure Shell (SSH) transport to configure a network. The client applications use this protocol to request information from the router and make configuration changes to it.

Before enabling NETCONF, make sure k9sec pie and mgbl pie software packages installed on the router and crypto keys are generated.

To enable the NETCONF protocol, complete these steps:

1. Enable the NETCONF protocol over an SSH connection. Example 8-37 shows the commands to enable the agent and set the ssh server port to 830 (default).

Example 8-37 *Enabling NETCONF in IOS-XR*

```
ssh server v2
ssh server netconf
netconf agent tty
netconf-yang agent ssh
  ssh server netconf port 830
```

2. You can verify the agent's status and statistics by using the command shown in Example 8-38 after sending NETCONF requests.

Example 8-38 *Checking NETCONF Statistics*

```
ASR9000-A# show netconf-yang statistics
Summary statistics        requests|           total time|    <snip>
other                           0|     0h  0m  0s   0ms|
close-session                   5|     0h  0m  0s   8ms|
kill-session                    0|     0h  0m  0s   0ms|
get-schema                      0|     0h  0m  0s   0ms|
get                             0|     0h  0m  0s   0ms|
get-config                      4|     0h  0m  0s   5ms|
edit-config                     6|     0h  0m  0s   6ms|
commit                          0|     0h  0m  0s   0ms|
cancel-commit                   0|     0h  0m  0s   0ms|
lock                            0|     0h  0m  0s   0ms|
unlock                          0|     0h  0m  0s   0ms|
discard-changes                 0|     0h  0m  0s   0ms|
validate                        0|     0h  0m  0s   0ms|
```

Using NETCONF Agent in IOS-XR

From the NETCONF client application, use data models to configure and manage the router. Before starting to manage configurations using data models, make sure to import the data model to the client application using a YANG tool. The next step is to configure the router using the imported model. For more information on the values of the data models that can be configured, refer to the *Programmability Configuration Guide for Cisco ASR 9000—IOS-XR 6.2.x* at https://hub.docker.com/signup.

Consider an example of configuring the CDP protocol. To start with, download the configuration YANG data model for CDP **Cisco-IOS-XR-cdp-cfg.yang** from the router. Import the data model to the client application using any YANG tool. Edit and modify the following leaf nodes of the CDP data model as needed.

- timer
- enable
- log adjacency
- holdtime
- advertise v1 only

With the edited CDP data model, like the one shown in Example 8-39, you can configure CDP in the device using NETCONF.

Example 8-39   *Configuring CDP Using NETCONF*

```
<edit-config>
  <target>
    <candidate/>
  </target>
  <config xmlns:xc="urn:ietf:params:xml:n:netconf:base:1.0">
    <cdp xmlns="http://cisco.com/ns/yang/Cisco-IOS-XR-cdp-cfg">
      <timer>80</timer>
      <enable>true</enable>
      <log-adjacency></log-adjacency>
      <hold-time>200</holdtime>
      <advertise-v1-only></advertise-v1-only>
    </cdp>
  </config>
</edit-config>
```

Note: You can also configure CDP under the interface configuration by augmenting the interface manager. Use the **Cisco-IOS-XR-ifmgr-cfg** YANG model to configure CDP under the interface configuration.

Enabling the NETCONF Agent in NX-OS

The Cisco NX-OS NETCONF Agent is a client-facing interface that provides secure transport for the client requests and server responses in the form of a YANG model, encoded in XML. Enable NETCONF with the command shown in Example 8-40.

Example 8-40 *Enabling NETCONF in NX-OS*

```
SW-N9K# config t
SW-N9K(config)# feature netconf
SW-N9K(config)#
```

Once NETCONF is enabled, it allocates TCP port 830, which can transport messages back and forth from the agent to the client. Example 8-41 shows the command to check the TCP socket allocated for NETCONF.

Example 8-41 *NETCONF TCP Sockets*

```
SW-N9K# show socket connection
Total number of netstack tcp sockets: 4
Active connections (including servers)
           Protocol State/          Recv-Q/    Local Address(port)/
                     Context        Send-Q     Remote Address(port)
<snip>
[host]: tcp(4/6) LISTEN           0          *(830)
                     Wildcard       0          *(*)
<snip>
SW-N9K#
```

Once the NETCONF is enabled, you can start a session from a client to access various data models and configure or manage a device.

Using NETCONF Agent in NX-OS

The NETCONF Agent supports a candidate configuration feature. The Candidate configuration datastore temporarily holds the candidate configuration and any changes you make without changing the running configuration. You can then choose when to update the configuration of the device with the candidate configuration when you commit and confirm the candidate configuration.

If you do not confirm the changes, exit from a nonpersistent NETCONF client session, or choose to cancel the commit after you commit the change, a system timer times out and rolls back the changes.

If you initiate a confirmed-commit operation with a persistent token, the NETCONF client session becomes a persistent process. In a persistent process, exiting the NETCONF client session will not call an automatic rollback, and the changes cannot be rolled back without the matching persistent token.

The candidate configuration can only be initialized with the contents of the running configuration. To initialize the candidate configuring datastore, send a Copy-Config request using SSH with candidate as the target and running as the source.

To read from the candidate configuration, send a get-config request with SSH, using candidate as the source. To write to the contents of the candidate configuration, send an Edit-Config request with SSH, using candidate as the target.

The candidate configuration workflow follows:

- Edit the candidate configuration file
- Validate the candidate configuration
- Commit the changes to the running configuration

Example 8-42 shows initiating a session to a Nexus switch using SSH over TCP port 830, which is allocated to the NETCONF agent. As you see, the NETCONF agent responds with a hello message describing the NETCONF agent's capabilities. Refer to Figure 8-11 to understand the communication between the NETCONF client and the agent.

Example 8-42 *SSH over TCP Port 830*

```
Ubuntu$ ssh -s admin@10.102.242.131 -p 830 NETCONF
User Access Verification
Password:
<?xml version="1.0" encoding="UTF-8"?>
<hello xmlns="urn:ietf:params:xml:ns:NETCONF:base:1.0">
    <capabilities>
        <capability>urn:ietf:params:NETCONF:base:1.0</capability>
        <capability>urn:ietf:params:NETCONF:base:1.1</capability>
        <capability>urn:ietf:params:NETCONF:capability:writable-running:1.0</capa-
bility>
        <capability>urn:ietf:params:NETCONF:capability:rollback-on-error:1.0</capa-
bility>

<capability>urn:ietf:params:NETCONF:capability:candidate:1.0</capability>
        <capability>urn:ietf:params:NETCONF:capability:validate:1.1</capability>
        <capability>urn:ietf:params:NETCONF:capability:confirmed-commit:1.1</capa-
bility>
        <capability>http://cisco.com/ns/yang/cisco-nx-os-device?revision=2018-
02-12&amp;module=Cisco-NX-OS-device&amp;deviations=Cisco-NX-OS-device-deviations</
capability>
    </capabilities>
    <session-id>2084777776</session-id>
</hello>
]]>]]>
```

Once an SSH session is initialized, you can send the edit-config operator. In Example 8-43, the attributes in **edit-config** identify the target on which the specific operation will be performed. With the **target** attribute set to **running**, the operation will be performed in the device's running configuration. The parameter that will be configured to 2.2.2.2 is **rtrId**, the Router ID for the BGP protocol.

Example 8-43   *Sending Edit-Config Operator*

```
<rpc message-id="101"
xmlns="urn:ietf:params:xml:ns:NETCONF:base:1.0"
xmlns:nc="urn:ietf:params:xml:ns:NETCONF:base:1.0">
    <edit-config>
        <target>
            <running/>
        </target>
        <config>
            <System xmlns="http://cisco.com/ns/yang/cisco-nx-os-device">
                    <bgp-items>
                        <inst-items>
                            <dom-items>
                                <Dom-list>
                                    <name>default</name>
                                        <rtrId>2.2.2.2</rtrId>
                                </Dom-list>
                            </dom-items>
                        </inst-items>
                    </bgp-items>
            </System>
        </config>
    </edit-config>
</rpc>
##
```

Besides **edit-config**, the NETCONF operation attribute can have the following values:

- create

- merge

- delete

As the names suggest, these attributes are used to create a new configuration, merge the configurations, or delete existing configurations, respectively. Example 8-44 shows how to delete the configuration of interface Ethernet 0/0 from the running configuration.

Example 8-44   *Deleting Configuration Under an Interface*

```
xmlns="urn:ietf:params:xml:ns:NETCONF:base:1.0">
    <edit-config>
        <target>
            <running/>
        </target>
        <default-operation>none</default-operation>
        <config xmlns:xc="urn:ietf:params:xml:ns:NETCONF:base:1.0">
            <top xmlns="http://example.com/schema/1.2/config">
                <interface xc:operation="delete">
                    <name>Ethernet0/0</name>
                </interface>
            </top>
        </config>
    </edit-config>
</rpc>]]>]]>
]]>]]>
```

Open-Source and Commercial Tools

This section takes a quick look at popular open source tools that developers commonly use to develop, test, and deploy applications. Even though the market is full of these tools, the discussion here will be limited to some of the most popular ones.

Linx

Linx is a low-code integrated development environment (IDE) and server infrastructure to build and automate back-end applications and web services. Linx is popular because it decreases the time it takes to design, develop, and automate business processes; integrate applications, systems, and databases; expose web services; and handle high workloads efficiently.

Highlights:

- Integrate any combination of applications, systems, or databases via a library of easy-to-use plug-ins. Integrate a web service, database, or application—public or proprietary, hosted on premise, or in the cloud—effortlessly.

- Define, execute, and manage multistep business processes as a single processing unit of work. Sync across multiple applications in real time with powerful data rules and triggers.

- Connect, transform, and automate data in limitless ways using the plug-in architecture. Linx excels in automating workflows for applications that require storing, querying, and manipulating data stored in ODBC, OLE DB, and NoSQL databases.

- Create a consolidated back end for disparate solutions or integrate specific back-end elements of different applications into one another. Easily store and reuse previous services as APIs, expose existing assets as services, or build and configure your own API.

- Compile, run, and execute processes for bugs using a dedicated window. Choose to step over values used in the execution of your process or add breakpoints to review functions values in detail.

Apache NetBeans

Apache NetBeans is an open source IDE and a free software development tool written in Java that develops world-class web, mobile, and desktop applications easily and quickly. It uses C/C++, PHP, JavaScript, and Java.

Highlights:

- Apache NetBeans offers editors, wizards, and templates to help you create applications in Java, PHP, C/C++, and many other languages.

- Apache NetBeans can be installed on all operating systems that support Java, such as Windows, Linux, macOS, and BSD. Write Once, Run Anywhere applies to NetBeans, too.

- Apache NetBeans highlights source code syntactically and semantically, and it enables you to easily refactor code, with a range of handy and powerful tools.

- Apache NetBeans allows its new developers to understand the structure of the application.

- It has support for fast code editing and efficient project management.

GitHub

GitHub allows developers to publish and review code, manage projects, and build software. It offers the right tool for different development jobs. GitHub is a powerful collaboration tool and development platform for code review and code management. With GitHub, users can build applications and software, manage projects, host code, and review code. With the rise of GitHub, Git has become a *de facto* standard and, according to several surveys, is now the most popular version control system among software developers.

Highlights:

- It is a unified place to publish all code, along with easy documentation.

- Developers can host their documentation directly from their repositories.

- It is free for open-source projects and public use.

- GitHub's project management tools help its users stay aligned, coordinate easily, and get their tasks done accordingly.

- GitHub offers enhanced code security, access control among team members, and integration with other tools.

- It runs on the Linux, Windows, and Apple macOS and can be hosted on servers and on a cloud platform.

Atom

Atom is a free open source text editor and source code editor. It is customizable to do anything to help developers write code and update.

Highlights:

- It supports operating systems such as macOS, Windows, and Linux.

- Atom has smart coding features for developers to compare codes, edit multiple files, and more.

- It allows you to view the whole project or multiple projects in one window.

- You can edit the look and feel of the user interface without editing the configuration file.

- It has a built-in package manager, smart autocomplete, multiple panes, and file system browser.

- Atom is used to build cross-platform applications with web technologies.

AWS Cloud9

Cloud9 is an integrated software development environment, with support for various programming languages like C, C++, PHP, Ruby, Perl, Python, JavaScript, and Node.js. Initially, it was open source, but since 2016 when it was acquired by Amazon Web Services, it became chargeable based on usage.

Highlights:

- It includes a browser-based editor that makes it easy to write, run, and debug your projects, with features such as code completion and code hinting suggestions.

- It supports more than 40 programming languages and application types, including JavaScript, Python, PHP, Ruby, Go, and C++.

- It comes with an integrated debugger, which provides commonly used capabilities such as setting breakpoints, stepping through code, and inspecting variables of any PHP, Python, JS/Node.js, or C/C++ app.

- It lets you share your development environment and makes it easy for multiple developers to actively see each other type and pair-program on the same file.

- It allows you to easily build serverless applications by providing an integrated experience to get started, write, and debug serverless application code. The Cloud9 development environment is prepackaged with SDKs, tools, and libraries needed for serverless application development.

Zend Studio

Zend Studio allows software developers to code faster and debug more easily. It is a next-generation PHP IDE designed to create mobile and web applications for boosting developer productivity. It scales according to the DPI settings of the underlying operating system.

Highlights:

- It boasts an intelligent code editor including intuitive code assist, smart code completion, refactoring, and real-time error validation and analysis. The intelligent code editor also supports the latest PHP 7, as well as the older versions of PHP for compatibility with legacy projects. And you can use it with HTML, CSS, and JavaScript.

- It supports Xdebug, Zend Debugger, and Z-Ray in Zend Server. You can dramatically boost efficiency by using Z-Ray with Zend Studio. Z-Ray provides real-time debugging and application-performance insights, along with other capabilities. And, if you have both products, you can open a debugging or profiling session in Z-Ray—and then fix the code and performance issues using Zend Studio.

- It helps developers create mobile applications—using PHP, HTML5, CSS, and JavaScript—that run on your existing PHP applications and servers.

- Enhanced source control integration helps you work smoothly with SVN, CVS, Git, and GitHub. You can easily import existing repositories into your workspace and collaborate with peers.

- Zend Studio includes new Docker tooling that supports the management of Docker images and containers. As a result, you can run, test, and debug PHP applications in Docker containers.

Eclipse

Eclipse is one of the most popular IDEs used by application developers. It is used to develop applications not only in Java but in other programming languages such as C, C++, C#, and PHP. The Eclipse Foundation, which oversees the development of the IDE, supports more than 250 open source projects, most of them related to development tools. There are also numerous plug-ins available to bring code quality, version control, and other capabilities to the development environment.

Highlights:

- It is an open-source group of projects, tools and collaborative working groups that play a key role in the development of new solutions and innovations.

- Its SDK is a free and open-source software

- It is used to create web, desktop, and cloud IDEs, which in turn delivers the wide collection of add-on tools for software developers.

- Advantages include refactoring, code completion, syntax checking, rich client platform, and error debugging.

Bootstrap

Bootstrap is an open-source and free framework to design faster and simpler websites using CSS, HTML, and JS. It contains design templates for typography, forms, buttons, navigation, and other interface components as well as optional JavaScript extensions. It has many built-in components, with which you can easily build responsive web pages.

Highlights:

- Because it is an open-source toolkit, you can customize it according to your project's requirement.

- Features such as responsive grid system, plug-ins, prebuilt components, sass variables, and mix-ins enable developers to build their applications.

- With its front-end web framework, you can do quick modeling of the ideas and build web applications.

- This tool guarantees consistency among all the developers or users working on the project.

Bitbucket

Bitbucket is a distributed, web-based version control tool for collaboration between software development teams (code and code review). It is used as a repository for source code and development projects. It integrates well with JIRA, a well-known project and issue-management application.

Highlights:

- Flexible deployment models, unlimited private repositories, and code collaboration

- Support of a few services such as code search, issue tracking, Bitbucket pipelines, integrations, and smart mirroring

- Organization of the repositories into the projects with which they can focus easily on their goals, processes, or products

- Controlled access permissions to ensure that only the right people can make changes to the code

- Integration into existing workflow to streamline the software development process

Node.js

Node.js is an open source, cross-platform and JavaScript run-time environment that is built to design a variety of web applications and to create web servers and networking tools. Node.js is a JavaScript runtime that uses an event-driven, nonblocking I/O model that makes it lightweight and efficient. According to its website, the Node.js package ecosystem, npm, is the largest ecosystem of open-source libraries in the world.

Key features:

- It is efficient and lightweight because it uses nonblocking and an event-driven I/O model.

- Developers use it to write server-side applications in JavaScript.

- Its modules provide rapid and well-organized solutions for developing a back-end structure and integrating with the front-end platforms.

As you have read, these tools bring unique capabilities and benefits toward application development and testing and integrate them into the workflow. Application developers' interest in these open-source tools is at an all-time high because they are easy to use to validate and prove a concept. With open-source tools maturing and community support growing, these tools are now used by numerous applications in today's enterprise/data center environment. It is highly recommended that you explore these open-source tools and use them to develop, test, and deploy applications for Cisco IOS-XE, IOS-XR, and NX-OS platforms.

Building and Deploying Container Images

This section discusses various tools, utilities, and documents available to containerize your applications and build a Docker image for scaled-up deployments.

Build Docker Images

In general, the workflow to build containerized applications looks like this:

1. Create and test individual containers for each component of your application by creating Docker images first.

2. Assemble your containers and supporting infrastructure into a complete application, expressed either as a Docker stack file or in Kubernetes YAML.

3. Test, share, and deploy your complete containerized application.

Dockerfile

As discussed in Chapter 7, a Docker image captures the private filesystem that the containerized processes will run in; you need to create an image that contains just what your application needs to run. A containerized development environment will isolate all the dependencies your app needs inside your Docker image, removing the need to install anything other than Docker on your development machine.

The following section considers an application referred to as **floodlight** that is developed in Python and made available for users to download at the GitHub. To download the application, refer to the *GitHub Floodlight Dockerfile* at https://hub.docker.com/_/registry.

Look at the file called Dockerfile in the root directory. Dockerfile describes how to assemble a private file system for a container. It also contains some metadata describing how to run a container based on this image. The Dockerfile for the specified application looks like the one in Example 8-45.

Example 8-45 *Dockerfile for Floodlight Application*

```
FROM alpine:latest

ARG BUILD_DATE
ARG VCS_REF

LABEL org.label-schema.build-date=$BUILD_DATE \
      org.label-schema.name="Floodlight" \
      org.label-schema.description="Python application to identify and display
unexpected control plane traffic on Cisco Nexus data center switches" \
      org.label-schema.vcs-ref=$VCS_REF \
      org.label-schema.vcs-url="https://github.com/ChristopherJHart/floodlight" \
      org.label-schema.schema-version="1.0"

RUN apk --update --no-cache add python3-dev git gcc g++ libxml2 libxslt-dev tshark
RUN pip3 install --upgrade pip
RUN mkdir /floodlight
ADD . /floodlight
RUN pip3 install -r /floodlight/requirements.txt
CMD [ "python3", "-u", "/floodlight/floodlight.py" ]
```

Writing a Dockerfile is the first step to containerizing an application. You can think of these Dockerfile instructions as a step-by-step recipe to build the image.

1. The FROM instruction sets the latest Alpine image as the base image for this application.

2. The ARG instruction defines a variable that developers can pass during the image build time.

3. The LABEL instruction adds metadata to the image.

4. The RUN instruction executes all commands. If the RUN instructions add anything as a new layer on top of the base image, it will be committed (in a shell form) and will be used for further instruction in the Dockerfile.

5. The ADD instruction copies any files or directories to the image's filesystem in the given path.

6. The CMD instruction provides the default settings or variables to execute the containerized application. The default settings or variables define an entry point for the application, such as printing a log message or setting a default directory.

This procedure looks similar to the steps you might have taken to set up and install your app on a host. However, capturing the instructions as a Dockerfile allows users to deploy applications in a portable fashion and at scale.

Docker Build

Now that you have some source code and a Dockerfile, it is time to build your first image and make sure the containers launched from it work as expected.

Make sure you are in the **floodlight** directory in a terminal, and build your image:

```
docker image build -t floodlight:1.0 .
```

You will see Docker step through each instruction in your Dockerfile, building up your image as it goes. If successful, the build process should end with the message "Successfully tagged floodlight:1.0."

Docker Run

Start a container based on your new image:

```
docker container run --publish 8000:8080 --detach --name FL
floodlight:1.0
```

The flags used in the command are described here:

- --publish asks Docker to forward traffic incoming on the host's port 8000 to the container's port 8080. Containers have their own private set of ports, so if you want to reach one from the network, you have to forward traffic to it in this way; otherwise, firewall rules prevent all network traffic from reaching your container as a default security posture.

- --detach asks Docker to run this container in the background.

- --name lets you specify a name with which you can refer to your container in subsequent commands—in this case, FL.

You can visit your application in a browser at localhost:8000 and verify that your floodlight application is up and running. At this step, ensure the containerized application works as expected, and run unit tests as needed.

If the test container is not needed anymore, delete the instance using the following command:

```
docker container rm --force FL
```

Publish Docker Images—Docker Hub

At this point, you have built a containerized application as discussed in the previous section. Now share the images on a registry such as Docker Hub so they can be easily downloaded and run on any destination device or cluster.

Docker Hub Account

Follow these steps to set up an account in Docker Hub, which will allow a user to share images there.

1. Visit the Docker Hub page and sign up at https://hub.docker.com/signup.

2. Fill out the form and submit it to create your Docker ID.

3. Click the Docker icon in your toolbar or system tray and click Sign In/Create Docker ID. Fill in your new Docker ID and password. If everything worked, your Docker ID will appear in the Docker Desktop drop-down menu instead of the Sign In option.

Note: You can create the docker hub account from the command line using the **docker login** command.

Docker Hub Repository

Now you will make your first repository and share the application there.

1. Access your Docker Hub account.

2. On the main page, navigate to Repositories -> Create Repository.

3. Fill out the Repository Name as floodlight. Leave all the other options as they are, and click Create at the bottom. Please note that, by default, the repository is public.

Docker Hub Publish

To share on the Docker Hub, images must be namespaced correctly. Specifically, images must be named like **<Docker Hub ID>/<Repository Name>:<tag>**. You can relabel the floodlight:1.0 image as shown in Example 8-46, and finally push the image.

Example 8-46 *Relabeling and Publishing a Docker Image*

```
docker image tag floodlight:1.0 UserID/floodlight:1.0
docker image push UserID/floodlight:1.0
```

Docker Pull

To download an image from the **Docker Hub**, use docker pull. If no tag is provided, Docker Engine uses the **:latest** tag as a default, as in the following command. To pull a specific image, use the tag as **<Docker Hub ID>/<Repository Name>:<tag>**.

```
docker pull UserID/floodlight:latest
```

Docker Registry

Docker Trusted Registry (DTR) is a commercial product that enables complete image management workflow, featuring LDAP integration, image signing, security scanning, and integration with Universal Control Plane. Use Registry if you want to do the following:

- Tightly control where images are being stored

- Fully own an image's distribution pipeline

- Integrate image storage and distribution into the development workflow

For these reasons, you can pull an image from a local Docker Hub Registry rather than from the Docker Hub. For more information, visit https://hub.docker.com/_/registry.

To install and activate a registry, run the following command, which pulls a registry image that contains an implementation of the Docker Registry HTTP API V2 for use with Docker 1.6+:

```
docker pull registry
```

Run the local registry:

```
$ docker run -d -p 5000:5000 --restart always --name registry
registry:2
```

Now the docker pull from the hosts or devices can be done, as shown in the following example:

```
$ docker pull registry.local:5000/testing/test-image
```

See the Docker Registry page at https://github.com/docker/distribution for further details.

Configuration and Application Management Tools

Configuration Management is the practice of defining performance, functional, and physical attributes of a product and then ensuring the consistency of a system's "configuration" throughout its life.

This practice has been widely used across IT systems management by many organizations large and small for a long time. Having proven successful with servers and applications, in recent years, it has extended to the network as well.

With these tools, you can define and enforce configuration related to system-level operations (that is, authentication, logging, image), interface-level configuration (that is, VLAN, QoS, Security), routing configurations (that is, OSPF or BGP specs), and much more.

Now you will look at popular management tools such as Puppet, Chef, and Ansible and how IOS-XE, IOS-XR, and NX-OS support them through local agents.

Ansible

Ansible is an open-source automation platform. It uses an agentless architecture, written in YAML, that allows you to describe your automation jobs in an easily readable format. Ansible has a powerful CLI templating engine that uses the Jinja2 language. CLI templating allows variables to be placed into a CLI configuration, which Ansible then replaces during playbook execution. Version 2.3 introduces support for NETCONF as well as persistent connections. Ansible is working on developing modules that use the NETCONF interface to provide declarative-type syntax, which is superior to CLI templating. Ansible is committed to developing its network automation capabilities and expects that by developing its network automation capabilities, by version 2.5 it will be a robust network management solution.

Puppet

Puppet is a Configuration Management Tool (CMT) used for centralizing and automating configuration management. Traditionally, Puppet has used an agent-based architecture, requiring a software agent to be installed on the device being managed. However, Puppet now supports direct NETCONF integration to Cisco IOS-XE devices. Puppet has a text file called a manifest that has details of what configuration should be pushed to what devices. It uses NETCONF to communicate with the switch. Therefore, any Cisco Catalyst switch capable of NETCONF will in theory be supported by Puppet. Cisco Nexus platforms now support agentless Puppet. The existing agent-based module can be updated to support the agentless mode of operation. This removes the requirement of having an agent installed in the device, and it makes the device interact with Open APIs that are natively provided by NX-OS.

Chef

Chef is a Configuration Management Tool (CMT) used for centralizing and automating configuration management. Traditionally, Chef has used an agent-based architecture, requiring a software agent to be installed on the device being managed. Chef has a text file called a cookbook that has details on what configuration should be pushed to what devices. Chef requires a software agent on the device under management. This requires Guest Shell running on the switch to host the Chef agent.

Cisco IOS-XE, IOS-XR, and NX-OS support Ansible, Puppet, and Chef. As most of the steps to configure, activate, and use these are similar, this section looks into these management tools, but each one for a specific operating system—how to enable and use Ansible in IOS-XE, Puppet in NX-OS, and Chef in IOS-XR.

Ansible and IOS-XE

In any Linux-based server infrastructure, check the Ansible version with commands shown in Example 8-47.

Example 8-47 *Checking Ansible Version*

```
Ubuntu$ ansible --version
ansible 2.5.3
  config file = None
  configured module search path = [u'/root/.ansible/plugins/modules', u'/usr/share/
  ansible/plugins/modules']
  ansible python module location = /usr/lib/python2.7/site-packages/ansible
  executable location = /usr/bin/ansible
  python version = 2.7.5 (default, Nov  6 2016, 00:28:07) [GCC 4.8.5 20150623 (Red
  Hat 4.8.5-11)]
```

Hosts File

The hosts file is where the devices under management are listed. A single device can be included in a single group or multiple groups. As you see in Example 8-48, the hosts file has two groups, called cat3000 and cat9000, which include two and four devices, respectively. As you see in Example 8-48, groups can also be nested like the **ios-xe** group, which includes both cat3000 and cat9000 groups. The default connection is set to **network_cli**, which replaces the connection **local** from release 2.5 onward.

Example 8-48 *Ansible Hosts File*

```
$ cat /etc/ansible/hosts

[ios-xe:vars]
ansible_network_os=ios
ansible_connection=network_cli

[cat3000]
cat3000-A
cat3000-B

[cat9000]
cat9000-A
cat9000-B
cat9000-C

[ios-xe:children]
cat3000
cat9000
```

Authentication

When communicating with remote machines, SSH keys are encouraged, but simple usernames and passwords can be used as well. To generate SSH keys in IOS-XE, follow the methods provided in the *IOS-XE Secure Shell Configuration User Authentication* guide given in the "References" section. A simple username and password are used for further discussion in this section.

There are several ways to provide a username and password in Ansible, but the following example shows how to define the username credential in the hosts file. Example 8-49 shows a sample user authentication configuration.

Example 8-49   *Ansible User Authentication*

```
[all:vars]
username=cisco
password=cisco123
auth_pass=cisco123
```

Note: Please be aware that the method of providing the username credential in a file is being deprecated.

Vault is a feature of Ansible that allows you to keep sensitive data such as passwords or keys in encrypted files rather than as plaintext in your playbooks, roles, or at runtime. These vault files can then be distributed or placed in source control. Please refer to the official documentation at https://puppet.com/blog/agentless-device-automation-puppets-cisco-nexus-module/.

Sample Playbook

In this initial playbook, you will provision a number of VRFs across all devices and purge any other VRF configured on the device. You will use the Ansible module called **ios_vrf** to automate this task, as shown in Example 8-50.

Example 8-50   *Ansible Playbook*

```
---

- name: configure vrfs and remove any other vrf configured
  hosts: ios-xe
  gather_facts: no

  tasks:
    - name: configure vfrs and purge all others
      ios_vrf:
```

```
        vrfs:
             - red
             - blue
             - yellow
        purge: yes
<snip>
```

As with all YAML files, the playbook starts with three dashes. **hosts** denotes the host or group of hosts that will have the tasks executed against, and **tasks** are the modules that are to be run. To make sure only the given list of VRFs are configured on the devices, a "purge" option is provided as well. The **purge** option removes all other VRFs existing in the device to standardize the configuration.

Running a Playbook

Assuming the preceding playbook is called ios_vrf.yaml, this task can be run from a terminal window. By default, Ansible uses the hosts file located in **/etc/ansible/hosts**; however, a different hosts file can be specified using the **-i** flag at runtime or defined in the **ansible.cfg** file. In Example 8-51, you will use the local hosts file. Please note that the password for the specific user had been provided through the command line with the -k option.

Example 8-51 *Running an Ansible Playbook*

```
$ ansible-playbook ios_vrf.yaml -u admin -k
SSH password:

PLAY [configure vrfs and remove any other vrf configured] **********************

TASK [configure vfrs and purge all others] *****************
changed: [cat3000-A]
changed: [cat3000-B]
changed: [cat9000-A]
changed: [cat9000-B]
changed: [cat9000-C]


PLAY RECAP *********************************************************************
cat3000-A               : ok=1    changed=1    unreachable=0    failed=0
cat3000-B               : ok=1    changed=1    unreachable=0    failed=0
cat9000-A               : ok=1    changed=1    unreachable=0    failed=0
cat9000-B               : ok=1    changed=1    unreachable=0    failed=0
cat9000-C               : ok=1    changed=1    unreachable=0    failed=0
```

The results reported under the "PLAY RECAP" section in the Example 8-51 indicate that all the changes executed by the playbook succeeded, with the **ok** flags set to 1 for all devices. Also, all five devices in the list have the **changed** flag set to 1, which means the configs are successfully changed, with no failures or unreachables.

NETCONF Operations with Ansible

NETCONF configuration operations have been supported in Ansible since release 2.3 by using the **netconf_config** core module. Example 8-52 provides a sample playbook to configure an interface's description and IP address in an IOS-XE device.

Example 8-52 *Ansible NETCONF Operations*

```
---

- name: configure IOS XE devices using NETCONF
  hosts: ios-xe
  vars:
      ansible_connection: netconf
      ansible_network_os: default
  gather_facts: no

  tasks:
  - name: set Gig0/3 interface description and primary IP address
    netconf_config:
      xml: |
        <config>
          <interfaces xmlns="urn:ietf:params:xml:ns:yang:ietf-interfaces">
            <interface>
              <name>GigabitEthernet0/3</name>
              <description>Managed by Ansible using netconf connection</description>
              <ip>
                  <address>
                     <primary>
                         <address>10.10.10.3</address>
                         <mask>255.255.255.0</mask>
                     </primary>
                  </address>
              </ip>
            </interface>
          </interfaces>
        </config>
<snip>
```

In Example 8-52, the objective is to connect to an IOS-XE device using the Ansible NETCONF connection to configure the device's GigabitEthernet 0/3 interface description, IP address, and mask.

A new connection specifically for NETCONF is introduced in Ansible release 2.5, which makes working with NETCONF operations much easier. In pre-2.5 releases, it is required that you set the connection type to be local when using networking modules. In other words, a playbook executes a local Python module and connects to the networking devices to perform tasks. In Ansible 2.5, the network_cli connection method becomes a top-level connection. This allows playbooks to have the same look and feel because the tasks are done on local Linux hosts.

Puppet and NX-OS

Puppet requires the Nexus devices to have an agent installed and activated in them. Puppet agents cannot run natively on Cisco Nexus platforms but can run in special virtual environments. As discussed in Chapter 7, Nexus platforms support different types of virtual environments such as Guest Shell, Bash, and Open Agent Containers (OAC), which can be used to install and activate Puppet agents.

Besides agent based, the configuration management of Cisco Nexus switches can be automated by Puppet with no agent installed on the devices. The existing agent-based module has been updated to support an agentless mode of operation. Now it is possible to manage all the Nexus platforms in an agentless manner that were once managed with agents. Please be aware that the upgraded module can still be used with the agent, but it is recommended to use the agentless approach.

Agent-based as well as agentless Puppet support are available for Nexus; the following section considers and uses the agent-based model.

Installing and Activating the Puppet Agent

1. Import the Puppet GPG keys. After activating the appropriate shell or OAC in the Nexus switch and verifying its network connectivity and proxy settings, import the Puppet GPG keys, as shown in Example 8-53.

Example 8-53 *Importing Puppet GPG Keys*

```
rpm --import http://yum.puppetlabs.com/RPM-GPG-KEY-puppetlabs
rpm --import http://yum.puppetlabs.com/RPM-GPG-KEY-reductive
rpm --import http://yum.puppetlabs.com/RPM-GPG-KEY-puppet
```

2. Choose the appropriate Puppet RPM for your agent environment—either Bash, Guest Shell, or OAC, as shown in Table 8-5.

Table 8-5 *Puppet RPM Download Location*

Environment	RPM Download URL
Bash	http://yum.puppetlabs.com/puppet5/puppet5-release-cisco-wrlinux-5.noarch.rpm
Guest Shell	http://yum.puppetlabs.com/puppet5/puppet5-release-el-7.noarch.rpm
OAC	http://yum.puppetlabs.com/puppetlabs-release-pc1-el-6.noarch.rpm

Note: The OAC RPM is now end of life. However, later versions of the RPM cannot be hosted in the OAC because of a Ruby version incompatibility. To continue using an OAC workflow, you must use a module version of 1.10.0 or earlier.

3. With the commands shown in Example 8-54, install the RPM and update the PATH variable. $PUPPET_RPM in the following example is the URL from the preceding table.

Example 8-54 *Installing Puppet*

```
yum install $PUPPET_RPM
yum install puppet
export PATH=/opt/puppetlabs/puppet/bin:/opt/puppetlabs/puppet/lib:$PATH
```

4. Add the Puppet server name. Configure the /etc/puppetlabs/puppet/puppet.conf file by adding your Puppet server name to the configuration file, as shown in Example 8-55. Optional: Use certname to specify the agent node's ID, provided that the hostname has not been set.

Example 8-55 *Adding Puppet Server Name*

```
[main]
  server   = mypuppetmaster.mycompany.com
  certname = this_node.mycompany.com
```

5. Install the gem module. The cisco_node_utils Ruby gem is a required component of the ciscopuppet module. This gem contains platform APIs for interfacing between the NX-OS CLI and Puppet agent resources. The gem can be installed manually or can be automatically installed by the Puppet agent by using the ciscopuppet::install helper class.

6. To automatically install the gem module, the ciscopuppet::install class is defined in the install.pp file in the examples subdirectory. Copy this file into the manifests directory, as shown here:

```
cd /etc/puppetlabs/code/environments/production/modules/
ciscopuppet/
cp examples/install.pp  manifests/
```

7. Next, update site.pp to use the install class. The following configuration causes the puppet agent to automatically download the current cisco_node_utils gem from the utils location and install it on the node.

```
node 'default' {
   include ciscopuppet::install
}
```

8. Once installed, the GEM will remain persistent across system reloads within the Guestshell or OAC environments; however, the bash-shell environment does not share this persistent behavior, in which case the ciscopuppet::install helper class automatically downloads and reinstalls the gem after each system reload.

9. Run the Puppet Agent in the device:

```
puppet agent -t
```

Using Puppet Agent

The following example demonstrates how to define a manifest that uses ciscopuppet to configure OSPF on a Cisco Nexus switch. Three resource types are used to define an OSPF instance, basic OSPF router settings, and OSPF interface settings:

- cisco_ospf

- cisco_ospf_vrf

- cisco_interface_ospf

The first manifest type should define the router instance using **cisco_ospf**. The title **'Sample'** becomes the router instance name.

```
cisco_ospf {"Sample":
    ensure => present,
}
```

The next type to define is **cisco_ospf_vrf**. As shown in Example 8-56, the title includes the OSPF router instance name and the VRF name. Note that a non-VRF configuration uses **'default'** as the VRF name.

Example 8-56 *Using Puppet Agent—OSPF VRF Configuration*

```
cisco_ospf_vrf {"Sample default":
    ensure => 'present',
    default_metric => '5',
    auto_cost => '46000',
}
```

Finally, define the OSPF interface settings. As you see in Example 8-57, the title here includes the Interface name and the OSPF router instance name.

Example 8-57 *Using Puppet Agent—OSPF Interface Configuration*

```
cisco_interface_ospf {"Ethernet1/2 Sample":
    ensure => present,
    area => 200,
    cost => "200",
}
```

Please see the *Cisco Network Puppet Module* provided in the "References" section for resources that include Cisco types and providers along with Cisco provider support for **netdev** and **stdlib** types. Installing the Cisco puppet module installs both the **ciscopuppet** and the **netdev_stdlib** modules.

Chef and IOS-XR

As you might have read in earlier sections, Chef is an open-source configuration management tool that can install, configure, and deploy various applications natively on Cisco IOS-XR. In this section, you will see how to configure an IOS-XR device as a Chef Client and install an application natively on IOS-XR.

To use Chef, you need the following components:

■ Chef Client RPM Version 12.5, or later for Cisco IOS-XR 6.0

■ Chef Server Version 12.4 or higher

■ Applications that are compatible with the Wind River Linux 7 environment of IOS XR

Three Chef built-in resources are needed to deploy your application natively on IOS-XR. The first three items in Table 8-6 are the built-in Chef Resources that are required; the last entry in the table is the location of IOS-XR Chef Client RPM.

Table 8-6 *Accessing Chef Resources*

Resource	Access URL
Package Resource	https://docs.chef.io/resource_package.html
File Resource	https://docs.chef.io/resource_file.html
Service Resource	https://docs.chef.io/resource_service.html
IOS-XR Chef Client	https://packages.chef.io/files/stable/chef/12.5.1/ios_xr/6/chef-12.5.1-1.ios_xr6.x86_64.rpm

Creating a Chef Cookbook with Recipes

On your Linux workstation, create a Chef cookbook with recipes and then copy it over to the Chef Server. After you install the Chef Client on IOS-XR, you can download the cookbook from the Chef Server and use it while running the Client.

Ensure the following requirements are met before you proceed:

■ You have access to the application package compatible with the native IOS-XR environment.

■ The target application package is hosted on an accessible repository or downloaded to a bootflash.

Once the requirements are met, use the following procedure to create a Chef recipe that starts the **bootlogd** service and installs iPerf on IOS-XR:

1. Create a cookbook on your Linux workstation by using the corresponding knife command:

```
knife cookbook create cisco-network-chef-cookbook
```

2. Create the Chef recipe file as shown in Example 8-58 to install iPerf. The IP address in this example is the Linux workstation's IP address, where the .rpm file is present.

3. The Chef recipe must be created in the cisco-network-chef-cookbook/recipes/ directory. For it to be loaded automatically by the Chef Client, the Chef recipe must be named default.rb.

Example 8-58   *Installing iPerf Using Chef*

```
package = 'iperf-2.0.5-r0.0.core2_64.rpm'
service = 'bootlogd'

remote_file "/#{package}" do
  source "http://<ip-address>/wrl7_yum_repo/#{package}"
  action :create
end

yum_package "#{package}" do
  source "/#{package}"
  action :install
end

service "#{service}" do
  action :start
end
```

Installing and Activating Chef Client

Follow the steps given below to install and activate Chef in an IOS-XR device.

1. Access Bash from the IOS-XR user prompt:

```
RP/0/RP0/CPU0:ios# bash
[xr-vm_node0_RP0_CPU0:~]$
```

Before installing and activating Chef in the Bash, verify the following:

- Your workstation is set up with the Chef repository and the Chef Development Kit. Refer to the *Chef Workstation Installation* page provided in the "References" section for more details.

- Chef Server Version 12.4 or higher installed and accessible from your Linux box.

- The Chef Server identification file availability.

- The right name server and domain name entries configured in the Linux environment (/etc/resolv.conf).

- The router using a valid NTP server.

- Proxy server configured as needed.

Note: For IOS-XR releases earlier to 6.0.2, the command is **run ip netns exec tpnns bash.**

2. Install the Chef Client:

   ```
   [xr-vm_node0_RP0_CPU0:~]$ yum install https://chef.io/chef/
   install.sh
   ```

3. The Chef install.sh script automatically determines the latest version of the Chef Client RPM for installation.

4. Copy the validation.pem file from the Chef Server to /etc/chef/validation.pem. Edit the Chef Client configuration file at /etc/chef/client.rb with the Chef Server identification and Client settings, as shown in Example 8-59.

Example 8-59   *Chef Client Configuration*

```
validation_client_name 'chef-validator'
chef_server_url 'https://my_chef_server.cisco.com/organizations/chef'
node_name 'asr9k-a.cisco.com' # "This" client device.
cookbook_sync_threads 5 # necessary for small memory switches (4G or less)
interval 30 # client-run interval; remove for "never"
```

Access the Chef Server from your Linux workstation and upload the cookbook to the server, with recipes shown in Example 8-59. Log in to the IOS-XR shell and run the Chef Client to load and execute the cookbook:

5. Run the Chef Client:

   ```
   [xr-vm_node0_RP0_CPU0:~]$ chef-client
   ```

When the **chef-client** command is executed, the Chef Client in the IOS-XR device registers and authenticates the node (the networking device running IOS-XR) to the Chef Server. The Chef Client accesses and pulls down the node objects from the server, which contains a run-list. By expanding this run-list, the Chef Client gets a list of all cookbook files like recipes, resources, libraries, attributes, and so on. For each cookbook, the Chef Client loads the attributes in the default.rb file and any other dependencies. As you may remember, the **cisco-network-chef-cookbook** that was created in the previous section has a recipe to install iPerf, as shown in Example 8-58. When all the attributes in the recipe are loaded and updated, the node object rebuild is complete. By executing each resource in the recipe, the Chef Client installs the iPerf application natively on IOS-XR and activates it.

> **Note:**   To run the client once, use the **chef-client --once** command. For more information, see the *Chef Client Overview* documentation provided in the "References" section.

Summary

This chapter introduced you to various Cisco application development tools and resources that are available, including Python APIs and NX-API in various Cisco platforms, and how these platforms support RESTCONF and NETCONF with YANG-based data. You saw simple examples of how to put these capabilities to use, with the goal of automating infrastructure management and monitoring.

There was a brief discussion of various open-source and commercial tools available in the marketplace that help developers create, test, and deploy applications and collaborate with their peers during the application development lifecycle.

This chapter concluded with a detailed look into various configuration and application management tools such as Ansible, Puppet, and Chef. You learned how the Cisco platforms support agents for these tools natively and how they can be leveraged to deploy applications at scale, with the highest level of consistency across your infrastructure.

The key takeaway from this chapter is this: Cisco IOS-XE, IOS-XR, and NX-OS platforms have built-in capabilities helping developers create, test, and deploy custom applications and bring intelligence closer to the end hosts and nodes and, more importantly, to the data these devices generate.

References

Cisco DevNet NX-SDK GitHub: https://github.com/CiscoDevNet/NX-SDK/blob/master/versions.md

Cisco DevNet GitHub Page for NX-SDK: https://hub.docker.com/r/dockercisco/nxsdk

Cisco DevNet GitHub Page for NX-SDK IP_Move Application: https://github.com/ChristopherJHart/NX-SDK/blob/master/ip_move/

Nexus 9000—Building and Packaging C++ Applications: https://www.cisco.com/c/en/us/td/docs/switches/datacenter/nexus9000/sw/92x/programmability/guide/b-cisco-nexus-9000-series-nx-os-programmability-guide-92x/b-cisco-nexus-9000-series-nx-os-programmability-guide-92x_chapter_010001.html#id_50768

DevHub Open NX-OS Repositories: https://devhub.cisco.com/artifactory/open-nxos/

DevNet Data Model Reference—NX-OS version 9.3(3): https://developer.cisco.com/site/nxapi-dme-model-reference-api/

Google Postman Download: https://www.getpostman.com/downloads/

Programmability Configuration Guide—Cisco IOS-XE Everest 16.6.x: https://www.cisco.com/c/en/us/td/docs/ios-xml/ios/prog/configuration/166/b_166_programmability_cg/b_166_programmability_cg_chapter_01011.html

Programmability Configuration Guide—Configuring NETCONF-YANG: https://www.cisco.com/c/en/us/td/docs/ios-xml/ios/prog/configuration/166/b_166_programmability_cg/configuring_yang_datamodel.html#id_32668

GitHub: YANG Models for Cisco IOS-XE: https://github.com/YangModels/yang/tree/master/vendor/cisco/xe

Programmability Configuration Guide—NETCONF Feature Information: https://www.cisco.com/c/en/us/td/docs/ios-xml/ios/prog/configuration/166/b_166_programmability_cg/configuring_yang_datamodel.html#id_44510

Programmability Configuration Guide for Cisco ASR 9000—IOS-XR 6.2.x: https://www.cisco.com/c/en/us/td/docs/routers/asr9000/software/data-models/guide/b-programmability-cg-asr9000-62x/b-data-odels-config-guide-asr9000_chapter_010.html#id_20896

GitHub: Floodlight Dockerfile: https://github.com/ChristopherJHart/floodlight/blob/master/Dockerfile

OS-XE Secure Shell Configuration User Authentication: https://www.cisco.com/c/en/us/td/docs/ios-xml/ios/sec_usr_ssh/configuration/xe-16-6/sec-usr-ssh-xe-16-6-book/sec-ssh-config-auth.html

DockerHub—Sign Up: https://hub.docker.com/

Docker Hub Registry: https://hub.docker.com/_/registry

GitHub Distribution—Docker: https://github.com/docker/distribution

Ansible Playbooks: Vault: http://docs.ansible.com/ansible/playbooks_vault.html

Cisco Network Puppet Module Reference: https://github.com/cisco/cisco-network-puppet-module/blob/master/README.md#resource-reference

Puppet: Agentless Nexus Automation: https://puppet.com/blog/agentless-device-automation-puppets-cisco-nexus-module/

Chef Workstation Installation: https://docs.chef.io/install_dk.html

Chef Client Overview: https://docs.chef.io/chef_client.html

Open Source and Commercial Application Development Tools:

Linx: https://linx.software/?utm=sth

NetBeans: https://netbeans.org/

GitHub: https://github.com/

Atom: https://atom.io/

Cloud9: https://c9.io/

Zend: http://www.zend.com/en/products/studio

Eclipse: http://www.eclipse.org/

Bootstrap: http://getbootstrap.com/

Bitbucket: https://bitbucket.org/

NodeJS: https://nodejs.org/en/

Relevant RFCs:

RFC 6241: Network Configuration Protocol (NETCONF)

RFC 6242: Using the NETCONF Protocol over Secure Shell (SSH)

RFC 6243: With-Defaults Capability for NETCONF

RFC 6020: YANG—A Data Modeling Language for the Network Configuration Protocol (NETCONF)

RFC 6022: YANG Module for NETCONF Monitoring

RFC 6991: Common YANG Data Types

RFC 5277: NETCONF Event Notificationsdraft-ietf-netconf-rfc5277-bis: Notification

RFC 6470: Network Configuration Protocol (NETCONF) Base Notifications

RFC 7950: The YANG 1.1 Data Modeling Language

RCF 7951: JSON Encoding of Data Modeled with YANG

RFC 7223: A YANG Data Model for Interface Management

RFC 7277: A YANG Data Model for IP Management

RFC 7224: IANA Interface Type YANG Module

## Chapter 9

Container Deployment Use Cases

In this chapter, you will learn the following:

- General use cases for enterprise, service provider, and data center networks

- The processes involved in creating and deploying containers to offer services in an enterprise network, to detect failures faster in a service provider network, and check health of the control plane in a data center network.

Numerous use cases put containers and application-hosting capabilities into practice, starting from day 0 operations to the complete lifecycle of hardware and software.

Day 0 is when businesses define the requirements and intended outcome of the investments and create the design and architecture of the infrastructure.

Day 1 is when engineering teams build the low-level design and install, set up, configure, test, and ensure compliance to the business policies and standards. Day 2 operations are the phase during which the infrastructure is fully operational and deemed "production ready." During this phase, the focus is on maintaining, operating, optimizing, and repairing (as needed through diagnosis, troubleshooting, and implementing corrective measures) to ensure the overall stability, security, and availability of the best possible services. Day 2 operations are mostly repetitive in nature, such as closely monitoring and reviewing resource usage across the infrastructure; addressing system-generated alerts, warnings, and failure logs; and incrementally improving or upgrading the system. Day 2 continues to day N when the system reaches end-of-life and is decommissioned or replaced with next-gen products. Compared to day 0 or day 1, day 2 lasts relatively longer and produces maximum outcome to the businesses in a sustained fashion.

As discussed extensively in Chapters 5, 6, and 7, with various features and capabilities available in IOS-XE, IOS-XR, and NX-OS, you can build containerized applications and host them in the Cisco routing and switching platforms to automate and scale. As far as general network design, deployment, and operations are concerned, common activities include (but are not limited to) the use cases discussed in the following section.

General Use Cases for Enterprise, Service Provider, and Data Center Networks

This section discusses general use cases for enterprise, service provider, and data center networks.

Inventory Management

As the name suggests, the support team maintains a list of inventory in its install base with product identification, serial numbers, and the like. The team tracks the inventory from the day of reception, to storage at warehouse, to installation, and in use. The team also tracks historical information on inventory and usage.

Hardware and Software Stability Check

Through this activity, the support team reviews crash, reset, reboot, and failover events that have been reported to closely monitor hardware and software uptime. Support teams analyze the generated reports, contact vendors for support, and implement corrective measures. The team tracks the historical information for these events to analyze product quality.

Control Plane Health Check

To achieve high availability of the network and to attain stability in the services offered, it is important to maintain a healthy control plane. As you may be aware, the available CPU, memory, and bandwidth resource are limited, and it is critical to implement strict control plane policies and restrict the scarce resource only to the needed traffic, such as that from OSPF Hello and BGP.

Resource Usage and Scalability Check

As the same suggests, this activity monitors resource usage in each of the installed devices and ensures they are not reaching their scale limit. Key resources monitored are the MAC Address tables, ARP caches, routing tables, and hardware TCAM. It is common to experience network instability when a device nears the vendor-provided scale limit on its resource usage.

Configuration Consistency Check

This activity checks the configuration of the devices in a network to confirm their configurations and operational states are consistent with the global templates. For example, this activity might check the switches on the third floor to ensure that all have VLAN 101 defined and active. Also, it might check a router on the second floor to make sure it has six /24 prefixes in the range of 10.10.15.0/24-10.10.20.0/24 available under the DC2_Business VRF.

Traffic Profiling and Top Talkers

This activity profiles the network traffic and determines the top talkers in terms of bandwidth usage. The support team uses SNMP or NetFlow-based network management applications to collect the traffic statistics. This data optimizes quality of service (QoS) policies and configurations to ensure that all services have fair access to common resources. Also, it detects any anomalous traffic in the network, thereby avoiding any DoS/DDoS type of attack and making the network more secure.

Monitor Operational Data to Detect Failures

In this use case, an application connects to the devices on the network, monitors and collects operational data (such as interface error counters), and proactively detects failures. Even though it may sound like regular SNMP-based network management tools, the application can leverage various programmability options and data modeling capabilities available in Cisco platforms to provide insights and detect failures proactively.

Build Infrastructure for Proof-of-Concept and Testing Purposes

In this use case, an infrastructure is built with containerized software components to help developers prove a concept or to develop and test applications, such as a containerized DNS service, DHCP service, or LDAP service. Through this capability, developers can quickly utilize the embedded capabilities in the Cisco switching and routing platforms to instantiate services like the ones mentioned and aid and expedite the development and testing processes. Beyond testing, the services can be used for production.

In this use case, you will deploy DHCP, DNS, and HAProxy Docker Containers in Catalyst 9000 platforms.

The main objective of this application is to demonstrate how a simple set of DHCP, DNS, and HAProxy Docker containers can be deployed in IOS-XE devices for testing and for production. The following section discusses at length the process involved in creating and deploying the containers. It also mentions the specific configuration of DHCP, DNS, and HAProxy.

Create and Deploy DHCP Docker Container

The premise behind this use case is a scenario in which an administrator wants to deploy a DHCP server for a branch using the Internet Systems Consortium's well-known DHCP server named **DHCPd**, as opposed to creating an additional configuration natively in IOS-XE.

Configure the Catalyst Switch for Application Hosting

To prepare a Catalyst 9000 switch for application hosting, follow the instructions at https://developer.cisco.com/docs/app-hosting/#!getting-cat9k-setup/installing-and-connecting-the-switch.

The steps for preparing the switch are shown in Example 9-1. To start, verify that the Catalyst 9000 device you are working with is running IOS-XE version 16.12 or greater.

Example 9-1 *Check IOS-XE Version*

```
CAT9300-A# show platform
Switch  Ports   Model       Serial No.    MAC address      Hw Ver.   Sw Ver.
------  -----   ---------   -----------   --------------   -------   -------
1       53      C9300L-48T-4G  FOC2320L02D  5c5a.c71f.1180  V01      16.12.1
Switch/Stack Mac Address : 5c5a.c71f.1180 - Local Mac Address
Mac persistency wait time: Indefinite
                                         Current
Switch#   Role       Priority     State
------------------------------------------------
*1        Active        1         Ready
```

As shown in Example 9-2, verify that the DNA-Advantage license is activated on the device because this is required to enable application hosting.

Example 9-2 *Check Device License*

```
CAT9300-A# show version
<snip>
Technology Package License Information:
-------------------------------------------------------------------------
Technology-package                              Technology-package
Current                      Type               Next reboot
-------------------------------------------------------------------------
network-advantage       Smart License               network-advantage
dna-advantage           Subscription Smart License  dna-advantage
```

Enable the application hosting framework (IOx) and verify the services are running as expected, as shown in Example 9-3.

Example 9-3 *Enable the IOx Framework*

```
CAT9300-A# configure terminal
CAT9300-A(config)# iox
CAT9300-A(config)# end
CAT9300-A#
CAT9300-A# show iox-service
IOx Infrastructure Summary:
---------------------------
IOx service (CAF)     : Running
IOx service (HA)      : Running
IOx service (IOxman)  : Running
Libvirtd              : Running
CAT9300-A#
```

Note: Before proceeding, ensure that you have correctly installed Docker on your local development machine. Because this process is heavily platform-independent, it is outside the scope of this procedure. If automation workflows (through Ansible, Puppet, Chef, and so on) already exist around the **DHCP** configuration, Docker can deploy the workflows in a scalable way (repeated at many switches or multiple sites).

Create Docker Containers

On your local development machine, create a new folder for the Docker containers and create a Docker container for each of the services (DHCP, DNS, and HAProxy) in the folder. Create two empty files—one named **Dockerfile**, and another named **dhcpd.conf**, as shown in Example 9-4.

Example 9-4   *Create Folders for Docker Container*

```
UBUNTU-SERV1:~ TestUser$
UBUNTU-SERV1:~ TestUser$ pwd
/Users/TestUser/
UBUNTU-SERV1:~ TestUser$ mkdir iox-automation
UBUNTU-SERV1:~ TestUser$ cd iox-automation/
UBUNTU-SERV1:iox-automation TestUser$
UBUNTU-SERV1:iox-automation TestUser$
UBUNTU-SERV1:iox-automation TestUser$ mkdir dhcp
UBUNTU-SERV1:iox-automation TestUser$ cd dhcp
UBUNTU-SERV1:dhcp TestUser$ touch Dockerfile
UBUNTU-SERV1:dhcp TestUser$ touch dhcpd.conf
UBUNTU-SERV1:dhcp TestUser$ ls -1
total 8
-rw-r--r--  1 TestUser  staff  0 Nov  6 20:16 Dockerfile
-rw-r-r--   1 TestUser  staff  0 Nov  6 20:16 dhcpd.conf
UBUNTU-SERV1:dhcp TestUser$
```

Use your favorite text editor to modify the **dhcpd.conf** file, as shown in Example 9-5.

Example 9-5   *Edit DHCPd Configuration*

```
subnet 10.0.2.0 netmask 255.255.255.0 {
    range 10.0.2.100 10.0.2.200;
    option routers 10.0.2.1;
    option domain-name-servers 10.0.2.10, 10.0.2.11;
    option domain-name example.com
}
```

Each entry in this file is explained here:

- **option domain-name:** Defines the organization-wide domain name for all DHCP pools.

- **subnet 10.0.2.0 netmask 255.255.255.0:** Defines a DHCP pool for the 10.0.2.0/24 subnet. The brackets indicate that the enclosed options are specific to this DHCP pool.

- **range 10.0.2.100 10.0.2.200:** Instructs the DHCP server to only lease addresses within the 10.0.2.100–10.0.2.200 range.

- **option routers 10.0.2.1:** Instructs the DHCP server to inform hosts that lease addresses that their default gateway has an IP address of 10.0.2.1.

- **option domain-name-servers 10.0.2.10, 10.0.2.11:** Instructs the DHCP server to inform hosts leasing addresses that DNS servers are located at IP addresses 10.0.2.10 and 10.0.2.11.

Note: You can find additional details regarding the specific syntax of the dhcpd.conf file at https://linux.die.net/man/5/dhcpd.conf.

In your preferred text editor, modify the contents of the Dockerfile file, as shown in Example 9-6.

Example 9-6   *Edit Dockerfile*

```
FROM alpine:latest

RUN apk add --no-cache dhcp
RUN touch /var/lib/dhcp/dhcpd.leases
COPY ./dhcpd.conf /etc/dhcp/dhcpd.conf
EXPOSE 67/udp 67/tcp
CMD ["/usr/sbin/dhcpd", "-4", "-f", "-d", "-cf", "/etc/dhcp/dhcpd.conf"]
```

Each entry in this file is explained here:

- **FROM alpine:latest:** Uses the latest version of the Alpine Linux container hosted on Docker Hub as the "base" for this container. Think of this as the starting template for the Docker container, where subsequent commands will further configure or modify this template.

- **RUN apk add –no-cache dhcp:** Executes the **apk add --no-cache dhcp** command within the container. This installs the **dhcp** package to the container, which houses the dhcpd process that will serve as the DHCP server. The **--no-cache** option forces the apk package manager to refresh its index on-the-fly instead of using a cached version.

- **RUN touch /var/lib/dhcp/dhcpd.leases:** Executes the **touch /var/lib/dhcp/dhcpd. leases** command, which creates an empty file at the provided filepath. The dhcpd process requires that this file is created within the container to function. The DHCP server uses this file to record DHCP lease activity.

- **COPY ./dhcpd.conf /etc/dhcp/dhcpd.conf:** Copies the **dhcpd.conf** file created earlier into the container's file system. The DHCP server process will use this configuration file.

- **EXPOSE 67/udp 67/tcp:** Instructs the Docker container to listen for UDP and TCP connections that use port 67. DHCP servers need to listen on this port to function as expected.

- **CMD:** Instructs the Docker container to execute the provided command when the Docker container is started. This command sequence starts the dhcpd daemon with specific parameters:

  - **-4:** Allows the DHCP server to service DHCPv4 requests.

  - **-f:** Executes the dhcpd process in the foreground instead of in the background (which is typically the default for daemon processes).

  - **-d:** Allows the DHCP server to log into the standard error descriptor (sometimes called **stderr**). This is important for use in a Docker container because Docker logs typically monitor either the stdout or the stderr file descriptors. This parameter allows you to easily check on the status of your container from within Docker using the **docker logs <container-name>** command. **-cf** specifies a filepath for a specific dhcpd configuration file to use. In this case, the **/etc/dhcp/dhcpd.conf** file path is provided immediately after the parameter is used.

Build the image for the new Docker container. The **-t** parameter specifies the tag to be used for the new Docker image, which is essentially the "name" to be used to refer to the Docker image. You can see in the output in Example 9-7 that each of the steps defined in the Dockerfile is executed.

Example 9-7 *Build Image for Docker Container*

```
UBUNTU-SERV1:dhcp TestUser$ docker build -t TestUser/dhcp .
Sending build context to Docker daemon  3.072kB
Step 1/6 : FROM alpine:latest
 ---> 5cb3aa00f899
Step 2/6 : RUN apk add --no-cache dhcp
 ---> Running in 2f91eff75d6d
fetch http://dl-cdn.alpinelinux.org/alpine/v3.9/main/x86_64/APKINDEX.tar.gz
fetch http://dl-cdn.alpinelinux.org/alpine/v3.9/community/x86_64/APKINDEX.tar.gz
(1/2) Installing libgcc (8.3.0-r0)
(2/2) Installing dhcp (4.4.1-r1)
Executing dhcp-4.4.1-r1.pre-install
Executing busybox-1.29.3-r10.trigger
OK: 10 MiB in 16 packages
Removing intermediate container 2f91eff75d6d
 ---> 357d05f1f755
Step 3/6 : RUN touch /var/lib/dhcp/dhcpd.leases
 ---> Running in 05cd5f036c59
```

```
Removing intermediate container 05cd5f036c59
 ---> be4eeae7740b
Step 4/6 : COPY ./dhcpd.conf /etc/dhcp/dhcpd.conf
 ---> 431be6a0529c
Step 5/6 : EXPOSE 67/udp 67/tcp
 ---> Running in f07491ba4340
Removing intermediate container f07491ba4340
 ---> bfc0a5943df5
Step 6/6 : CMD ["/usr/sbin/dhcpd", "-4", "-f", "-d", "-cf", "/etc/dhcp/dhcpd.conf"]
 ---> Running in 1aa49bcf8950
Removing intermediate container 1aa49bcf8950
 ---> d7890c38f5ed
Successfully built d7890c38f5ed
Successfully tagged TestUser/dhcp:latest
```

Create a tarball from your newly built Docker image, as shown as Example 9-8.

Example 9-8　*Create Docker Image Archive*

```
UBUNTU-SERV1:dhcp TestUser$
UBUNTU-SERV1:dhcp TestUser$ docker save TestUser/dhcp:latest -o TestUser-dhcp.tar
UBUNTU-SERV1:dhcp TestUser$
```

Install and Activate DHCP Docker Container in Catalyst 9000

Transfer this tarball to the Catalyst device where the container will be deployed and installed, as shown in Example 9-9. As you notice, the state of the deployed application is reported as DEPLOYED, which indicates the service is successfully deployed.

Example 9-9　*Install DHCP Docker*

```
CAT9300-A#
CAT9300-A# dir | inc dhcp
16407  -rw-        10664960    Nov 7 2019 02:57:50 +00:00  TestUser-dhcp.tar
CAT9300-A#
CAT9300-A# app-hosting install appid TestUser-dhcp package flash:TestUser-dhcp.tar
Installing package 'flash:TestUser-dhcp.tar' for 'TestUser-dhcp'.
  Use 'show app-hosting list' for progress.
CAT9300-A#
CAT9300-A# show app-hosting list
App id                            State
---------------------------------------------------------------
dhcpd                             DEPLOYED
CAT9300-A#
```

In IOS-XE, configure the IOx application for the DHCP package. With the commands shown in Example 9-10, the clients are bridged to the DHCP Server container in VLAN 10 through the AppGigabitEthernet1/0/1 interface.

Example 9-10 *Configure IOx for DHCP Package*

```
CAT9300-A#
CAT9300-A# show run interface AppGigabitEthernet1/0/1
interface AppGigabitEthernet1/0/1
 switchport mode trunk
 switchport trunk allowed vlan 10
CAT9300-A#
CAT9300-A# show run | sec dhcpd
app-hosting appid dhcpd
 app-vnic AppGigabitEthernet trunk
  vlan 10 guest-interface 0
   guest-ipaddress 10.0.2.5 netmask 255.255.255.0
 app-resource profile custom
  cpu 100
  memory 100
CAT9300-A#
```

Activate and run the IOx container with the commands shown in Example 9-11.

Example 9-11 *Activate and Run the Application*

```
CAT9300-A#
CAT9300-A# app-hosting activate appid dhcpd
CAT9300-A# app-hosting start appid dhcpd
CAT9300-A#
```

At this point, the DHCP container and the service it offers should be active and running. Test it by using the **show app-hosting** command. As you saw in Example 9-9, this command helps you verify the operational state of the service.

Create and Deploy DNS Docker Container

The premise behind this use case is a scenario in which an administrator wants to deploy a DNS server for a branch using the Internet Systems Consortium's well-known BIND (Berkeley Internet Name Domain) 9 DNS server, as opposed to creating additional configuration natively in IOS-XE. This is particularly useful if existing automation workflows (such as through Ansible, Puppet, Chef, and so on) already exist around BIND 9 configuration.

Prepare to Create DNS Docker Container

Create a new folder for the DNS Docker container. Create three empty files, as shown in Example 9-12.

- **Dockerfile:** File with list of commands that will be used to assemble a docker image

- **named.conf:** Bind configuration file

- **db.foobar.local:** Zone configuration file

Example 9-12 *Create Folders for a Docker Container*

```
UBUNTU-SERV1:iox-automation TestUser$ mkdir dns
UBUNTU-SERV1:iox-automation TestUser$ cd dns
UBUNTU-SERV1:dns TestUser$ touch Dockerfile
UBUNTU-SERV1:dns TestUser$ touch named.conf
UBUNTU-SERV1:dns TestUser$ touch db.foobar.local
```

Use your favorite text editor to modify the **named.conf** file, as shown in Example 9-13.

Example 9-13 *Edit Nameserver Daemon Configuration*

```
options {
    directory "/var/bind";
    recursion;

    forwarders {
        8.8.8.8;
        8.8.4.4;
    };

    listen-on {
        any;
    };

    allow-transfer {
        none;
    };

};

zone "foobar.local" {
    type master;
    file "/etc/bind/zones/db.foobar.local";
```

The exact syntax of BIND's configuration file is outside the scope of this book. However, at a high level, this configuration defines three key factors:

- The IP addresses of upstream DNS forwarders that BIND can use to send DNS requests it cannot locally resolve

- The IP addresses or interfaces which BIND should listen to for incoming DNS requests (set to **any** interface)

- The definition of the **foobar.local** zone, the details of which are defined in the **/etc/bind/zones/db.foobar.local** file

Use your favorite text editor to modify the **db.foobar.local** file, as shown in Example 9-14.

Example 9-14 *BIND Configuration*

```
$TTL    604800          ; 1 week
@       IN      SOA     ns1.foobar.local. admin.foobar.local (
                3       ; config edit
                604800  ; refresh  - 1 week
                86400   ; retry - 24 hours
                2419200 ; expiration - 4 weeks
                604800  ; minimum - 1 week
                }
; NS Records
        IN      NS      ns1.foobar.local.
        IN      NS      ns2.foobar.local.


; A Records
dns01.foobar.local.     IN      A       10.0.2.10
dns02.foobar.local.     IN      A       10.0.2.11
```

The second line configures Start of Authority (SOA) for the records, which lists **ns1. foobar.local** and **admin.foobar.local** as identified authorities for the DNS records. The first entry right after the SOA entries tracks the number of edits done to the BIND configuration. The timers provided in the example define the time interval before refreshing an entry, time interval to retry, entry expiration time, and minimum time duration to maintain entries. The configuration is followed by Name Server (NS) and Address (A) records. The A records are added to the configuration for the hosts belonging to the zone and whose names should end with the domain name given.

Use your favorite text editor to modify the Dockerfile file, as shown in Example 9-15.

Example 9-15   *Edit Dockerfile*

```
FROM alpine:latest

RUN apk add --no-cache bind

COPY ./named.conf /etc/bind/named.conf
COPY ./db.foobar.local /etc/bind/zones/db.foobar.local

EXPOSE 53/udp 53/tcp

CMD ["/usr/sbin/named", "-4", "-c", "/etc/bind/named.conf", "-f"]
```

Each entry in the Dockerfile is explained next:

- **FROM alpine:latest:** Uses the latest version of the Alpine Linux container hosted on Docker Hub as the "base" for this container. Think of this as the starting template for the Docker container, where subsequent commands further configure or modify this template.

- **RUN apk add –no-cache bind:** Executes the **apk add --nocache bind** command within the container. This installs the **bind** package to the container, which contains the bind process that will serve as the DNS server. The **--no-cache** option forces the apk package manager to refresh its index on-the-fly instead of using a cached version.

- **COPY ./named.conf /etc/bind/named.conf:** Copies the **named.conf** file created earlier into the container's file system. This configuration file will be used to configure the DNS server (BIND) process.

- **COPY ./db.foobar.local /etc/bind/zones/db.foobar.local:** Copies the **db.foobar.local** file created earlier into the container's file system. This configuration file will be used to configure the **foobar.local** zone as defined by the **named.conf** BIND configuration file.

- **EXPOSE 53/udp 53/tcp:** This instructs the Docker container to listen for UDP and TCP connections that use port 53. DNS servers need to listen on this port to function as expected.

- **CMD:** This instructs the Docker container to execute the provided command when the Docker container is started. This command sequence starts the BIND/named daemon with specific parameters:

    - **-4:** This allows the DNS server to service IPv4 DNS requests.

    - **-c:** This specifies a file path for a specific BIND configuration file to use. In this case, the **/etc/bind/named.conf** file path is provided immediately after the parameter is used.

- **-f:** This allows the DNS server daemon to work in the foreground instead of in the background (which is typically the default for daemon processes). Running it in the foreground, with logs generated, helps to identify if there is any startup problems and also to debug it.

Note: You can find additional information about the syntax used to build a Docker container at https://docs.docker.com/engine/reference/builder/.

Create DNS Docker Containers

Build the image for the new Docker container. The **-t** parameter in Example 9-16 specifies the tag to be used for the new Docker image, which is essentially the "name" to refer to the Docker image. From the results shown in the example, you can see that the **docker build** command executes each instruction in the Dockerfile step by step.

Example 9-16 *Build Image for Docker Container*

```
UBUNTU-SERV1:dns TestUser$
UBUNTU-SERV1:dns TestUser$ docker build -t TestUser/dns .
Sending build context to Docker daemon  15.24MB
Step 1/6 : FROM alpine:latest
 ---> 5cb3aa00f899
Step 2/6 : RUN apk add --no-cache bind
 ---> Using cache
 ---> 6bb2150dd0db
Step 3/6 : COPY ./named.conf /etc/bind/named.conf
 ---> Using cache
 ---> 48ec7d0abbfc
Step 4/6 : COPY ./db.foobar.local /etc/bind/zones/db.foobar.local
 ---> Using cache
 ---> 9c206c2dead2
Step 5/6 : EXPOSE 53/udp 53/tcp
 ---> Using cache
 ---> 0f3b19d8baf5
Step 6/6 : CMD ["/usr/sbin/named", "-4", "-c", "/etc/bind/named.conf", "-f"]
 ---> Using cache
 ---> 3589722a2e5e
Successfully built 3589722a2e5e
Successfully tagged TestUser/dns:latest
UBUNTU-SERV1:dns TestUser$
```

Create a tarball from your newly built Docker image, as shown in Example 9-17.

Example 9-17 *Create Docker Image Archive*

```
UBUNTU-SERV1:dns TestUser$
UBUNTU-SERV1:dns TestUser$ docker save TestUser/dns:latest -o bind.tar
UBUNTU-SERV1:dns TestUser$
```

Install and Activate DNS Docker Container in Catalyst 9000

Install the application after transferring the tarball to the catalyst switch where you plan to deploy the container, as shown in Example 9-18.

Example 9-18 *Install DNS Docker Container*

```
C9500# dir | inc tar
97362  -rw-        15233024  Nov 20 2019 20:24:55 +00:00  bind.tarC9500#
C9500# app-hosting install appid bind package bootflash:bind.tar
Installing package 'bootflash:bind.tar' for 'bind'. Use 'show app-hosting list' for
  progress.
C9500#
C9500#
C9500# show app-hosting list
App id                          State
---------------------------------------------------------
bind                            DEPLOYED
C9500#
```

In IOS-XE, configure the IOx application for the BIND package, as shown in Example 9-19. Through the commands shown in Example 9-19, the clients are bridged to the DNS Server container in VLAN 10 through the AppGigabitEthernet1/0/1 interface.

Example 9-19 *Configure IOx for DNS Package*

```
C9500# show run interface AppGigabitEthernet1/0/1
interface AppGigabitEthernet1/0/1
 switchport mode trunk
 switchport trunk allowed vlan 10
C9500#
C9500# show run | sec bind
app-hosting appid bind
 app-vnic AppGigabitEthernet trunk
  vlan 10 guest-interface 0
   guest-ipaddress 10.0.2.10 netmask 255.255.255.0
 app-resource profile custom
  cpu 100
  memory 100
C9500#
```

Activate and start the IOx container with commands shown in Example 9-20.

Example 9-20 *Activate and Run Docker Container*

```
C9500#
C9500# app-hosting activate appid bind
C9500# app-hosting start appid bind
C9500#
C9500#show app-hosting list
App id                              State
----------------------------------------------------------
bind                                RUNNING
C9500#
```

At this point, the DNS container and the service it offers should be up and running. Test it! As you might have noticed, only one instance of the DNS server offering its service at 10.0.2.10 has been instantiated. The same procedure can be used to create another instance of DNS, say at 10.0.2.11 or more instances as required.

Create HAProxy and Node Containers

The premise behind this use case is a scenario wherein an administrator wants to deploy a high-availability load balancer or proxy server to act as a front end for a set of existing back-end services. This capability is demonstrated by deploying HAProxy, an opensource, load-balancing solution, to provide high-availability access to two web servers (deployed using a simple HTTP server hosted through **Node.js**).

Note that in this example, all three containers are made accessible through the management interface of the Catalyst switch in the **Mgmt-vrf VRF**. In a production environment, you would likely need to deploy this service in the default or other non-management VRFs so that the service can access front-panel ports.

The DHCP and DNS services discussed earlier in this chapter can also be deployed in the management VRF, which would be a low-cost name servers deployment for the management network.

Project Initiation

Create a new folder for the HAProxy Docker container solution. Create two subfolders inside—one for HAProxy and one for the **Node.js** web server, as shown in Example 9-21.

Example 9-21 *Create Folders for HAProxy and Node.js*

```
[admin@TestUser-playground ~]$
[admin@TestUser-playground ~]$ mkdir haproxy-solution/
[admin@TestUser-playground ~]$ ls -al | grep haproxy
drwxrwxr-x.  4 admin admin       33 Nov 19 16:11 haproxy-solution
[admin@TestUser-playground ~]$ mkdir HAProxy/
```

```
[admin@TestUser-playground ~]$ mkdir Node/
[admin@TestUser-playground haproxy-solution]$ ls -al
total 4
drwxrwxr-x.  4 admin admin   33 Nov 19 16:11 .
drwx------. 20 admin admin 4096 Nov 20 16:33 ..
drwxrwxr-x.  2 admin admin   62 Nov 20 15:52 HAProxy
drwxrwxr-x.  2 admin admin   40 Nov 19 16:12 Node
[admin@TestUser-playground haproxy-solution]$
```

Setting Up Web Server

Within the Node directory, create two empty files—one for your Dockerfile and the other for the JavaScript file to be used by Node.js to host a simple web server, as shown in Example 9-22. Node.js has a built-in HTTP module, which allows Node.js to communicate and transfer data over HTTP.

Example 9-22   *Create Folders for Dockerfile and JavaScript*

```
[admin@TestUser-playground haproxy-solution]$
[admin@TestUser-playground haproxy-solution]$ cd Node/
[admin@TestUser-playground Node]$ touch Dockerfile
[admin@TestUser-playground Node]$ touch index.js
[admin@TestUser-playground Node]$
```

Using your favorite text editor, modify the index.js file, as shown in Example 9-23.

Example 9-23   *Edit JavaScript File Used by Node.js*

```
var http = require("http");
var os = require("os");

http.createServer(function (req, res) {
    res.writeHead(200, {"Content-Type": "text/html"});
    res.end('<h1>You have accessed container ${os.hostname()}</h1>');
}).listen(8080);
```

This code creates a simple web server through JavaScript. When accessed, the web server will report the hostname of the server it is running on. The hostname of a Docker container corresponds with the container's ID. As a result, when this solution is deployed via Docker, the container ID of the Docker container will be reported when the web server is accessed.

Using your favorite text editor, modify the Dockerfile file, as shown in Example 9-24.

Example 9-24 *Edit Dockerfile*

```
FROM node:latest
COPY index.js /app/index.js
EXPOSE 8080
CMD [ "node", "/app/index" ]
```

Each entry in this file is explained here:

- **FROM node:latest:** Uses the latest version of the Node container hosted on Docker Hub as the "base" for this container. Think of this as the starting template for the Docker container, where subsequent commands will further configure and modify this template.

- **COPY index.js /app/index.js:** Copies the **index.js** file created earlier into the container's file system. This file will later be executed by **Node.js.**

- **EXPOSE 8080:** This instructs the Docker container to listen for any traffic destined for port 8080, which is what the **Node.js** web server will be listening on.

- **CMD:** This instructs the Docker container to execute the **index.js** file using Node.

Create Docker Image

Build the image for the new Docker container. The **-t** parameter specifies the tag to be used for the new Docker image, which is essentially the "name" to be used to refer to the Docker image. You can see in Example 9-25 that each of the steps defined in the Dockerfile is executed.

Example 9-25 *Create Image for Docker Container*

```
UBUNTU-SERV1:Node TestUser$ docker build -t custom-node:latest .
Sending build context to Docker daemon  3.072kB
Step 1/4 : FROM node
 ---> 1a77bcb355eb
Step 2/4 : COPY index.js /app/
 ---> 2fadb03cbe2c
Step 3/4 : EXPOSE 8080
 ---> Running in ddf1b1b41e34
Removing intermediate container ddf1b1b41e34
 ---> f3828781ea73
Step 4/4 : CMD [ "node", "/app/index" ]
 ---> Running in 5695b4c9046f
Removing intermediate container 5695b4c9046f
 ---> a27b21a0031c
Successfully built a27b21a0031c
Successfully tagged custom-node:latest
UBUNTU-SERV1:Node TestUser$
```

Create a tarball from your newly built Docker image, as shown in Example 9-26, and transfer the file to the Catalyst device where you plan to deploy the container.

Example 9-26   *Create Image Archive for Docker Container*

```
UBUNTU-SERV1:Node TestUser$
UBUNTU-SERV1:Node TestUser$ docker save custom-node:latest -o node.tar
UBUNTU-SERV1:Node TestUser$ ls -al | grep node
-rw-------  1 TestUser  staff  962044928 Nov 20 15:44 node.tar
UBUNTU-SERV1:Node TestUser$
```

Deploy, Install, and Activate Web Server Docker Containers

To properly demonstrate the load-balancing capabilities of HAProxy, you need to install two separate containers using the Node.js Web Server Docker container. Install two applications on Catalyst 9000 from the same node.tar package. See Example 9-27.

Example 9-27   *Install Node.js Docker Container*

```
C9500#
C9500# app-hosting install appid node1 package bootflash:node.tar
Installing package 'bootflash:node.tar' for 'node1'. Use 'show app-hosting list' for
  progress.
C9500#
C9500# app-hosting install appid node2 package bootflash:node.tar
Installing package 'bootflash:node.tar' for 'node2'. Use 'show app-hosting list' for
  progress.
C9500#
C9500# show app-hosting list
App id                          State
--------------------------------------------------------------
node1                           DEPLOYED
node2                           DEPLOYED
C9500#
```

In IOS-XE, configure two separate IOx applications for both Node.js web servers. Example 9-28 shows the configurations applied to the Web Server nodes. Both nodes communicate through guest-interface 0 and have IP address 10.0.2.10 and 10.0.2.11, respectively.

Example 9-28   *Configure IOx for Node.js Package*

```
C9500#
C9500# show run | sec node
app-hosting appid node1
 app-vnic management guest-interface 0
  guest-ipaddress 10.0.2.10 netmask 255.255.255.0
```

```
app-default-gateway 10.0.2.1 guest-interface 0
 app-resource profile custom
  cpu 100
  memory 100
app-hosting appid node2
 app-vnic management guest-interface 0
  guest-ipaddress 10.0.2.11 netmask 255.255.255.0
 app-default-gateway 10.0.2.1 guest-interface 0
 app-resource profile custom
  cpu 100
  memory 100
C9500#
```

Activate and run both containers for the Node.js web servers, as shown in Example 9-29.

Example 9-29   *Activate and Run Node.js Docker Container*

```
C9500#
C9500#app-hosting activate appid node1
node1 activated successfully
Current state is: ACTIVATED
C9500#
C9500#app-hosting activate appid node2
node2 activated successfully
Current state is: ACTIVATED
C9500#
C9500#show app-hosting list
App id                                      State
-----------------------------------------------------------
node1                                       ACTIVATED
node2                                       ACTIVATED
C9500#
C9500#
C9500#app-hosting start appid node1
node1 started successfully
Current state is: RUNNING
C9500#
C9500#app-hosting start appid node2
node2 started successfully
Current state is: RUNNING
C9500#
C9500#show app-hosting list
App id                                      State
-----------------------------------------------------------
node1                                       RUNNING
node2                                       RUNNING
C9500#
```

Confirm that both web servers are accessible from their provided guest IP addresses using port 8080. Each unique web server should report a different hostname, which maps to the internal Docker container ID. This is demonstrated in Example 9-30 using the **Curl** command.

Example 9-30 *Verify Container Accessibility*

```
[admin@TestUser-playground ~]$ curl 10.0.2.10:8080
<h1>You have accessed container a8f42b84b6e9</h1>
[admin@TestUser-playground ~]$ curl 10.0.2.11:8080
<h1>You have accessed container 9bb21101804d</h1>
```

HAProxy Load Balancer Setup

Within the **HAProxy** directory originally created, create two empty files—one for your Dockerfile and the other for the HAProxy configuration file, as shown in Example 9-31.

Example 9-31 *Create Folders for Dockerfile and Configuration*

```
[admin@TestUser-playground ~]$
[admin@TestUser-playground ~]$ cd haproxy-solution/
[admin@TestUser-playground haproxy-solution]$ ls -al
total 4
drwxrwxr-x.  4 admin admin   33 Nov 19 16:11 .
drwx------. 20 admin admin 4096 Nov 20 16:33 ..
drwxrwxr-x.  2 admin admin   62 Nov 20 15:52 HAProxy
drwxrwxr-x.  2 admin admin   40 Nov 19 16:12 Node
[admin@TestUser-playground haproxy-solution]$ cd HAProxy/
[admin@TestUser-playground HAProxy]$ touch Dockerfile
[admin@TestUser-playground HAProxy]$ touch haproxy.cfg
[admin@TestUser-playground HAProxy]$ ls -al
total 92340
drwxrwxr-x. 2 admin admin      62 Nov 20 15:52 .
drwxrwxr-x. 4 admin admin      33 Nov 19 16:11 ..
-rw-rw-r--. 1 admin admin      73 Nov 18 21:14 Dockerfile
-rw-rw-r--. 1 admin admin     180 Nov 18 21:36 haproxy.cfg
[admin@TestUser-playground HAProxy]$
```

Using your favorite text editor, modify the **haproxy.cfg** file, as shown in Example 9-32.

Example 9-32 *Edit HAProxy Load-Balancing Configuration*

```
frontend public_facing
    bind *:80
    default_backend node_servers
backend node_servers
    balance roundrobin
    server server1 10.0.2.10:8080
    server server2 10.0.2.11:8080
```

This configuration is a basic HAProxy load balancer that is split into two parts:

- **Front end:** The "public" element of the load balancer facing the enterprise where incoming requests ingress

- **Back end:** The "private" element of the load balancer facing the servers to which you want to load balance requests

The front-end element listens on the default HTTP port 80, and a default back end named **node_servers** is defined. The back-end element defines both **Node.js** servers that were previously deployed and specifies that requests to those servers should be load balanced in a round-robin fashion.

Using your favorite text editor, modify the **Dockerfile** file, as shown in Example 9-33.

Example 9-33   *Edit Dockerfile*

```
FROM haproxy:latest
COPY haproxy.cfg /usr/local/etc/haproxy/haproxy.cfg
```

Both entries in this file are explained here:

- **FROM haproxy:latest:** Uses the latest version of the HAproxy container hosted on Docker Hub as the "base" for this container. Think of this as the starting template for the Docker container, where subsequent commands will further configure or modify this template.

- **COPY haproxy.cfg /usr/local/etc/haproxy/haproxy.cfg:** Copies the **haproxy.cfg** file created earlier into the container's file system. This file is placed in the default location that HAProxy references.

Create Docker Image

Build the image for the new Docker container. The **-t** parameter specifies the tag to be used for the new Docker image, which is essentially the "name" to be used to refer to the Docker image. You can see in the output shown in Example 9-34 that each of the steps defined in the Dockerfile is executed.

Example 9-34   *Build Image for Docker Container*

```
[admin@TestUser-playground HAProxy]$ docker build -t custom-haproxy:latest .
Sending build context to Docker daemon 3.072 kB
Step 1/2 : FROM haproxy:latest
 ---> 643ee56fee48
Step 2/2 : COPY haproxy.cfg /usr/local/etc/haproxy/haproxy.cfg
 ---> Using cache
 ---> 359df688a63c
Successfully built 359df688a63c
[admin@TestUser-playground HAProxy]$
```

Create a tarball from your newly built Docker image and transfer it to the Catalyst device(s) where you plan to deploy the container, as shown in Example 9-35.

Example 9-35　*Build Image Archive for Docker Container*

```
[admin@TestUser-playground HAProxy]$ docker save TestUser-haproxy:latest -o haproxy.
  tar
[admin@TestUser-playground HAProxy]$ ls -al | grep haproxy.tar
-rw-------. 1 admin admin 94544896 Nov 20 15:52 haproxy.tar
[admin@TestUser-playground HAProxy]$
```

Install, Activate, and Run HAProxy Docker Containers

Install the application in the Catalyst 9000 switch, as shown in Example 9-36.

Example 9-36　*Install HAProxy Docker Container*

```
C9500#
C9500# app-hosting install appid haproxy package bootflash:haproxy.tar
Installing package 'bootflash:haproxy.tar' for 'haproxy'. Use 'show app-hosting
  list' for progress.
C9500#
C9500# show app-hosting list
App id                                State
---------------------------------------------------------
node1                                 RUNNING
node2                                 RUNNING
haproxy                               DEPLOYED
C9500#
```

In IOS-XE, configure the IOx application for HAProxy, as shown in Example 9-37.

Example 9-37　*Configure the IOx Package for the HAProxy Docker Container*

```
C9500# show run | sec haproxy
app-hosting appid haproxy
 app-vnic management guest-interface 0
  guest-ipaddress 10.0.2.15 netmask 255.255.255.0
 app-default-gateway 10.0.2.1 guest-interface 0
 app-resource profile custom
  cpu 100
  memory 100
C9500#
```

Activate and run the HAProxy container, as shown in Example 9-38.

Example 9-38 *Activate and Run HAProxy Docker Container*

```
C9500# app-hosting activate appid haproxy
haproxy activated successfully
Current state is: ACTIVATED
C9500#
C9500#show app-hosting list
App id                                  State
---------------------------------------------------------
node1                                   RUNNING
node2                                   RUNNING
haproxy                                 ACTIVATED
C9500#
C9500# app-hosting start appid haproxy
haproxy started successfully
Current state is: RUNNING
C9500#
C9500#show app-hosting list
App id                                  State
---------------------------------------------------------
node1                                   RUNNING
node2                                   RUNNING
haproxy                                 RUNNING
C9500#
```

Confirm that when accessing the HAProxy container's IP from a web browser, your HTTP request is successfully passed through to one of the underlying **Node.js** Docker containers. This is best demonstrated using the **Curl** command, as shown in Example 9-39. As you can see, the command accesses the containers a8f42b84b6e9 and 9bb21101804d in a round-robin fashion.

Example 9-39 *Verify Container Accessibility*

```
[admin@TestUser-playground HAProxy]$ curl 10.0.2.15
<h1>You have accessed container a8f42b84b6e9</h1>
[admin@TestUser-playground HAProxy]$ curl 10.0.2.15
<h1>You have accessed container 9bb21101804d</h1>
[admin@TestUser-playground HAProxy]$ curl 10.0.2.15
<h1>You have accessed container a8f42b84b6e9</h1>
[admin@TestUser-playground HAProxy]$ curl 10.0.2.15
<h1>You have accessed container 9bb21101804d</h1>
[admin@TestUser-playground HAProxy]$ curl 10.0.2.15
<h1>You have accessed container a8f42b84b6e9</h1>
[admin@TestUser-playground HAProxy]$ curl 10.0.2.15
```

```
<h1>You have accessed container 9bb21101804d</h1>
[admin@TestUser-playground HAProxy]$ curl 10.0.2.15
<h1>You have accessed container a8f42b84b6e9</h1>
[admin@TestUser-playground HAProxy]$ curl 10.0.2.15
<h1>You have accessed container 9bb21101804d</h1>
```

Figure 9-1 shows a logical representation of containers that have deployed services with Dockerized DHCP, DNS, and web servers with a load-balancer.

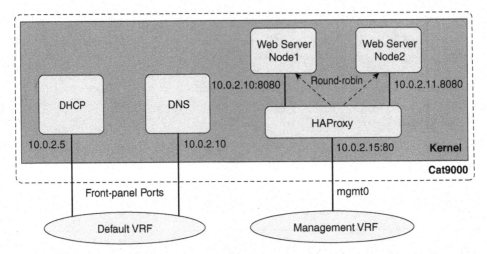

Figure 9-1 *Containerized DHCP, DNS, and HAProxy Services in IOS-XE*

Network administrators and operators are encouraged to leverage these simple procedures to deploy the services discussed, as well as any similar services, into production. Also, you can assist developers to prove a concept or test their applications.

IOS-XR Use Case: Disaggregated Seamless BFD as a Virtual Network Function for Rapid Failure Detection

Network function disaggregation is not a new term for those who are in the networking industry. At one end of the spectrum, disaggregation can be considered the concept of decoupling the control plane from the underlying proprietary hardware; on the other end of the spectrum, the control plane itself can be disaggregated into multiple independent network functions. Imagine choosing each network function such as NAT, ACL, and OSPF from different vendors and instantiating them as stand-alone containers on any compute platform. Although it looks good, the concept of disaggregating independent network functions will open up interoperability issues between different disaggregated functions, which can create other issues. When all the network functions are coupled as one software component from the same vendor, the interprocess or interfunction communication is locally significant and can be defined using any proprietary method. But when the functions are disaggregated, the interprocess or interfunction communication needs to be standardized to ensure seamless communication between network functions from different vendors.

To avoid such issues while realizing the benefits of disaggregation, a good starting point is to identify some of the leaf applications that do not have minimal dependency on other functions. This sample use case explained one such network function that can be disaggregated and instantiated as a container for a path and node liveliness check.

Seamless BFD Overview

Seamless BFD is a relatively new continuity check protocol that was designed by extending the traditional BFD protocol to address some of the common challenges observed with BFD. Figure 9-2 takes a quick look at the challenges raised by the traditional BFD.

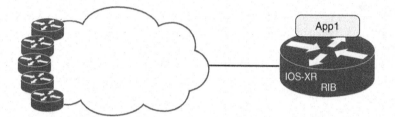

Figure 9-2 *Multiple Ingress Nodes Checking Availability of App1*

In Figure 9-2, multiple ingress nodes utilize a service hosted on the XR device on the right side of the topology. The ingress nodes are intended to check the availability of the function App1 on the XR and take necessary action when the function fails on XR. If you use traditional BFD, you will end up creating many state entries on the IOS-XR node, causing scale issues depending on the number of ingress nodes that rely on App1. Further, each ingress must learn the discriminator value for each function hosted.

S-BFD addresses these challenges by introducing the following characteristics:

- Preassigns and advertises a domain-wide unique discriminator using IGP protocol extensions

- Creates one reflector session that reflects the control packet if the "Your Discriminator" value in the received packet matches the local reflector session "Discriminator" value

As illustrated in Figure 9-3, there are two components of S-BFD:

- S-BFD Discriminators

- S-BFD Reflector session

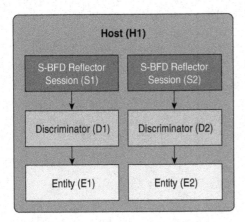

Figure 9-3   *S-BFD Components—Logical View*

S-BFD Discriminator

A pair of discriminators negotiated between BFD neighbors identifies a BFD session. In a traditional BFD, the discriminator is negotiated as part of a three-way handshake. With seamless BFD, each network entity within the same administrative domain will be preassigned with a minimum of one domain-wide unique discriminator, and it will be advertised using IGP protocol extensions.

It is the operator's responsibility to maintain the domain-wide uniqueness of the S-BFD discriminator, just like the system or router ID of the IGP protocol. Although the simple option is for operators to arbitrarily and manually allocate from a pool of discriminators, other options can be considered. For example, when the underlying IGP protocol is OSPF, the uniqueness of the 32-bit router identifier can be leveraged and can use the same as the S-BFD discriminator. Alternatively, a centralized intelligence such as SDN can be leveraged to dynamically assign from a pool. Cisco implementation supports leveraging the loopback IPv4 address as a discriminator.

In Figure 9-3, each entity that needs to be monitored will be assigned a unique S-BFD discriminator. As shown in Figure 9-3, Host H1 assigns discriminator D1 for entity E1 and discriminator D2 for entity E2. When any node within the domain is required to monitor entity E1 within host H1, it will send an S-BFD control packet to H1 and set the control packet details in S-BFD as your discriminator (YD)=D1 and my discriminator (MD)=local-random-value.

This enhanced characteristic of S-BFD eliminates the need for a handshake or discriminator negotiation between endpoints to monitor a path or local resources. It drastically reduces the time taken by the initiator to create a session; consequently, this augments the swiftness for the path and resource liveliness validation.

S-BFD Reflector Session

Each network entity participating in the S-BFD architecture will create one or more reflector sessions. The intention of the reflector session is to respond to a received S-BFD control packet with "Your Discriminator" (YD) as any of the locally assigned S-BFD discriminators.

The routers can have multiple reflector sessions with the associated S-BFD discriminator. This is required when the S-BFD discriminator is used for services other than basic connectivity. For example, a router can assign an S-BFD discriminator to any local service and create a reflector session for the service S-BFD discriminator. The router will respond to the control packet until the associated service is up. If service failure occurs, the associated reflector session will be disabled, and no response will be sent, which will cause the session to fail on the initiator if necessary actions are not taken.

This aspect of S-BFD eliminates the need for a per-session state entry in each BFD neighbor.

Creating and Hosting S-BFD as a Virtual Network Function

To demonstrate the use case of running a vNF as a container on IOS-XR, you will use S-BFD and develop a simple prototype by disaggregating the S-BFD protocol as shown here:

- **Reflectorbase:** The reflector entity that creates the reflector session and reflects the control plane if the local discriminator matches

- **Clientbase:** The client that generates control plane packets and expects a response

Each of these entities is developed as independent Docker container images.

The reflectorbase is instantiated on the relevant devices and can use any programming extensions to monitor an external entity and to modify the status of the reflector session. See the sample topology in Figure 9-4.

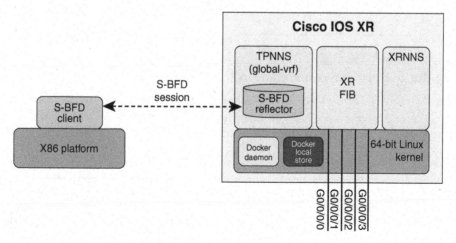

Figure 9-4 *Containerized S-BFD Reflector and Client*

The S-BFD reflectorbase is instantiated as a Docker container in the TPNNS namespace of the Cisco IOS-XR device, and the S-BFD client is instantiated in a remote x86 platform as a Docker container. The next section examines the procedures to instantiate the container for a liveliness check and validation.

S-BFD Docker Images

The Docker images for S-BFD Reflectorbase and SBFDClient are shown in Example 9-40.

Example 9-40 *Docker Images for Reflectorbase and SBFDClient*

```
root@kvmserver:/home/ubuntu/sbfd/new/reflect1# docker images
REPOSITORY      TAG           IMAGE ID          CREATED         SIZE
reflectbase     latest        6c0652f06829      6 days ago      11.3MB
sbfdclient      latest        99400707b608      5 days ago      11.2MB
root@kvmserver:/home/ubuntu/sbfd/new/reflect1#
```

Note: The development environment used for developing this prototype is C-based, so **base-rootfs** was used as the base image to convert the source code into Docker images. Using Alpine or any other Linux distribution increases the size of the image to about 100 MB.

The sample Dockerfile used to convert the **reflect** and **register_disc** app functions to a Docker image is shown in Example 9-41.

Example 9-41 *Edit Dockerfile*

```
FROM devhub-docker.cisco.com/iox-docker/ir800/base-rootfs
COPY reflect /opt/apps/
COPY register_disc /opt/apps/
CMD ["/opt/apps/reflect"]
```

Hosting the S-BFD Reflectorbase on the XR Device

Chapter 6 discussed ways of pulling Docker images to Cisco IOS-XR for application hosting. Any of the mechanisms discussed there can be used to pull the Docker image to the local image store, as shown in Example 9-42.

Example 9-42 *Docker Pull Images*

```
RP/0/RP0/CPU0:ios#
RP/0/RP0/CPU0:ios# bash
Wed Nov 13 14:29:34.010 UTC
[host:~]$ sudo -i
[host:~]$ docker images
```

```
REPOSITORY        TAG        IMAGE ID        CREATED        SIZE
reflectbase       latest     6c0652f06829    6 days ago     11.25 MB
alpine-iproute2   latest     9f259bb8a391    5 weeks ago    10.76 MB
nginx             latest     f949e7d76d63    7 weeks ago    126 MB
ubuntu            latest     2ca708c1c9cc    7 weeks ago    64.18 MB
alpine            latest     961769676411    12 weeks ago   5.577 MB
[host:~]$
```

The Docker command shown in Example 9-43 instantiates the S-BFD reflector function as a container on a Cisco IOS-XR device. The S-BFD "Discriminator" value for the reflector function is configured in the **/opt/apps/register_disc** file.

Example 9-43 *Instantiate S-BFD Reflector Container*

```
[host:~]$ sudo -i
[host:~]$ docker run -it --name sbfd --net=host --cap-add=NET_ADMIN reflectbase /
  bin/ash
/ # cd /opt/apps
/opt/apps # more register_disc
10
20
89
59
/opt/apps #
```

Because the container is instantiated with the host network option, all the device inter-faces and IP addresses reflect on the S-BFD reflector function container as well. Upon instantiating the function, it creates a netstat entry in the host data path to punt traffic received with the UDP port 7784 to the container, as shown in Example 9-44.

Example 9-44 *Container Network Interfaces and Layer 4 Ports*

```
[host:~]$
[host:~]$ netstat -nlp
Active Internet connections (only servers)
Proto Recv-Q Send-Q Local Address      Foreign Address  State    PID/Program name
tcp        0      0 127.0.0.53:53       0.0.0.0:*        LISTEN   -
tcp        0      0 127.0.0.1:58742     0.0.0.0:*        LISTEN   -
udp        0      0 0.0.0.0:7784        0.0.0.0:*                 -
udp        0      0 127.0.0.53:53       0.0.0.0:*                 -
Active UNIX domain sockets (only servers)
[host:~]$
```

Note: Traditional BFD uses UDP port 3784, whereas Seamless BFD uses 7784 as the destination UDP port. In the output shown in Example 9-44, note that the netstat entry accepts any packet with a destination IP matching one of the local IP address with destina-tion port 7784.

Hosting the S-BFD Client on the Server

In this example, the S-BFD client is hosted as a Docker container in a remote x86 platform. The client is not necessarily required to be directly connected to the Cisco-IOS-XR device. It can be a centralized entity performing the liveliness check.

The Docker image for the S-BFD client was created using the same **base-rootfs** file from Cisco devhub. The size of the image file is about 11 MB, as shown in Example 9-45.

Example 9-45   *SBFDClient Docker Image*

```
root@kvmserver:~#
root@kvmserver:~# docker images sbfdclient
REPOSITORY      TAG        IMAGE ID        CREATED          SIZE
sbfdclient      latest     99400707b608    6 days ago       11.2MB
root@kvmserver:~#
```

The S-BFD client is instantiated using the Docker command shown in Example 9-46 on the x86 platform. The S-BFD client is expected to have basic reachability to the Cisco IOS-XR device on which the S-BFD reflectorbase is instantiated. The sample output is shown in Example 9-46.

Example 9-46   *Run SBFDClient Docker Container*

```
root@kvmserver:~#
root@kvmserver:~# docker run -itd sbfdclient /bin/sh
ed682d289e2621ee5cc835892578e521f566352c4c5e424c25350c06f6558e41
root@kvmserver:~#
root@kvmserver:~# docker ps
CONTAINER ID  IMAGE       COMMAND     CREATED        STATUS PORTS NAMES
ed682d289e26  sbfdclient  "/bin/sh"   3 seconds ago    Up 3 sec silly_bhaskara
root@kvmserver:~#
```

Now log in to the container and configure the client, as shown in Example 9-47.

Example 9-47   *Access SBFDClient Docker Container*

```
root@kvmserver:~#
root@kvmserver:~# docker exec -it silly_bhaskara /bin/sh
/ #
/ # cd /opt/apps/
/opt/apps # ./cli
boot start up config........
done
Enter H for help
Enter your inputs: H
Enter "Add -i <ip address> -y <Your_Discr value> -m <multiplier>" for adding,
```

```
     example: "add -i 127.0.0.1 -y 10 -m 3"
             "a -i 127.0.0.1 -y 20"
             "a -i 127.0.0.1 -y 30 -m 4"
   Enter "Delete -i <ip address> -y <Your_Discr value>" for adding,
    example: "delete -i 127.0.0.1 -y 89"
             "d -i 127.0.0.1 -y 89"
   Enter "W" for storing all the inputs into the file
   Enter "H" for help
   Enter H for help
   Enter your inputs: add -i 172.17.0.4 -y 89
   Enter your inputs: s
   TYPE          LD/RD        IP            STATE   timer   Multiplier
   Ipv4          2/89         172.17.0.4    UP    1 sec   3
   Enter H for help
   Enter your inputs:
   <snip>
```

In Example 9-47, you created a client session from the S-BFD client container to the destination IP address 172.17.0.4 and "Your Discriminator" of 89. As long as the remote reflector session is up, the session state will be up, and any failure in the path or the remote reflector session can be rapidly detected.

This disaggregated S-BFD as a virtual network function is a flexible approach of instantiating OAM functionality only on the relevant devices by leveraging the virtualization capability of the Cisco devices.

NX-OS Use Case: Control Plane Health Check Using an Anomaly Detector

Chapter 8, "Application Developers' Tools and Resources," discussed the Floodlight application, which was developed, containerized, and run in a Docker environment. This section dives deep into the application to see how it helps to check control plane health.

Objective of the Application

Running as a Docker container, the application captures all packets going through the inband to the CPU/control plane. It also compares the characteristics of the traffic captured against the device configuration and classifies them into **expected traffic** and **unexpected traffic** categories. Lastly, it generates a PCAP file with the **unexpected traffic** for further processing. The objective here is to notify users of malicious traffic hitting the control plane in an on-demand fashion.

Build and Host the Anomaly Detector Application in Docker—High-Level Procedure

Figure 9-5 is a logical representation of the workflow to develop and host an application using Docker.

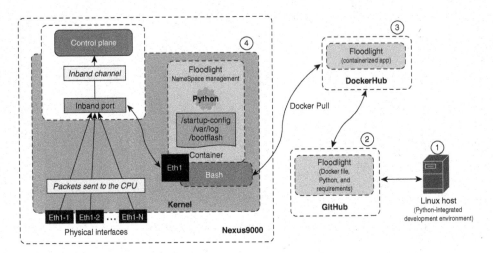

Figure 9-5 *NX-OS Anomaly Detector—Development and Hosting Workflow*

Even though there are different ways to develop an application, containerize it, and run it in a Docker environment, here are the simple steps for this use case:

1. Develop the application in an integrated development environment (IDE) setup in a Linux server.

2. Build a GitHub repository with the Python application, Dockerfile, and all other requirements and dependencies.

3. Build a DockerHub repository by leveraging the feature in DockerHub to connect to a GitHub repository.

4. In NX-OS, a Docker container is instantiated running a specific application, and it mounts necessary filesystems such as **/bootflash** and **/startup-config**. The application hosted in the container executes its routine and functions to achieve the objective.

Floodlight Application

Floodlight is a Dockerized Python application that identifies unexpected control plane traffic on Docker-capable Cisco Nexus data center switches and displays the top talkers of unexpected traffic. The startup configuration of the switch is analyzed to determine what traffic should be expected and what traffic should not be expected. Usage of the application is discussed in the following section.

To start, create a Docker container running the **floodlight** application, as shown in Example 9-48.

Example 9-48 *Using the Docker Create Command to Instantiate a Docker Container*

```
docker create --name=floodlight --net=host -e CAPTURE_TIME=300 -e EXPORT=/
  bootflash/pcap_filename.pcap -e DEBUG=1 -v /var/sysmgr/startup-cfg/ascii/system.
  cfg:/startup-config -v /var/log/:/var/log/ -v /bootflash:/bootflash chrisjhart/
  floodlight
```

The configuration parameters given in the **docker create** command follow:

- **--net=host:** Shares Docker host networking with the container, which is required for Floodlight to properly capture control plane traffic for analysis.

- **-e CAPTURE_TIME=:** An integer representing the number of seconds that Floodlight should capture control plane traffic for analysis. If it is not defined, the default is 60 seconds.

- **-e EXPORT=:** An absolute file path that defines where a PCAP containing all unexpected traffic is to be stored. In addition to setting this environmental variable, the directory must be mounted as a volume into the container for unexpected traffic to be exported.

- **-e DEBUG=:** When set to **1**, it enables debug logging in the **/var/log/floodlight.log** file. This should be used for troubleshooting; it is not recommended that you enable this in a production environment.

- **-v /var/sysmgr/startup-cfg/ascii/system.cfg:/startup-config:** Mounts the Nexus device's startup configuration into the container to determine what control plane traffic is to be expected. If this file is not mounted or Floodlight does not recognize the file as a valid NX-OS configuration, all control plane traffic will be considered unexpected.

- **-v /var/log:/var/log:** Allows logging to /var/log/floodlight.log on the Docker host. This is useful for debugging purposes and determining when the application was last executed.

- **-v /bootflash:/bootflash:** Mounts the bootflash directory of the Nexus device inside the container to allow for a PCAP of unexpected traffic to be stored. In addition to mounting this directory, the **EXPORT=** environmental variable must be set to an absolute filepath inside the bootflash directory for unexpected traffic to be exported.

If desired, the user can also utilize **Docker Compose** to run this application. The **docker-compose.yml** file shown in Example 9-49 may be used as a baseline.

Example 9-49   *Using Docker-Compose to Instantiate a Docker Container*

```
version: "3"
services:
  floodlight:
    image: chrisjhart/floodlight:latest
    container_name: floodlight
    volumes:
      - /var/sysmgr/startup-cfg/ascii/system.cfg:/startup-config
      - /var/log/:/var/log/
      - /bootflash:/bootflash
    environment:
      - DEBUG=1
      - CAPTURE_TIME=300
      - EXPORT=/bootflash/example_pcap.pcap
    network_mode: "host"
```

Docker Compose is a tool used to define and run Docker applications, with details provided in the **docker-compose.yml** file. It is easier to instantiate a Docker application
through Docker Compose than through a long **docker create** command with multiple
options, as given in Example 8-48. Docker Compose can be used to create an application
development environment with dependencies such as databases and caches and interact
with it. Moreover, Docker Compose is user-friendly in automated testing environments
as well as in hosting multicontainer Docker applications. Docker Compose is not available by default in NX-OS switches. Users need to install it on the switch, as mentioned at
https://docs.docker.com/compose/install/#install-compose. For more information about
Docker Compose on Cisco NX-OS, refer to the Cisco documentation available at
https://www.cisco.com/c/en/us/support/docs/switches/nexus-9000-series-switches/
213961-install-docker-compose-in-nx-os-bash-she.html.

Capturing Traffic

As shown in Example 9-50, the application captures the traffic received on the eth1 interface using the **tshark** command and saving them to a **.pcapng** file, after setting a capture
timeout. **tshark** is a network protocols analyzer that helps users capture the packet
received on an interface or read the packets saved in a capture file.

Example 9-50   *SPython Application Capturing Traffic*

```
<snip>
cap_timeout = 60 * capture_time
log.info("[CAPTURE] Beginning packet capture, be back in %s seconds...", cap_timeout)
tshark_cmd = "tshark -n -i eth1 -a duration:{} -w /tmp/floodlight.pcapng > /dev/
  null 2>&1".format(cap_timeout)
subprocess.Popen(tshark_cmd, shell=True).wait()
packets = rdpcap("/tmp/floodlight.pcapng")
log.info("[CAPTURE] Packet capture finished! %s packets in capture", len(packets))
<snip>
```

After capturing packets for the predefined duration and saving them as PCAPng file, it is read back using Scapy to analyze the captured packets. Scapy is a powerful interactive packet manipulation Python program that can forge or decode packets, send or capture packets, match requests and replies for a given flow, and more. Scapy can also perform tasks such as scanning, probing, tracerouting, network discovery, and more. For more information on Scapy, access the URL provided at https://scapy.net/.

Classifying Expected and Unexpected Control Plane Traffic

As discussed earlier, the application builds a filter based on the **startup-config** for a small set of commonly used protocols in Cisco Nexus data center switches; however, this list in the current code is not exhaustive by any means. If a protocol is in use in your environment and not caught by an existing filter, refer to the *Contributing* section of the repository to find out how to add the protocol to this application.

The following list of control plane protocols is currently supported by Floodlight:

- **OSPF:** Open Shortest Path First

- **EIGRP:** Enhanced Interior Gateway Routing Protocol

- **BGP:** Border Gateway Protocol

- Spanning Tree Protocol

- **HSRP:** Hot Standby Router Protocol

- **VRRP:** Virtual Router Redundancy Protocol

- **SSH:** Secure Shell

- **vPC:** Virtual PortChannel peer-keepalive heartbeat

- Cisco Discovery Protocol

- **LLDP:** Link Layer Discovery Protocol

If Floodlight reports a false positive (unexpected traffic that is expected), and the protocol is in the supported list just shown, ensure that the startup configuration of the device has been updated by the **copy running-config startup-config** command.

Example 9-51 shows a snippet of the code that is building filter for the OSPF protocol.

Example 9-51 *Python Application—OSPF Filter*

```
def filter_ospf(parse, filters):
<snip>
    if parse.find_objects("^feature ospf"):
        log.debug("[FILTER] OSPF feature is enabled")
        if parse.find_objects("^router ospf"):
            log.info("[FILTER] OSPF feature and configuration found!")
            filters["ip"] += ["224.0.0.5", "224.0.0.6"]
```

```
        filters["ip_protocol_type"].append("89")
        filters["protocols"].append("OSPF")
    else:
        log.warning("[FILTER] OSPF feature is enabled, but no
  configuration found!")
        return None
<snip>
```

Once Floodlight has completed scanning through the startup configuration and building the list of filters, the filter looks like the one in Example 9-52.

Example 9-52 *Python Application—Filter List for Expected Traffic*

```
filters["ip"] = ["224.0.0.5", "224.0.0.6", "224.0.0.10", ......]
filters["mac"] = ["01:80:c2:00:00:00", "01:00:0c:cc:cc:cc", ......]
filters["ip_protocol_type"] = ["88", "89", "112", ......]
filters["ports"] = [{"transport": "TCP", "port": "179"}, {"transport": "TCP",
  "port": "22"}, ......]
```

The final step is to run these filters against the PCAP collected and filter the unexpected traffic, as shown in Example 9-53.

Example 9-53 *Python Application—Apply Filter to PCAP Traces*

```
def expected_packet(filters, packet, idx):
    log.debug("[PKT-CHECK][%s] Checking packet...", idx)
    if (filtered_ip(filters["ip"], packet, idx) or
            filtered_mac(filters["mac"], packet, idx) or
            filtered_protocol_types(filters["ip_protocol_type"], packet, idx) or
            filtered_ports(filters["ports"], packet, idx)):
        log.debug("[PKT-CHECK][%s] Packet is expected!", idx)
        return True
    if "complex" in filters.keys():
        for complex_filter in filters["complex"]:
            if "vPC" in complex_filter["protocol"]:
                if filtered_vpc(complex_filter, packet, idx):
                    return True
    else:
        log.debug("[PKT-CHECK][%s] Packet is ~NOT~ expected!", idx)
    return False
```

Running the App in NX-OS

Example 9-54 shows that the app is run with the **docker-compose up** command. This command executes the **docker-compose.yml** file shown in this example. You can use any text editor to create this file and then copy it over to the Nexus switch. Notice that a Docker container is instantiated by pulling the latest Floodlight image, mounting the specified volumes (**/bootflash**, **/startup-config**, and so on), and setting the container network mode to **host**.

Example 9-54   *Run App—NX-OS Anomaly Detector*

```
N93180# conf t
N93180(config)# feature bash-shell
N93180(config)# end
N93180# run bash sudo su -
root@N93180# ip netns exec management bash
root@N93180#
root@N93180# cd floodlight/
root@N93180# ls -l
-rw-r--r-- 1 root root 316 Jan 16 14:24 docker-compose.yml
root@N93180#
root@N93180# more docker-compose.yml
version: "3"
services:
  floodlight:
    image: chrisjhart/floodlight:latest
    container_name: floodlight
    volumes:
      - /var/sysmgr/startup-cfg/ascii/system.cfg:/startup-config
      - /var/log/:/var/log/
      - /bootflash:/bootflash
    environment:
      - DEBUG=1
      - CAPTURE_TIME = 60
      - EXPORT=/bootflash/example_pcap.pcap
    network_mode: "host"
root@N93180#
root@N93180# docker-compose up
Starting floodlight ... done
Attaching to floodlight
floodlight   INFO [LOG] Debug logging level set!
floodlight   INFO [SETUP] NX-OS startup-config file detected
floodlight   INFO [FILTER] OSPF feature and configuration found!
floodlight   INFO [FILTER] HSRP configuration not found, skipping...
<snip>
floodlight   INFO    ==== FILTERS ====
floodlight   | 'ip': ['224.0.0.5', '224.0.0.6'],
floodlight   | 'ip_protocol_type': ['89'],
<snip>
floodlight   | 'protocols': ['OSPF', 'BGP', 'Spanning Tree Protocol', 'SSH', 'CDP',
  'LLDP']}
```

```
floodlight  INFO [CAPTURE] Beginning packet capture, be back in 60 seconds...
floodlight  INFO [CAPTURE] Packet capture finished! 259 packets in capture
floodlight  INFO [UNEXPECTED] Number of unexpected packets: 138
floodlight  INFO           ===== RESULTS =====
floodlight  INFO    14,879 bytes (123 packets) | TCP   (TCP ) 00:01:02:03:04:05 10.
  150.53.63:50449  -> 10.150.53.229:2345 00:de:fb:fa:64:c7
<snip>
floodlight  INFO [WRITE-PCAP] Successfully wrote unexpected packets to PCAP at /
  bootflash/example_pcap.pcap
floodlight exited with code 0
root@N93180#
```

The **docker-compose up** command captures the traffic sent to the control plane for 60 seconds, classifies the packets into expected and unexpected traffic, and builds a PCAP file with just traffic that is not expected to be seen in the control plane. As shown in Example 9-54, the app has filtered 138 packets as **unexpected** and listed the top talkers. The one with the most packets indicates a flow from 10.150.53.63:50449 to 10.150.53.229:2345.

As you have learned, the floodlight application can be deployed in advance, not just in one but in multiple switches at the same time, and can be used on demand to troubleshoot a specific switch in the network. This simple containerized application empowers and enables network engineers to capture the traffic on demand and bring the troubleshooting time down as it automatically and unexpectedly filters the traffic sent to the control plane.

NX-OS Use Case: NX-OS Docker Health Check

This use case involves a Dockerized application that checks the system health of a Nexus switch and generates a comprehensive report. This section dives deep into the application so you can see how it helps to check the system health.

Objective of the Application

Running as a Docker container, the application runs key commands and captures relevant results to check the system health of the Nexus switches provided as input to the script. It also generates a comprehensive report for further use.

Build and Host the Application in Docker—High-Level Procedure

Following are the steps for this use case, in which you develop the application and host it in a Nexus device. These steps are the same as those for the Floodlight use cases discussed earlier in this chapter.

1. Develop the application in an IDE, set up in a Linux server.

2. Build a GitHub repository with the Python application (**.py** file), Dockerfile and all other requirements and dependencies.

3. Build a DockerHub repository by leveraging the feature in DockerHub to connect to a GitHub repository.

4. In NX-OS, a Docker container is instantiated running a specific application and mounting necessary filesystems, like /bootflash and /startup-config. The application hosted in the container executes its routine and functions to achieve the objective.

NX-OS Docker Health Check Application

As the name suggests, the NX-OS Docker Health Check application is a Dockerized Python application that checks the health of the Nexus switches listed in the ./**config.ini** file.

As you have seen in the NX-OS Floodlight use case in this chapter, **Docker Compose** is used for this use case, too. The **docker-compose.yml** file shown in Example 9-55 may be used as a baseline.

Example 9-55 *Docker Compose to Instantiate NX-OS Health Check Container*

```
version: "3"
services:
  nxos-health-check:
    image: TestUser/nxos-docker-health-check:latest
    container_name: nxos-health-check
    environment:
      - DEBUG=True
    volumes:
      - /var/log/:/var/log/
      - ./example_config.ini:/app/config.ini
```

Example 9-56 shows the content of the config.ini file, which lists the devices the **NX-OS Health Check** application is going to perform a health check for. The application uses the credentials provided in the config.ini file to log in to the devices.

Example 9-56 *Docker Container config.ini File*

```
[Devices]
Device-1 = 192.168.2.10
Device-2 = 192.168.2.20
Device-3 = 192.168.2.30

[Credentials]
username = example_username
password = example_password
```

Performing Health Check

The Dockerized application acts as an NX-API client checking the health of the devices listed in the config.ini file, as depicted in Figure 9-6.

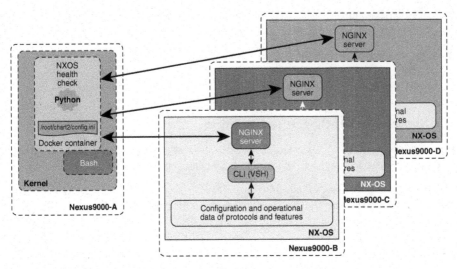

Figure 9-6   *NX-OS Health Check*

As Example 9-57 shows, the application checks Control Plane Policing (CoPP) counters in the devices to see if there is any violation. If there is, the application reports the class-map, module, and violations detected.

Example 9-57   *Python Application—CoPP Counters*

```
for device in devices:
        nxapi_conn = NXAPI(
            device["ip"], credentials["username"], credentials["password"]
        )
        # Verifies:
        # - Device model/modules
        # - Device NX-OS software release
        # - Device module diagnostic tests have passed
        nxapi_conn.check_device_modules()
        log.info(
            "[DEV] Device with IP %s is a %s running NX-OS %s",
            nxapi_conn.ip,
            nxapi_conn.model,
            nxapi_conn.nxos_version,
        )
<snip>
def report_copp_counters(counters):
    issue_found = False
    for cmap in counters.keys():
        for module in counters[cmap].keys():
            violations = int(counters[cmap][module]["violate_bytes"])
```

```
            if violations != 0:
                issue_found = True
                log.error(
                    "[DEV] \tCoPP violation %s on module %s: %s",
                    cmap,
                    module,
                    violations,
                )
    if not issue_found:
        log.info("[DEV] \tNo non-zero CoPP violation counters")
<snip>
```

When this book was written, the application was built to check very few health parameters:

- Interface status
- Interface error counters
- CoPP violation counters

For more details, see the GitHub repository at https://github.com/ChristopherJHart/nxos-docker-health-check. You are encouraged to fork this repository and develop it further by adding more health checks routines, such as these:

- Module diagnostic failures
- File system usage
- Memory and CPU usage

Running the App in NX-OS

Example 9-58 shows that the app is run with the **docker-compose up** command. This command executes the **docker-compose.yml**. You can use any text editor to create this file and then copy it to the Nexus switch. As you notice in the file, a docker container is instantiated by pulling the latest image and mounting the specified volume.

Example 9-58 *Run App—NX-OS Health Check*

```
RTP-HOM-VTEP-1# conf t
RTP-HOM-VTEP-1(config)# feature bash-shell
RTP-HOM-VTEP-1(config)# end
RTP-HOM-VTEP-1# run bash sudo su -
root@RTP-HOM-VTEP-1#
root@RTP-HOM-VTEP-1# cd nxos-docker-health-check/
root@RTP-HOM-VTEP-1# ls -l
-rw-r--r-- 1 root root 316 Nov 12 03:02 docker-compose.yml
root@RTP-HOM-VTEP-1#
root@RTP-HOM-VTEP-1# cat docker-compose.yml
```

```
version: "3"
services:
  nxos-health-check:
    image: TestUser/nxos-docker-health-check:latest
    container_name: nxos-health-check
    environment:
      - DEBUG=True
    volumes:
      - ./example_config.ini:/app/config.ini
root@RTP-HOM-VTEP-1#
root@RTP-HOM-VTEP-1# cat config.ini
[Devices]
RTP-HOM-VTEP-2 = 10.122.140.114
RTP-LAC-VTEP-1 = 10.122.140.123
RTP-LAC-VTEP-2 = 10.122.140.86
RTP-SUG-BGW-1 = 10.122.140.92
RTP-SUG-BGW-2 = 10.122.140.93
SJC-BCM-VTEP-2 = 10.122.140.103
RTP-BCM-SP-1 = 10.122.140.101
RTP-BCM-SP-2 = 10.122.140.100
[Credentials]
username = admin
password = cisco!123
root@RTP-HOM-VTEP-1#
root@RTP-HOM-VTEP-1# docker-compose up
latest: Pulling from chrisjhart/nxos-docker-health-check
Status: Downloaded newer image for chrisjhart/nxos-docker-health-check:latest
2019-11-12 03:14:41,253 INFO   [                main] [INIT] Initializing health check
2019-11-12 03:14:41,254 INFO   [                main] [CFG] Analyzing configuration...
2019-11-12 03:14:41,254 INFO   [                main] [HLTH] Performing health check
   on 8 devices
2019-11-12 03:14:41,330 INFO   [                main] [DEV] Device with IP 10.122.
   140.114 is a N9K-C93180YC-FX running NX-OS 9.2(3)
2019-11-12 03:14:41,330 INFO   [                main] [DEV] Diagnostics passing: True
2019-11-12 03:14:42,964 INFO   [ report_interfaces] [DEV]   No non-zero interface
   error counters
2019-11-12 03:14:43,072 INFO   [report_copp_counters] [DEV]   No non-zero CoPP
   violation counters
2019-11-12 03:14:43,287 INFO   [ report_intf_status] [DEV]   No interfaces in an
   unexpected status
2019-11-12 03:14:45,424 INFO   [                main] [DEV] Device with IP
   10.122.140.123 is a N9K-C92304QC running NX-OS 7.0(3)I7(7)
2019-11-12 03:14:45,424 INFO   [                main] [DEV] Diagnostics passing: True
2019-11-12 03:14:47,566 INFO   [ report_interfaces] [DEV]   No non-zero interface
   error counters
```

```
2019-11-12 03:14:47,846 INFO    [report_copp_counters] [DEV]   No non-zero CoPP
   violation counters
2019-11-12 03:14:48,196 INFO    [ report_intf_status] [DEV]   No interfaces in an
   unexpected status
2019-11-12 03:14:50,335 INFO    [              main] [DEV] Device with IP
   10.122.140.86 is a N9K-C92304QC running NX-OS 7.0(3)I7(7)
2019-11-12 03:14:50,336 INFO    [              main] [DEV]   Diagnostics passing:
   True
2019-11-12 03:14:52,483 INFO    [  report_interfaces] [DEV]   No non-zero interface
   error counters
2019-11-12 03:14:52,766 INFO    [report_copp_counters] [DEV]   No non-zero CoPP
   violation counters
2019-11-12 03:14:53,116 INFO    [ report_intf_status] [DEV]   No interfaces in an
   unexpected status
2019-11-12 03:14:54,198 INFO    [              main] [DEV] Device with IP
   10.122.140.92 is a N9K-C93180YC-EX running NX-OS 9.3(1)
2019-11-12 03:14:54,198 INFO    [              main] [DEV]   Diagnostics passing:
   True
2019-11-12 03:14:56,028 INFO    [  report_interfaces] [DEV]   No non-zero interface
   error counters
2019-11-12 03:14:56,173 INFO    [report_copp_counters] [DEV]   No non-zero CoPP
   violation counters
2019-11-12 03:14:56,408 INFO    [ report_intf_status] [DEV]   No interfaces in an
   unexpected status
2019-11-12 03:14:57,494 INFO    [              main] [DEV] Device with IP
   10.122.140.93 is a N9K-C93180YC-EX running NX-OS 9.3(1)
2019-11-12 03:14:57,494 INFO    [              main] [DEV]   Diagnostics passing:
   True
2019-11-12 03:14:59,260 INFO    [  report_interfaces] [DEV]   No non-zero interface
   error counters
2019-11-12 03:14:59,414 INFO    [report_copp_counters] [DEV]   No non-zero CoPP
   violation counters
2019-11-12 03:14:59,662 INFO    [ report_intf_status] [DEV]   No interfaces in an
   unexpected status
2019-11-12 03:15:00,730 INFO    [              main] [DEV] Device with IP
   10.122.140.103 is a N9K-C9372PX running NX-OS 7.0(3)I7(4)
2019-11-12 03:15:00,731 INFO    [              main] [DEV]   Diagnostics passing:
   True
2019-11-12 03:15:04,291 INFO    [  report_interfaces] [DEV]   No non-zero interface
   error counters
2019-11-12 03:15:04,408 INFO    [report_copp_counters] [DEV]   No non-zero CoPP
   violation counters
2019-11-12 03:15:04,657 INFO    [ report_intf_status] [DEV]   No interfaces in an
   unexpected status
2019-11-12 03:15:06,805 INFO    [              main] [DEV] Device with IP
   10.122.140.101 is a N9K-C9500 running NX-OS 7.0(3)I7(5a)
2019-11-12 03:15:06,805 INFO    [              main] [DEV]   Diagnostics passing:
   True
2019-11-12 03:15:19,229 INFO    [  report_interfaces] [DEV]   No non-zero interface
   error counters
```

```
2019-11-12 03:15:19,800 INFO       [report_copp_counters] [DEV]    No non-zero CoPP
  violation counters
2019-11-12 03:15:20,260 INFO       [ report_intf_status] [DEV]    No interfaces in an
  unexpected status
2019-11-12 03:15:21,370 INFO       [                main] [DEV] Device with IP
  10.122.140.100 is a N9K-C9500 running NX-OS 7.0(3)I7(5a)
2019-11-12 03:15:21,370 INFO       [                main] [DEV]    Diagnostics passing:
  True
2019-11-12 03:15:33,520 ERROR      [  report_interfaces] [DEV]    Interface
  Ethernet1/1 error counter eth_rcv_err: 15
2019-11-12 03:15:33,521 ERROR      [  report_interfaces] [DEV]    Interface
  Ethernet1/1 error counter eth_giants: 15
2019-11-12 03:15:34,194 INFO       [report_copp_counters] [DEV]    No non-zero CoPP
  violation counters
2019-11-12 03:15:34,639 INFO       [ report_intf_status] [DEV]    No interfaces in an
  unexpected status
```

As you might have noticed in Example 9-58, the **docker-compose up** command has instantiated a Docker container pulling the latest version of the application from the DockerHub. It has initialized a health check in each device listed in the **config.ini** file with the relevant results reported.

The beginning of this chapter discussed general container deployment use cases for enterprise, data center, and service provider environments. Even though the application in this use case does a health check on the Nexus switches, you can modify the Python scripts to check other operational states or parameters, such as the OSPF adjacency state. You can do the same checks through SNMP-based Network Management Servers (NMS), which may be behind a firewall or have limited or restricted access.

Having a Dockerized application running on one of the networking switches and checking the health or other operational parameters in other devices overcomes the accessibility limitation. In reference to Figure 9-6, the Nexus running the application and the three devices being checked are in the same network or VRF, with no firewall in between. One other key advantage of the containerized application running on a networking device is that it enables you to check multiple devices on demand and at the same time.

Summary

In this chapter, you learned how to leverage cutting-edge containers and application-hosting capabilities in the Cisco platforms running IOS-XE, IOS-XR, and NX-OS for some of the key network operational activities and how to deploy simple services such as DHCP. You can also leverage these built-in capabilities to deploy, provision, and test the infrastructure at scale.

## Chapter 10

Current NFV Offering and Future Trends in Containers

In this chapter, you will learn the following:

- Various open-source and certified third-party applications and the use cases for each

- Summary of various VNF service offerings from Cisco beyond the basic application hosting

- Challenges and future development in an application-hosting space

Bringing the flexibility of hosting any third-party applications on the Cisco software architecture is irrefutably a revolutionary step from Cisco that opened the ecosystem for new and innovative operational use cases to meet and exceed market demands. One of the main objectives for bringing this application-hosting capability to the Cisco platforms is to allow users to leverage existing open-source tools or to build applications in a language-agnostic and environment-agnostic manner and to host the tools seamlessly on the devices. A plethora of open-source network operational tools, such as iPerf, tcpdump, are available for consumption and can be preinstalled in a Linux distribution. Now that the Docker daemon is native to Cisco platforms, you can leverage the Docker image repository base that is supported by a strong developer community. Also, users can build their own applications and convert the code into Docker images.

By now, you are familiar with how to host and run virtual network functions (VNFs) and cloud-native network functions (CNFs) directly on the Cisco platforms. This chapter looks at some of the readily available network operational service applications, and then it examines the Cisco VNF that goes beyond basic application hosting. Lastly, it looks at what the future might hold in terms of network functions.

App Hosting Services

There is no single Internet repository available that consolidates all the open-source tools. You must search and identify the tools that match your requirements. You will look at some of the well-known network services that are readily available to be hosted. This chapter is a nonexhaustive list that includes both open-source applications that are freely available and licensed products from Cisco or other third parties. It offers a glimpse of the commonly available tools, but it is not intended to be an exhaustive list.

Solenoid

Solenoid, a route injection agent, is a custom-built routing application that disaggregates the control plane further by running the BGP protocol as a third-party container. The Solenoid application leverages exaBGP, which is an open-source BGP protocol–enabled SDN tool that is capable of receiving BGP updates and converting the routing content into a user-friendly and readable format, such as plaintext or JSON. A simple topology using Solenoid is shown in Figure 10-1.

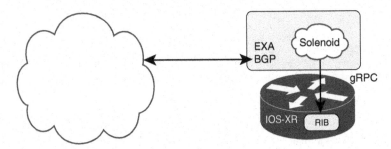

Figure 10-1   *A Solenoid App-Hosted Network*

Solenoid leverages exaBGP to establish the control plane neighborship with one or more remote nodes and to receive the prefix updates from the neighbor. exaBGP converts the update into JSON, which is further used by the Solenoid application to program the Routing Information Base (RIB) table of the Cisco devices using gRPC. The ability to disaggregate the route-learning and route-injection functions by using the Solenoid application introduces the flexibility of applying policies or other machine-learning capabilities.

Solenoid is a Linux application developed for IOS-XR devices, and the application is available in GitHub for download. The rootfs file with the preinstalled Solenoid application is instantiated as an LXC container on the IOS-XR platform.

Further details about the installation and configuration of Solenoid tools are available at https://xrdocs.io/application-hosting/tutorials/2016-09-28-solenoid-inject-routes-into-cisco-s-rib-table-using-grpc/.

Note: The Solenoid application, developed by Cisco, is free at https://github.com/ios-xr/Solenoid.

Two-Way Active Measurement Protocol (TWAMP)

TWAMP is a UDP-based network measurement protocol used to measure the round-trip metrics between two endpoints, as shown in Figure 10-2.

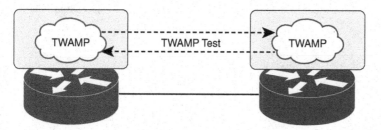

Figure 10-2   *TWAMP Test Scenario*

One end acting as the TWAMP client will send the measurement control probe that is reflected by the remote end acting as the TWAMP server. The client uses the time difference between sending the probe and receiving the response to measure the round-trip time between the endpoints. Because the round trip is measured based on the sent and received timestamp on the client, TWAMP is useful when the timestamp is not synchronized between devices.

The TWAMP tool is available as both a native Linux application and as a Docker image that can be instantiated for round-trip measurement on IOS-XE, IOS-XR, and NXOS platforms.

Note: The One-Way Active Measurement Protocol (OWAMP) was initially proposed to measure the one-way delay from the client to the server. The TWAMP architecture is derived from OWAMP and developed further to accommodate the different use cases. The ability to request and carry metrics in the probe payload helps with performance measurement and thereby makes it more powerful than the traditional ICMP. More details about the TWAMP protocol are available in RFC 5357.

Some platforms natively support TWAMP as part of the IP SLA configuration. The ability to host the TWAMP application comes with additional programmability benefits, where the reaction to any failure can be programmed with the device's SDK extensions.

tcpdump

tcpdump is a packet-capture and analyzer tool that dissects and displays the content of the captured IP packets. It is an open-source and CLI-based tool that is an alternative for Wireshark, which is another well-known packet-capture tool. tcpdump is developed to work on most of the UNIX and Linux distributions. When the application is hosted using host networking, all the host interfaces are listed in the application, and the CLI can trigger packet capture on any of the host interfaces.

Note that this tool is natively available in some of the Cisco platforms, such as IOS-XR, and NXOS, which comes with access to the Bash shell. However, tcpdump is a useful addition for other platforms, such as IOS-XE, where there is no native Bash shell.

The tcpdump tool is available as both a native Linux application and as a Docker image that can be instantiated for packet capture and analysis purposes on IOS-XE, IOS-XR, and NXOS platforms.

Note: The Docker image for tcpdump is an Alpine distribution–based image that runs the Alpine Linux container with the tcpdump tool preinstalled.

Cisco Kinetic EFM Module

Cisco Kinetic is a cloud-based IoT platform that is responsible for extracting, processing, and moving the data from the sensors or things to the relevant apps running in the cloud, as shown in Figure 10-3. One of the Kinetic components is the Edge and Fog Processing Module (EFM) that runs on the edge node as close as possible to the sensors for processing and reducing the volume of the data sent to the cloud app, based on the data relevancy.

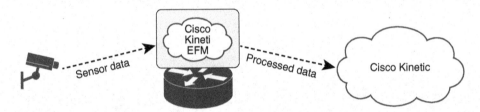

Figure 10-3   *Cisco Kinetic Module*

Any IOS-XE platforms connecting the sensor network can act as an edge or fog node device, and the computing resource of this edge node can be leveraged to run the Kinetic EFM service. The Cisco Kinetic EFM module is available as an application that can be instantiated with IOX-CAF on IOS-XE platforms.

Note: Cisco Kinetic is a cloud offering from the Cisco IoT product portfolio. It is not an open-source tool and may need additional licensing to be purchased to install and enable the service on Cisco platforms.

perfSONAR

perfSONAR is a network measurement toolkit that comprises a collective set of open-source tools, such as OWAMP, TWAMP, Ping, iPerf, and nuttcp, which are brought together for end-to-end network measurements. Although there are many integrated tools, the scheduler component efficiently fires up the relevant process and executes the task. perfSONAR is powered with the GUI interface that allows the users to manage the tool through web browsers. perfSONAR is available as a Docker image that can be natively instantiated on Cisco IOS-XR and NXOS platforms.

DNS/DHCP

DNS and DHCP are common application hosting services. The DNS server is responsible for offering naming conversion that resolves the IP address associated with the host name or the URL. The DHCP server is responsible for securely assigning and managing IP addresses to the endpoints. The choice of running the DHCP or DNS service directly on the devices is a good option for branch or other small sites because it helps eliminate one or more dedicated servers for this purpose; therefore, it reduces the hardware devices to manage. While some of the Cisco devices, such as IOS-XE platforms that natively support these services, the flexibility to host open-source DNS/DHCP as virtual entities on Cisco platforms, enables the users to add any new or proprietary features.

Various open-source applications and Docker images are available to run these services as containers on Cisco platforms. Although the application can be hosted on any Cisco platform, IOS-XE devices are the most common in branch and small sites.

Note: At the time this book was written, proof-of-concept testing is actively under investigation to run Cisco Umbrella services on Cisco IOS-XE platforms.

NetBeez Agent

NetBeez is a real-time, performance-monitoring agent that proactively monitors the network and detects issues. It is composed of a central server that runs in the cloud or in another centralized location. An agent is instantiated on the switches. A sample topology running NetBeez as an application on a Cat 9000 series switch is shown in Figure 10-4.

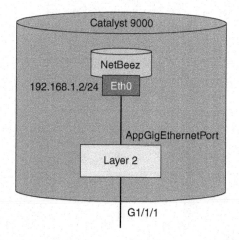

Figure 10-4 *Network Monitoring Application*

NetBeez Agent is available as both a Service Container image and a Docker image, and it is targeted primarily for IOS-XE platforms.

Note: A detailed instruction about the installation, configuration, and use of NetBeez Agent is available at https://netbeez.zendesk.com/hc/en-us/articles/360028594831-Cisco-Catalyst-NetBeez-App-Hosting-with-Docker.

App Hosting Summary

Although the previous section lists some of the well-known applications that are popularly used, the application hosting capability and the programmability can be used to develop native applications. The availability of the applications may vary depending on the platform on which the application is targeted to be hosted. A list of open-source applications available on the Cisco DevNet page for IOS-XE platform is shown in Figure 10-5.

Figure 10-5   *Open-Source Applications*

Further details about open-source and certified third-party commercial applications available for hosting are found at https://developer.cisco.com/app-hosting/opensource/ and https://developer.cisco.com/ecosystem/spp/#deploymentModel=763& technology=Networking.

The built-in SDK toolkits available for each platform, along with the programmability and application hosting capability of various Cisco platforms, can be combined to unleash the power of innovation.

Note: There is no better way to learn the technology than to get your hands dirty. Cisco provides a free sandbox on the Cisco DevNet website and other environments for you to experiment and learn application hosting.

Cisco NFV Offerings

There are other virtualization services beyond the application hosting capability that Cisco offers. To meet the business goals and demands of the market, various new NFV solutions surface from time to time. As discussed in previous chapters, it is beneficial to run some of the applications directly on the network devices. But depending on the type of the service offered by the NFV and the resource requirements imposed by such NFVs, it may not be practical to run all such applications directly on the network devices.

Cisco offers a whole suite of virtualization services that provide the foundation for an agile and elastic network. The Cisco NFV reference architecture is derived based on the ETSI model, as shown in Figure 10-6.

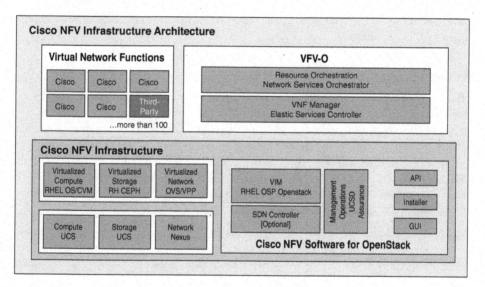

Figure 10-6   *Cisco NFV Infrastructure Architecture*

The main components of the Cisco NFV reference architecture are shown here:

- **NFV Infrastructure (NFVI):** This component is the basic infrastructure component that offers the computing, network, and storage resources for a carrier class, reliable, and feature-rich infrastructure.

- **NFV Orchestration (NFVO):** This component is composed of the orchestration and management functions that are responsible for orchestrating and managing resources and services with a holistic view of the network.

- **Virtual Network Function (VNF):** This component runs the actual network functions as a virtual entity by leveraging the infrastructure component provided by NFVI.

Just as Rome was not built in a day, neither was the NFV offering from Cisco. Over the past few years, various products and service offerings have evolved to satisfy the business demands and needs related to NFV. The next section examines some of the NFV-related products and services that Cisco offers.

Compute Platforms

Although most of the NFV products from Cisco can be instantiated on any x86-based computing platforms, Cisco also offers a purpose-built computing product line that has a whole suite of solutions from the underlying computing infrastructure. This approach helps the supportability aspect of the solution. Cisco computing platforms offer multi-core, high-speed CPUs and superfluous units of memory and storage that play key roles in providing the NFV Infrastructure. The following sections outline some of the computing platforms Cisco offers.

Cisco Unified Computing Servers (UCS)

The Cisco UCS family of products are x86 platform computing resources that come in two form factors: UCS Rack servers and UCS Blade servers. The former is a standalone server that can operate independently, whereas the latter is a blade that sits inside a chassis. This bare-metal x86 platform supports most of the major hypervisors, such as VMware, Hyper-V, and Xen. UCS also supports Network Function Virtualization Infrastructure Software (NFVIS), which is more than a simple hypervisor. NFVIS is the software platform that implements the full lifecycle-management of virtualized services from a central orchestrator APIC-EM. The Cisco UCS product portfolio is listed in Figure 10-7.

The virtual interface cards (VIC) that come with UCS platforms are accelerated NICs that are capable of offloading services such as NVGRE and VxLA. This VIC card helps accelerate the performance of the virtual network services.

ENCS

Enterprise Network Compute System (ENCS) is the compute platform in the Enterprise NFV solution that aims to reduce the number of hardware elements in a branch site by running them as virtual instances on a computing resource. ENCS platforms are available in different configurations, as shown in Figure 10-8.

ENCS also supports NFVIS, which provides the virtualization layer along with the controller used to create and manage the lifecycle of virtual instances such as virtual routers, virtual firewalls, and virtual WLC.

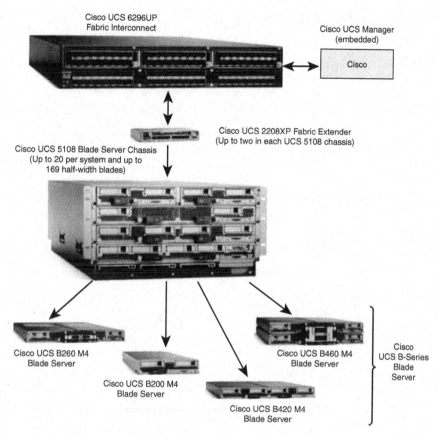

Figure 10-7   *Cisco UCS Platform Portfolio*

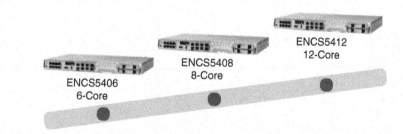

	ENCS5406	ENCS5408	ENCS5412
CPU	6-core, 1.9GHz	8-core, 2.0GHz	12-core, 1.5GHz
PoE	No	200W	200W
Capacity Guidance	ISRv + 2 VNFs	ISRv + 3 VNFs	ISRv + 5 VNFs

Figure 10-8   *Cisco ENCS Platform Portfolio*

Virtual Routers and Switches

One of the first NFV offerings from Cisco is the virtualized routing and switching elements that decouple the software from the underlying proprietary hardware. Virtual routers are not just control planes; they come with a powerful data plane component that supports different I/O modes and accelerates the data forwarding performance. A comprehensive list of virtual routers and switches available from Cisco as NFV offerings is shown in Figure 10-9. Although XRv 9000 and CSR1000v are available for production use, Nexus 9000v is for demo purposes, and it is not recommended for use in a production network.

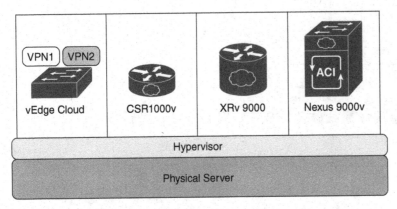

Figure 10-9 *Virtual Routers and Switches*

Most of the recent versions of the virtual routers are supported by different hypervisors such as VMware, Hyper-V, and Xen. Example 10-1 shows using KVM to instantiate IOS-XRv 9000.

Example 10-1 *KVM Command Line*

```
/usr/bin/kvm \
-smbios type=1,manufacturer="cisco",product="Cisco IOS XRv 9000",uuid=97fc351b-431d-
   4cf2-9c01-43c283faf2a4 \
-cpu host \
-drive file=/home/ubuntu/XR2/disk2.raw,if=virtio,format=raw,media=disk,index=1 \
-drive file=/home/ubuntu/XR2/xrv9k-fullk9-x.vrr-7.0.1.iso,media=cdrom,index=2 \
-m 20480 \
-smp cores=4,threads=1,sockets=1 \
-enable-kvm \
-daemonize \
-display none \
-rtc base=utc \
-name IOS-XRv-9000:root \
-netdev tap,id=host1,ifname=Lx4,script=no,downscript=no \
-netdev tap,id=host2,ifname=Lx5,script=no,downscript=no \
-netdev tap,id=host3,ifname=Lx6,script=no,downscript=no \
```

```
-device virtio-net-pci,romfile=,netdev=host1,id=host1,bus=pci.0,mac=53:46:1A:1A:37:
  E6,csum=off,guest_csum=off \
-device virtio-net-pci,romfile=,netdev=host2,id=host2,bus=pci.0,mac=53:46:47:22:5D:
  11,csum=off,guest_csum=off \
-device virtio-net-pci,romfile=,netdev=host3,id=host3,bus=pci.0,mac=53:46:01:A6:3B:
  F7,csum=off,guest_csum=off \
-netdev tap,id=data1,ifname=Xr4,script=no,downscript=no \
-netdev tap,id=data2,ifname=Xr5,script=no,downscript=no \
-netdev tap,id=data3,ifname=Xr6,script=no,downscript=no \
-device e1000,romfile=,netdev=data1,id=data1,bus=pci.0,mac=53:46:F8:B8:27:88 \
-device e1000,romfile=,netdev=data2,id=data2,bus=pci.0,mac=53:46:C4:09:B0:ED \
-device e1000,romfile=,netdev=data3,id=data3,bus=pci.0,mac=53:46:11:1D:50:8B \
-monitor telnet:0.0.0.0:11073,server,nowait \
-serial telnet:0.0.0.0:10721,nowait,server \
-serial telnet:0.0.0.0:15713,nowait,server \
-serial telnet:0.0.0.0:19090,nowait,server \
-serial telnet:0.0.0.0:18181,nowait,server \
-boot once=d &
```

Cisco Ultra Service Platform

Cisco Ultra Service Platform is a family of software products from Cisco that rearchitect the 5G packet core network into an API-driven NFV model by completely virtualizing mobility network functions for the evolving 5G and Wi-Fi networks. Cisco Ultra Service Platform leverages the Control Plane and User Plane Separation (CUPS) architecture that disaggregates the control plane from the user plane for mobility services, as shown in Figure 10-10.

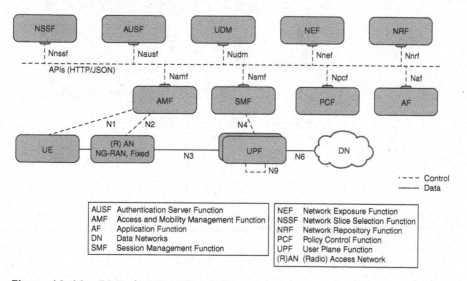

Figure 10-10 *5G Packet Core Network*

The User Plane component known as the Cisco User Plane Function (UPF) is a virtual network function that is designed to provide a high-performance forwarding engine. The UPF uses Vector Packet Processor (VPP), an open-source high-performance forwarding engine from Cisco.

The control plane components such as MME, AMF, and SMF, and policy planes such as NSSF and PCRF, are developed as cloud native virtual components that can be instantiated on any x86 platforms.

Cisco Container Platforms

Based on the proven benefits of using the microservice architecture for end applications, the industry is shifting gears to focus more on containerized network services by developing cloud-native network functions (CNFs). The use of Kubernetes is becoming a popular and de-facto industry standard for the orchestration and management of the containers. Deploying and setting up Kubernetes to manage containers in a multicloud environment is a real challenge.

Cisco Container Platform (CCP) is an offering from Cisco that addresses the mentioned challenge. CCP is a production-grade platform with programmable API extensions to deploy and manage multiple Kubernetes clusters in a multicloud environment. Simply put, this can be considered a "Kubernetes-as-a-Service" offering from Cisco. The architecture is shown in Figure 10-11.

Cisco Container Platform Architecture

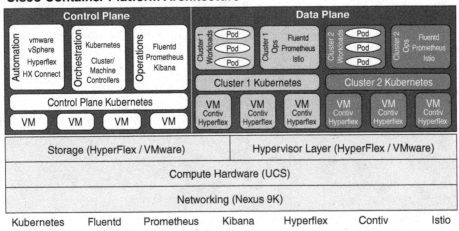

Figure 10-11 *Cisco Container Platform*

CCP is a bundle that comprises open source components as listed here:

- **Container Runtime:** Docker CE
- **Operating System:** Ubuntu

- **Orchestration:** Kubernetes

- **Infrastructure:** HyperFlex

- **Container Network Interface:** ACI, Contiv, Calico

- **Service Mesh:** Istio

- **Monitoring:** Prometheus, Grafana

Note: For those who would like to get their hands dirty with CCP, there are many sand-boxes available in DevNet for learning CCP.

Consolidated View

As you might have noticed, the VNF offering from Cisco spans multiple market verticals with extreme flexibility in choosing the relevant component from different layers of virtualization architecture. A consolidated view of different VNF offerings from Cisco is shown in Figure 10-12.

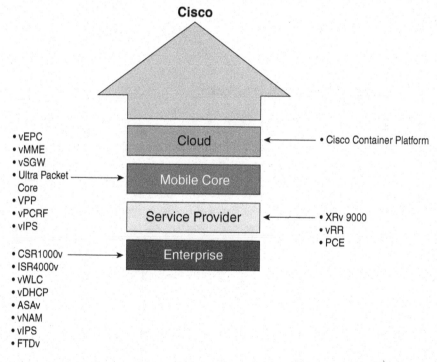

Figure 10-12 *Cisco VNF Offerings*

In addition, Cisco collaborates and opens up the ecosystem for other third-party vendors to submit and get their VNFs tested and certified to guarantee that they work seamlessly on the Cisco VNF infrastructure. Some of the certified vendors and their VNFs are listed in Table 10-1.

Table 10-1   *Third-Party Vendor-Certified VNF*

Partnering Vendor	Description
AVI Networks	The AVI Vantage platform offers an application delivery solution.
Fortinet	FortiGate firewalls offer security solutions.
A10 Networks	vThunder offers secure application services.
Netscout	Virtual Arbor Edge Defense offers a DDoS attack mitigation solution.
CTERA	Enterprise File Service Platform offers file sharing and collaboration services.

Note: Cisco Enterprise NFV Open Ecosystem is a program for testing and certifying third-party VNF that is open to all vendors. Any vendors interested can approach Cisco by contacting nfv-ecosystem@cisco.com. The list in Table 10-1 is not exhaustive and may change in the future.

Containers and Service Chaining

Over the past decade, the prospect and expectancy of the service offering have significantly matured beyond basic connectivity to additional value-add and critical services for differentiated service delivery. The introduction of virtualization allowed vendors to disaggregate such basic and value-added network service into VNFs and CNFs and run them independently as containers or virtual machines in any x86-based computing platform. Although VNFs and CNFs bring a load of benefits, the users are challenged with steering the traffic over ordered lists of such network functions running in different parts of the network. The migrated network from traditional to VNF-based networks is shown in Figure 10-13.

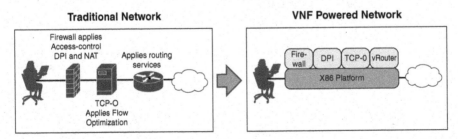

Figure 10-13   *Traditional to VNF-Powered Network*

Any traffic from the user is expected to steer through the firewall appliance to apply access control, DPI, and address translation services. This traffic is further steered to the flow optimization service and then to the router for WAN forwarding. The mentioned ordered list of services is applied by connecting different appliances inline to the traffic data path. In the migrated network, network functions are running as virtual entities and need some intelligence to steer the traffic over the relevant network functions to apply the same in the required order.

The concept of applying an ordered list of services for any traffic flow is known as service chaining. The industry is actively working on the following two standards to apply service chaining:

- Network Service Header (NSH)

- Segment Routing v6 (SRv6)

Network Service Header

To address the need of carrying service layer instruction details, IETF developed **Network Service Header (NSH)**, which allows users to steer traffic over a specific set of service functions and carry additional metadata. The format of the NSH header is shown in Figure 10-14.

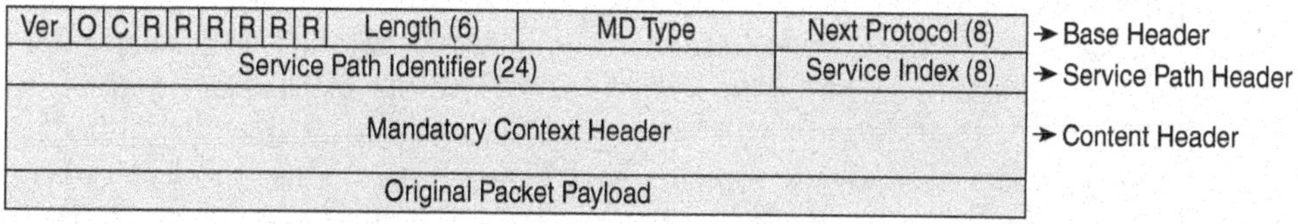

Ver	O	C	R	R	R	R	R	R	Length (6)	MD Type	Next Protocol (8)	→ Base Header
Service Path Identifier (24)											Service Index (8)	→ Service Path Header
Mandatory Context Header												→ Content Header
Original Packet Payload												

Figure 10-14 *Network Service Header*

NSH is a new data plane overlay header to encapsulate the original packet or frame and carry service path information that steers the packet over an ordered list of service functions. The NSH header is also flexible in carrying optional metadata details that can be used by the service function for service treatment. To accommodate this diverse set of information, the NSH is formatted as follows:

- **Base Header:** Carries payload details, type of context header, TTL, and so on.

- **Service Path Header:** Carries Service Path ID and Service Index. The combination is used to identify the service function to be applied on the encapsulated frame/packet.

- **Context Header:** Carries the metadata details. The MD type defined in the base header outlines whether the context header is fixed size or variable size.

IETF has done extensive work to make NSH transport agnostic to accommodate a broad set of use cases without a topology or network dependency. Accordingly, NSH is flexible and can use any type of transport layer encapsulation that is imposed on an NSH header, including VXLAN, VxLAN-GPE, GRE, Ethernet, and MPLS.

To accommodate diverse use cases without impacting the performance, an NSH header is structured to carry metadata in a fixed or variable context header, which is differentiated by the MD-Type field in Base Header. MD-Type 1 defines a fixed mandatory context header, whereas MD-type 2 defines a variable context header that can carry different TLVs.

Active standardization efforts are progressing in IETF to develop an MD-type 1–based NSH context header for mobility and data center use cases. Equal efforts are being spent developing the different TLVs to be carried in an MD-type 2 context header.

Note: Followed by the immense standardization efforts from IETF that resulted as RFC 8300, open source development bodies such as FD.IO and OpenFlow have developed feature support for NSH encapsulation in DPDKs like VPP and Open Virtual Switch (OVS).

To learn more about Service Chaining architecture, refer to RFC 7665, and to learn more about NSH, refer to RFC 8300.

Segment Routing

Segment routing is a new architecture that leverages the source routing paradigm and encodes the path information directly in the packet header as a stack of segments to steer the packet over any specific path. Each segment can be considered a forwarding instruction that steers the packet to a specific node or through a specific link. This architecture can be applied for both the MPLS (SR-MPLS) and the IPv6 (SRv6) data plane. When the architecture is applied for the MPLS data plane, the label is the segment identifier, and the label stack is then used to carry the stack of segments. On the other hand, when the architecture is applied for the IPv6 data plane, the 128-bit IPv6 address acts as the segment identifier and a new IPv6 extension header known as SRH is introduced to carry the segments. The format of the IPv6 header with SRH is shown in Figure 10-15.

The Ingress SRv6 node encodes the list of segments to be executed in the SRH and copies the first segment to the destination address field of the IPv6 header. The packet, upon reaching the node in the destination address, will be rewritten based on the next segment in the SRH. This approach allows the packet to be steered over a specific path by carrying the entire path information in the SRH.

Segment Routing v6 (SRv6) introduces the notion of an application-engineered network by infusing the function code and Args in the 128-bit segments identifier and carrying the same as part of the packet header. The 128-bit segment identifier can be dissected into <LOC>:<FUNC><Args> fields, as shown in Figure 10-16.

The LOC (also known as locator) is similar to the IPv6 prefix that delivers the packet to the node. The FUNC and Args are local values used by the node to execute instructions.

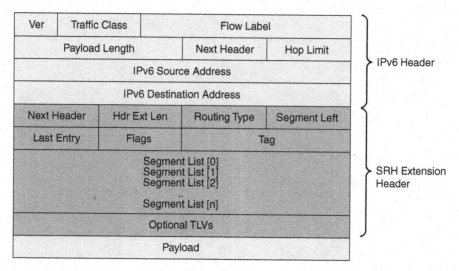

Figure 10-15 *Segment Routing Header*

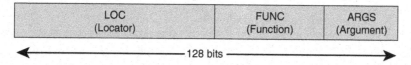

Figure 10-16 *SRv6 Addressing Format*

This notion of carrying instruction as part of a 128-bit segment identifier and using the SRH to carry a stack of such segments allows you to apply service chaining with SRv6 as the overlay header. The network services will be assigned with a unique LOC

Note: The standard definition for applying SRv6 for service chaining is a work under progress in IETF at the time this book was written. More details about applying service chaining using SRv6 are available in draft-ietf-spring-sr-service-programming.

Serverless Computing and Network Functions

The amazing journey of computer evolution right from vacuum tubes to containers has not stopped, and the industry is still technology voracious. "Serverless computing" is the technology buzzword that the industry is humming currently. Many of the key cloud technology companies, such as Amazon and Google, are already offering the service in one or another. What is serverless? You might be wondering if this is a technology that can execute any application without servers. On the contrary, it still needs servers and computing resources. Although the term used to define this technology does not reflect the actual meaning, it appears to bring benefits primarily in terms of resource conservation and pecuniary benefits. Function as a Service (FaaS) is the term that better defines this technology.

Serverless or FaaS is a new cloud service offering that offloads the application execution responsibility to the cloud provider. Users are only required to maintain the stateless function code. A quick comparison of different computing offerings is shown in Figure 10-17.

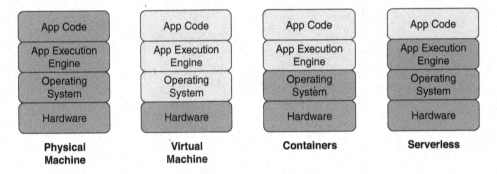

Figure 10-17 *Evolution to Serverless Computing*

The versatility introduced by cloud computing rapidly upsurges the productivity of the end users by bringing the virtual machines or containers in a few seconds with a couple of button clicks. FaaS primarily focuses on preserving the resource and the cost associated in managing the cloud entities. There are modern applications or microservices within an application that are sparsely executed. For example, Smart Cities and other IoT use cases collect the data from one or more sensors at a low frequency and process that data using an application before sending the processed data to the analytics server. Although the data collection frequency can be a few minutes or even hours, the time taken by the application to process is only a few seconds. In such use cases, running the application in an "always-on" mode is not computing resource or cost efficient.

FaaS helps in such scenarios by running the function code in the cloud and leveraging the execution engine offered by the cloud provider to execute the function based on a certain trigger. The trigger can be an interesting request or a cronjob. Bringing up the function only when required and charging the user based on the execution drastically reduces the cost compared to the service offered by a container or a virtual machine running the same function code. If you are wondering if FaaS is going to be the future architecture for application development, you are not alone. However, there are valid reasons why FaaS may not replace the existing software development architecture. When the FaaS engine continuously executes function code with no time interval to bring the runtime down, it is equivalent to running the function in a container. Therefore, FaaS is not a choice for function codes that are expected to be heavily executed. FaaS also may not be a choice if the function is delay sensitive. As you might have observed, FaaS, upon receiving the trigger, needs some time to bring the runtime of the function code up.

Various open-source initiatives are available to bring the serverless framework for a Kubernetes environment. Kubeless and Knative are two such frameworks that introduce a way to deploy functions and leverage API gateways or other execution engines to execute code. Fission is another framework for serverless functions on Kubernetes; it comparatively improves the performance and addresses the delay to a certain extent. Fission maintains a pool of warm containers and uses one of them to execute the function upon receiving a trigger. This allows users to reduce the delay to around 100 msec, which is pretty good compared to the other alternatives.

The ever-evolving market demand on network services fuels vendors to evaluate a serverless architecture for network service development to improve the velocity of the service delivery. Various universities and research communities are actively testing the feasibility of developing network functions using serverless architecture. It is possible that serverless network services will be common in the future.

Summary

This chapter reviewed various open-source and third-party applications that are available for hosting on Cisco platforms. It covered some of the commonly deployed applications along with the use cases and pointers to the location to obtain additional details such as configurations or applications. The chapter explained the other VNF offering from Cisco that spans across various market and business verticals. It summarized different VNF services and product portfolios.

The chapter explained the operational challenges of applying services in the expected order due to the disaggregation and covered different service chaining solutions that are standardized and available in the industry. Finally, the chapter closed with a summary of future trending and where the industry is heading to improve the efficiency of network services.

References

Open Source Application for Catalyst k Switches: https://developer.cisco.com/app-hosting/opensource/

Solution Partner Program: https://developer.cisco.com/ecosystem/spp/#deploymentModel=763&technology=Networking

Two-Way Active Measurement Protocol (TWAMP): https://tools.ietf.org/html/rfc5357

Cisco Kinetic for Internet of Things: https://www.cisco.com/c/en/us/solutions/internet-of-things/iot-kinetic.html

Cisco Enterprise NFV Infrastructure: https://www.cisco.com/c/en/us/products/routers/enterprise-nfv-infrastructure-software/index.html

Cisco Ultra Service Platform: https://www.cisco.com/c/en/us/solutions/service-provider/mobile-internet/index.html#ultra

Cisco Container Platform: https://www.cisco.com/c/en/us/products/cloud-systems-management/container-platform/index.html

Segment Routing Extension Header for SRv6: https://datatracker.ietf.org/doc/draft-ietf-6man-segment-routing-header/

Serverless Architecture for Kubernetes: https://kubeless.io/docs/quick-start/

Knative: https://knative.dev/docs/

Index

O

Q-R

S

W

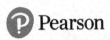